The Hardball Times Season Preview 2008

Featuring contributions by THT's staff writers and some of the best baseball bloggers on the Internet:

Joe Aiello • Sal Baxamusa • John Brattain
John Beamer • Brian Borawski • Larry Borowsky
Chris Constancio • Bradford Doolittle • Cork Gaines
Lisa Gray • Brandi Griffin • Justin Inaz
Ben Jacobs • Eric Johnson • Pat Lackey
Scott Lucas • Larry Mahnken • Jim McLennan
Chris Needham • Mike Pindelski • Ryan Richards
Jeff Sackmann • Aaron Sapiro • Sean Smith
Craig Strain • Dave Studenmund • Jeff Sullivan • Tuck
Steve Treder • Jason Weitzel • Geoff Young • Will Young

Produced by David Gassko
Edited by Bryan Tsao, Carolina Bolado and Joe Distelheim

ACTA SPORTS

The Hardball Times Season Preview 2008
New articles daily at www.hardballtimes.com

Edited by Bryan Tsao, Carolina Bolado, and Joe Distelheim
Projections developed by David Gassko and Chris Constancio
Cover design by Tom Wright
Typesetting by Dave Studenmund

Published by: ACTA Sports
                 5559 W. Howard Street
                 Skokie, IL 60077
                 1-800-397-2282
                 info@actasports.com
                 www.actasports.com

ISBN: 978-0-87946-346-5
ISSN: 1940-798X
Printed in the United States of America by Total Printing Systems.
Year: 12 11 10 09 08 07 06
Printing: 10 9 8 7 6 5 4 3 2 1

What's Inside

Read This First! 5
by David Gassko
Projected 2008 Standings 8

Team Essays and Player Projections
Arizona Diamondbacks 9
by Jim McLennan
Atlanta Braves...................................... 16
by John Beamer
Baltimore Orioles................................. 23
by Jeff Sackmann
Boston Red Sox 29
by Ben Jacobs
Chicago Cubs 36
by Joe Aiello
Chicago White Sox 43
by Mike Pindelski
Cincinnati Reds.................................... 50
by Justin Inaz
Cleveland Indians................................ 58
by Ryan Richards
Colorado Rockies 64
by Brandi Griffin
Detroit Tigers....................................... 71
By Brian Borawski
Florida Marlins..................................... 77
By Craig Strain
Houston Astros.................................... 83
by Lisa Gray
Kansas City Royals.............................. 90
by Bradford Doolittle
Los Angeles Angels of Anaheim............. 99
by Sean Smith
Los Angeles Dodgers........................ 106
by Aaron Sapiro
Milwaukee Brewers 113
by Eric Johnson

Minnesota Twins 119
by Will Young
New York Mets.................................. 126
by Dave Studenmund
New York Yankees............................. 132
by Larry Mahnken
Oakland Athletics............................... 139
by Sal Baxamusa
Philadelphia Phillies 147
by Jason Weitzel
Pittsburgh Pirates 154
by Pat Lackey
San Diego Padres.............................. 160
by Geoff Young
San Francisco Giants 166
by Steve Treder
Seattle Mariners 172
by Jeff Sullivan
St. Louis Cardinals 180
by Larry Borowsky
Tampa Bay Rays 186
by Cork Gaines
Texas Rangers 194
by Scott Lucas
Toronto Blue Jays.............................. 201
by John Brattain
Washington Nationals 208
by Chris Needham

Extra Innings
Star Maps 215
by John Burnson
Projecting Career Statistics 218
by David Gassko
Rookies to Watch in 2008................... 225
by Chris Constancio
Player Index..................................... 230

Read This First!

by David Gassko

Somehow, we got it done. When I first conceived of publishing *The Hardball Times Season Preview*, for some reason I thought that putting out a book would be a fairly easy project. It doesn't take a genius to figure out I was wrong, though I suppose that says nothing good about my intelligence.

Yet my job was actually much easier than I should have expected, a great credit to the fantastic team of writers and editors that worked so hard on this book. We recruited some of the best baseball scribes on the internet to write about their favorite teams and players, and they delivered. The bulk of the *Season Preview* consists of concise but incisive player comments and succinct team essays written in the style of Bill James' old "team in a box" reviews. I hope you enjoy them as much as I do.

For those of you who just want the stats, we have plenty of those too, with projections for almost every player who will appear in the major leagues next season. Those were developed by Chris Constancio and yours truly; we used three years of detailed data and just about anything else we could think of to build what I think will prove to be a very accurate model.

We've gone out and built projections for the next three years, so alongside our projections for 2008, you'll find the predicted change in ERA or OPS over the next three years for almost every player (with very old major leaguers the exception). Cincinnati outfielder Jay Bruce, for example, projects to go from an .840 OPS in 2008 to .925 in 2010, an increase of 85 points. Joel Pineiro, meanwhile, goes from a respectable 4.41 ERA projection in '08 to a not-so-respectable 5.02 in 2010, a 61 point increase.

That's not all. Besides projecting basic stats, we also have two more features that are fairly unique to the *Season Preview*. The first is projected fantasy dollar values. With the help of blogger extraordinaire "SG" and Hardball Times writer John Beamer (who doubles as the author of the Braves chapter), we constructed depth charts and simulated 100 seasons using our projections, recording the runs scored and batted in for hitters and wins and saves (which are not the same as the team-independent estimates listed in our projections) for pitchers to more accurately calculate team-dependent statistics. We then combined those with the rest of our projections to calculate fantasy dollar values based on a standard 12-team, 5x5 league. On page 8, we also print our projected standings based on those simulations.

The second thing I think you'll enjoy is our projected fielding grades. Utilizing detailed zone-based data provided to us by Baseball Info Solutions, we have projected how many runs, adjusted for park, above or below average each fielder should be at his main position, and to compensate for the uncertainty in our understanding of fielding performance, we replaced those with fielding grades printed with each hitter's projection. For those interested, here is how the grades correspond to runs above or below average per 150 games:

-15 runs above average or worse	F-
-9 to -15	F
-3 to -9	D
-3 to +3	C
+3 to +9	B
+9 to +15	A
+15 or better	A+

Fielders rated "F-" are bad enough that their teams should strongly consider moving them to an easier position, while "A+" fielders should be perennial Gold Glovers. We've compressed this scale in half for catchers (i.e., a catcher has to be projected at +7.5 runs above average or better per 150 games to garner an "A+") because their ratings tend to be closer to average. You'll notice that minor league players also have projected fielding ratings—all the credit for that goes to Chris, who put in a lot of time creating a zone rating-like statistic using minor league data provided by the MLB. The quality of a team's fielders is included in our pitcher projections—White Sox pitchers are really hurt by this.

If you tire of the player projections, we also have some cool content at the back of the book for you. I've already mentioned the projected standings, but right next to that is an essay on projecting career milestones by yours truly, with projected career statistics and odds of reaching various goals (500 home runs, 3000 hits, 300 wins, etc.) for pretty every much player of interest. We also have an essay from Chris that touches upon all the best rookies that might play in 2008 and some cool graphs from John Burnson, editor of *The Graphical Player*, that will help fantasy players better visualize which players will help most in what categories. Continuing with the graphical angle, we commissioned "Tuck," our in-house artiste, to illustrate nine different baseball-related cartoons which you'll find sprinkled throughout the book. As you'll see, Tuck has his own, very different set of predictions for the 2008 season.

But with all that said, I find myself returning to my favorite part of the book—its lifeblood really—and that is the writing. With a gargantuan helping hand from editor Joe Distelheim, who deserves a medal of some sort, our writers have put together a product that, I hope, will not only entertain and enlighten now, but years from now as well. There are some things that can only be gleaned from following a team every day of the season, and the team essays and player comments are full of those kinds of insights.

Before I let you go, I do want to give thanks where it is due. First and foremost, I want to thank Dave Studenmund for somehow tolerating me, helping at every stage of putting this book together, and then typesetting the whole monster. If Joe deserves a medal, Dave deserves a car, though he'll have to settle for a thank you note. Editing along with Joe were Bryan Tsao and Carolina Bolado, both of whom can turn lemons into, um, discerning baseball writing. And of course, I'd like to thank the folks at ACTA Sports for agreeing to publish this book, designing a beautiful cover, and being generally great to work with. With the orchestra playing in the background, I'll thank just one more person: You, the reader. We wouldn't be doing this book if you weren't reading it, so thank you for purchasing *The Hardball Times Season Preview 2008*—I hope you enjoy what's ahead.

Note: The projections printed in this book as well as full career projections can be downloaded from http://hardballtimes. com/THT2008Preview/. The username is "preview08" and the directions for the password can be found at http://www.hardball-times.com/main/content/preview08/. This page will also include any corrections or updates to the Preview.

You'll find a wealth of interesting information in the next 200 pages, including team projections and reports, player comments and projections. Each player projection includes a number of statistics; here are the definitions of each one:

Batter Statistics

PA – Plate appearances. This projection is based on a player's past playing time and does not take into account his projected major league role.

R – The listed runs projection is based on a player's basic statistics, unadjusted for lineup or playing time.

H – Hits.

2B – Doubles.

3B – Triples.

HR – Home runs.

RBI – Runs batted in. As with runs, we use a basic formula to calculate a player's projected RBI from his basic statistics without adjusting for lineup position or playing time.

SO – Strikeouts.

BB – Walks.

SB – Stolen bases.

CS – Caught stealing.

BA – Batting average: Hits/At-bats.

OBP – On-base percentage: (Hits + Walks + Hit-by-pitch)/(Plate appearances – Sacrifice hits).

SLG – Slugging average: (Hits + Doubles + 2*Triples + 3*Home Runs)/At-bats.

OPS – On-base plus slugging: OBP + SLG.

3 Yr. – The projected change in a hitter's OPS in the next three years. A positive number indicates that the hitter is expected to improve from 2008 to 2010, while a negative number indicates he is expected to get worse. Very old players are difficult to project over long periods of time, so we don't list this statistic for them.

Fld – We project how many runs above or below average each fielder will be, but because fielding ratings contain some uncertainty, we've listed grades to avoid any false precision. The scale ranges from "A+" to "F-." An "A+" fielder should be winning Gold Gloves most years, while an "F-" fielder should probably be moved to an easier position. Fielders with an "A" rating are very good; "B" fielders are above average; "C" fielders are average; "D" fielders are below average; and "F" fielders are pretty bad.

F$ – This is a player's projected fantasy value in a standard 12-team, 5x5, 23 player roster league. We built depth charts for each team so as to adjust player statistics for playing time and simulated 100 seasons using those depth charts to project team dependent statistics such as runs and RBI. The fantasy values are based on those numbers.

Pitcher Statistics

W – Wins as listed in our projections are not adjusted for a player's team or projected role.

L – Losses, also not adjusted for a player's team or projected role.

ERA – Earned run average. This projection takes each team's projected defensive ability into account.

IP – Innings pitched. This projection is based on a player's past playing time and does not take into account his projected major league role.

TBF – Total batters faced.

Hit – Our hits projection takes into account each team's projected defensive strength. In fact, a ground-ball pitcher's hits total will benefit more from a good infield than a fly ball pitcher's, and vice-versa.

HR – Home runs.

SO – Strikeouts.

BB – Walks.

HBP – Hit-by-pitch.

3 Yr. – The projected change in a pitcher's ERA in the next three years. A positive number indicates that the pitcher is expected to decline from 2008 to 2010, while a negative number indicates he is expected to improve. Very old players are difficult to project over long periods of time, so we don't list this statistic for them.

F$ – This is a player's projected fantasy value in a standard 12-team, 5x5, 23-player roster league. We built depth charts for each team so as to adjust player statistics for playing time and simulated 100 seasons using those depth charts to project team dependent statistics such as wins and saves. The fantasy values are based on those numbers.

FEARLESS PREDICTIONS, 2008: STILL MORE HEARINGS...

Projected 2008 Standings

American League						
East	**W**	**L**	**RS**	**RA**	**DIV**	**WC**
Boston	97	65	850	690	66.5	23.5
Yankees	93	69	919	778	27.0	39.5
Toronto	84	78	774	742	6.5	15.0
Tampa Bay	75	87	773	843	0.0	0.0
Baltimore	69	93	752	865	0.0	0.0
Central	**W**	**L**	**RS**	**RA**	**DIV**	**WC**
Cleveland	90	72	866	761	53.0	5.5
Detroit	88	74	871	787	40.0	8.5
Minnesota	79	83	733	756	4.5	2.5
White Sox	75	87	812	868	1.0	0.5
Kansas City	73	89	784	879	1.5	0.0
West	**W**	**L**	**RS**	**RA**	**DIV**	**WC**
Angels	89	73	783	706	74.5	2.0
Texas	79	83	832	855	8.5	2.5
Seattle	77	85	725	779	10.0	0.0
Oakland	77	85	748	803	7.0	0.5
National League						
East	**W**	**L**	**RS**	**RA**	**DIV**	**WC**
Mets	92	70	802	700	48.5	20.0
Philadelphia	90	72	867	772	36.5	19.5
Atlanta	84	78	815	783	13.0	7.0
Washington	70	92	740	849	2.0	0.0
Florida	63	99	721	892	0.0	0.0
Central	**W**	**L**	**RS**	**RA**	**DIV**	**WC**
Milwaukee	88	74	826	752	43.0	11.8
Cubs	87	75	852	785	35.0	7.0
Cincinnati	82	80	833	824	12.5	6.5
St. Louis	78	84	790	830	5.5	0.0
Houston	73	89	762	858	4.0	2.0
Pittsburgh	70	92	720	837	0.0	0.0
West	**W**	**L**	**RS**	**RA**	**DIV**	**WC**
San Diego	86	76	754	708	31.0	5.0
Arizona	85	77	785	727	28.5	7.0
Colorado	85	77	845	795	27.0	7.8
Dodgers	82	80	764	764	12.5	6.3
San Francisco	70	92	654	765	1.0	0.0

Notes

- The projected standings are based on 100 computer simulations of the 2008 season, including individual player projections.
- Projected team wins (W) and losses (L), runs scored (RS) and runs allowed (RA) are the average outcome of the 100 simulations.
- The "DIV" and "WC" columns represent the number of times, out of the 100 simulations, that the team won the Division title or qualified for the Wild Card.
- These results were calculated before Johan Santana was traded from the Twins to the Mets.

Arizona Diamondbacks

by Jim McLennan of AZ Snakepit (azsnakepit.com)

2008 Projections

Record: 85-77
Division Rank: 2nd, one game back
Runs Scored: 785
Runs Allowed: 727

2007 in a Nutshell

Our win differential is more important than your run differential.

Your Arizona Diamondbacks: driving stats geeks frothing mad everywhere. Arizona didn't just win its division; the D-backs had the best record in the National League, despite allowing more runs than they scored. This was caused by a phenomenal 32-20 record in one-run games, combined with a fondness for losing blowouts; take July 26-Aug. 5, when they won eight of 10, yet were outscored by seven runs. Their two losses were 14-0 and 11-0. The offense struggled terribly, finishing last in the league in OBP, but was bailed out by a heroic pitching staff, particularly the bullpen, which rarely had much of a lead to play with and did excellent work in keeping what they were given.

It was not exactly easy, with Arizona never leading by more than five games and clinching a playoff spot only after the 160th game of the season. But the Diamondbacks ended up taking the National League West by one game, then swept the Cubs in the Division Series, restricting Chicago to a total of six runs over the three games. However, turnabout proved to be fair play, and Arizona was swept in the Championship Series, scoring eight runs in four games. Still, given a payroll ranked 26th of the 30 major league teams on Opening Day, the season can be regarded only as a major success, despite the disappointing way it ended.

General Comments

Team Strengths

In Brandon Webb, the team has one of the best pitchers in baseball, and overall, Arizona's ERA+ of 114 was second-best in the National League. As noted, the relief corps was particularly strong; Jose Valverde, Tony Peña, Juan Cruz and Brandon Lyon combined for 284.2 innings at a 2.94 ERA, a stunningly-good performance in a hitter-friendly environment like Chase Field.

Team Weaknesses

Despite said environment, the offense struggled, outscoring only the woeful Giants and Nationals. The long ball wasn't a problem, with Arizona's 171 homers right at the league median. It was an overall batting average of .250 that was striking; three points lower than the 2004 Diamondbacks, who lost 111 games. The shortstop and right field positions delivered particularly poor production.

The General Manager is Known for...

Josh Byrnes likes pitchers who are "innings eaters"; he's traded for Livan Hernandez, Doug Davis and Dan Haren as starters, while Chad Qualls is also among the tops for innings by a reliever in the past three years. Byrnes seems to be of a sabermetric bent in general, and he has largely avoided the free-agent market, preferring to fill gaps through trades.

The Manager is Known for...

Bob Melvin appears to have a phobia about using the same batting order twice: last year, we got 146 different ones, and that's excluding the pitcher, while 15 different players started in the No. 7 spot. He plays the "hot hand" and tends to use pitching match-ups to decide the lineup. In games, he will rarely yank a starter if he has a chance at a win, but he does prefer to use the bullpen in well-defined roles. He was significantly more aggressive in 2007, with stolen bases increasing from 76 to 109.

Ballpark Characteristics

Not that you'd know it by Arizona's performance last year, but the park remains one of the most hitter-friendly ones in the major leagues. Second only to Colorado in altitude, Arizona's dry, warm climate helps the balls fly, even with the roof closed. The outfield has a number of interesting nooks, and Chase Field saw more triples last season (53) than any other park in the National League. Phoenix does tend to be a bandwagon town, and it'll be interesting to see if the fans come out to support the new division champions in greater numbers this year—passionate support was often hard to find at Chase in 2007.

The Minor League System is...

Arizona prospects are a lot thinner, both in number and quality, than they were at this time last year. This is partly due to the likes of Mark Reynolds, Chris Young and Justin Upton becoming major league regulars, but also because the top remaining candidate, outfielder Carlos Gonzalez—with a number of others—was shipped off to Oakland in the deal for Dan Haren. However, that should not be too much of a problem, since second base is likely the only position where the Diamondbacks are not settled for the foreseeable future. First-round pick Max Scherzer may see a September call-up.

Favorite Team Blogs

AZ Snakepit (http://azsnakepit.com/)

Diamondbacks Bullpen (http://forum.diamondbacksbullpen.org/)

Diary of a Die Hard (http://www.diarydiehard.com/)

Keys for 2008

Players Lost from Last Year's Team

Jose Valverde, Jeff DaVanon, Tony Clark (almost certainly), Livan Hernandez (ditto).

Players Acquired

Dan Haren, Chad Qualls, Chris Burke.

Reasons to be Optimistic

The majority of the team will be a year older and a year better. Haren forms a one-two punch with Webb that's among the best in the majors; Peña proves just as good a closer in 2008 as Valverde was in 2007.

Reasons to be Pessimistic

Randy Johnson's back could flare up again, the offense might not improve as much as needed, and the bullpen could revert to the mediocre levels of production. Eric Byrnes' three-year, $30 million contract might turn into an albatross.

Due for a Better Season

Stephen Drew, and the occupant of right field—almost certainly Justin Upton—will be an improvement on the late, lamented Carlos Quentin.

Likely to Have a Worse Season

Davis needs to stop walking people, and he dodged bullets from the mound with Matrix-like finesse last year. It's difficult to see how everyone in the bullpen can repeat their 2007 performances, but Lyon's peripherals are perhaps the shakiest.

Still Left to Do

Arizona needs to work out the bullpen roles, decide who's going to be the No. 6 starter—who could see a lot of activity depending on Johnson's back—and decide how to play or platoon Chad Tracy, Reynolds and Conor Jackson at first and third base.

Most Likely Team Outcome

Additional runs will be scored and probably about the same number allowed, fewer wins (but still some) over performance against Pythagoras, 90 wins again and another division title, though not by much.

Player Projections

Batters

Emilio Bonifacio (Second Base)

PA	R	H	2B	3B	HR	RBI	SO	BB	SB	CS	BA	OBP	SLG	OPS	3 Yr	Fld	F$
565	57	131	18	6	2	38	104	25	17	8	.248	.282	.316	.598	.042	C	$1

The second-base prospect was called up from Double-A in September, but is likely to start the season back in Triple-A. His best tool is his speed, having stolen 40-plus bases each of the last four seasons in the minors. He'll need to improve his hitting, though, if he's going to stick at a higher level.

Chris Burke (Second Base)

PA	R	H	2B	3B	HR	RBI	SO	BB	SB	CS	BA	OBP	SLG	OPS	3 Yr	Fld	F$
439	55	103	23	3	8	45	64	30	12	3	.265	.327	.401	.728	.004	C	$1

If his shoulder has finally healed this winter, he should be a very good hitter for Arizona. It is difficult to judge his fielding ability at second, as he has spent so few innings there in the majors. However, he was a very good second baseman in the minors.

Eric Byrnes (Left Field)

PA	R	H	2B	3B	HR	RBI	SO	BB	SB	CS	BA	OBP	SLG	OPS	3 Yr	Fld	F$
593	83	143	31	4	18	74	88	42	29	4	.267	.325	.440	.765	-.030	A	$18

Many fans were surprised by Byrnes being signed to a three-year contract during last season; others were delighted. Brynes' season falls off a cliff at the All-Star break, with startling inevitability. After eight years, his first-half career batting average is .306; in the second half, it's only .258. Arizona can expect more of the same mix—brilliance and incompetence—with maddening frequency through 2010.

Tony Clark (First Base/DH)

PA	R	H	2B	3B	HR	RBI	SO	BB	SB	CS	BA	OBP	SLG	OPS	Fld	F$
301	42	73	14	1	18	53	70	30	0	1	.275	.349	.538	.887	C	$1

Clark's contract is up, and he will likely not return to Arizona. His numbers in 2007 were not bad, but conceal the facts that he failed to hit lefties (.219 in only 32 at-bats) or on the road (.202/.288/.317, over 57 games). He's looking for more at-bats and won't get them with the Diamondbacks; a switch to the American League, where he can DH between starts at first, might be best.

Stephen Drew (Shortstop)

PA	R	H	2B	3B	HR	RBI	SO	BB	SB	CS	BA	OBP	SLG	OPS	3 Yr	Fld	F$
543	67	128	27	6	14	62	91	48	6	1	.265	.330	.433	.763	.016	F	$3

Drew was one of the big disappointments. A career .299 hitter in the minors, and with a .316 average in his rookie season, his 2007 offense was basically the same as the man he replaced, Craig Counsell. In his defense, and in contrast to Reynolds, Drew's BABIP was almost freakishly low, at .267 (NL avg = .301). This year will show whether that was bad luck, or if he's one of those players doomed by their style.

Orlando Hudson (Second Base)

PA	R	H	2B	3B	HR	RBI	SO	BB	SB	CS	BA	OBP	SLG	OPS	3 Yr	Fld	F$
557	70	140	28	7	10	57	75	51	7	2	.284	.349	.429	.778	-.029	B	$6

Hudson's year was cut short by a thumb injury, suffered while sliding into base, and he missed the team's playoff run. That should be no problem for 2008, and as this is his contract year, don't be surprised if he has another good performance–the desert climate suits him, as his two seasons in Arizona have been significantly better than any in Toronto. He's cracked .800 in OPS both times.

Conor Jackson (First Base)

PA	R	H	2B	3B	HR	RBI	SO	BB	SB	CS	BA	OBP	SLG	OPS	3 Yr	Fld	F$
485	64	124	30	2	14	63	58	53	3	1	.295	.375	.476	.851	.025	D	$7

Outside of a dismal April, when he batted .217, Jackson was the team's best hitter, improving as the year went on. In the second half, he had a line of .308/.371/.555, though he was somewhat protected from right-handed pitching by a platoon with Tony Clark. The next season may bring more of the same, with Chad Tracy replacing Clark as Jackson's partner.

Miguel Montero (Catcher)

PA	R	H	2B	3B	HR	RBI	SO	BB	SB	CS	BA	OBP	SLG	OPS	3 Yr	Fld	F$
368	44	86	15	2	13	47	54	27	1	1	.261	.322	.436	.758	.011	C	$1

Montero's ceiling was considered higher than Chris Snyder's, but a disappointing season has left him sitting in the backup spot once again. He had only one month batting better than .250, and his defense proved another area of concern. He showed decent power (10 home runs in 214 at-bats), so he will get pinch-hit duty and the occasional spot start.

Augie Ojeda (Shortstop)

PA	R	H	2B	3B	HR	RBI	SO	BB	SB	CS	BA	OBP	SLG	OPS	3 Yr	Fld	F$
339	35	72	13	2	1	23	37	32	2	1	.248	.332	.317	.649	-.018	D	$1

Likely replacing Callaspo as first backup in the middle infield is Ojeda, who returned to the big leagues for the first time since 2004. He won a lot of fans with his hustle, but he is only a .232 career hitter, and he is now 33, so any kind of rejuvenation seems unlikely.

Mark Reynolds (Third Base)

PA	R	H	2B	3B	HR	RBI	SO	BB	SB	CS	BA	OBP	SLG	OPS	3 Yr	Fld	F$
509	63	115	22	4	22	71	132	42	2	1	.252	.317	.462	.779	.020	C	$4

Reynolds was almost unknown before the year, getting his break straight from Double-A after injuries removed Tracy and others in his way. He seized the chance, batting .356 in his first 20 games, including one where he went 5-for-5 with two homers. Inevitably, regression followed, but his OPS was above .900 in August and September, and he seems likely to be starting at third on Opening Day. His BABIP was .378 though, very likely unsustainable.

Jeff Salazar (Center Field)

PA	R	H	2B	3B	HR	RBI	SO	BB	SB	CS	BA	OBP	SLG	OPS	3 Yr	Fld	F$
518	65	116	25	7	11	52	87	55	10	4	.257	.337	.417	.754	-.008	D	$1

He'll reprise his second-half role as a fourth outfielder. He had only one homer last year: a three-run, two-out, bottom-of-the-ninth pinch-hit shot that gave Arizona a victory in San Francisco. He probably won't have many more in 2008, but he should be serviceable enough and can play any of the three spots if needed.

Chris Snyder (Catcher)

PA	R	H	2B	3B	HR	RBI	SO	BB	SB	CS	BA	OBP	SLG	OPS	3 Yr	Fld	F$
371	47	88	20	1	13	50	66	38	0	2	.273	.353	.462	.815	.010	B	$1

Before we started 2007, it seemed possible Chris Snyder was going to be supplanted by Miguel Montero as the everyday catcher. It didn't happen, with Snyder batting .292 after the break and posting an OPS of .889, among the best for a regular at the position. His defense was also impressive, and he called all of Brandon Webb's starts, including the 42-inning scoreless streak. Snyder's spot now seems very secure.

Chad Tracy (Third Base)

PA	R	H	2B	3B	HR	RBI	SO	BB	SB	CS	BA	OBP	SLG	OPS	3 Yr	Fld	F$
407	53	103	24	3	14	56	70	36	1	1	.284	.349	.483	.832	.004	C	$1

Tracy's status is currently uncertain, after knee surgery brought a premature end to his 2007 season. A blood clot at Thanksgiving set his recovery back, and no one knows if he'll be ready for Opening Day. Whenever he's ready, expect him to see time both at first and third, in particular against right-handed pitching; his career OPS is 271 points better than against lefties.

Justin Upton (Right Field)

PA	R	H	2B	3B	HR	RBI	SO	BB	SB	CS	BA	OBP	SLG	OPS	3 Yr	Fld	F$
530	69	125	26	5	16	64	99	52	8	4	.269	.345	.449	.794	.068	D	$1

The first overall pick in the 2005 draft made his debut in August, three years to the day after brother B.J. (both were also aged 19). The results were unsurprisingly mixed; no teenager has posted an OPS+ better than 100 since Ken Griffey Jr. in 1989. With the departure of Carlos Quentin, he'll be the starting right fielder for Arizona. Time is definitely on his side.

Chris Young (Center Field)

PA	R	H	2B	3B	HR	RBI	SO	BB	SB	CS	BA	OBP	SLG	OPS	3 Yr	Fld	F$
554	78	127	31	4	26	84	114	45	17	4	.256	.320	.492	.812	.034	B	$15

Young's season was a mix of the sublime and the ridiculous. Thirty-two home runs was the most by a rookie center fielder since Jimmie Hall in 1963, but he also struck out 141 times and became the first player in history to hit 30 home runs, steal 20 bases and have an OBP below .300. If he can learn to take a few walks, he'll be a monster, but that's certainly an "if."

Pitchers

Juan Cruz (Relief Pitcher)

W	L	ERA	TBF	IP	Hit	HR	SO	BB	HBP	3 Yr	F$
1	4	4.24	298	68	61	7	73	33	4	0.54	$1

Reverting to a full bullpen role in 2007, Cruz didn't need to pace himself and struck out 87 batters in only 61 innings, a pace beaten only by Jonathan Papelbon (minimum 30 innings pitched) last year. Right handers batted .143/.211/.277; left handers were significantly higher, so I'd expect Cruz to be platooned more strictly in the coming season. However, 17 of his 53 appearances lasted more than an inning.

Doug Davis (Starting Pitcher)

W	L	ERA	TBF	IP	Hit	HR	SO	BB	HBP	3 Yr	F$
10	10	4.62	791	179	185	20	134	86	5	0.39	$1

How Davis managed an ERA+ of 111 with a WHIP of 1.59, is a mystery—no player has had a WHIP that high, and an ERA+ better than 110, since Bump Hadley in 1934. His control proved problematic—Davis placed second in the league for walks—for the third straight season, and his peripherals continued to drift in the wrong direction. Still, he had his first winning record since 2001, albeit only by a single game.

Edgar Gonzalez (Starting/Relief Pitcher)

W	L	ERA	TBF	IP	Hit	HR	SO	BB	HBP	3 Yr	F$
6	7	4.50	482	113	118	16	71	33	5	-0.33	$1

You name it, Edgar did it for Arizona. He made 12 starts, and his relief appearances also spanned every inning from the first (after a failed Byung-Hyun Kim outing) to the 11th. This flexibility enhances his value, and he'll probably start the season in the bullpen, as the long relief/spot starter.

Dan Haren (Starting Pitcher)

W	L	ERA	TBF	IP	Hit	HR	SO	BB	HBP	3 Yr	F$
14	9	3.56	825	203	192	23	186	41	6	0.12	$24

Haren was reputed to be homer-prone based on his 2005-2006 seasons. That's not really fair; last year's edition of this book showed he was unlucky with gopher balls in 2006. So it was no surprise when his home run rate fell in 2007 and Haren had a banner year. There's no reason to think that his home run rate will rise again, once you adjust for his homer-happy new digs in Arizona.

Haren probably won't be as good as he was last year, but he is a solid bet as starting pitchers go. His strikeout rate has increased every year, he has never been injured and he's just entering his late 20s.

Livan Hernandez (Starting Pitcher)

W	L	ERA	TBF	IP	Hit	HR	SO	BB	HBP	3 Yr	F$
9	12	5.19	825	187	212	27	93	70	5	0.41	$1

Opponents hit .308 off Livan last year, and he was also in the NL top 10 for walks, yet he exhibited a Houdini-like tendency to get out of jams when necessary. Opponents' OPS fell by 150 points when he had runners on base,

(.938 to .783), and he also coaxed more hitters into double plays than Brandon Webb's sinker. Free agency will be kind to him in a thin market for starters, likely more so than his 2008 performance will deserve.

Randy Johnson (Starting Pitcher)

W	L	ERA	TBF	IP	Hit	HR	SO	BB	HBP	3 Yr	F$
8	5	3.84	488	119	111	16	114	29	5		$9

Josh Byrnes rolled the dice on the Big Unit, but Johnson's season was over before June ended, a relapse of the herniated disk in his back leading to further surgery. When he pitched, Johnson was effective, posting a 3.81 ERA in 10 starts, with 72 strikeouts against 13 walks. If he's that good again and can last longer, Arizona will have a very formidable 1-2-3 at the top of the rotation. Thirty starts is optimistic, but Arizona would likely settle for 25.

Brandon Lyon (Relief Pitcher)

W	L	ERA	TBF	IP	Hit	HR	SO	BB	HBP	3 Yr	F$
4	4	4.32	296	69	70	7	42	25	2	0.47	$5

Lyon will probably reprise his setup role from last year, when he kept the ball in the park with almost impossible skill: two homers in 74 innings. Prior to 2007, Lyon's home run frequency was about five times higher. He is that rarity, a reliever who has four pitches, but a regression to the mean for him seems inevitable.

Brandon Medders

W	L	ERA	TBF	IP	Hit	HR	SO	BB	HBP	3 Yr	F$
4	4	4.85	323	73	75	9	53	35	2	0.12	$1

After two brilliant seasons, combining for 102 innings at a 3.09 ERA, Medders took a step back in 2007. Overall, his stats weren't bad, but he gave up nine homers in fewer than 30 innings—the most infamous, a first-pitch grand-slam in a May 9 game, when Arizona led 3-0. He was sent to Triple-A in June and his future is sketchy.

Dustin Nippert (Relief Pitcher)

W	L	ERA	TBF	IP	Hit	HR	SO	BB	HBP	3 Yr	F$
5	5	4.75	413	93	94	11	80	45	4	0.11	$1

Nippert's 2007 campaign was marked by inconsistency. For every outing where he'd look rock solid, he'd have another where he couldn't get anyone out—after a 3.05 first-half ERA, he allowed 13 earned runs in 10.1 innings from July 19 to Aug. 2, on his way to a second-half figure of 7.66. His fate may not be decided until the end of spring training.

Micah Owings (Starting Pitcher)

W	L	ERA	TBF	IP	Hit	HR	SO	BB	HBP	3 Yr	F$
8	8	4.81	623	143	148	19	98	53	9	-0.09	$1

An 8-8 record with a 4.30 ERA is not bad for a 24-year-old rookie, and Owings will be the No. 5 starter for Arizona this year. However, it was his batting which perhaps drew more attention, as he hit .333, including a two-homer, four-hit, six-RBI game in Atlanta. If he can keep that up—and there seems no reason why not—he will become a true double threat. Don't be surprised to see him batting outside the ninth spot and even used as a pinch hitter or DH this year.

Jailen Peguero (Relief Pitcher)

W	L	ERA	TBF	IP	Hit	HR	SO	BB	HBP	3 Yr	F$
4	4	4.59	318	72	67	8	61	38	4	0.11	$1

Peguero is now 27, and his upside is evaporating. He did reach the majors last year, but 13 walks in 14.2 innings didn't impress anyone. However, down at Triple-A Tucson—another hitter's park—he had a 1.89 ERA in 66.2 innings, striking out more than a batter per inning. He's a dark horse candidate for more action in 2008.

Tony Peña (Relief Pitcher)

W	L	ERA	TBF	IP	Hit	HR	SO	BB	HBP	3 Yr	F$
5	4	4.43	338	79	78	10	54	29	4	-0.10	$1

The most likely candidate to replace Jose Valverde is Peña, a flame-throwing righty who occupied the seventh-inning spot last season. In his first full year, the 25-year-old fit in nicely, with an ERA+ of 144, appearing in a team-high 75 games. However, he will be a largely unproven commodity as a closer (three career major league saves) and his projections are unimpressive.

Yusmeiro Petit (Starting Pitcher)

W	L	ERA	TBF	IP	Hit	HR	SO	BB	HBP	3 Yr	F$
8	8	4.86	619	144	144	25	90	51	5	-0.41	$1

Brought from Florida in a trade for Jorge Julio, Petit replaced Johnson in the rotation, becoming known to fans as the "Petit Unit." Any time a replacement pitcher, especially a 22-year-old, delivers a 103 ERA+, you'll be happy, and as a result, Petit and Edgar Gonzalez are likely first-line replacements in 2008 if a starter goes down. However, he was very homer-prone (12 in 57 innings), and Chase Field is not the best home park to deal with that issue.

Chad Qualls (Relief Pitcher)

W	L	ERA	TBF	IP	Hit	HR	SO	BB	HBP	3 Yr	F$
5	3	4.15	328	76	78	7	59	29	3	0.36	$1

A good seventh- or eighth-inning righty who has averaged 84 innings the past three years, he's a fastball/slider type who induces a lot of ground balls. I didn't see any evidence that he was on a downhill trend.

Doug Slaten (Relief Pitcher)

W	L	ERA	TBF	IP	Hit	HR	SO	BB	HBP	3 Yr	F$
3	3	4.42	229	52	52	6	46	23	2	0.16	$1

It was thought that he would be an extended lefty specialist, capable of facing more than one batter and getting right-handers out too. But he ended up with only 36.1 innings pitched, despite appearing in 61 games. His "one and done" usage, combined with the effectiveness of his colleagues, likely helped contribute to his 2.72 ERA—a .275 OBP is a better mark of his talents. He'll be the left-handed specialist again in 2008.

Brandon Webb (Starting Pitcher)

W	L	ERA	TBF	IP	Hit	HR	SO	BB	HBP	3 Yr	F$
15	8	3.26	849	207	196	13	157	60	5	0.28	$21

Webb followed up his Cy Young-winning season by improving his ERA, win-loss record, strikeout numbers and opponents' batting average figures, but he didn't receive a single first-place vote for the award. However, he was arguably the MVP of the team that won the division title. More of the same can be expected in 2008, and he starts the year as one of the preseason favorites for the Cy Young.

Atlanta Braves

by John Beamer of The Hardball Times

2008 Projections

Record: 84-78
Division Rank: 3rd, 8 games back
Runs Scored: 815
Runs Allowed: 783

2007 in a Nutshell

In what was billed as a super-competitive NL East, the Braves were first out of the starting blocks, going 24-12 and reprising the glories of years gone by. The rotation turned out to be the weak point as the Tomahawks lost their way in early summer and at one point fell below the .500 mark.

A recovery ensued.

General manager John Schuerholz obliterated the farm to acquire Mark Teixeira from the Rangers and Teixeira provided the big bat that catapulted the Braves back into playoff contention. The Mets never could string enough wins together to put the division beyond reach, and coming into September the Braves were in the hunt for both the division and wild card. Alas, it was the Phillies who staged a remarkable sprint to nip the Mets for the division crown. The Braves weren't even able to secure the wild card berth. It was a year that promised much but ultimately delivered little.

General Comments

Team Strengths

One word: hitting.

Since the Smoltz-Glavine-Maddux triumvirate was dislodged in the early 2000s, the Braves had become a hitting team and 2007 was no different, with Atlanta boasting the second best park-adjusted offense on the National League.

Chipper Jones pieced together an MVP-caliber season, hitting .337/.425/.604. Edgar Renteria was equally good, but with less power (.332/.390/.470), while Matt Diaz, Teixeira and Yunel Escobar all comfortably cleared a .300 batting average. Of the starting eight, only Andruw Jones and Scott Thorman had a sub-100 OPS+.

Team Weaknesses

To the surprise of no one, starting pitching was the quagmire this time around. Apart from Tim Hudson and John Smoltz, who both had sub-3.50 ERAs, the rotation was sub-par. Chuck James looked good in the first half of the season but lost a run per nine innings after the break. The remaining starters read like a who's who of replacement pitching: Buddy Carlyle (5.21 ERA), Kyle Davies (5.76 ERA), Jo-Jo Reyes (6.22 ERA), Lance Cormier (7.09 ERA) and the ghastly Mark Redman (11.63 ERA—that isn't a typo).

The General Manager is Known for...

This was the year Schuerholz decided to move into a more comfortable chair upstairs, leaving his protégé, Frank Wren, in the hot seat. One worry for Braves fans is that Wren doesn't quite have the gilt-laden CV of his predecessor. His only other stint as a GM was with the Orioles, where he was fired after barely one year in charge.

The signs are that he'll be a canny GM very much in the Schuerholz mode. Indeed, his first act was to restock a depleted farm by trading Renteria for a couple of prospects. The odds are that the Braves will continue along a path of developing a strong regional youth network, supplemented by trading for critical pre-arbitration players where necessary and rounding off the team with some experienced veterans. Also, don't be surprised if he locks up some of the arb and free-agency years of his better young hitters.

The Manager is Known for...

Getting ejected. In 2007, Bobby Cox finally passed John McGraw's milestone of 131 career ejections. There was never much doubt about him passing the mark and he now stands alone on 133 with nary a challenger in sight.

Cox has other qualities, in spades. Not only is he a born winner, but he builds cohesive teams by showing and demanding unswerving loyalty to the Atlanta cause. On more than one occasion, this has caused consternation among Braves fans as Cox would place blind faith in players who just weren't very good—people half expected Cox to bring the ossified Brian Jordan back.

Ballpark Characteristics

A look at both single- and multi-year park factors shows that Turner Field is a slight pitcher's park. The irony is that since Camden Yards, ballparks have been designed to be individualistic yet are all, in some absurd way, slightly derivative.

The Ted is no different. There is nothing unpleasant about it; in fact, it is a great venue with a massive Jumbotron, a good beer tent and comfortable seats. But there is nothing about the yard that really stands out. The field is boringly uniform; it feels neither cavernous nor intimate. And, sadly, snaring a ticket is easy because it is rarely full. As a result the atmosphere is often subdued, which is a pity. Maybe a strong run in 2008 will rekindle the atmosphere.

The Minor League System is...

The organization is recovering after being blitzed over the summer by the Rangers. Losing Jarrod Saltalamacchia, Neftali Feliz, Matt Harrison and Elvis Andrus put a big dent in the farm, but some good front office work has led a recovery.

Some believe that Jason Heywood, whom the Braves selected with their first pick of the 2007 draft, has the potential to be a standout player. Add in Jair Jurrjens and Gorkys Hernandez, who were picked up on the back end of the Renteria trade, and the Braves have started to address their minor league worries.

The other spot of good news is that Jordan Schafer took several huge strides forward at Rome and Myrtle Beach, hitting a combined .312/.374/.513 in what are ostensibly pitcher parks. Better yet, Schafer is a sprightly 22 years old with a ton of upside. Few could imagine the farm would be this healthy after the Texan garroting.

Favorite Team Blogs

Chop-n-Change (http://mvn.com/mlb-braves/)
Talking Chop (http://www.talkingchop.com/)
Braves Journal (http://www.bravesjournal.com/)

Keys for 2008

Players Lost from Last Year's Team

The highest profile departure was Andruw Jones, though considering he hit a bulimic .221/.311/.413 Braves fans won't miss him as much as they once feared. Other notable departures include Cormier; Edgar Renteria, who was traded to the Tigers; Pete Orr, who failed to make the 40-man roster; Ron Mahay, who was offered arbitration but declined and signed with the Royals; and Octavio Dotel, who signed with the White Sox. Jose Ascanio was sent to the Cubs, while Willie Harris was non-tendered and snapped up by the Nationals. Oscar Villarreal was sent to Houston for outfielder Josh Anderson.

Players Acquired

The highest-profile acquisition is Tom Glavine, who elected not to exercise his $13 million option with the Mets and finish his career in a Braves uniform. Despite imploding in September, Glavine had a fine season and should be a welcome addition to an under-strength rotation. Mike Hampton isn't really an acquisition, but it feels like it, since he has been on the DL for an eternity. Quiz question: Will the Braves have the oldest rotation in the majors this year?

Other acquisitions includer Jurrjens and Hernandez from the Tigers (for Renteria), Omar Infante and Will Ohman from the Cubs, Javy Lopez in a minor league deal and Anderson from the Astros

Reasons to be Optimistic

Smoltz, Hudson and Glavine aren't a bad front three for the rotation. If you add in a healthy Hampton and James, the rotation might actually be above average. Everyone knows that Rafael Soriano is one of the best relievers out there and with Mike Gonzalez due back in the early part of the season, the Braves have the stuff to win plenty of close games.

On the other side of the ledger, you can be sure the Braves will score a barrage of runs. Jeff Francoeur and Brian McCann will be a year older and better—Frenchy could even combine some of the plate discipline he showed in 2007 with his 2006 power. Chipper Jones, as ever, will produce a solid season with the timber and Teixiera will be out to score the loot in his free agency year. With the Mets and Phillies both struggling to assemble a decent pitching staff, the Braves have a great shot at capturing the NL East

Reasons to be Pessimistic

Despite the confident overtones of the Braves front office, namely that the rotation problems are fixed, starting pitching is decidedly shaky. Glavine and Smoltz are aged hurlers who are prone to injury or, at the least, bouts of ineffectiveness. Also, Hudson almost certainly pitched above station last year and is likely to end 2008 with an ERA is the 4s. And, as for Hampton ... he'll struggle to pitch a tent let alone 150 innings.

The Braves offense wildly outperformed last season. Escobar is not a .300 hitter; neither is Diaz. After a relatively healthy 2007, Chipper Jones is due a stint on the DL. Can he really string together two consecutive MVP seasons? No, it is very unlikely.

Defense also will take a hit. Although Andruw Jones was abominable at the plate, he is still one of the best center fielders in the bigs. It is unclear how the Braves will replace Jones, but a combination of Diaz in left and Kotsay in center won't be the same.

Also, if Soriano gets hurt or Gonzalez fails to return from the DL, the Braves could struggle to break .500. And with an unsigned Teixiera approaching free agency, this could be the Tomahawks' last shot at the postseason for some time.

Due for a Better Season

Hampton isn't only due a better season, he's due any season. Even if the Braves can eke out 100 innings from the veteran sinkerballer, it will be a huge bonus. Anything approaching a 4.00 ERA is gravy.

After challenging for a batting title in 2006, McCann was a disappointment in 2007, hitting only .270/.320/.452—a classic sophomore slump. Don't be fooled. As much as Heap played above his ceiling in 2006, he was below in 2007—expect the middle road in 2008.

Don't be surprised to see Francoeur have a breakout year. We've seen immense power since he burst onto the scene and last year we witnessed a bit more patience at the plate. This could be the year he finally pulls it all together.

Likely to Have a Worse Season

In this spot last year I predicted that Renteria and Chipper Jones would play worse than advertised, so get the salt out. Again, I'll plump for Chipper to slide down the age performance curve. I mean the man had an MVP season last year—he won't repeat it, surely.

On the staff, expect Hudson to regress some. Huddy had his finest year in a Braves uniform, finally vindicating the decision to snatch him from Oakland three years ago. This was partly because he was locating his splitter and sinker better but also because of luck. A three-year view would say that he outperformed in 2007 and we should expect an ERA in the 4.00 zone in 2008. Consider this little tidbit: Pre-break his OPS against was .646 and his ERA was 3.54; post-break his ERA was lower at 3.08 but OPS against was higher at .678—work that one out.

Still Left to Do

Not much. Perhaps a few more arms for the bullpen and don't be surprised to see a late veteran pick-up to fill out a couple of roster spots. Given the payroll constraints and pre-Christmas activity don't expect too much action before Opening Day.

Most Likely Team Outcome:

The NL East will likely remain a three-horse race with the Mets, Phillies and Braves all in contention for both the division and wild card. The Nationals and Marlins don't have enough talent to make a run just yet, maybe in 2009. Although the Braves aren't the strongest of the trio, expect all three to hover within 10 games of .500 for most of the season. It won't take much to break away … the team that is hottest in September will likely take the division. Will it be the Braves? Who knows, but the team is good enough to be playing for a postseason berth to the very death.

Player Projections

Batters

Josh Anderson (Center Field)

PA	R	H	2B	3B	HR	RBI	SO	BB	SB	CS	BA	OBP	SLG	OPS	3 Yr	Fld	F$
574	63	141	20	5	1	40	86	24	21	6	.267	.306	.329	.635	.001	C	$2

Anderson is a left-handed hitting center fielder who actually can hit the other way and walk. He's a good runner who can steal bases and is an above-average fielder who gets excellent jumps on the ball. He won't be mistaken for Jim Edmonds 2004, but he seems to be a prototypical center fielder.

Matt Diaz (Left Field)

PA	R	H	2B	3B	HR	RBI	SO	BB	SB	CS	BA	OBP	SLG	OPS	3 Yr	Fld	F$
392	51	112	22	3	11	52	66	19	3	1	.310	.351	.479	.830	-.046	A	$4

Diaz has an uncanny ability to hit for average. However, his plate discipline is poor and his glove work has been much criticized in the past. Amazingly, in the field we think he'll be above average. That isn't an aberration. Most other fielding systems thought he was at least that good in 2007. Diaz remains an important part of the lineup going into 2008. The downside is that if his batting average on balls in play is unlucky, his line could look a little ugly.

Yunel Escobar (Shortstop)

PA	R	H	2B	3B	HR	RBI	SO	BB	SB	CS	BA	OBP	SLG	OPS	3 Yr	Fld	F$
402	47	96	21	2	14	54	78	25	1	1	.261	.309	.443	.752	.016	B	$1

Escobar is projected to be a contact hitter without displaying a heap of power, despite hitting .295/.368/.413 in the minors. Digging a little deeper reveals that Yunel struggled in Double-A. Whether that is a reflection of true talent or is an aberration is unclear. If the latter, Yunel will be a serious downgrade on Renteria; if the former, expect the Braves' offensive juggernaut to steam ahead.

Jeff Francoeur (Right Field)

PA	R	H	2B	3B	HR	RBI	SO	BB	SB	CS	BA	OBP	SLG	OPS	3 Yr	Fld	F$
616	78	163	34	3	21	86	113	33	4	2	.286	.330	.467	.797	.051	C	$16

2007 heralded some improved plate discipline from the free-swinging Francoeur, and we expect that to continue in 2008. He has a cannon arm, but his positional play and range are sub-par, which means overall he is mediocre in the field. Overall there is considerable upside in these numbers, particularly in hitting. Jeff is a supremely talented ball player with the ability to hit for power. Last year he traded some of that power for patience. This year, I'd expect him to be challenging the 30-homer mark. Oh, and if you are in a fantasy league that relies on count stats, Jeff is your man—Cox plays him in almost every game.

Omar Infante (Shortstop)

PA	R	H	2B	3B	HR	RBI	SO	BB	SB	CS	BA	OBP	SLG	OPS	3 Yr	Fld	F$
288	34	70	15	2	6	31	48	17	4	1	.266	.312	.407	.719	.013	C	$1

Infante already has been dealt twice this offseason, finally landing with the Braves. Infante broke out in 2004 with a solid season, but that's now three seasons removed, so while Infante is still just 27, it's hard to tell what you will get from him. He'll probably start the season as a utility player for the Braves, but with an injury or two and some solid work with the bat, he could find himself in a starting role in the second half of the season.

Kelly Johnson (Second Base)

PA	R	H	2B	3B	HR	RBI	SO	BB	SB	CS	BA	OBP	SLG	OPS	3 Yr	Fld	F$
455	61	106	21	5	12	51	84	58	6	3	.274	.368	.447	.815	.016	D	$3

KJ was a revelation at second base last year. It was not so much for his work with the leather, although that wasn't bad, but because he was solid with the lumber. A projected OPS of .815 might seem on the low side, but he has the potential to beat that mark. Last year, he slugged 16 home runs. He'll be disappointed if he doesn't beat that mark this year.

Chipper Jones (Third Base)

PA	R	H	2B	3B	HR	RBI	SO	BB	SB	CS	BA	OBP	SLG	OPS	Fld	F$
527	78	137	32	2	23	83	75	74	3	2	.308	.404	.545	.949	B	$20

Larry's demise has been prognosticated for many years now, ever since his languid 2004, when he had a .248 batting average. In the last two seasons he has been a .320 hitter, which has vastly exceeded expectations. At 36 and with a mounting injury record, 2008 could be the year where the decline starts. It is all relative, though—expect Chipper to be good for 25 long balls and a low .300 batting average. A few more seasons like this and he'll be in the reckoning for the Hall of Fame.

Mark Kotsay (Center Field)

PA	R	H	2B	3B	HR	RBI	SO	BB	SB	CS	BA	OBP	SLG	OPS	3 Yr	Fld	F$
380	44	93	20	1	7	41	40	36	2	1	.277	.346	.405	.751	-.045	C	$1

When his back problems aren't keeping him out of games, they are sapping him of his range and his power. A microdiscectomy last April was supposed to have solved the issue, but the back problems recurred and cut his season short. Even if he's healthy, age may have taken the edge off his game. He still has a sniper's arm, though, and will make a lazy baserunner look foolish.

Brian McCann (Catcher)

PA	R	H	2B	3B	HR	RBI	SO	BB	SB	CS	BA	OBP	SLG	OPS	3 Yr	Fld	F$
558	73	146	35	2	20	81	75	47	1	3	.294	.356	.493	.849	.063	C	$11

McCann is one of the best hitting catchers in the league. The only area that lets him down is his plate discipline. It's not as though he strikes out a lot—he doesn't—but he walks infrequently. If he adds some walks, his OBP will edge up toward the .390 mark and he will establish himself as the cornerstone of the Braves offense.

Mark Teixiera (First Base)

PA	R	H	2B	3B	HR	RBI	SO	BB	SB	CS	BA	OBP	SLG	OPS	3 Yr	Fld	F$
583	86	146	32	2	30	97	105	75	1	1	.296	.391	.551	.942	-.003	B	$25

In terms of raw stats, Texeira's numbers are remarkably similar to Chipper's, though he has a little extra oomph. With Andruw Jones heading to Hollywood, Teixiera projects to have the most homers of any Atlanta hitter. All Wren needs to do now is to tie him to four-year contract. Chances of that happening? Zero.

Scott Thorman (First Base)

PA	R	H	2B	3B	HR	RBI	SO	BB	SB	CS	BA	OBP	SLG	OPS	3 Yr	Fld	F$
402	47	96	21	2	14	54	78	25	1	1	.261	.309	.443	.752	.016	B	$1

Thorman is one of those infuriating hitters who you know should be able to make a big league impact but hasn't. There has been speculation that Thorman will either be released or traded and by the time you read this he may have been. Only 26, he could break out, but you fear if he doesn't do so this season his career in the bigs is destined to be short and not especially sweet.

Pitchers

Blaine Boyer (Relief Pitcher)

W	L	ERA	TBF	IP	Hit	HR	SO	BB	HBP	3 Yr	F$
4	5	5.25	375	81	87	8	59	49	5	0.13	$1

Make no mistake; Boyer is good reliever with upside. An uneducated look at his stats might make you slightly worried but entering his age 26 season his career ERA is a healthy 3.71. However, the real issue is health: After facing seven batters in 2006, he faced 26 in the bigs last year. Because of that, and because of some inauspicious minor league numbers, our projections include a healthy dose of regression to the mean. If he gets called up to the 25-man roster, he should best that comfortably.

Buddy Carlyle (Relief Pitcher)

W	L	ERA	TBF	IP	Hit	HR	SO	BB	HBP	3 Yr	F$
6	9	5.06	583	134	143	21	105	47	6	0.31	$1

What Smoltz is to war horses, Carlyle is to journeymen. His 2007 W-L record was a respectable 8-7, though his ERA bordered on replacement level at 5.21. If he hits his projection, he could have some value to the ballclub this year. A poll of Braves fans will tell you that is a little optimistic.

Tom Glavine (Starting Pitcher)

W	L	ERA	TBF	IP	Hit	HR	SO	BB	HBP	F$
10	10	4.49	780	180	199	19	90	59	6	$1

How Glavine continues to get batters out is a mystery. His fastball has no particular life, and umpires no longer give him the outside corner. But he throws a changeup that is unlike any other major league pitcher's, and that appears to get the job done most of the time. When you watch him pitch, you can't help feeling that the genie will let the cat out of the bag at any moment.

Mike Gonzalez (Relief Pitcher)

W	L	ERA	TBF	IP	Hit	HR	SO	BB	HBP	3 Yr	F$
3	2	3.36	182	43	35	3	42	22	2	0.38	$1

The southpaw pitcher was super-effective last year before succumbing to a season-ending injury that required Tommy John surgery. That means he'll likely return after the All-Star break and probably will be used sparingly for the remainder of the season.

Mike Hampton (Starting Pitcher)

Given that Hampton hasn't thrown a pitch in anger in over two years, we haven't been able to include him in our projections. Suffice to say he could play an important role for the Braves in 2008. A rotation of Hampton, Glavine, Smoltz, James and Hudson isn't half bad. Beyond that. you'll get the heebie-jeebies.

Tim Hudson (Starting Pitcher)

W	L	ERA	TBF	IP	Hit	HR	SO	BB	HBP	3 Yr	F$
11	10	4.07	820	192	208	16	112	59	8	0.38	$4

Hudson showed Cy Young form with a 1.77 ERA through his first nine starts, pitching fewer than seven innings only once. The numbers predict a decline in strikeouts, which would run counter to his recent performance. Hudson is close to peak value and would be a good trade candidate provided the Braves could get a decent offer. Given the state of the pitching market, that shouldn't be difficult.

Chuck James (Starting Pitcher)

W	L	ERA	TBF	IP	Hit	HR	SO	BB	HBP	3 Yr	F$
8	9	4.76	672	156	156	26	117	56	6	0.08	$1

The most worrying aspect for Braves fans is James' inconsistency. He'll string together a couple of good starts only to get routed in the next five. Just as you think he should be demoted to Triple-A, he bounces back with a shutout, giving him leeway to lose another bunch of games. Despite the negativity, our projected ERA of 4.76 might be a touch bearish. His cumulative ERA in the bigs stands at 4.00, and that is largely as a starter. Expect something closer to his 4.24 mark of 2007.

Jair Jurrjens (Starting Pitcher)

W	L	ERA	TBF	IP	Hit	HR	SO	BB	HBP	3 Yr	F$
7	9	4.96	617	140	154	18	80	53	7	-0.71	$1

While Jurrjens was one of the Tigers' top five prospects heading into 2007, he pitched surprisingly well for the major league team when injuries did a number on their rotation in the second half. His low strikeout rate at the big league level was a little cause for concern, but he should still be fighting for a spot at the back of the Braves' rotation in 2008.

Peter Moylan (Relief Pitcher)

W	L	ERA	TBF	IP	Hit	HR	SO	BB	HBP	3 Yr	F$
4	4	4.42	335	75	76	6	58	40	5	0.46	$1

Moylan proved to be the pick of the Braves' relievers last year, recording an ERA of 1.80 over 90 innings. The worry is that his so-called breakout season came at age 28. Was it a fluke? This season will tell us for sure. If his ERA is 4.42 as projected, he'll have missed fans' expectations.

Chad Paronto (Relief Pitcher)

W	L	ERA	TBF	IP	Hit	HR	SO	BB	HBP	3 Yr	F$
3	4	4.56	281	64	68	6	39	28	3	0.40	$1

Paronto should secure a spot among the relief corps in spring training, although that may not be the correct decision. The last two years he has recorded a sub-4 ERA. Rather worryingly, last year, walks exceeded strike-outs—Paronto likes to get hitters out on ground balls. If that continues, expect his ERA to balloon and a trip to Triple-A will beckon.

Jo-Jo Reyes (Starting Pitcher)

W	L	ERA	TBF	IP	Hit	HR	SO	BB	HBP	3 Yr	F$
7	9	5.29	660	146	150	20	104	82	8	-0.40	$1

It is uncertain whether Reyes has a future as a starter in the major leagues. The problem last year was that he walked 20 percent more batters than he struck out. The worrying thing is that the THT numbers project he'll reverse that ratio but his ERA will remain stubbornly high. What with a veteran rotation and the uncertain form and health of Hampton, Reyes probably will be pegged as the No. 6 starter. Braves fans should start praying for the health of the other five immediately.

John Smoltz (Starting Pitcher)

W	L	ERA	TBF	IP	Hit	HR	SO	BB	HBP	F$
13	8	3.47	791	193	183	18	162	46	6	$21

Noun: an aged pitcher who has an uncanny ability to churn out 200-plus innings a season while recording an infinitesimally small ERA. Synonym: war horse.

When an athlete is as old as Smoltz the risk of spending time on the sidelines increases. The good news for Braves fans is that he re-signed with Atlanta on favorable terms partway through the 2007 season. Don't be surprised if he rewards the team with another Cy Young.

Rafael Soriano (Relief Pitcher)

W	L	ERA	TBF	IP	Hit	HR	SO	BB	HBP	3 Yr	F$
5	3	3.44	284	70	57	8	68	21	2	0.30	$14

Mariners fans are still bristling at how the Braves managed to snare one of the best young relievers in the game for Horacio Ramirez, but they did. After the ousting of Bob Wickman last year, Soriano was the designated closer, which is a role he is expected to keep in 2008. He strikes out one per inning and has reasonable control. A projected ERA of 3.44 doesn't smell of elite closer, but this kid is the real deal.

Tyler Yates (Relief Pitcher)

W	L	ERA	TBF	IP	Hit	HR	SO	BB	HBP	3 Yr	F$
4	3	4.11	288	66	60	6	61	35	3	0.28	$1

The one thing that Tyler Yates has going for him is that he throws the ball with some serious heat. He can touch 97 on the gun without too much difficulty but he is wild, typically walking a batter every other inning. His career ERA is 5.15 (his 2007 ERA was 5.18) so it is hard to see how he'll get close to his projection.

Baltimore Orioles

by Jeff Sackmann of The Hardball Times

2008 Projections

Record: 69-93
Division Rank: Last, 28 games back
Runs Scored: 752
Runs Allowed: 865

2007 in a Nutshell

It wasn't pretty, but it wasn't unexpected. Back in spring training, optimistic fans could construct a plausible scenario that would get the O's to 75 or even 80 wins. But there were too many weak offensive performances at the corners (Jay Payton, AL left fielder?), and never enough starting pitching to get the team through a week unscathed.

There was plenty to root for, namely the emergence of Nick Markakis and the studliness of Erik Bedard. Jeremy Guthrie proved to be a tremendous waiver-wire pickup, and ... well, that's about it. Whether due to an unimaginative front office staff or the micromanagement of Peter Angelos, there's no clear plan in place. It's been the same story for years: The O's were going to lose with or without veterans such as Miguel Tejada; they chose to lose with them.

General Comments

Team Strengths

Markakis and Brian Roberts are quality offensive players, and depending on Adam Loewen's recovery, Baltimore could end up with three above-average starting pitchers. Middle relief is a likely asset, though aging and pricey.

Team Weaknesses

It wouldn't be surprising if six or seven guys in the Opening Day starting lineup were average or worse at their position. No single player is the problem, especially now that Payton won't be starting in a corner, but that's a lot of mediocrity for a lineup without Albert Pujols in it. On the other side of the bat, there's a lot of finger-crossing that passes for solutions in the back of the starting rotation.

The General Manager is Known for...

He follows orders. Angelos is in charge here regardless of what Mike Flanagan's title is, and he's late, indecisive or both when it comes to just about any important decision. Tejada was finally dealt, and Bedard and/or Roberts could be next, but when forecasting the future in Baltimore, it's always best to err on the side of indecision and overspending.

The Manager is Known for...

When we find out, we'll let you know. Dave Trembley was a midseason replacement, and it's his first try in the bigs. The O's were as bad under him as they were under Sam Perlozzo. If he is particularly skilled, we probably won't figure it out in 2008.

Ballpark Characteristics

Historically, Camden Yards is pretty, and pretty close to neutral.

The Minor League System is...

It's getting better. Angelos surprised nearly everybody by selecting and then signing slugging catcher Matt Wieters in the '07 draft. Wieters is a bright spot among a very small group of quality hitters. There's a lot of upside among the hurlers in the system, though it's tough not to think of the recent Pirates farm: lots of arms, lots of highly-ranked prospects, and ... lots of injuries.

Favorite Team Blogs

Camden Chat (http://www.camdenchat.com/)
Oriole Magic (http://mvn.com/mlb-orioles/)

Keys for 2008

Players Lost from Last Year's Team

Catcher Paul Bako, outfielder Corey Patterson, infielder Miguel Tejada, pitcher Steve Trachsel.

Players Acquired

Pitcher Matt Albers, Greg Aquino, Dennis Sarfate, Troy Patton and Lance Cormier; outfielders Chris Roberson and Luke Scott.

Reasons to be Optimistic

The Tejada trade makes the team younger, and Flanagan has done a nice job of bringing in high-upside relief arms such as Aquino and Sarfate. The farm system should start making meaningful contributions by 2009.

Reasons to be Pessimistic

There's an awful lot of dead weight on this team, and most of it is on the wrong side of 30. Adding insult to injury, Tampa Bay is slowly turning things around, making a fifth place finish a plausible outcome in Baltimore.

Due for a Better Season

One of these years, Daniel Cabrera will put things together. Danys Baez can't be as bad as he was last year, and there are enough projects in the bullpen that O's fans will get a surprise from somebody.

Likely to Have a Worse Season

Markakis won't bomb, but it's likely he was playing over his head in 2007. Expect a step back to the tune of 30-50 OPS points. While he may have a bright future, Guthrie is another young player for whom the wattage will come down some in '08.

Still Left to Do

Who will play shortstop? Tejada left a gaping hole without any semblance of an internal solution. Center field is another question mark, though with Roberson and Payton in the mix, someone will go out there every day and run fast.

Most Likely Team Outcome

While the Yankees and Red Sox fight it out for playoff spots in September, the O's will find themselves in a heated battle with the Rays for fourth place, 70 wins, and whatever is left of their dignity.

Player Projections

Batters

Paul Bako (Catcher)

PA	R	H	2B	3B	HR	RBI	SO	BB	SB	CS	BA	OBP	SLG	OPS	Fld	F$
263	25	55	10	1	3	21	60	25	1	1	.236	.310	.326	.636	C	$1

The Orioles certainly didn't pony up for four years of Hernandez with the expectation that Paul Bako would ever play in 60 games. But he did and, well, let's hope that doesn't happen again. Bako is almost as good as Gary Bennett in inspiring fans to think, "Give me a million bucks and I can slug .229, too!" and he should probably enter the Triple-A player-coach phase of his career soon. But meanwhile, hey, they say he can call a good game.

Freddie Bynum (Shortstop)

PA	R	H	2B	3B	HR	RBI	SO	BB	SB	CS	BA	OBP	SLG	OPS	3 Yr	Fld	F$
236	30	54	10	4	4	22	53	16	10	2	.253	.309	.394	.703	-.007	C	$1

Among the flotilla of middle infielders who will fight it out in Orioles camp this spring, Bynum probably has the best chance of a steady job. That's doesn't mean he'd get one with very many of the other 29 teams, but he stumbled into an ideal situation. His versatility makes it difficult to evaluate him as a defender, with only a handful of games at each position in any given year, but if he can hack it at shortstop, his .700ish OPS will make him a credible option, and put him squarely on the Craig Counsell career path. It's the stuff that dreams are made of.

Brandon Fahey (Shortstop)

PA	R	H	2B	3B	HR	RBI	SO	BB	SB	CS	BA	OBP	SLG	OPS	3 Yr	Fld	F$
440	45	95	12	5	2	28	65	29	9	4	.239	.294	.309	.603	.001	C	$1

With Tejada gone, anything's possible. Even Brandon Fahey getting some starts at short. We project him to just peek over the .600 OPS mark, which suggests he'd be stretched as a starter in the International League, but desperate times call for desperate measures. He may compete for a starting job, but if he gets 250 at-bats again, the Rays probably will charge into fourth place unimpeded.

Jay Gibbons (Left Field)

PA	R	H	2B	3B	HR	RBI	SO	BB	SB	CS	BA	OBP	SLG	OPS	3 Yr	Fld	F$
369	44	89	20	1	13	50	54	26	1	1	.265	.317	.446	.763	-.027	C	$1

It's unclear what will be worse for Gibbons' career—admitting to HGH use, or ceasing his HGH use. Gibbons' stats over the last few years are exactly the sort of thing that get people riled up about PEDs. His solid years came with a healthy dose of slugging, and everything good about his game went missing in 2007. I suspect that's not just HGH detox, but whatever it is, it doesn't bode well for Gibbons' chances of ever getting 300 at-bats again.

Ramon Hernandez (Catcher)

PA	R	H	2B	3B	HR	RBI	SO	BB	SB	CS	BA	OBP	SLG	OPS	3 Yr	Fld	F$
443	53	109	22	1	14	57	62	34	1	1	.274	.334	.439	.773	-.036	C	$1

In two years, Hernandez has gone from a high-profile signing to a stopgap while the O's wait for uber-prospect Matt Wieters to develop. The 2007 season was his worst power year since 2002 by a huge margin, meaning he should be in for something of a rebound—we're optimistically projecting him to gain 50 points of SLG, putting him higher than his career average. That's always iffy for an aging catcher, especially one who has started fewer than 110 games in three of the last four years. If Hernandez does stay healthy and productive, he's likely to find himself in a new uniform long before his four-year contract expires.

Aubrey Huff (Designated Hitter)

PA	R	H	2B	3B	HR	RBI	SO	BB	SB	CS	BA	OBP	SLG	OPS	3 Yr	Fld	F$
548	67	132	27	2	18	71	78	50	2	3	.270	.338	.444	.782	-.034	C	$6

The Orioles under Flanagan and Angelos seem to really like their veteran corner guys. Huff is an ideal solution then: He's a veteran, and he can play all the corners. Even DH! Huff isn't a bad player, nor is he even bad at his current price ($8 million in both '08 and '09), but he's little more than an expensive wall hanging for the Orioles at this point.

Nick Markakis (Right Field)

PA	R	H	2B	3B	HR	RBI	SO	BB	SB	CS	BA	OBP	SLG	OPS	3 Yr	Fld	F$
595	78	152	32	3	18	77	91	53	10	4	.287	.352	.460	.812	.031	B	$15

Finally, a hitter from the farm made it, and made good! Markakis is the real thing, a toolsy player with the skills to convert those tools to wins. He outperformed all but the most optimistic projections for 2007 with a 900+ OPS as a 23-year-old. Unsurprisingly, we're projecting a step back; after all, at this point two years ago, he didn't have a single major league at-bat. The rosy path to superstardom is a possibility, but even the middle road represents a very good outcome for the Orioles. Solid defense only makes him more valuable.

Kevin Millar (First Base)

PA	R	H	2B	3B	HR	RBI	SO	BB	SB	CS	BA	OBP	SLG	OPS	Fld	F$
516	64	114	24	1	14	59	80	66	1	2	.262	.365	.418	.783	D	$1

Millar is clearly on the decline, but when a slide starts from an OBP in the .380 range, it can be a long, gentle slope. His power took a hit in 2007, but he kept walking, even reaching base safely in 52 consecutive games at one point. Millar probably won't be a full-time player on a contender again, but it's easy to imagine him following in Scott Hatteberg's footsteps as a platoon on-base specialist. The Orioles don't have any better options unless they want to put Aubrey Huff in the field, so expect another 450-500 plate appearances.

Melvin Mora (Third Base)

PA	R	H	2B	3B	HR	RBI	SO	BB	SB	CS	BA	OBP	SLG	OPS	Fld	F$
545	67	132	23	1	15	65	83	50	8	2	.276	.346	.422	.768	C	$6

Our projections still reflect a bit of that mid-decade magic, the two years when Mora slugged over .500 and was a genuine star. The two more pertinent years, though, are the most recent ones in which Mora looks like the same guy he was in his late 20s: a player without a good enough bat to deserve a permanent home at a corner, and not quite enough glove to earn him a spot up the middle. The glove certainly isn't getting any better, and while I don't like to bet against algorithms, I'd happily wager that his bat is headed in the same direction.

Corey Patterson (Center Field)

PA	R	H	2B	3B	HR	RBI	SO	BB	SB	CS	BA	OBP	SLG	OPS	3 Yr	Fld	F$
493	66	119	20	3	12	55	79	26	33	7	.266	.309	.405	.714	-.033	A	$1

Patterson has been impressing and letting down and generally confusing onlookers for so long that it's tough to remember that he's still 28 years old. He's offered everything from a half-season of near-All-Star numbers to a

2005 that made Bill Bergen rush to protect his place in the history books. All of which is a long way of saying that this is one tough dude to project. The speed will be there, the on-base skills won't, but everything else? Your guess is as good as ours.

Jay Payton (Left Field)

PA	R	H	2B	3B	HR	RBI	SO	BB	SB	CS	BA	OBP	SLG	OPS	Fld	F$
480	54	121	21	3	10	52	47	28	3	1	.276	.320	.405	.725	B	$1

Payton is a useful player. Every team should have one. No team, however, should give him more than a handful of starts in a corner. The odds are high that he'll outperform his dreadful .256/.292/.376 performance from 2007, but the chances are slim he'll do so by a wide enough margin to earn more than a couple hundred at-bats.

Tike Redman (Center Field)

PA	R	H	2B	3B	HR	RBI	SO	BB	SB	CS	BA	OBP	SLG	OPS	3 Yr	Fld	F$
450	50	109	18	5	2	34	49	26	15	4	.264	.307	.346	.653	-.035	D	$1

Maybe it's just me, but whenever a player spends a full year out of the big leagues, I tend to assume he's washed up, and by extension, about 37 years old. So while Tike put together an above-average half-season, I was more shocked by his age (he'll turn 31 in March) than his out-of-nowhere production.

Brian Roberts (Second Base)

PA	R	H	2B	3B	HR	RBI	SO	BB	SB	CS	BA	OBP	SLG	OPS	3 Yr	Fld	F$
620	90	156	35	4	12	68	78	68	36	5	.289	.365	.435	.800	-.030	A	$24

Roberts is one of only two true assets in the Baltimore offense, which means trade rumors are likely to continue right up to the day he tries on a new uniform. For Roberts, 2005 and '06 were a roller-coaster ride, with his OPS falling almost 150 points, but '07 was a respectable middle road that gives us a much better idea of what to expect in the future.

Luke Scott (Left Field)

PA	R	H	2B	3B	HR	RBI	SO	BB	SB	CS	BA	OBP	SLG	OPS	3 Yr	Fld	F$
477	66	112	25	4	20	68	96	55	3	1	.272	.359	.497	.856	-.027	C	$1

A good-hitting lefty corner outfielder, he hits both southpaws and right handers and hits for power. He is above average as a right fielder and has a powerful and reasonably accurate arm. He isn't especially fast, and won't steal bases, but he doesn't get himself out on the basepaths. He hits best if played every day; he's a poor pinch hitter.

Pitchers

Matt Albers (Starting Pitcher)

W	L	ERA	TBF	IP	Hit	HR	SO	BB	HBP	3 Yr	F$
6	10	5.77	654	141	162	20	72	77	9	-0.41	$1

Right-hander Albers seemed to have a lot more potential than he showed when he arrived in Houston. His minor league numbers were excellent, but in in the majors, he had a great deal of difficulty, giving up more more hits and three times as many home runs. Unless a miracle occurs, he's going to have some serious trouble facing AL East lineups.

Danys Baez (Relief Pitcher)

W	L	ERA	TBF	IP	Hit	HR	SO	BB	HBP	3 Yr	F$
3	4	4.54	261	59	59	7	35	28	3	0.28	$1

Here's an interesting thought: Baez has 114 career saves, including 25 or more in three separate seasons, but he's never been more valuable than he was as a starter in 2002, going 10-11 with an ERA of 4.41 in 165 innings. He's basically Joe Borowski without the benefit of a winning team to support his 5.00+ ERA, a so-called power reliever without the strikeout numbers to back up any claim that he uses the power effectively.

Erik Bedard (Starting Pitcher)

W	L	ERA	TBF	IP	Hit	HR	SO	BB	HBP	3 Yr	F$
12	7	3.33	710	171	150	15	172	61	5	0.30	$18

Before the 2007 season, most of us knew that Bedard was good, but this? Way more than a strikeout per inning, a strikeout-to-walk ratio (K/BB) ratio of nearly four to one, barely a baserunner per frame … wow. It's still in the air whether Bedard will be pitching for the Orioles come April, but it's abundantly clear that regardless of the uniform, he'll dominate.

Rob Bell (Relief Pitcher)

W	L	ERA	TBF	IP	Hit	HR	SO	BB	HBP	3 Yr	F$
5	8	5.69	512	113	133	19	59	48	4	0.32	$1

Fun facts: Rob Bell has pitched in parts of six major league seasons, has only once posted an ERA under 5.00, and is a righty. It's refreshing to know that such a thing is still possible, at least as long as you don't give that guy too many innings, or you trade him to a division rival that is inexplicably enamored with his stuff. By this point, a few years after his transition to the bullpen, Bell is a known quantity, one that our projections suggest will post a 5.69 ERA with just barely as many strikeouts as walks.

Chad Bradford (Relief Pitcher)

W	L	ERA	TBF	IP	Hit	HR	SO	BB	HBP	3 Yr	F$
4	3	4.10	282	65	73	4	35	21	3	0.38	$1

Bradford is a rare creature: a consistently effective right-handed specialist, and as long as Dave Trembley remembers to use him that way, he's likely to keep performing. He has had a full-season ERA over 4.00 only once in his career, suggesting that our projected 4.10 ERA is conservative. He may not last in Baltimore if management decides to sell off the veterans, but he'll keep getting guys out somewhere.

Brian Burres (Relief Pitcher)

W	L	ERA	TBF	IP	Hit	HR	SO	BB	HBP	3 Yr	F$
5	8	5.54	526	114	125	17	79	63	6	0.09	$1

If the Orioles are going to get better performance out of the 121 innings that Burres pitched last year, they better hope that they don't have to give them to Burres again. He is a useful enough player, a sort of stereotype of a weak team's sixth starter, but there's little in his history to suggest he'll develop into anything more.

Daniel Cabrera (Starting Pitcher)

W	L	ERA	TBF	IP	Hit	HR	SO	BB	HBP	3 Yr	F$
10	10	4.32	796	180	167	19	154	100	8	0.13	$1

Everybody knows that Cabrera has an uneasy relationship with the strike zone. He's about to turn 27 and he hasn't shown improvement, so it's reasonable to assume he'll walk a guy every other inning as long as the O's keep sending him out there. The surprise in 2007 was his home run rate, which skyrocketed. With Cabrera, it's best to accept the bases on balls and fervently hope that the wind is blowing in.

Jeremy Guthrie (Starting Pitcher)

W	L	ERA	TBF	IP	Hit	HR	SO	BB	HBP	3 Yr	F$
8	9	4.69	657	150	156	20	95	61	6	0.48	$1

Now, this you don't see every day. A 28-year-old rookie makes 26 starts and manages an ERA of 3.70? The peripherals are a bit shaky: While a two-to-one K/BB ratio is nice, there aren't that many strikeouts to start with. Despite the caveats, even a disappointing sophomore season from Guthrie will be very useful in Baltimore. If he comes close to his projection, that'll mean he's doing his part to keep the likes of Steve Trachsel and Victor Zambrano out of the O's organization.

Radhames Liz (Relief Pitcher)

W	L	ERA	TBF	IP	Hit	HR	SO	BB	HBP	3 Yr	F$
5	10	6.71	639	133	148	25	103	95	10	-0.29	$1

Liz is sort of like a young version of Daniel Cabrera, only better. Or so the Orioles hope. He's got the strikeouts, he's got the walks, and in his first try in Baltimore, he got the pummeling. Bringing the 24-year-old Liz up from Double-A might not have been the smartest move in his development—he's still a top prospect, and it would've taken an unexpectedly poised performance to put him in the running for a spot on the 2008 Opening Day roster. As is, he's still something of a project, albeit one that could pay big dividends in 2009 and beyond. Or, of course, turn into Cabrera.

Adam Loewen (Starting Pitcher)

W	L	ERA	TBF	IP	Hit	HR	SO	BB	HBP	3 Yr	F$
5	5	4.96	427	93	95	10	68	58	5	-0.23	$1

So much promise, so much time on the disabled list. A return from the operating table of Dr. James Andrews usually isn't a rapid process, so Loewen is far from a lock to be in the Opening Day starting rotation. Uncertainty aside, he is one of the better options for the middle of the O's rotation, despite his lack of an extensive statistical track record.

Garrett Olson (Starting Pitcher)

W	L	ERA	TBF	IP	Hit	HR	SO	BB	HBP	3 Yr	F$
7	9	5.60	671	147	162	24	102	73	9	-0.29	$1

A glance at Olson's stat line—23 years old, 7.79 ERA in seven starts—suggests he was rushed to the bigs, but his minor league stats do a good job of describing someone who was ready for the jump. He's still a top-10 prospect in Baltimore, but I can't imagine that he'll retain that status if he coughs up another seven starts like the ones from his first time around the league. He is a lefty, so middle relief is always a reasonable backup plan. But given the O's lack of depth in the rotation, anything better than 7.79 will probably keep Olson working on Plan A.

Chris Ray (Relief Pitcher)

W	L	ERA	TBF	IP	Hit	HR	SO	BB	HBP	3 Yr	F$
4	2	3.80	240	57	49	7	51	24	2	-0.06	$1

Ray is out, likely until 2009, recovering from Tommy John surgery. This is one of those rare times the O's look smart: Not only did they pass on B.J. Ryan (who also missed lots of time to injury) to go with the cheap, in-house alternative, but they also spent big on middle relief the very year they needed a closer by committee to replace Ray.

Jamie Walker (Relief Pitcher)

W	L	ERA	TBF	IP	Hit	HR	SO	BB	HBP	F$
4	3	4.23	267	62	62	8	42	21	2	$1

His usage patterns are about as lefty-specialist typical as they come, but in his given role, Walker is really, really good. Our projections are pessimistic, figuring that like any reliever, he'll regress toward the mean with a vengeance, but he's one of the few middle relievers with a track record that points toward continued success.

Boston Red Sox

by Ben Jacobs of The Hardball Times

2008 Projections

Record: 97-65
Division Rank: 1st, by four games
Runs Scored: 850
Runs Allowed: 690

2007 in a Nutshell

The Red Sox couldn't have scripted the first half of the season any better. While the Yankees struggled out of the gate, Boston could hardly lose over the first two months. At the end of May, the Red Sox were 36-16, 10 games ahead of second-place Baltimore and 13.5 games ahead of the last-place Yankees.

The Red Sox hit some speed bumps the rest of the season while the Yankees recovered, and the division lead dwindled almost to nothing at times in September. But the Red Sox ultimately kept the Yankees at bay and held the lead in the AL East from April 18 through the end of the season to win their first division title since 1995.

Boston easily swept the Angels in the first round of the playoffs and took the first game from Cleveland in the ALCS before things went south and the Indians took three in a row. A gem from Josh Beckett got the Red Sox back on track, and they used their own three-game streak to win the pennant before going on to sweep the Rockies for their second World Series title in four years.

The biggest key to the season for the Red Sox was the trade they made with the Marlins the year before. In 2006, Beckett wasn't the ace he was supposed to be, struggling to a 5.01 ERA while Mike Lowell helped salvage the trade a little by posting an .814 OPS. Lowell was even better in 2007, posting an .879 OPS and setting career highs in RBIs, batting average and on-base percentage. This time, Beckett held up his end of the bargain as well, going 20-7 with a 3.27 ERA to finish second in the Cy Young voting.

As good as they were, however, the Red Sox did have some disappointments. Boston spent a bundle of money in the offseason on free agents Julio Lugo and J.D. Drew, and neither of them played up to expectations. Lugo played solid defense but had an anemic .643 OPS while Drew posted a .796 OPS and became the player Red Sox fans loved to hate until his key grand slam in the sixth game of the ALCS.

General Comments

Team Strengths

The Red Sox were very balanced in 2007, allowing the fewest runs in the AL while scoring the third most. The biggest strength was the bullpen. Jonathan Papelbon and Hideki Okajima handled the last two innings of most close games and combined for a 2.05 ERA in 127.1 innings. Manny Delcarmen, Mike Timlin, Javier Lopez and Kyle Snyder were also solid for the Red Sox out of the bullpen.

The starting pitching (particularly Beckett and Curt Schilling) was mostly very good, and the lineup had one great hitter (David Ortiz) and several good hitters (Kevin Youkilis, Dustin Pedroia, Lowell and Manny Ramirez).

Team Weaknesses

If the Red Sox had a real weakness, it was that the team lacked the home run power that had made the offense so scary in recent seasons. After averaging 213 homers per season from 2003-06 (with a low of 192 in 2006), the Red Sox hit only 166 in 2007. Ortiz led the team with 35 and nobody else hit more than 21. Those 56 homers from Boston's top two power hitters paled in comparison to the numbers Ortiz and Ramirez posted in 2006 (89 combined homers), 2005 (92) and 2004 (84).

The General Manager is Known for...

At this point, Theo Epstein is known more as the man who helped turn the Red Sox into one of baseball's elite franchises than as the guy who was the youngest GM in baseball.

He looks for bargains where he can find them, particularly with hitters, but he is more than willing to dip into Boston's deep bank account to sign the players he thinks he needs. He tends to build his bullpens in bulk, signing a bunch of guys to one-year deals and then seeing who works out, rather than committing several years to one reliever he really likes.

The Manager is Known for...

With two championships under his belt, Terry Francona is starting to get much more respect as a manager. He's a player's manager who generally seems to have a good grasp of how to keep guys happy and performing well. He's certainly not a master strategist, but he doesn't make obvious blunders very often, either. He used to struggle managing his relievers, but his bullpen use in 2007 was generally good. Of course, it helps to have a very good bullpen at your disposal.

Ballpark Characteristics

Fenway Park was more favorable to hitters in 2007 than it had been in any season since 1993. Between those seasons, it had mostly checked in as a slightly above-average park for hitters, so the sudden spike in 2007 was probably just random. Still, Fenway is a tiny park and will likely always be at least something of a boon to hitters.

The Minor League System is...

The upper levels have been stripped in the last two seasons by trades (Hanley Ramirez and Anibel Sanchez) and promotions (Jonathan Papelbon, Dustin Pedroia, Jacoby Ellsbury and Clay Buchholz). The best prospects left in the high minors are shortstop Jed Lowrie (.896 OPS between Double-A and Triple-A in 2007) and pitchers Michael Bowden (3.34 ERA with 128/41 strikeout-to-walk ratio (K/BB) in 142.2 innings between Single-A and Double-A) and Justin Masterson (4.33 ERA with 115/40 K/BB ratio in 153.2 innings between Single-A and Double-A).

The lower levels of the system have much more talent. The Red Sox have not been shy about using their money in the last three drafts to ensure that they get more talent than a team drafting in their slot probably should.

Favorite Team Blogs

Keys to the Game (http://keystothegame.blogspot.com/)

The Soxaholix (http://www.soxaholix.com/)

Over the Monster (www.overthemonster.com).

Feeding the Monster (http://www.sethmnookin.com/blog/)

Yanksfan vs. Soxfan (http://yanksfansoxfan.typepad.com/ysfs/)

Keys for 2008

Players Lost from Last Year's Team

Pitcher Eric Gagne, outfielder Bobby Kielty, infielders Royce Clayton and Eric Hinske.

Players Acquired

None.

Reasons to be Optimistic

The Red Sox are coming off a World Series championship and didn't lose a single important player. Even more, youngsters Ellsbury and Buchholz will be with the major league team for a full season instead of just as late-season call-ups. Japanese import Daisuke Matsuzaka may be more effective in his second season in the majors after turning in a decent rookie season while dealing with a difficult transition.

Reasons to be Pessimistic

The only thing Red Sox fans could possibly be unhappy about on Opening Day is that the much-discussed trade for Johan Santana never happened. And even so, the Red Sox will open the season as favorites to win a third World Series in five years. If there's one thing to worry about at all, it's that several key pieces of the team (Ramirez, Jason Varitek, Schilling, Tim Wakefield and Lowell) are getting old and could stop producing without warning.

Due for a Better Season

Lugo had the worst offensive season of his career and should bounce back at least a little. Drew also didn't play up to his abilities, hitting significantly worse than he had over the previous four seasons. Ramirez posted his worst season since his rookie year, and he could easily rebound to his normal levels. Matsuzaka wasn't bad, but he clearly struggled at times and with a year of adjustment under his belt, he could be significantly better.

Likely to Have a Worse Season

Lowell will be 34 when the season starts, so he's more likely to decline at least a little bit than anything else. Pedroia surprised a lot of people with his offensive production on the way to winning the Rookie of the Year award, but it wouldn't be a shock to see him slump a little as a sophomore. And Okajima may not be quite so dominant now that major league hitters have had a chance to face him for a year and study him.

Still Left to Do

Sign backup position players.

Most Likely Team Outcome

Win AL East and advance to at least the American League Championship Series.

Player Projections

Batters

Alex Cora (Second Base)

PA	R	H	2B	3B	HR	RBI	SO	BB	SB	CS	BA	OBP	SLG	OPS	3 Yr	Fld	F$
304	34	70	15	3	3	26	36	20	2	1	.262	.324	.374	.698	-.044	A+	$1

Cora is one of those rare players who can't hit for average, can't hit for power and can't draw walks. That makes him pretty useless in general on offense, but he plays solid defense at both middle infield positions. He can look okay at the plate for two- to three-week stretches, but he's strictly backup material.

Coco Crisp (Center Field)

PA	R	H	2B	3B	HR	RBI	SO	BB	SB	CS	BA	OBP	SLG	OPS	3 Yr	Fld	F$
532	69	133	30	4	8	54	76	42	23	4	.280	.336	.410	.746	-.034	B	$2

It's seems strange that a player would produce two nearly identical seasons followed by two nearly identical seasons of a different caliber, but that's exactly what Crisp has done. His last two years in Cleveland, he had OBPs of .344 and .345 and SLGs of .446 and .465. His first two years in Boston, he had OBPs of .317 and .330 and SLGs of .385 and .382. For whatever reason, it's clear that Crisp is no longer the hitter he was those last two seasons with the Indians. He can hit .270, maybe .280, with a bunch of doubles and a handful of triples and homers, but he's not going to hit .300 with 15 homers again any time soon.

J.D. Drew (Right Field)

PA	R	H	2B	3B	HR	RBI	SO	BB	SB	CS	BA	OBP	SLG	OPS	3 Yr	Fld	F$
514	67	117	29	4	12	57	89	75	3	2	.272	.380	.441	.821	-.032	C	$3

Drew exhibits great patience at the plate, but he sometimes passes on quality pitches and drew the ire of Red Sox fans last year by striking out frequently in important situations. Still, he's always struck out a lot and he's rarely been as unproductive at the plate as he was in 2007. His power should bounce back at least somewhat in 2008.

Jacoby Ellsbury (Center Field)

PA	R	H	2B	3B	HR	RBI	SO	BB	SB	CS	BA	OBP	SLG	OPS	3 Yr	Fld	F$
540	67	135	25	6	1	40	76	34	24	3	.274	.327	.355	.682	.001	C	$5

For some reason, our projections really don't like Ellsbury. He's clearly not going to match the .903 OPS he posted in limited playing time last year, mostly because he's not going to hit .353. But he makes good contact, has blazing speed and showed power in the majors that he never really displayed in the minors. A conservative estimate for what he might do in his rookie season would probably be a .340 OBP and .400 SLG.

Eric Hinske (First Base)

PA	R	H	2B	3B	HR	RBI	SO	BB	SB	CS	BA	OBP	SLG	OPS	3 Yr	Fld	F$
327	42	74	20	2	10	41	73	37	3	1	.261	.349	.452	.801	-.026	C	$1

Hinske's fallen hard since his impressive rookie season. He still has a bit of power and some patience at the plate, but he rarely shows much ability to hit for a decent average any more. He is versatile; he's a solid fielder at all four corner positions.

Mike Lowell (Third Base)

PA	R	H	2B	3B	HR	RBI	SO	BB	SB	CS	BA	OBP	SLG	OPS	3 Yr	Fld	F$
583	72	148	38	1	15	74	67	50	2	1	.284	.345	.447	.792	-.043	D	$8

Lowell's 2007 season was a bit misleading because he actually displayed significantly less power than in 2006 if you take into account that his batting average was 40 points higher in 2007. If Lowell's batting average returns to a level more in line with the rest of his career, you can expect overall production closer to his 2006 level. Either way, it's clear now that either something was wrong with him in 2005 or he just had one of those fluky bad years.

Julio Lugo (Shortstop)

PA	R	H	2B	3B	HR	RBI	SO	BB	SB	CS	BA	OBP	SLG	OPS	3 Yr	Fld	F$
558	72	134	32	3	7	54	76	47	29	5	.271	.334	.390	.724	-.040	C	$11

Most of Lugo's 2007 numbers fit right in with the rest of his career. He hit 36 doubles and eight home runs, drew 48 walks and struck out 82 times. None of that is out of the ordinary for him. The trouble came with hitting singles. He averaged a single every 6.4 at-bats in 2007 after averaging one every five at-bats the previous three seasons. Give him just 14 extra singles over the season, bringing him to one every 5.5 at-bats, and his OPS rises from .643 to .690. He did have his best base-stealing season with 33 in 39 attempts, so his speed isn't fading as he ages past 30.

Doug Mirabelli (Catcher)

PA	R	H	2B	3B	HR	RBI	SO	BB	SB	CS	BA	OBP	SLG	OPS	Fld	F$
230	28	50	11	0	8	30	59	20	1	1	.246	.319	.418	.737	C	$1

Our projections for Mirabelli seem very generous. His assets have always been a bit of power and, since joining Boston, the ability to catch the knuckleball. He still has those assets to some degree, but they don't overcome the fact that he can't get hits in general. He has a .206 batting average over the last three seasons and he struggles to make contact, as shown by him striking out more than a third of the time in that span.

Brandon Moss (Right Field)

PA	R	H	2B	3B	HR	RBI	SO	BB	SB	CS	BA	OBP	SLG	OPS	3 Yr	Fld	F$
531	57	116	31	3	9	53	134	43	3	2	.242	.303	.375	.678	.027	B	$1

Moss strikes out a ton, but he's shown great doubles power and some home run pop in the minors to go with solid patience at the plate. In his brief major league call-up, he showed that he can stay disciplined at the plate and get some hits, including a few for extra bases. He should at least be able to produce enough to be a nice fourth outfielder at this point in his career.

David Ortiz (Designated Hitter)

PA	R	H	2B	3B	HR	RBI	SO	BB	SB	CS	BA	OBP	SLG	OPS	3 Yr	Fld	F$
617	99	152	36	1	38	114	102	106	2	1	.304	.423	.608	1.031	-.029	C	$33

Despite hitting his fewest home runs since 2003, Ortiz actually had his best offensive season in 2007, setting career highs in batting average, on-base percentage and doubles. Ortiz showed his versatility on offense as he compensated for his decrease in home run power, presumably due to the injuries that bothered him in 2007, with an increase in singles and doubles. That versatility should allow him to continue to be productive in the coming years.

Dustin Pedroia (Second Base)

PA	R	H	2B	3B	HR	RBI	SO	BB	SB	CS	BA	OBP	SLG	OPS	3 Yr	Fld	F$
541	65	141	34	3	6	54	43	42	4	1	.294	.357	.415	.772	.017	D	$4

Pedroia's a difficult case to figure out because he hit better than most people expected his rookie year, and if not for an abysmal performance in April, he actually could have done even better. With almost no home run power, his value comes entirely from his ability to hit for a decent average, draw a walk every now and then and hit 35-40 doubles. If his batting average even drops to .300, he goes from a very nice .822 OPS to a merely okay .775 OPS.

Manny Ramirez (Left Field)

PA	R	H	2B	3B	HR	RBI	SO	BB	SB	CS	BA	OBP	SLG	OPS	Fld	F$
544	80	135	29	1	26	87	91	82	1	1	.300	.408	.541	.949	F-	$19

After hitting 88 homers between 2004 and 2005, Ramirez hit only 55 the past two seasons. It's possible that his days of hitting 40-plus homers in a season are over, but he's still a very dangerous hitter. While getting older may be robbing him of some power and his ability to play 150-plus games, he's still capable of hitting around .300 while drawing 75-plus walks and pounding out 50-60 extra-base hits.

Jason Varitek (Catcher)

PA	R	H	2B	3B	HR	RBI	SO	BB	SB	CS	BA	OBP	SLG	OPS	Fld	F$
487	61	107	23	2	16	60	104	65	1	1	.260	.364	.442	.806	C	$1

When Varitek's offense bottomed out in 2006, it looked like there was at least a decent chance that he was simply going through what many 34-year-old catchers have gone through before him. But he bounced back nicely in 2007 and while his days of posting an OPS+ in the 120 range are probably gone, he's still capable of producing league-average offense. That's all the Red Sox really need from him.

Kevin Youkilis (First Base)

PA	R	H	2B	3B	HR	RBI	SO	BB	SB	CS	BA	OBP	SLG	OPS	3 Yr	Fld	F$
556	73	131	35	2	13	65	95	71	2	2	.280	.381	.447	.828	-.025	B	$6

Youkilis saw a nice bump in his production from his first full season in the majors to his second, but that's probably the ceiling of what he can do. It's unlikely that he'll ever hit more than 20 homers, so he's going to be a viable starter at first base only as long as he can get on base nearly 40 percent of the time. Fortunately for him, patience is something that should be fairly consistent from year to year, so there's no reason to expect him to decline too much any time soon.

Pitchers

Josh Beckett (Starting Pitcher)

W	L	ERA	TBF	IP	Hit	HR	SO	BB	HBP	3 Yr	F$
12	8	3.79	759	184	174	18	164	50	6	0.12	$18

After a tough first year in the AL, Beckett adjusted nicely and performed even better than his years in the NL indicated he should. In addition to having excellent stuff and a nice repertoire of pitches, Beckett is one of the few pitchers who seem to have the ability to step up and pitch their best in the most important games. As long as he can stay healthy, he should be one of the better pitchers in the game for quite some time.

Clay Buchholz (Starting Pitcher)

W	L	ERA	TBF	IP	Hit	HR	SO	BB	HBP	3 Yr	F$
8	7	4.71	594	137	136	16	128	57	6	-0.12	$1

Buchholz grabbed everybody's attention by throwing a no-hitter in his second major league start, but he didn't come out of nowhere. He has a devastating curveball and is easily Boston's best under-25 pitcher. His control deteriorated in his major league stint (he walked only 35 in 125 minor league innings and then walked 10 in 23 innings in the majors), but he was so hard to hit that it didn't matter.

Manny Delcarmen (Relief Pitcher)

W	L	ERA	TBF	IP	Hit	HR	SO	BB	HBP	3 Yr	F$
4	4	4.14	302	70	67	5	62	31	3	-0.04	$1

Delcarmen throws very hard, and last year he turned hard pitches into hard pitches to hit. He still struggles with his control, but his ability to blow batters away earned him the chance to pitch more important innings as the season went along. He's unlikely to continue to allow quite so few hits, but he should still be a dependable reliever.

Brendan Donnelly (Relief Pitcher)

W	L	ERA	TBF	IP	Hit	HR	SO	BB	HBP	F$
3	2	4.02	198	47	45	4	35	17	2	$1

Donnelly was pitching well for the Red Sox before suffering an injury that required Tommy John surgery. With his age (36), the fact that he was mentioned in the Mitchell report in December and the fact that he won't be able to pitch again until at least August (by which time he'll be 37), it's entirely possible that he doesn't have much of a career left. If he can maintain his solid control and not lose much off his stuff, however, somebody will take a shot on him.

Jon Lester (Starting Pitcher)

W	L	ERA	TBF	IP	Hit	HR	SO	BB	HBP	3 Yr	F$
7	8	5.35	632	140	154	16	94	71	6	-0.32	$1

Lester hasn't pitched like a star, but holding your own in the majors at age 22 and 23 while batting cancer in the offseason is still pretty impressive. He struggles with his command periodically and he's rarely shown the ability to pitch deep into games. While he doesn't have the ceiling of some other impressive young pitchers, his fastball/change-up/slider combination should allow him to continue to pitch effectively.

Javier Lopez (Relief Pitcher)

W	L	ERA	TBF	IP	Hit	HR	SO	BB	HBP	3 Yr	F$
3	4	4.63	269	60	65	3	38	31	3	0.35	$1

Lopez has pitched well despite the fact that he doesn't throw hard or have good control. He pitches from a variety of arm angles and is frequently used as a lefty specialist, but lefties hit much better against him than righties in 2007 for the first time in his career. He'll probably never be a top option out of the bullpen, but he can continue to pitch effectively thanks to his deceptive delivery.

Daisuke Matsuzaka (Starting Pitcher)

W	L	ERA	TBF	IP	Hit	HR	SO	BB	HBP	3 Yr	F$
11	9	4.47	783	183	178	21	171	69	9	0.18	$8

Matsuzaka has a dazzling array of pitches, but he seemed to lose command of some of them from time to time, leading to more walks than you'd like to see. He also appeared to wear down as the season went along, and September was by far his worst month. After getting a year to adjust to the new country and league and pitching in a five-man rotation, Matsuzaka should feel more comfortable and pitch more effectively in his second season.

Hideki Okajima (Relief Pitcher)

W	L	ERA	TBF	IP	Hit	HR	SO	BB	HBP	3 Yr	F$
4	4	4.02	293	69	68	6	58	25	2	0.43	$1

Okajima has excellent control, a funky delivery and a variety of pitches. It remains to be seen what was more responsible for his excellent rookie season—the control and quality pitches or the unusual pitching motion. He should still be a good pitcher because of the former, but he may not be quite as dominant once hitters start to adjust to the latter.

Jonathan Papelbon (Relief Pitcher)

W	L	ERA	TBF	IP	Hit	HR	SO	BB	HBP	3 Yr	F$
5	2	3.09	272	68	52	6	78	20	3	0.12	$17

Papelbon seems almost perfectly suited to the closer's role: He has a bulldog attitude and a big-time fastball. The ability to control a mid-90s heater that has late movement is what makes him so dominant. He has secondary pitches, but his command of them isn't as good and he doesn't always need them to get through an inning.

Curt Schilling (Starting Pitcher)

W	L	ERA	TBF	IP	Hit	HR	SO	BB	HBP	F$
10	8	4.33	681	164	178	21	126	29	4	$8

The great fastball isn't there any more, so Schilling relies on his excellent control and pitching smarts to get hitters out. Since he has a much smaller margin for error than he used to, he'll have games where he gets hit hard. Overall, though, he's still a very effective pitcher when he's healthy enough to take the mound.

Kyle Snyder (Relief Pitcher)

W	L	ERA	TBF	IP	Hit	HR	SO	BB	HBP	3 Yr	F$
3	5	5.23	306	69	79	7	44	28	3	0.36	$1

Snyder turned in a surprisingly good season after four years of injuries and ineffectiveness, but that was probably the best you could expect from him. He still throws fairly hard after a couple arm surgeries, but he got away with laughably bad control in 2007 (32 walks in 54.1 innings). Expect a major regression in 2008, even if he does lower the walk rate.

Julian Tavarez (Relief Pitcher)

W	L	ERA	TBF	IP	Hit	HR	SO	BB	HBP	3 Yr	F$
6	8	5.06	552	125	143	12	72	50	6	0.52	$1

His biggest asset is his versatility, as he can pitch in any role and not be a complete disaster. He walks way too many batters, especially for somebody without dominant stuff, but he's capable of eating up innings while performing around the league average.

Mike Timlin (Relief Pitcher)

W	L	ERA	TBF	IP	Hit	HR	SO	BB	HBP	F$
4	3	4.44	263	61	66	6	37	19	2	$1

Timlin's longevity is amazing. He'll be 42 next season, and he just completed his 13th consecutive season of pitching better than the league average. The key for him always has been his control. He hasn't walked more than 20 batters in a season since 2000 and that precision has allowed him to continue to succeed as his stuff has faded.

Tim Wakefield (Starting Pitcher)

W	L	ERA	TBF	IP	Hit	HR	SO	BB	HBP	F$
10	9	4.65	735	173	176	22	105	57	6	$1

For somebody who makes a living with such an unpredictable pitch, the knuckleballer has been remarkably consistent with seven consecutive seasons of league-average or better performance. Wakefield gives up more than his share of walks (when his knuckler moves too much) and homers (when it doesn't move enough), but he can make hitters look silly when he's on.

Chicago Cubs

by Joe Aiello of View From the Bleachers (viewfromthebleachers.com)

2008 Projections

Record: 87-75
Division Rank: 2nd, one game back
Runs Scored: 852
Runs Allowed: 785

2007 in a Nutshell

For the first time since the magical 2003 season, the Cubs qualified for postseason play by winning the NL Central. After a very slow start, the team reached a turning point after a Carlos Zambrano fight with Michael Barrett in the dugout and a Lou Piniella explosion directed at a third base umpire that brought a multi-game suspension. From that point, the team began a stretch in which it was the best in baseball. Unfortunately for the team and its hopeful fans, the Cubs laid an egg in the first playoff round, swept at the hands of the Arizona Diamondbacks.

General Comments

Team Strengths

By far, the strongest cog in the Cubs machine was the pitching staff . The starters ranked second in baseball in combined ERA and the bullpen shook off an early funk to finish seventh. All five starters posted an ERA+ above the 100 threshold, and one could argue that they were the healthiest bunch in baseball. The Cubs were also the hardest team to manufacture a run against, says the 2008 Bill James Handbook.

Team Weaknesses

Patience at the plate continues to elude the team. This year, their 500 walks drawn ranked them 26th in baseball. That patience problem routinely allowed opposing starting pitchers to work deep into the game and save their bullpens for critical times in the series.

The General Manager Is Known for...

His ability to acquire talent via trade is one of his best assets. Some of the more notable achievements during his tenure were deals that brought in Nomar Garciaparra, Aramis Ramirez, Kenny Lofton, Derrek Lee and Matt Clement.

Last season, Hendry moved disappointing catcher Michael Barrett for Rob Bowen and a former first-round pick, Kyler Burke. Bowen flopped and was flipped to Oakland for a struggling Jason Kendall. Kendall resurrected a sorry season with a relatively strong finish

that gave the team some much needed stability behind the plate.

A knock on Hendry is his love for weak-hitting middle infielders. Neifi Perez, Erique Wilson and Tony Womack are a few of the names littering the roster over the past years of Hendry's tenure as GM.

The Manager is Known for...

Uncle Lou Piniella is one of the top managers in the game and knows how to win. With a World Series ring from Cincinnati, Piniella brings a winning attitude to complement his no-nonsense attitude toward fundamentals. When he is not happy with you, you can bet he will let you know it, most of the time laced with expletives.

Ballpark Characteristics

The second oldest ballpark in the majors behind Fenway Park, Wrigley Field is known for its party atmosphere, green ivy-laden outfield walls, and an atrocious playing field that sloped so badly Piniella could not see his outfielders completely while sitting in the dugout. The field has been redone this past offseason and should be much improved.

The groundskeepers are known for keeping the grass fairly long in the infield. A tough evening sun makes right field one of the toughest in baseball.

The Minor League System is...

The farm system has notoriously not produced the building blocks that other teams have over the years. Looking at the roster, it has always been tough to identify home-grown talent making a difference. Recently, the system has begun to take a turn for the better with names like Carlos Zambrano, Rich Hill and Carlos Marmol beginning to be contributors. The recent addition of Tim Wilken as director of scouting, after a fine tenure in Tampa Bay, has the fan base excited about the promise of prospects making a major difference for a team that has spent quite a bit via free agency over the past few years.

Tyler Colvin comes into the 2008 season as one of the top prospects in the farm system and appears to be roughly a year and a half away. Many considered the power-hitting outfielder from Clemson to be a bit of an overdraft when the Cubs picked him in the first round in 2006. Colvin has recently been named to MiLB.com's Top 50 prospects list. Assuming he progresses consistently, the Cubs could find themselves moving new import Kosuke Fukudome to center field to make room for Colvin.

Jeff Samardzija was a major reason why the critics claimed Colvin was an overdraft. The former Notre Dame receiver turned pro ballplayer was selected in the fifth round but received first-round money and a big league contract in the 2006 draft. Samardzija struggled to find his command while in High-A early in the year, posting a 1.65 WHIP, and was eventually promoted to Double-A for a change of scenery. The change seemed to be the ticket: Samardzija saw his numbers improve. He should start in Double-A with the opportunity to move up to Triple-A midseason.

Favorite Team Blogs

The Cub Reporter (www.mvn.com/mlb-cubs/)
Bleed Cubbie Blue (www.bleedcubbieblue.com/)

Keys for 2008

Players Lost from Last Year's Team

Jacque Jones finally got his wish for a new team and new fans when the Cubs dealt him to Detroit. The "savior" Mark Prior was non-tendered and signed with his hometown San Diego Padres. Will Ohman, who burned a good many bridges late in the year when he claimed the team pitched him while he was injured, was moved to the Braves in a change-of-scenery deal.

Players Acquired

The primary target of Hendry's offseason wish list, a left-handed corner outfielder, was addressed with the signing of Fukudome. He becomes the team's first Japanese player and has been labeled as a 4.5-tool player, with the half being his power. He figures to fit in between Lee and Ramirez in the heart of the lineup and should provide some lefty-righty balance that the team lacked last year.

At this writing, there have been rumors that the team is trying to acquire leadoff man Brian Roberts from the Orioles, despite Baltimore reassuring fans that Roberts would remain an Oriole. The team signed ex-Cub Jon Lieber to compete for a back-of-the-rotation spot.

Reasons to Be Optimistic

Besides the fact that Cubs fans are always optimistic, there are reasons to be excited about the season. The Cubs should be the favorite to repeat as Central Division champion. Returning basically the same team that won the division last year, the Cubs have added a much-needed piece in Fukudome. The pitching rotation was one of the best in baseball and has remained intact. If Zambrano can pitch the way his contract would warrant, the Cubs could have one of the most underrated rotations in the game.

Reasons to Be Pessimistic

Is this a rhetorical question? With 100 years of futility on the burner?

The Cubs enter the season with a major question mark in center field. Felix Pie is one of the prized prospects fans have heard about for years, but his performance in 2007 failed to justify the hype. Fans see the gaudy numbers put up in Iowa and salivate, envisioning what they could mean in the majors. Unfortunately, the name Corey Patterson still rings in our minds.

Due for a Better Season

Hill pitched well out of the rotation last year, but his numbers have yet to reach his minor league record. He began the season 3-1 with a 1.77 ERA in April. His youth and inexperience showed in May as he constantly fidgeted with holding runners on. When he began to relax late in the season, he began to show, once again, the promise the Cubs have for him. With a full season under his belt, Hill should begin to grow as a pitcher. Look for him to win 15-plus games and eclipse the 200-K mark in 2008.

Likely To Have a Worse Season

Ted Lilly slots in as the No. 2 man in the rotation, but many think he was the ace of the staff in 2007. With a career ERA of 4.46, one would think that Lilly's 3.83 ERA in '07 was both a product of the move to the National League and the result of a career year. Or was it? Just because Lilly is placed in this section doesn't mean he's due for a "bad" year. I simply think we'll see him regress closer to that career ERA in 2007 and take his rightful place behind Zambrano and Hill on the staff.

Carlos Marmol has nowhere to go but down after his remarkable burst onto the scene last year. He still has tremendous talent, but expecting numbers like he delivered last year is a bit unrealistic.

Most Likely Team Outcome

The team played most of the first half of the year drastically under its Pythagorean record and finished two wins shy of the 87 predicted based on the formula. With Fukudome providing balance and fundamentals, the Cubs should have no problem improving on their 85 wins from '07 and could be in line for a 90-93 win season.

Player Projections
Batters

Henry Blanco (Catcher)

PA	R	H	2B	3B	HR	RBI	SO	BB	SB	CS	BA	OBP	SLG	OPS	Fld	F$
214	23	51	12	1	5	25	33	15	0	1	.266	.319	.418	.737	D	$1

Blanco spent most of the year on the disabled list, but has recovered from his neck injury and played winter ball. Expect him to begin the year as Geovany Soto's backup and continue to be the focus of the Hank White Fan Club started by Desipio.com. He'll hit the occasional homer, but his ability to play the position is what makes Blanco one of the best, and highest paid, backup catchers in the game.

Ronny Cedeno (Shortstop)

PA	R	H	2B	3B	HR	RBI	SO	BB	SB	CS	BA	OBP	SLG	OPS	3 Yr	Fld	F$
442	53	115	20	4	10	50	75	25	7	2	.289	.331	.434	.765	.014	C	$1

The key to Cedeno finding success in the regular season is to tell him that he is playing in the Venezuelan Winter League, where he always shines like a star. Cedeno is out of options, so the team has a decision to make. Either Cedeno makes the team, or the Cubs expose him to waivers in an attempt to demote him.

Mark DeRosa (Second Base)

PA	R	H	2B	3B	HR	RBI	SO	BB	SB	CS	BA	OBP	SLG	OPS	3 Yr	Fld	F$
505	61	125	28	2	11	58	86	49	1	1	.282	.358	.429	.787	-.038	C	$2

The super-utility man was tremendous for the team last season, but has questioned what his role is this year, with the rumors that the team was pursuing a second baseman in the offseason. Hendry has promised that DeRosa will get his 400 to 500 at-bats. His greatest strength is his ability to play virtually anywhere on the diamond effectively.

Mike Fontenot (Second Base)

PA	R	H	2B	3B	HR	RBI	SO	BB	SB	CS	BA	OBP	SLG	OPS	3 Yr	Fld	F$
463	57	114	24	6	7	45	76	41	6	2	.277	.343	.415	.758	-.004	D	$1

He spent most of the season as a reserve and figures to do the same in '08. Fontenot needs to improve his strike-out-to-walk ratio to have a chance to break into the everyday lineup; he averaged one walk for every two strikeouts last season. He plays primarily as a second baseman, but can fill in at shortstop as well.

Kosuke Fukudome (Right Field)

PA	R	H	2B	3B	HR	RBI	SO	BB	SB	CS	BA	OBP	SLG	OPS	Fld	F$
440	65	111	29	3	14	65	82	53	7	3	.290	.382	.491	.873	C	$24

The Japanese outfielder was the Cubs' primary target in the offseason and fills a tremendous need for the team. He is reportedly a fine defender with great strike zone judgment that should help set the table for the sluggers in the lineup. There's no word yet on where Piniella plans to hit him in the lineup, but between Lee and Ramirez seems to make the most sense, since it would set up a right-left-right mix in the middle of the lineup.

Derrek Lee (First Base)

PA	R	H	2B	3B	HR	RBI	SO	BB	SB	CS	BA	OBP	SLG	OPS	3 Yr	Fld	F$
526	75	135	32	1	21	79	94	65	5	3	.300	.390	.516	.906	-.027	B	$17

After injury cut 2006 short for Lee, many expected him to return to his 2005 numbers and become a poor man's Albert Pujols. While Lee continued to hit for average and get on base at a great clip, his home run production decreased from 46 in 2005 to just 22 in 2007. Lee will continue to play a Gold Glove first base and be an on-base machine. The big question is whether the power stroke will return. Look for Lee to improve on the 22 long balls but not hit more than 30 this season.

Matt Murton (Left Field)

PA	R	H	2B	3B	HR	RBI	SO	BB	SB	CS	BA	OBP	SLG	OPS	3 Yr	Fld	F$
456	58	119	22	2	13	58	64	40	3	2	.292	.358	.452	.810	-.006	B	$4

Acquired in the trade that brought Garciaparra to Chicago, Murton has failed to find his niche with the team. Murton has good plate discipline, but doesn't possess the power typically associated with a corner outfielder. His role on the team figures once again to be that of a fourth outfielder, but there have been numerous rumors that the team is shopping him.

Felix Pie (Center Field)

PA	R	H	2B	3B	HR	RBI	SO	BB	SB	CS	BA	OBP	SLG	OPS	3 Yr	Fld	F$
517	67	132	25	7	13	60	101	33	11	6	.280	.328	.446	.774	.055	C	$8

With the departure of Jones to Detroit, the center field spot should be his for the taking. To this point, talk about him has always included the word "but". He has great speed, *but* he needs to work on his base running. He has leadoff potential, *but* he needs to learn how to bunt. He has good power, *but* he needs to work on his strike zone judgment. It's time for him to turn the "buts" into assets.

Aramis Ramirez (Third Base)

PA	R	H	2B	3B	HR	RBI	SO	BB	SB	CS	BA	OBP	SLG	OPS	3 Yr	Fld	F$
543	76	145	32	3	26	89	66	42	0	1	.298	.356	.536	.892	-.031	D	$19

Most know about the stick this guy carries to the plate, but few know about the ever-improving glove of A-Ram. After coming over from Pittsburgh as a disaster in the field, Ramirez has also worked to improve his fielding.

Alfonso Soriano (Left Field)

PA	R	H	2B	3B	HR	RBI	SO	BB	SB	CS	BA	OBP	SLG	OPS	3 Yr	Fld	F$
594	91	154	36	3	33	105	122	39	23	6	.285	.335	.546	.881	-.035	C	$34

The Cubs paid $9 million for Soriano's services last season, a pretty good bargain. As the team begins to feel the weight of a back-loaded, eight-year, $136 million contract, it remains to be seen if he was indeed worth the money. Soriano has great ability to throw runners out from left field, yet runners and coaches continued to test that scouting report.

After going down with a hamstring injury late in the year, he recovered quickly and seemed to show no ill effects. The mystery will be how it affects his running game. If he runs less, his value as a leadoff hitter, already compromised by his propensity for striking out, is significantly decreased.

Geovany Soto (Catcher)

PA	R	H	2B	3B	HR	RBI	SO	BB	SB	CS	BA	OBP	SLG	OPS	3 Yr	Fld	F$
457	60	116	27	1	17	66	98	46	0	1	.288	.360	.487	.847	.037	D	$2

Soto enters the season as the primary option for the Cubs at catcher. A fringe prospect for most of his career, Soto had a breakout year in Triple-A in 2007. Hitting .353/.424/.652 in his third go-round with Iowa, Soto got called up late in the year and produced a 175 OPS+ in 54 at-bats. He has soft hands behind the plate and an effectively accurate arm, and has been said to call an above-average game, especially for a youngster. His ability to handle a pitching staff of veterans, especially an ornery Zambrano, remains to be seen.

Ryan Theriot (Shortstop)

PA	R	H	2B	3B	HR	RBI	SO	BB	SB	CS	BA	OBP	SLG	OPS	3 Yr	Fld	F$
525	61	128	25	4	2	41	57	39	17	4	.271	.326	.354	.680	-.027	D	$1

"The Riot" is a fan favorite, but fan love doesn't assure success in the majors. Theriot should be the starting shortstop out of spring training, but could be on a short leash if he struggles and Ronny Cedeno shows some success.

Daryle Ward (First Base)

PA	R	H	2B	3B	HR	RBI	SO	BB	SB	CS	BA	OBP	SLG	OPS	3 Yr	Fld	F$
253	32	60	15	1	8	33	41	34	0	2	.280	.380	.472	.852	-.061	C	$1

Many believe that Ward is one of the better pinch hitters in the game, but is that the case? In his career as a pinch hitter, Ward has a .249/.335/.400 line in 328 plate appearances. That's far from pinch-hitting greatness. What Ward brings is versatility and good plate discipline off the bench. He should once again be Lee's backup at first base and an additional outfielder in a pinch.

Pitchers

Ryan Dempster (Starting Pitcher?)

W	L	ERA	TBF	IP	Hit	HR	SO	BB	HBP	3 Yr	F$
4	4	3.90	300	70	65	5	59	32	3	0.28	$1

Dempster has expressed a desire to be part of the starting rotation ever since he was asked to move to the bullpen in 2003. In 2008, he'll get his shot. Though his projection calls for a sub-4.00 ERA, that's based on his numbers as a reliever over the past three years, and Dempster's career ERA as a starter is closer to 5.00. However, most of those starts came early in his career, so Dempster should find more success in this go-round. The biggest question will be his ability to stand up to a 200-inning season.

Scott Eyre (Relief Pitcher)

W	L	ERA	TBF	IP	Hit	HR	SO	BB	HBP	F$
4	3	4.21	268	61	56	6	56	33	2	$1

After a career year in San Francisco in 2005, Eyre has seen his ERA and WHIP increase each year. At 36 and in the last year of his contract, Eyre could be pitching for his baseball life. If he comes out struggling, he could force the Cubs to make a move and look to a guy like Neal Cotts or Carmen Pigniatello to fill the lefty role in the bullpen for a cheaper price.

Rich Hill (Starting Pitcher)

W	L	ERA	TBF	IP	Hit	HR	SO	BB	HBP	3 Yr	F$
11	9	4.04	743	177	159	25	174	61	9	0.11	$14

Mentioned earlier as someone who is due for a better season, Hill comes in with two seasons of big league pitching under his belt. He has a wicked curveball that drops off the table and pairs it with 90-92 mph heat and a change-up that is steadily improving. He struggles with trusting his stuff and just going out there and pitching. He's a mild-mannered kid who needs to come out and dominate.

Bobby Howry (Relief Pitcher)

W	L	ERA	TBF	IP	Hit	HR	SO	BB	HBP	3 Yr	F$
5	4	3.44	318	78	68	8	65	21	3	0.26	$15

Howry has been exactly what the Cubs wanted when they acquired him. The ninth inning was Howry's most effective inning last season; he allowed an opponent batting average of just .220. He figures to get the first shot at the closer role, with Marmol and Kerry Wood close behind.

Jon Lieber (Starting Pitcher)

W	L	ERA	TBF	IP	Hit	HR	SO	BB	HBP	F$
7	6	4.34	511	121	131	16	74	28	5	$1

Lieber replaced Brett Myers in the Philly rotation after Lieber's own audition in the bullpen failed miserably. He was soon lost to season-ending surgery to repair a ruptured tendon in his left foot. For a short period before the injury, he pitched quite well.

Ted Lilly (Starting Pitcher)

W	L	ERA	TBF	IP	Hit	HR	SO	BB	HBP	3 Yr	F$
10	10	4.33	757	179	173	26	150	62	5	0.40	$7

He's a durable, take-the-ball-every day type of starter. He is tough on lefties, but tends to keep the ball up in the zone when he's struggling. As a result, he allowed 28 home runs, most on the staff.

Carlos Marmol (Relief Pitcher)

W	L	ERA	TBF	IP	Hit	HR	SO	BB	HBP	3 Yr	F$
6	6	4.45	465	106	91	13	109	57	7	-0.04	$2

Marmol has flat-out nasty stuff with great movement, but needs to stop nibbling himself deep into counts and just go after the hitters. When he trusts his stuff and pitches aggressively, he's nearly impossible to hit.

Jason Marquis (Starting Pitcher)

W	L	ERA	TBF	IP	Hit	HR	SO	BB	HBP	3 Yr	F$
9	11	5.01	773	177	188	27	94	70	10	0.54	$1

Marquis has a career ERA of 4.97 in the second half of the year. Last season, he saw his ERA jump more than two full points in the second half. If the Cubs see him struggle again, look for them to move him into the bullpen and give a shot to someone like Sean Gallagher or Kevin Hart.

Sean Marshall (Starting Pitcher)

W	L	ERA	TBF	IP	Hit	HR	SO	BB	HBP	3 Yr	F$
7	8	4.76	582	133	140	18	84	55	6	-0.12	$1

For some reason, people are not sold on Marshall. He came up in 2006 and made 24 starts in a ravaged rotation. After a setback in spring training last year, Marshall took the place of Wade Miller in the rotation and finished with an ERA of 3.92 and an ERA+ of 119. He's a groundball pitcher, which fits well at Wrigley Field, as a result of a good sinker. He throws only about 50 percent of his first pitches for strikes, which tends to get him in trouble.

Kerry Wood (Relief Pitcher)

W	L	ERA	TBF	IP	Hit	HR	SO	BB	HBP	3 Yr	F$
3	2	4.20	188	44	40	6	43	19	2	0.27	$1

It's hard to believe that Wood has been a part of the system for 12 years. He enters 2008 on a one-year deal with a chance to impress and take over the closer role. His biggest asset used to be his sweeping hook of a curveball; it's since been scrapped in favor of a slider, which puts less pressure on his arm. One concern about throwing Wood into the closer role is that he never pitched three consecutive outings last year

Michael Wuertz (Relief Pitcher)

W	L	ERA	TBF	IP	Hit	HR	SO	BB	HBP	3 Yr	F$
5	3	3.78	311	73	63	7	79	34	3	0.42	$1

Wuertz is the what-you-see-is-what-you-get reliever essential to every bullpen. He won't dominate, but won't kill you, either. Wuertz should continue to fill the middle relief role for the team and pitch primarily in the sixth and seventh innings. He'll get his 60-plus innings and finish with an ERA somewhere around 4.00.

Carlos Zambrano (Starting Pitcher)

W	L	ERA	TBF	IP	Hit	HR	SO	BB	HBP	3 Yr	F$
13	9	3.72	820	195	164	20	163	87	9	0.05	$15

Most Cub fans would tell you they are thrilled that Zambrano re-signed with the Cubs, but deep down inside, most are worried. Worried about what? Take these numbers, for example. Zambrano's ERAs from 2004 to 2007 are as follows: 2.75, 3.26, 3.41 and 3.95. He's also seen his pitches per plate appearance increase, a product of a decrease in control over recent years. It's hard to get a good read on Zambrano. If he can get his head screwed on straight, he could be in line for a 20-win season.

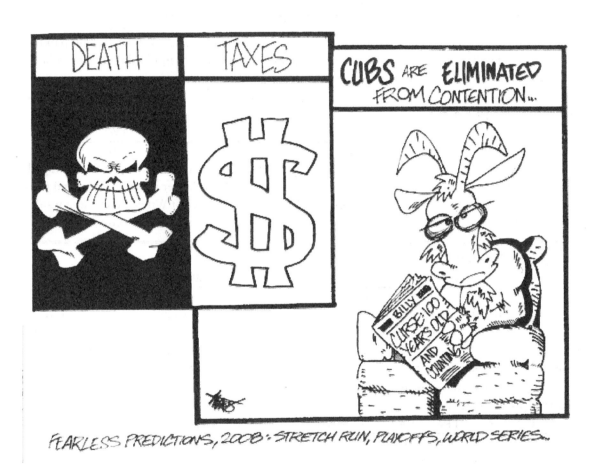

FEARLESS PREDICTIONS, 2008 - STRETCH RUN, PLAYOFFS, WORLD SERIES...

Chicago White Sox

by Mike Pindelski of The Bard's Room (mvn.com/mlb-whitesox)

2008 Projections

Record: 75-87
Division Rank: 4th, 15 games back
Runs Scored: 812
Runs Allowed: 868

2007 in a Nutshell

Just one full season removed from winning the World Series, the White Sox essentially went into a season-long slump in 2007, losing 90 games for the first time since 1989. The high point of the White Sox season came on April 24, when they had a share of first place in the AL Central. It would be their last and only day in first place on the season.

At the beginning of June, the Sox found themselves a mediocre 25-25. They were 7.5 games out of first place, and though the season was far from over, fans started to get the feeling the team needed to pick things up to survive in the very competitive AL Central. The Sox would go 10-18 in June, though, and find themselves 35-43 when July began; 12.5 games back in the division.

Things didn't get any easier from there as the Sox went 14-15 in July; when August began, they were essentially out of the playoff picture. To put it in simple terms, the Sox never really stood a chance in this division, nor would they have in any division in baseball.

General Comments

Team Strengths

There aren't too many, but the White Sox do have a few bright spots. The front end of their rotation was quite good last season: Mark Buehrle and Javier Vazquez formed a strong one-two punch. Assuming Buehrle doesn't revert to his 2006 form and Vazquez continues to harness his impressive arsenal, it should be another strong spot this season.

The Sox also feature one of the league's better closers in Bobby Jenks. Last season, Jenks went 40-for-46 in save opportunities and tied a major league record by retiring 41 consecutive batters. Assuming Jenks remains healthy; the Sox won't have to worry about the ninth inning much in 2008.

Team Weaknesses

The Sox' biggest weakness last season was their bullpen. Even with Jenks' valiant efforts, the Sox bullpen managed to blow 23 saves, the fourth-worst total in the AL. A number of pitchers in the bullpen have the ability to succeed in the majors, but it seems like everyone's production went south at the same time. The addition of Scott Linebrink may help, but expecting everyone in the bullpen to step up is a bit much.

The Sox offense was also a major disappointment last season. They were dead last in the AL in runs with 693 and the team OPS of .722 ranked 12th in the league.

The General Manager is Known for...

Ken Williams talks about his team in a cool and confident matter, but rarely reels in the big fish in the free agent or trade market. This past winter, Williams failed to land high-profile free agents Torii Hunter and Aaron Rowand (both of whom could have helped) or acquire Miguel Cabrera, a player the Sox were supposedly "aggressively" pursuing. His unexpected grab of Nick Swisher from the Athletics helped offset those losses.

Maybe because Williams doesn't have the resources to compete with other big market clubs, he has said the White Sox will not be chasing top free agents. Williams won't even negotiate with Scott Boras clients.

Instead, he's relied on a slew of minor moves to improve his team. The Chris Carter-Carlos Quentin swap and the Jon Garland-Orlando Cabrera trade will probably help the Sox in '08. So will Alexei Ramirez, an affordable Cuban defector who figures to slide into a regular role sometime this season, perhaps in center field.

In past years, Williams has been heralded around Chicago as a creative dealmaker. The Scott Podsednik-Carlos Lee trade before the 2005 championship supposedly gave the Sox the financial flexibility needed to sign Tadahito Iguchi, Orlando Hernandez, A.J. Pierzynski and Jermaine Dye. Williams also pulled the trigger on the Jose Contreras-Esteban Loaiza trade on the trade deadline of the 2004 season. Though Contreras isn't the same pitcher he was a couple of years ago, he was crucial during the stretch run in the team's 2005 championship season.

The Manager is Known for...

Outside of the occasional outburst on Chicago Sun-Times columnist Jay Mariotti or the fact he encourages his pitchers to retaliate when one of his hitters is hit by a pitch, Ozzie Guillen is known by Sox fans as a National League manager managing an American League team. Though the 2007 White Sox didn't steal as many bases as they did in 2006 or in 2005, Guillen remains a manager who will send runners on the basepaths. He isn't afraid to initiate the hit and run and the Sox are typically among the league leaders in sacrifice hits. Guillen handles his pitching staff well, rarely allowing his starters to run into dangerous pitch count totals.

Ballpark Characteristics

It's known around the sabermetric community as a very hitter-friendly stadium. Otherwise, U.S. Cellular Field is known as the "other" ballpark in Chicago. While "The Cell" will always be overshadowed by the Friendly Confines of Wrigley Field, the organization has done an excellent job making improvements around the ballpark, upgrading the bleachers and adding the FUNdamentals area for kids to learn to basics of baseball.

The Minor League System is…

It's weak to say the least. They traded their two best arms to the A's for Nick Swisher, and the Sox don't have one true positional prospect in the minors worth getting excited about.

The Sox finally moved away from their low-risk, low-reward draft strategy, selecting left-hander Aaron Poreda in last year's draft. Poreda is still raw, but he does have the size and the stuff to dominate. Many scouts are torn as to whether Poreda's big league future is in a starting rotation or in a bullpen.

Center fielder John Shelby (.301/.352/.508 at Low-A in 122 games) and toolsy 19-year-old outfielder Jose Martinez are worth taking flyers on, but the White Sox are an organization lacking any depth of young positional talent.

Favorite Team Blogs

South Side Sox (http://www.southsidesox.com/)
Sox Machine (http://www.soxmachine.com/)

Keys for 2008

Players Lost from Last Year's Team

The big name loss this winter was Garland from the starting rotation. Former fan favorite Podsednik was designated for assignment.

Players Acquired

Cabrera was the return for Garland. Quentin, who will likely begin the year as the Sox' starting left fielder, came for Carter, a first base prospect. Linebrink, likely the primary right-handed setup man, signed a four-year/$19 million contract. Ramirez, who signed a four-year, $4.75 million deal, figures to open the season in

the minor leagues, but should find himself in a regular role somewhere in 2008. And, of course, Nick Swisher will provide a big upgrade to the offense.

Reasons to be Optimistic

Though the Sox are an old team, there's hope some of the young guns can improve in 2008. John Danks and Gavin Floyd will likely fill in the back end of the rotation and though each struggled in 2007, both have the ability to be above-average starters, and it's up to the Sox coaching staff to guide their development. There's also Josh Fields, who likely will begin the season as the starting third baseman. He struggled making contact last season, but he has plenty of power and should hit better than .221/.275/.367, the collective batting line of Sox third basemen last season.

There's also the hope that Jim Thome will remain healthy and that Paul Konerko and Dye will bounce back from relatively disappointing seasons. If these factors pan out, the Sox should have a very strong 3-4-5 combo of hitters. The additions of Swisher, Quentin, Ramirez and Cabrera should also improve the Sox offense.

Reasons to be Pessimistic

The Sox still don't present a very strong lineup despite the additions. The back of the starting rotation is a big question mark. I'm optimistic about the development of both Danks and Floyd, but nothing is a certainty. The bullpen, which didn't hold too many leads last season, doesn't figure to be one of the team's strong points in 2008. The Linebrink signing was one of this winter's most controversial moves and may backfire.

The Sox are a pretty old team that just got another year older. As players age, there's an increased chance of regression or injury.

Due for a Better Season

Given his resurgence following the All-Star break, I believe Dye will have a strong comeback season in 2008. He battled injuries through most of the first half, but once healthy he really took off, hitting .298/.368/.579 following the midsummer classic. The projection systems I've seen agree that Dye is due for a better season in 2008, health permitting.

Contreras is another guy who should improve following his god-awful 2007 season.

Likely to Have a Worse Season

Buehrle looked like a rejuvenated pitcher in 2007, but he seems like the most likely candidate to regress in 2008. A guy who strikes out slightly more than five hitters per nine innings needs Chien-Ming Wang groundball tendencies to keep his ERA in the mid-threes consistently. Buehrle doesn't possess that ability. Perhaps more importantly, the mileage is starting to pile up on his left arm. Buehrle once was considered a lock for 200-plus innings a season, but his totals have declined each of the last three seasons and he's starting to show fatigue as September arrives.

Still Left to Do

It's been a busy winter for Williams, and he may not be done trading yet. He has a surplus of infielders. Joe Crede and Juan Uribe are two of Williams' top trading chips: They're blocked by Fields and Cabrera, respectively. Neither will bring the White Sox top-tier talent in return, but my guess is that Williams will continue to shop these two.

Most Likely Team Outcome

It's difficult to imagine the White Sox making a run at the postseason in 2008. The American League Central may be the most competitive division in baseball, and the Tigers and Indians are far superior teams.

Last season's White Sox went 72-90, and with the moves Williams made this winter, I expect improvement in 2008. At the high end, I could see the Sox flirting around .500 and possibly even finishing third, but given the ages of a few of the team's key players (Thome, Dye) and the uncertainty as to whether the team's young players will progress (Danks, Floyd, Fields), this team could just as easily finish last.

Player Projections

Batters

Brian Anderson (Center Field)

PA	R	H	2B	3B	HR	RBI	SO	BB	SB	CS	BA	OBP	SLG	OPS	3 Yr	Fld	F$
340	39	77	16	1	10	41	74	27	3	1	.251	.312	.407	.719	.023	B	$1

Guillen never gave Anderson an opportunity to recover from a very poor rookie season in 2006. He saw very little time in the majors last season and his time at Triple-A wasn't very good (.255/.318/.435 in 200 at-bats). He is a fairly good athlete, however, and his defense in center field is quite good. Chances of him picking up a starting gig with the Sox are slim, but he could make a difference elsewhere.

Orlando Cabrera (Shortstop)

PA	R	H	2B	3B	HR	RBI	SO	BB	SB	CS	BA	OBP	SLG	OPS	3 Yr	Fld	F$
615	76	154	32	1	11	66	57	47	19	3	.278	.335	.399	.734	-.040	C	$11

The wizard of OC turned in a fine season, hitting over .300 for the first time in his career, scoring more than 100 runs, and winning a Gold Glove. He'll be 33 this year, so it's unlikely he can improve on or even match last season. But he's a very smart player who's an excellent baserunner and rarely makes a mistake.

Joe Crede (Third Base)

PA	R	H	2B	3B	HR	RBI	SO	BB	SB	CS	BA	OBP	SLG	OPS	3 Yr	Fld	F$
348	43	85	18	0	15	52	46	22	0	1	.269	.319	.468	.787	-.026	A+	$1

Crede's ailing back finally got the best of him last year, and he went under the knife in June to repair herniated disks. His back problems clearly contributed to his poor showing throughout his shortened season: He hit a mere .216/.258/.317 in 178 plate appearances. Though he should be ready in time for Opening Day, he wasn't much of a hitter before his breakout 2006 season and his career power numbers show he likes cozy U.S. Cellular Field, a place he may not see so often, since he's a prime trade candidate. On the bright side, his defense is among the best.

Jermaine Dye (Right Field)

PA	R	H	2B	3B	HR	RBI	SO	BB	SB	CS	BA	OBP	SLG	OPS	3 Yr	Fld	F$
539	75	133	28	1	30	93	102	51	2	2	.279	.351	.531	.882	-.035	F	$16

After a terrible first half (.214/.271/.402), Dye took off following the All-Star game and the Sox inked him to an extension shortly after the July 31 trade deadline. Dye is a lot like Thome: He has a chance to be a force in the Sox lineup, but health is a major issue at his age (34).

Josh Fields (Third Base)

PA	R	H	2B	3B	HR	RBI	SO	BB	SB	CS	BA	OBP	SLG	OPS	3 Yr	Fld	F$
572	72	130	27	1	24	81	148	55	5	3	.259	.335	.461	.796	.024	F	$8

Fields sprays fly balls to all parts of the diamond and could easily hit 30 or more homers playing half of his games at U.S. Cellular Field. But he struck out at an alarming rate last season (33.5 percent) and his defense is no better than average at third. Fields is still learning to work walks, but he will hit for power.

Toby Hall (Catcher)

PA	R	H	2B	3B	HR	RBI	SO	BB	SB	CS	BA	OBP	SLG	OPS	3 Yr	Fld	F$
272	29	66	14	0	6	31	30	15	0	0	.264	.307	.392	.699	-.019	F	$1

After tearing the labrum of his right shoulder during spring training, Hall missed all of April in 2007 and never really got rolling when he returned. He has never been much of an offensive catcher and his defense took a step back last year.

Paul Konerko (First Base)

PA	R	H	2B	3B	HR	RBI	SO	BB	SB	CS	BA	OBP	SLG	OPS	3 Yr	Fld	F$
589	82	145	29	0	31	98	96	70	0	1	.286	.372	.526	.898	-.035	C	$19

It looked as if Konerko was having a difficult time hitting the ball on the nose last year, compared to recent seasons, and his batting average clearly suffered. The ability to hit line drives is something that fluctuates greatly, but if Konerko starts hitting the ball a bit more cleanly in 2008, he's a good bounce-back candidate.

Jerry Owens (Center Field)

PA	R	H	2B	3B	HR	RBI	SO	BB	SB	CS	BA	OBP	SLG	OPS	3 Yr	Fld	F$
565	65	131	17	3	3	41	88	44	29	9	.256	.316	.319	.635	-.011	C	$1

Owens' finest asset is his speed: He stole 32 bases with the White Sox in only 93 games last season. He doesn't offer much in the way of plate discipline, however, and his power is essentially nonexistent. He could be a pretty good bench player, especially if he starts making more contact like he did in the minors.

Pablo Ozuna (Second Base)

PA	R	H	2B	3B	HR	RBI	SO	BB	SB	CS	BA	OBP	SLG	OPS	3 Yr	Fld	F$
220	25	55	11	1	2	20	26	12	5	2	.279	.326	.375	.701	-.030	C	$1

Ozuna's season was cut short at the end of May by a fractured right fibula. Though he's never been much of a hitter, he does have value. Ozuna is a speed guy who can play every position on the diamond but catcher, which will get you a job somewhere in today's baseball world.

A.J. Pierzynski (Catcher)

PA	R	H	2B	3B	HR	RBI	SO	BB	SB	CS	BA	OBP	SLG	OPS	3 Yr	Fld	F$
499	58	124	24	0	15	64	70	30	1	2	.273	.326	.425	.751	-.027	F	$1

Known around baseball as being one of the sporting world's hated athletes, Pierzynski is a decent offensive catcher whom the White Sox value for his ability to handle a pitching staff and play solid defense behind the plate. It didn't look like Pierzynski was making solid contact with the ball last season: His batting average dropped to .263; the lowest of his career.

Carlos Quentin (Right Field)

PA	R	H	2B	3B	HR	RBI	SO	BB	SB	CS	BA	OBP	SLG	OPS	3 Yr	Fld	F$
457	61	102	27	2	14	57	78	39	3	1	.261	.355	.447	.802	.030	B	$1

Carlos Quentin was the biggest disappointment of the 2007 season for Arizona. Expected to be the right fielder for years to come, he lost the first two weeks to injury and never recovered. Pitchers exploited his willingness to swing at any pitch down and away, and he was sent to Triple-A in July after batting .210 in 66 games. He had surgery on his rotator cuff and labrum in October and finally was traded to the White Sox.

Danny Richar (Second Base)

PA	R	H	2B	3B	HR	RBI	SO	BB	SB	CS	BA	OBP	SLG	OPS	3 Yr	Fld	F$
564	61	125	23	6	12	56	98	37	5	4	.243	.294	.382	.676	.013	C	$1

Though none of his skills are outstanding, Richar does everything well with both the bat and the glove and I believe he has a pretty good chance of being a productive big league second basemen. Richar hits fastballs and off-speed stuff equally well. He has a chance to prove himself if he wins the White Sox job at second base for 2008.

Nick Swisher (Center Field)

PA	R	H	2B	3B	HR	RBI	SO	BB	SB	CS	BA	OBP	SLG	OPS	3 Yr	Fld	F$
593	82	129	28	1	28	88	122	88	2	2	.263	.379	.496	.875	.002	F	$13

After he hit 35 homers in 2006, many were disappointed with only 22 dingers in 2007. Don't be: According to Hit Tracker, many of his 2006 homers barely cleared the fence. Nothing happened to his power stroke; those 13 homers that he lost in 2007 were offset by 12 more doubles, and his production was basically identical by Runs Created and OPS+. Bump that slugging a little bit now that he's playing at the Cell.

Jim Thome (Designated Hitter)

PA	R	H	2B	3B	HR	RBI	SO	BB	SB	CS	BA	OBP	SLG	OPS	F$
504	75	111	21	0	30	86	118	92	0	1	.276	.413	.553	.966	$15

Thome is the Sox's most productive hitter, but health is the biggest concern for him at this point. With age comes injury risk, and Thome will be 38 in August. He was limited to 130 games in 2007 due to a strained rib cage and back spasms. When healthy, however, he was the same Jim Thome. As usual, he showed a ton of power and patience; 27.2 percent of his fly balls went for homers and his .410 on-base percentage was far and away the highest on the team.

Juan Uribe (Shortstop)

PA	R	H	2B	3B	HR	RBI	SO	BB	SB	CS	BA	OBP	SLG	OPS	3 Yr	Fld	F$
517	59	117	24	2	20	70	91	32	2	4	.250	.300	.439	.739	-.029	C	$1

Over the past few seasons, Uribe has tweaked his batting stance a number of times, but at the end of the year we see the same result: a disappointing season. Uribe has very good range at shortstop and a cannon of an arm, but he's a very impatient hitter who seems to get ahead of himself in the batter's box, resulting in plenty of meaningless flyball outs.

Pitchers

Mark Buehrle (Starting Pitcher)

W	L	ERA	TBF	IP	Hit	HR	SO	BB	HBP	3 Yr	F$
10	10	4.57	777	184	201	24	105	47	6	0.44	$1

After suffering the worst year of his career in 2006, Buehrle bounced back nicely in 2007 on both the statistical and scouting front. Not only did Buehrle's peripherals take a step forward, his fastball showed better life, his cutter was cutting and his curveball was much sharper. That being said, his days as a No. 1 starter are probably over. He's highly reliant on the defense behind him and his groundball tendencies have deteriorated over the past few seasons.

Jose Contreras (Starting Pitcher)

W	L	ERA	TBF	IP	Hit	HR	SO	BB	HBP	F$
10	10	4.55	770	181	188	22	113	58	8	$1

Contreras' major league career has been one heck of a roller coaster ride, with his lowest point possibly being last season. Not only did Contreras' peripherals worsen significantly, so did his stuff. His fastball, which once showed great life in the mid-90s, was dull and stayed in the low 90s most of the year. His forkball didn't bite nearly as much and found itself up in the zone as well. The decline in Contreras' repertoire may be the result of a chronic problem in the sciatic nerve in his back. At this point, Contreras' health is anything but a certainty; he looks like he's 60 years old on the mound and on the diamond.

John Danks (Starting Pitcher)

W	L	ERA	TBF	IP	Hit	HR	SO	BB	HBP	3 Yr	F$
6	10	5.68	639	144	156	26	108	64	6	-0.38	$1

Danks tends to struggle at new levels of play and he did just that in his first major league season. Danks has above-average velocity for a lefty, usually sticking in the low 90s with his fastball, and mixes in a pretty good curveball and change-up. He kept the ball up in the zone last season, which led to a lot of big flies. He's still a work in progress, particularly in regard to throwing strikes and keeping the ball in the ballpark, but the talent is there.

Dewon Day (Relief Pitcher)

W	L	ERA	TBF	IP	Hit	HR	SO	BB	HBP	3 Yr	F$
3	3	5.63	260	56	59	6	50	38	4	0.21	$1

Day looked like a major sleeper last season after striking out 17.28 hitters per nine innings at Double-A before being called up in May. At 26, he was old for his level, but that is a figure you simply cannot ignore. He throws a pretty good sinking fastball in the low 90s, but his out pitch is a sharp-breaking slider. His major league debut was pretty uninspiring (11.25 ERA in 12 innings), but his minor league dominance should get him another look at the big league level.

Gavin Floyd (Starting Pitcher)

W	L	ERA	TBF	IP	Hit	HR	SO	BB	HBP	3 Yr	F$
7	10	5.77	696	155	177	25	96	69	8	-0.33	$1

Floyd's entire major league career has been a struggle, and a change of scenery apparently didn't help. Always high on talent, Floyd throws a fastball in the low 90s, mixing in a slider, change-up and curveball, the latter being his finest pitch. Like Danks, Floyd is still young and talented and may just need guidance from the coaching staff. Unlike Danks, he continues to struggle in different stops in the major leagues and he may be running out of chances.

Charlie Haeger (Starting/Relief Pitcher)

W	L	ERA	TBF	IP	Hit	HR	SO	BB	HBP	3 Yr	F$
6	10	5.89	676	147	162	19	80	89	8	-0.37	$1

The first true new knuckleballer baseball has seen for a while, Haeger will mix in a mid-80s fastball, but it's mostly just the knuckleball. He's struggled at the major league level, but he's still young and looks a lot like a young Tim Wakefield.

Bobby Jenks (Relief Pitcher)

W	L	ERA	TBF	IP	Hit	HR	SO	BB	HBP	3 Yr	F$
5	2	3.43	278	67	57	5	64	28	2	0.09	$10

Overall, 2007 was a very nice year for Jenks with his 40 saves and his record-tying 41 consecutive batters retired. He did, however, take a step back in the strikeout department and his velocity decreased compared to previous seasons. The guy who once was clocked at 102 mph wasn't even throwing in the upper 90s much last year. Outside of his famous hammer curveball, Jenks also started using a slider more last season.

Scott Linebrink (Relief Pitcher)

W	L	ERA	TBF	IP	Hit	HR	SO	BB	HBP	3 Yr	F$
3	5	5.18	299	68	74	10	46	28	2	0.53	$1

Linebrink went from San Diego to Milwaukee last season in what seemed to be a bit of a panic move on Doug Melvin's part, and while he did pitch well for the Brewers, it's hard to ride 25 set-up innings into the playoffs, no matter how good they are. With the Brewers, Linebrink found the strikeouts he'd lost earlier in the year, but his walk rate also went up. He probably won't be as mediocre as he was at the beginning of 2007, but 2004 and '05 probably aren't coming back either.

Boone Logan (Relief Pitcher)

W	L	ERA	TBF	IP	Hit	HR	SO	BB	HBP	3 Yr	F$
3	4	4.87	264	60	62	7	46	28	3	-0.20	$1

Logan reminds me quite a bit of Matt Thornton—a big power left hander struggling with control. Though his strikeout totals don't indicate it, his fastball and slider are both above-average pitches while his change-up is still a work in progress. Logan had a difficult time throwing his slider and change for strikes last season. He also has a tendency to keep his fastball up in the zone, which can make him quite hittable.

Mike MacDougal (Relief Pitcher)

W	L	ERA	TBF	IP	Hit	HR	SO	BB	HBP	3 Yr	F$
3	3	4.56	239	54	56	4	46	27	2	0.35	$1

MacDougal throws two above-average pitches, a sinker with electric life and a sharp-breaking slider. His problem is that he has a difficult time controlling those pitches, leading to high walk totals. If he's going to rebound in 2008, he needs to harness his stuff, which is good enough to dominate. On the downside, his right shoulder continues to act up and DL stints may be in the cards for the rest of his career.

Andrew Sisco (Relief Pitcher)

W	L	ERA	TBF	IP	Hit	HR	SO	BB	HBP	3 Yr	F$
4	7	5.64	437	96	98	14	72	60	4	-0.22	$1

Sisco is a very talented left-handed pitcher who needs to harness his arsenal. At 6-foot-10 and around 270 pounds, Sisco looks a lot like Randy Johnson on the mound. He typically sits in the low to mid-90s with a moving fastball and mixes in a sweeping slider and change-up, using the latter only on occasion. Control was a major problem last season. It's worth noting the White Sox are interested in using him as a starting pitcher.

Matt Thornton (Relief Pitcher)

W	L	ERA	TBF	IP	Hit	HR	SO	BB	HBP	3 Yr	F$
3	4	4.71	268	61	59	7	55	33	2	0.48	$1

Thornton is a big power lefty who can get his fastball in the mid-to-upper 90s with ease, but he has a difficult time throwing his sharp slider for strikes. Even as a southpaw, left-handed hitters found him very hittable last season, teeing off for an .800 OPS against. His potential is sky high, but throwing strikes is essential.

Javier Vazquez (Starting Pitcher)

W	L	ERA	TBF	IP	Hit	HR	SO	BB	HBP	3 Yr	F$
11	10	4.42	795	191	189	27	172	51	8	0.46	$11

Always high on talent but low on results, Vazquez finally put together a very strong season, posting his highest ERA+ (127) since 2003. His arsenal features a moving fastball he usually keeps in the low 90s, complemented with a couple of breaking balls and a change-up, all plus pitches. He has the stuff to dominate—he reached double-digit strikeout totals in four starts last season—but he tends to develop gopheritis when he gets the ball up. Luckily for Vazquez, 19 of the 29 home runs he surrendered last season were solo shots.

Cincinnati Reds

by Justin Inaz of On Baseball & the Reds (jinaz-reds.blogspot.com)

2008 Projections

Record: 82-80
Division Rank: 3rd, 6 games back
Runs Scored: 833
Runs Allowed: 824

2007 in a Nutshell

The Reds seemed on pace for another .500 season through April, but the wheels fell off during a catastrophic May in which they went 9-21, spiraling to the bottom of the NL Central. Their 10-16 June wasn't much of an improvement, ultimately spelling the end of Jerry Narron's tenure as Reds manager.

Enter Pete Mackanin, former Reds advance scout, who was hired as interim manager. Mackanin, told by general manager Wayne Krivsky that he wouldn't guarantee the job for more than a week, entered determined to make the most of his time at the Reds' helm. What followed was a remarkable turnaround. Under Mackanin, the Reds were 41-40, and climbed out of the basement to finish fifth (13 games out) in the awful National League Central division. The surge was the result of a revitalized offense and a surprisingly effective bullpen … and a fair bit of luck: The Reds' Pythagorean record under Mackanin was just 38-43.

In terms of individual performances, the positive highlights were the emergences of newcomers Josh Hamilton, Jared Burton, Norris Hopper and Jeff Keppinger as effective contributors. Brandon Phillips had the best overall season of any Reds position player, while Aaron Harang continued as the Reds' ace and David Weathers had another solid season anchoring the Reds' otherwise shaky bullpen.

General Comments

Team Strengths

Despite their reputation, the Reds no longer have a dominant offense. But the '07 offense was decent (4.8 runs per game), capable of scoring in a variety of ways via a combination of power-oriented and contact-and-speed players. The outfield was a source of offensive strength for the ballclub, and the Reds got surprisingly good production from their middle infielders. The pitching staff had a solid ace and a passably effective closer, with some very promising youth beginning to contribute. The Reds also had very good defense up the middle, most notably due to the play of Phillips and David Ross.

Team Weaknesses

Overall team defense continues to be a problem, particularly in the corner outfield spots. Defense down the line in both the infield and outfield was poor last season, and that was a big reason the Reds gave up runs at the second-highest rate in the league last year (5.7 per game). Another reason, of course, was the pitching. With the exceptions of Harang, Weathers and Burton, it ranged from average to awful.

The General Manager is Known for...

Krivsky's mode of operation is absurd secrecy. It's really hard to know what goes on in his head, because he is very reluctant to talk about anything for fear of giving up competitive advantage. The joke at the winter meetings among reporters covering the Reds was whether Krivsky would confirm that he was actually at those meetings.

Nevertheless, two years into his tenure with the Reds, we can start to see some trends and patterns. Krivsky has been skilled (or lucky?) at finding and acquiring quality talent on the cheap, as showcased by the acquisitions of Scott Hatteberg (free agent), Phillips (trade), Hamilton (Rule 5 trade), Burton (Rule 5), Keppinger (trade) and Jon Coutlangus (waivers). Furthermore, his first major acquisition—Bronson Arroyo for Wily Mo Pena at the start of the '06 season—continues to balance well in his favor despite Arroyo's regression back toward mediocrity in '07.

At the same time, he has shown remarkable lapses in judgment, most strikingly with the awful trade in July 2006 of Austin Kearns and Felipe Lopez for Bill Bray, Gary Majewski and Brendan Harris. That deal might still have looked far better than it does now except that Harris was subsequently traded to the Devil Rays for a player to be named later/cash to make room on the 40-man roster for, uh, Jeff Conine. Furthermore, while the offseason addition of Francisco Cordero clearly improves the bullpen, most estimates by sabermetricians around the 'net indicated that Coco will be overpaid by roughly $20 million over his four-year, $46 million contract.

Despite his occasional flashes of brazen activity, Krivsky can be surprisingly conservative, especially with respect to his young players. Despite the Reds being out of contention by the end of May, Joey Votto had to wait until September for a call-up after a fine season at Triple-A. Jay Bruce, the Baseball America and Sporting News Minor League Player of the Year, was not invited to the big league club in September, even after Ken Griffey went down with a groin injury. Sometimes being conservative is a good thing, though—one wonders if Krivsky's conservative treatment of phenom prospect Homer Bailey may have helped prevent an injury cascade stemming from his strained groin.

The Manager is Known for...

There may be no other manager who generates such divergent opinions as the new Reds skipper, Dusty Baker. Baseball insiders often herald him as a terrific manager and superb communicator, a guy who really takes the time to know his players. He's a guy who "gets the most out of his players," someone who guys "really like to play for." I think a lot of that is probably true.

On the other hand, outside observers sometimes criticize him as among the worst managers in baseball. The biggest harping point is his use, and arguably abuse, of young pitchers while with the Chicago Cubs. While he may not be exclusively to blame for their career-stunting injuries, alarmingly high pitch counts on then-young Mark Prior and Kerry Wood did routinely occur on Baker's watch. With so much of the Reds' future falling on the backs and arms of guys like Bailey, Johnny Cueto and Edinson Volquez, this is a concern.

Dusty also has a reputation of strongly favoring veterans over youngsters ... though he would respond that he didn't have a lot of young guys to work with on the veteran-heavy Giants and Cubs teams he managed. The legitimate young talents that he did get—Wood, Prior, Corey Patterson, Rich Aurilia, Bill Mueller, Russ Ortiz, Kirk Rueter and Shawn Estes in particular—seemed to have gotten plenty of playing time.

One thing that is clear is that Baker has little use for modern baseball statistics—in his words, walks and on-base percentage are "overrated."

Ballpark Characteristics

Great American Ballpark has been cited by TV analysts, fans and players as one of the great hitters' parks in the National League. Statheads, on the other hand, have observed that while home run rates do tend to be well above average in Cincy, the overall effect of this park on runs scored compared to a neutral park is surprisingly modest. The trend over the last three years has been toward higher park factors, but in the two years before that, it was a pitchers' park overall.

At this point, I view GABP as a moderate hitters' park, though its five-year regressed park factor (courtesy of Brandon Heipp) comes out to a very reasonable 1.01. Nevertheless, it is the case that GABP is extremely permissive with home runs (which has not been good news to the Reds' flyball-friendly pitching staff over the last several years).

The Minor League System is...

The farms gradually are becoming a genuine strength. Two of the Reds' top three prospects (Bailey and Votto) made their big league debuts in 2007, while the third (Bruce) won Baseball America's Player of the Year award. At the same time, Cueto emerged as a top pitching prospect, while a number of lesser prospects—including several members of the 2007 draft class—made important strides in the right direction.

Furthermore, 2007 saw surprisingly few significant injuries in the minor leagues. That might be luck, but it also might reflect the Reds' increased emphasis on treating pitchers on a case-by-case basis. This offseason, respected minor league evaluator John Sickels said this regarding the Reds system: "Good Lord. This system is loaded. ... Take heart, Reds fans. You have a lot to look forward to." It's been decades since someone outside the Reds organization said something like that about their minor league system.

Favorite Team Blogs

Red Reporter (http://www.redreporter.com/)
Redleg Nation (http://www.redlegnation.com/)
Church of Baseball (http://baseballchurch.blogspot.com/)
Redleg Rundown (http://mvn.com/mlb-reds/)
Red Hot Mama (http://www.red-hot-mama.com/)
Reds and Blues (htttp://www.redsandblues.com/)
Cincinanti Reds Blog (http://shawns.blogspot.com/)
The Reds Rocket (http://theredsrocket.blogspot.com/)
Reds Minor League (http://www.redsminorleagues.com/)
Reds Insider (http://frontier.cincinnati.com/blogs/redsinsider/)
Baseball Minutia (http://www.baseballminutia.com/)

Keys for 2008

Players Lost from Last Year's Team

Pitchers Kirk Saarloos, Eric Milton, Eddie Guardado, Phil Dumatrait and Michael Gosling, outfielders Josh Hamilton, Buck Coats and Jason Ellison, infielders Mark Bellhorn, Jorge Cantu and Pedro Lopez , catcher Ryan Jorgensen.

Players Acquired

Pitchers Francisco Cordero, Edinson Volquez and Sergio Valenzuela, outfielder Danny Herrera.

Reasons to be Optimistic

There's a lot of good young talent already on this ballclub, and four top-rated rookies are set to either make debuts or establish themselves in the big leagues in 2008. A young rotation including Bailey, Cueto and Volquez—not to mention Harang and Arroyo—has a lot of potential, especially in the second half. Defense up the middle is above-average, and the bullpen should be significantly better with the addition of Cordero. With the exception of center field, all major roles on this club are set, and most are occupied by legitimately talented players.

Reasons to be Pessimistic

The pitching rotation after Harang and (maybe) Arroyo is a potential disaster, depending on the strides the young guys make in their development. The defense in the infield and outfield corners ranges from poor to terrible. And the offense is no longer the powerhouse it once was, especially after the loss of Hamilton. Some of the most reliable talent on the '06 and '07 teams is aging, and that often brings declines in production.

Due for a Better Season

David Ross, Edwin Encarnacion, Bronson Arroyo, Matt Belisle, Volquez, and Mike Stanton.

Likely to Have a Worse Season

Brandon Phillips, Ken Griffey Jr., Alex Gonzalez, Francisco Cordero, David Weathers, Scott Hatteberg, Jeff Keppinger and Norris Hopper.

Still Left to Do

The Reds must develop their young starting pitchers and prevent Baker from breaking them. And they must decide on a center fielder.

Most Likely Team Outcome

The easy, and perhaps safest, thing would be to say that the Reds are a terrible team and will continue their streak of sub-.500 seasons in 2008. But hope springs eternal, and there's a foundation of good, young talent here, with more on the way. If that youth can live up to its potential, no one regresses horrifically, and everyone stays healthy, this team can be a surprise contender in the weak NL Central. It'll likely take some luck for them to win in '08, but if you write off the Reds before the season starts, you might end up regretting it.

Player Projections

Batters

Jay Bruce (Center Field)

PA	R	H	2B	3B	HR	RBI	SO	BB	SB	CS	BA	OBP	SLG	OPS	3 Yr	Fld	F$
521	71	130	32	5	23	80	123	39	4	3	.275	.330	.510	.840	.085	D	$1

Bruce skyrocketed through the minors last year, starting in A-ball and reaching (and dominating) Triple-A by the end of the season. As arguably the No. 1 prospect in the country, his arrival in Cincinnati—whenever it happens—may be the biggest Reds event of the year. The Reds tend to handle their prospects conservatively, and he's only 20, so it seems unlikely Bruce will make the team out of spring training. Nevertheless, the trade of Hamilton opens a major hole in center field, and Bruce has a way of advancing faster than the Reds seem to anticipate. No matter what, he seems like a lock to arrive by midseason.

Adam Dunn (Left Field)

PA	R	H	2B	3B	HR	RBI	SO	BB	SB	CS	BA	OBP	SLG	OPS	3 Yr	Fld	F$
595	88	124	27	1	35	99	154	99	5	1	.256	.385	.533	.918	-.025	D	$20

Dunn put to rest concerns about early decline last year by posting his third outstanding offensive season in the last four. His power was back in full, and his batting average was its highest since '04, pushing his OBP back up to his typical .380ish levels. This improvement was caused in part by better luck (he was rather unlucky in '06), and in part by a slight decrease in his strikeout rates. The main weakness in Dunn's game is his defense; So, to quote the late Joe Nuxhall, "he's not great, but he's not terrible, either." A move to first base might help, though Votto's presence makes that unlikely.

Edwin Encarnacion (Third Base)

PA	R	H	2B	3B	HR	RBI	SO	BB	SB	CS	BA	OBP	SLG	OPS	3 Yr	Fld	F$
512	67	128	29	1	17	69	85	41	5	1	.281	.350	.461	.811	.038	F	$8

Eddie struggled in early 2007, on both offense and defense, and was demoted to Triple-A for a few weeks to figure things out. When he returned, his defense did seem better, and most estimates have him now just slightly below average at third base. He hit better upon returning as well, especially during his torrid final two months. He became a bit more aggressive last season, cutting down on strikeouts and raising his average, but also cutting down on his walk, line drive and power rates. I'm not sure that it was a good tradeoff. Overall, last season wasn't really the step forward many of us thought he'd take. This may be the make-or-break year of his career.

Ryan Freel (Center Field)

PA	R	H	2B	3B	HR	RBI	SO	BB	SB	CS	BA	OBP	SLG	OPS	3 Yr	Fld	F$
392	51	91	19	2	4	34	63	33	23	6	.263	.336	.365	.701	-.040	A	$1

Freel was just brutal last season. He started the season slowly, and a concussion in late May sidelined him for over a month. Upon his return, he just never seemed right. While a bad knee ultimately ended his season, it's his head I'm worried about. The Ryan Freel of old was a guy who took a lot of pitches, struck out a fair bit, but also walked enough and hit enough singles to have respectable value despite minimal power. I'm not sure if we'll ever see that guy again.

Alex Gonzalez (Shortstop)

PA	R	H	2B	3B	HR	RBI	SO	BB	SB	CS	BA	OBP	SLG	OPS	3 Yr	Fld	F$
439	51	106	25	1	12	54	72	27	1	1	.267	.319	.425	.744	-.027	B	$1

Gonzalez had the best year of his career in '07 statistically, posting career highs in OBP, SLG and OPS+ at age 30. Particularly impressive was Gonzalez's power surge, which may have been helped by playing in homer-friendly GABP. Unfortunately, Gonzalez missed a great deal of time while attending to his ill child. That allowed Jeff Keppinger to establish himself as a viable option at shortstop, further limiting Gonzalez's playing time. Gonzalez is a plus (though perhaps overrated) defender, but he will likely regress offensively this season, and may have to fight for playing time if Keppinger continues to hit.

Ken Griffey Jr. (Right Field)

PA	R	H	2B	3B	HR	RBI	SO	BB	SB	CS	BA	OBP	SLG	OPS	Fld	F$
548	75	130	25	1	27	86	90	67	3	1	.276	.365	.505	.870	F-	$16

During 2007's first half, he was a monster, seemingly putting to rest concerns generated during his sub-par '06 season. His second half was pedestrian (.761 OPS). Perhaps he was just tired—his 623 plate appearances last season were his highest total since 2000. But he's also 38. His isolated power has declined for two straight years, and the primary reason his overall numbers looked so much better in '07 was a massive improvement in his walk rate (8 percent in '06 vs. 14 percent in '07).

Griffey can still be a dangerous hitter, and the move to right field helped his fielding numbers considerably. He's no longer a superstar, but he's a valuable guy to have in the lineup.

Scott Hatteberg (First Base)

PA	R	H	2B	3B	HR	RBI	SO	BB	SB	CS	BA	OBP	SLG	OPS	Fld	F$
458	56	111	23	1	9	50	46	57	0	1	.283	.375	.416	.791	C	$1

Hatteberg's rebirth with the Reds over the past two years has surprised a lot of people. How many other players reverse a multi-year decline at age 36 to post the two best consecutive seasons of their careers? Nevertheless, one should expect a drop in his plate appearances. Hatteberg has been used by the Reds as a strict platoon player since his arrival in Cincinnati, and this season he will compete with top prospect Joey Votto for starts against right-handed pitchers. Unless Votto struggles, Hatteberg may be relegated to a pinch-hitting role.

Norris Hopper (Center Field)

PA	R	H	2B	3B	HR	RBI	SO	BB	SB	CS	BA	OBP	SLG	OPS	3 Yr	Fld	F$
393	44	107	14	2	3	35	41	19	10	4	.295	.331	.369	.700	-.042	B	$1

Hopper quickly became a fan favorite last season with his combination of scrappy small-ball play and excellent defense. Hopper is not a particularly good hitter, and has absolutely no power, but he has good speed, which works with his aggressive style of hitting to result in a good number of infield hits.

Jeff Keppinger (Shortstop)

PA	R	H	2B	3B	HR	RBI	SO	BB	SB	CS	BA	OBP	SLG	OPS	3 Yr	Fld	F$
497	58	136	23	2	8	53	42	34	3	2	.306	.356	.421	.777	-.019	F	$1

Keppinger began the season in Triple-A, but when he finally joined the club in July, he flat-out hit. He eventually all but took over the starting shortstop position. While Keppinger has always been a high-average hitter, his .477 slugging average in the major leagues last season was higher than any he'd ever posted in the minors. I think it's unlikely that, at 27, he suddenly discovered a power stroke upon arriving in the big leagues, so look for his power to decline as per THT's projections.

Andy Phillips (First Base)

PA	R	H	2B	3B	HR	RBI	SO	BB	SB	CS	BA	OBP	SLG	OPS	3 Yr	Fld	F$
428	53	107	19	2	16	59	70	35	2	2	.281	.342	.467	.809	-.033	A	$1

Phillips hit very well for a second baseman in the minors, but didn't field well enough. He fielded very well for a first baseman, but didn't hit well enough. The Yankees gave him a shot the past couple of years, and all he did was confirm their doubts.

Brandon Phillips (Second Base)

PA	R	H	2B	3B	HR	RBI	SO	BB	SB	CS	BA	OBP	SLG	OPS	3 Yr	Fld	F$
596	81	151	27	3	21	80	95	33	23	4	.277	.325	.453	.778	-.009	B	$20

While he's a decent hitter and, of course, now a card-carrying 30/30 man, Phillips is probably a bit overrated. His OBP always has been rather low, mostly due to a reluctance to walk. And his power surge in '07 may have been the result, at least in part, of some good fortune: According to HitTrackerOnline.com, Phillips was tied for third in baseball with seven "lucky" home runs (home runs that wouldn't have been were it not for the weather). Despite his offensive flaws, Phillips is a very good all-around player, and an essential cog in the Reds' plans.

David Ross (Catcher)

PA	R	H	2B	3B	HR	RBI	SO	BB	SB	CS	BA	OBP	SLG	OPS	3 Yr	Fld	F$
351	45	78	17	0	19	57	81	33	1	1	.254	.327	.496	.823	-.029	A+	$1

Ross had a spectacular year in 2006 (.932 OPS), and the Reds hoped for more of the same in '07. Instead, they got .203/.271/.399. Which is the real Ross? While his flyball percentage was down a tad last year, his line drive percentage was actually up to 19 percent. Despite this, his batting average on balls in play was just .220. So was he just unlucky? THT's projections sure think so, forecasting a fine season from Ross in '08. If he can produce close to those numbers, the Reds will be ecstatic, because Ross is a plus defensive catcher with a cannon for an arm … and the Reds simply don't have any other options.

Javier Valentin (Catcher)

PA	R	H	2B	3B	HR	RBI	SO	BB	SB	CS	BA	OBP	SLG	OPS	3 Yr	Fld	F$
307	36	76	17	1	8	37	38	27	0	1	.278	.342	.435	.777	-.055	C	$1

Valentin was used almost exclusively as a pinch hitter in the first half, with ex-manager Jerry Narron giving much of the backup catching starts job to Chad Moeller. As a result, he had trouble getting and staying in any sort of groove. Valentin's playing time picked up in the second half, and he hit closer to his '06 rates during that stretch, but he was still a far cry from his breakout performance in 2005. Even so, Valentin's a decent-hitting backup catcher with some pop.

Joey Votto (First Base)

PA	R	H	2B	3B	HR	RBI	SO	BB	SB	CS	BA	OBP	SLG	OPS	3 Yr	Fld	F$
583	74	137	28	1	22	80	118	58	8	5	.266	.340	.453	.793	.022	B	$1

Given his phenomenal September debut in '07, you might find THT's projections for Votto to be pessimistic. However, there are some questions about Votto's power. While he's always gotten on base at a fine clip, Votto posted a SLG over .500 only once in minor leagues above rookie ball. The Reds haven't had a power-hitting first baseman in ages, and I'm not sure that Votto will be that guy. Even so, he should turn out to be a capable hitter with decent pop.

Pitchers

Jeremy Affeldt (Starting/Relief Pitcher)

W	L	ERA	TBF	IP	Hit	HR	SO	BB	HBP	3 Yr	F$
3	4	4.63	286	64	63	7	48	37	2	0.38	$1

Word is that the Reds will try Affeldt in the starting rotation, though our projections are based on his experience as a reliever. This will either turn out to be a good move by Cincinnati, or Affeldt will be remembered in Colorado for his George Kostanza-esque ability to leave before his weaknesses are exposed.

Bronson Arroyo (Starting Pitcher)

W	L	ERA	TBF	IP	Hit	HR	SO	BB	HBP	3 Yr	F$
11	10	4.45	823	194	202	25	132	56	8	0.33	$4

Bronson predictably regressed last season after his impressive (and hit-lucky) 2006. His peripherals didn't change much, with only a slight decrease in strikeouts and increase in walks, indicating little change in actual skill by the 30-year old. One thing we have learned is that he's susceptible to decline based on workload—from '06 through mid '07, he performed about a half-run better after throwing fewer than 110 pitches in the previous start. How that tendency will interact with Dusty Baker's tendency to rack up high pitch counts among his starters remains to be seen.

Homer Bailey (Starting Pitcher)

W	L	ERA	TBF	IP	Hit	HR	SO	BB	HBP	3 Yr	F$
7	7	4.75	560	127	121	15	95	69	7	-0.47	$1

Bailey's was the most anticipated debut of a Reds prospect since ... well ... it's hard to exaggerate how long it's been. In the end, his performance was rather disappointing. Sometimes he looked just like the guy we all hoped we'd see. Other times, he really struggled, particularly with his control and consistency. Bailey is at a crossroads. If he can pitch reasonably well this season, he'll still be considered among the game's top young pitchers. Remember, the guy doesn't turn 22 until May. Don't give up on him too quickly.

Matt Belisle (Starting Pitcher)

W	L	ERA	TBF	IP	Hit	HR	SO	BB	HBP	3 Yr	F$
7	10	5.01	659	152	175	21	103	43	7	0.16	$1

Last season was Belisle's first full year as a starter in the major leagues. His ERA indicates that it didn't go so well. But his peripherals look similar to Arroyo's—slightly lower strikeout rate, but also slightly lower walk rate. The difference: Belisle gave up too many big flies: Six of his 26 home runs allowed resulted in three or more runs (compared to two of 28 for Arroyo), including three grand slams. Belisle's not great, but capable of posting a 4.50 ERA in 180-200 innings.

Bill Bray (Relief Pitcher)

W	L	ERA	TBF	IP	Hit	HR	SO	BB	HBP	3 Yr	F$
3	3	3.90	224	53	48	6	52	20	2	-0.05	$1

Bray suffered a broken finger early in the season, but his "rehab" in Triple-A went on for a surprisingly long time. When he returned, Bray seemed to struggle, posting a 6+ ERA in 14 innings. His peripherals, however, told a different story—almost a strikeout per inning innings, a 3:1 strikeout-to-walk ratio, and a sparkling 3.24 FIP. Bray will be 25 this season. Look for him to take a step forward as one of the better left-handed setup men in baseball.

Jared Burton (Relief Pitcher)

W	L	ERA	TBF	IP	Hit	HR	SO	BB	HBP	3 Yr	F$
3	4	4.79	265	60	60	7	49	30	3	0.07	$1

Rule 5 pick Burton took a while to adjust to the big leagues, but in July he took over the eighth-inning relief job. One of his most successful pitches is a cutter, which several analysts studying Pitch f/x data have noted bears a remarkable resemblance to Mariano Rivera's signature pitch. He's unlikely to approach Rivera's excellence, of course, but he doesn't have to in order to be valuable. The biggest red flag in his peripherals was his walk rate, but his dominance over the last two months coincided with a dramatic improvement in his control.

Todd Coffey (Relief Pitcher)

W	L	ERA	TBF	IP	Hit	HR	SO	BB	HBP	3 Yr	F$
4	4	4.32	323	75	81	8	57	25	4	0.11	$1

Coffey may have been more prone to the walk last year, but his strikeout rates improved, as did his groundball rate (57 percent in 2007). Yet he allowed a ridiculous 12 home runs in 57 innings. The reasonable interpretation of those data is that he was darn unlucky, which is supported by his absurd 25 percent home run-to-fly ball ratio last year. The thing is, this nonsense kept happening *all season long.*

Francisco Cordero (Relief Pitcher)

W	L	ERA	TBF	IP	Hit	HR	SO	BB	HBP	3 Yr	F$
5	3	3.39	283	69	57	7	79	24	2	0.32	$13

Unhittable, almost literally so, at the beginning of the year, Cordero struggled a little during the summer, but overall was a welcome comfort blanket for Brewers fans after the squirm-inducing tenure of Derrick Turnbow as closer. He posted the highest strikeout rate (by almost two K/9) and lowest walk rate of his career, and his lowest FIP and xFIP in the last four years. He's truly one of the elite relievers in the game, a distinction that has absolutely nothing to do with finishing second in the NL in saves.

Jon Coutlangus (Relief Pitcher)

W	L	ERA	TBF	IP	Hit	HR	SO	BB	HBP	3 Yr	F$
3	4	5.11	270	60	61	7	49	35	4	0.16	$1

Jon is a converted outfielder and left-handed sinkerballer. Compared to his minor league rates, his strikeouts with Cincinnati last year seemed a bit high, but so did his walks. His future will depend in large part on whether he can improve his control. If he can, look for him to become a good middle/late inning option from the left side of the mound.

Johnny Cueto (Starting Pitcher)

W	L	ERA	TBF	IP	Hit	HR	SO	BB	HBP	3 Yr	F$
7	10	4.99	655	152	158	25	123	49	12	-0.47	$1

Cueto was dominant across three levels as the Reds' minor league pitcher of the year in 2007. He posted excellent strikeout numbers and a five-strikeouts-per-walk ratio in one of the more impressive runs through the minors since ... well, Homer Bailey's 2006 season. In some recent prospect rankings, Cueto has been placed higher than Bailey. Given the Reds' conservatism with their prospects and the acquisition of Edinson Volquez, it would be surprising for Cueto to start the season with the big league club. But a midseason call-up is likely.

Aaron Harang (Starting Pitcher)

W	L	ERA	TBF	IP	Hit	HR	SO	BB	HBP	3 Yr	F$
12	10	4.04	837	201	200	25	173	51	7	0.57	$15

Harang has quietly turned in three superb seasons. He's finally getting some credit for it, as evidenced by his fourth-place finish in the NL Cy Young voting. Harang has a plus fastball and slider, as well as a decent curve and change-up, but his excellence seems to stem largely from his excellent control. His one weakness is that he induces lots of fly balls, which makes him prone to home runs. Even so, few pitchers have been more reliable than Harang over the past several years.

Bobby Livingston (Starting Pitcher)

W	L	ERA	TBF	IP	Hit	HR	SO	BB	HBP	3 Yr	F$
7	10	5.42	664	151	186	23	74	43	6	-0.14	$1

Livingston's final line doesn't show it, but he was an essential part of the Reds rotation for a few months last season. He didn't strike anybody out, but he also didn't walk anyone, and the result was a very serviceable pitcher. His FIP was a heck of a lot better than his ERA, and I think it was a pretty good indication of his true skill. Unfortunately, his shoulder blew out, which puts his ability to pitch again in the major leagues—much less in 2008—in doubt. Shame.

Gary Majewski (Relief Pitcher)

W	L	ERA	TBF	IP	Hit	HR	SO	BB	HBP	3 Yr	F$
4	3	4.43	290	67	72	6	41	26	3	0.13	$1

Majewski has essentially been injured since arriving in Cincinnati in what Reds fans still call (with bitterness) The Trade. His strikeouts were way down (even by his standards) in his limited playing time last season, so there's reason to think that he was still not healthy even after missing the first half with shoulder weakness. He'll still be just 28 this season, however, so there's reason to hope that he can heal and be effective. If healthy, Majewski can be a groundball machine and a serviceable middle reliever.

Mike Stanton (Relief Pitcher)

W	L	ERA	TBF	IP	Hit	HR	SO	BB	HBP	F$
3	4	4.54	277	64	66	7	43	25	3	$1

When he signed, there was talk that he would be the co-closer with Weathers. Ultimately, he never got a save, and never seemed even to put together more than a few solid appearances in a row. His peripherals and high BABIP indicate that he was terribly unlucky last season, but he also showed a big increase in his home runs allowed rate, in part due to GABP, and in part due to a declining groundball percentage.

Edinson Volquez (Starting Pitcher)

W	L	ERA	TBF	IP	Hit	HR	SO	BB	HBP	3 Yr	F$
8	10	4.89	696	159	152	24	142	79	8	-0.18	$1

Texas sent Volquez down to High-A Bakersfield last year in an attempt to correct the control issues that jeopardized his future. He didn't show any improvement there, but displayed much better control in Double-A and Triple-A, cutting his walks by 40 percent with no detriment to his terrific strikeout rate. Back in Texas, he still struggled with free passes at times, but otherwise looked like a major league pitcher. If he can complete the development of his curve to accentuate his mid-90s fastball and killer change-up, he'll be Cincinnati's second-best starter.

David Weathers (Relief Pitcher)

W	L	ERA	TBF	IP	Hit	HR	SO	BB	HBP	F$
4	4	4.43	316	74	71	9	48	30	3	$1

I've been predicting Stormy Weathers' decline for years now, but he just keeps proving me wrong. Last season, he reversed what appeared to be a major decline in his peripherals and posted yet another fine season. I still see major reasons for concern. Weathers' strikeout rates have dropped three consecutive years, dipping to below average last season. Similarly, his groundball rates have declined dramatically, dipping to an alarming 35 percent in 2007. With any similar pitcher entering his age-38 year, I'd guarantee that he would be about to implode. But given how many times he's proven me wrong, I'll just say that I continue to be really worried about him.

Cleveland Indians

by Ryan Richards of Let's Go Tribe (letsgotribe.com)

2008 Projections

Record: 90-72
Division Rank: 1st, by two games
Runs Scored: 866
Runs Allowed: 761

2007 in a Nutshell

The Indians won 96 games and the AL Central, thanks in large part to winning five of their last six games with the Detroit Tigers. The Indians had just one losing month (July, 12-14), and went 36-20 over the final two months of the season.

General Comments

Team Strengths

The pitching staff, which ranked third in AL ERA. The starting staff allowed the fewest walks in the AL, which led to Cleveland's rotation leading the league in innings pitched. Their starters going deeper into games ensured that the Indians' three key relievers (Joe Borowski, Rafael Betancourt and Rafael Perez) wouldn't be overused. And because the Indians had those three consistent relievers all season, there weren't many late-inning meltdowns.

Team Weaknesses

Infield defense remained a problem for the Indians; their Revised Zone Rating of .758 ranked next to last in the American League.

The General Manager is Known for...

Mark Shapiro rebuilt the Indians from basket case to good team in three seasons, and to a playoff team in five. He decided to tear down the Indians completely in June 2002, after his initial plan of a more gradual rebuild blew up in his face. The Bartolo Colon trade netted, among others, Grady Sizemore, and an offseason deal landed Travis Hafner. Those two, along with C.C. Sabathia and Victor Martinez, formed a young core that Shapiro would build around.

Shapiro has kept his priorities on developing the major league club through the minor league system even as the team became competitive. Most recent expenditures have been on extending players already on the roster; the Indians have not been major players in the free-agent market.

The Manager is Known for...

Eric Wedge is a conventional tactician. He has been able to get his players to buy into the organizational philosophy. He takes an active role in player evaluation, behaving in the offseason more like an NFL head coach than an MLB manager.

Ballpark Characteristics

Jacobs Field, which played as a hitters' paradise when it first opened, has become a slight pitchers' park since the turn of the century. The left field wall is 19 feet high, while the rest of the park's dimensions are conventional.

The Minor League System is ...

It's deep, but not as talented as in years past.

Adam Miller is the headliner, a big right hander with a lot of upside but also lot of health issues. Miller has an excellent fastball/slider combo, and assuming he can stay available, he can help the Indians this season.

First baseman-outfielder Jordan Brown hit .331/.421/.484 at Double-A Akron, walking more (63) than striking out (56). If he can play left field, he could be a midseason call-up. Left-hander Chuck Lofgren probably needs another year of seasoning, but he has a very good fastball and three other decent-to-good pitches (curve, slider, change) in his repertoire.

Favorite Team Blogs

The DiaTribe (http://www.clevelandtribeblog.blogspot.com/)

Mistake By the Lake (http://mistakesports.blogspot.com/)

Keys for 2008

Players Lost from Last Year's Team

Outfielders Kenny Lofton and Trot Nixon were still unsigned as of press date, but they won't be returning to Cleveland. Infielder Chris Gomez has signed with Pittsburgh. Prospects Brian Barton and Matt Whitney were selected in the Rule 5 draft.

Players Acquired

The Indians have added two players to their major league roster since the end of the season: They signed Japanese free agent reliever Masahide Kobayashi, and traded for infielder Jamey Carroll. Because Carroll's primary position is second base, it will allow Asdrubal

Cabrera to serve as both the starting second baseman and the primary backup at shortstop; this should allow the Indians to keep Andy Marte on the 25-man roster. Kobayashi will add quality set-up depth to a bullpen that needed an extra high-leverage reliever.

Reasons to be Optimistic

Virtually every contributing player from last year's division winner will return. Organizational starting pitching depth is substantial: The Indians' rotation possibilities go at least seven deep. If the both the Indians and Tigers have to dip into their reserves, the Indians probably will win the division.

Reasons to be Pessimistic

The Indians still will get less production from their corners than most of their peers. It remains to be seen how Fausto Carmona will react to throwing a lot of innings the season before, and they might lose Paul Byrd to an early-season suspension (he admitted to using HGH). If Hafner can't regain his pre-2007 form, the offense won't be able to keep up with other American League offenses.

Due for a Better Season

David Dellucci is a better hitter than his 2007 performance indicated, though the Indians still should be looking for someone better.

Likely to Have a Worse Season

Carmona pitched 230 innings last season, counting the postseason; that's almost 130 more innings than he pitched in 2006. Rafael Betancourt pitched 33 more innings and in 25 more games than in 2006. Both those pitchers are going to feel the effects of that jump in workload this season.

Still Left to Do

The Indians still need to sort out their infield for the long term. Involved in that sorting out will be the fates of Marte and Josh Barfield. They may need to acquire a left fielder if Dellucci can't bounce back. And above all, they need to extend Sabathia.

Most Likely Team Outcome

A season-long battle with the Detroit Tigers for the AL Central crown.

Player Projections

Batters

Josh Barfield (Second Base)

PA	R	H	2B	3B	HR	RBI	SO	BB	SB	CS	BA	OBP	SLG	OPS	3 Yr	Fld	F$
478	55	122	25	2	8	51	84	26	10	2	.277	.316	.397	.713	.013	C	$3

It's hard to imagine many things going wrong with a 96-win team, but Barfield's implosion was a big problem. Not only was his spot in the lineup an automatic out, but his defense was poor. Barfield's still in the Indians' long-term plans, but thanks to Cabrera's late-season heroics, he's probably not in this year's outlook. A modest offensive rebound, as suggested by his projection, would open up several interesting possibilities.

Casey Blake (Third Base)

PA	R	H	2B	3B	HR	RBI	SO	BB	SB	CS	BA	OBP	SLG	OPS	3 Yr	Fld	F$
560	69	130	29	2	18	71	106	53	3	3	.265	.342	.443	.785	-.048	D	$5

A versatile player, Blake moved over from first after Andy Marte got hurt. He proceeded to give the Indians a very adequate season at the hot corner. He's considered the starter at third, but his shelf life as a viable third baseman isn't long (it was defense that moved him off the position a few years ago), and they really need to find out if Marte is their future at the position. He'd probably be best used as an outfielder or super utility player.

Asdrubal Cabrera (Shortstop)

PA	R	H	2B	3B	HR	RBI	SO	BB	SB	CS	BA	OBP	SLG	OPS	3 Yr	Fld	F$
550	62	131	27	5	6	49	81	40	10	5	.265	.322	.377	.699	.056	D	$1

Boxed into a corner after Josh Barfield's flameout, the Indians plucked 21-year-old Cabrera out of the minors, not expecting much. But Cabrera, a natural shortstop, played a good second base and showed surprising plate discipline. Because Cabrera can play shortstop, the Indians can now start to think about moving Jhonny Peralta.

David Dellucci (Left Field)

PA	R	H	2B	3B	HR	RBI	SO	BB	SB	CS	BA	OBP	SLG	OPS	3 Yr	Fld	F$
314	41	72	14	3	11	40	63	36	2	1	.265	.354	.461	.815	-.046	D	$1

Dellucci was supposed to be that corner power bat the Indians had lacked in previous years. But in his 175 at-bats before going on the DL, David slugged just .382. The Indians are naively banking on a comeback: David's at an age where corner outfielders' power can disappear in a hurry.

Ben Francisco (Center Field)

PA	R	H	2B	3B	HR	RBI	SO	BB	SB	CS	BA	OBP	SLG	OPS	3 Yr	Fld	F$
482	58	114	24	3	11	53	87	32	10	4	.262	.315	.406	.721	.003	C	$1

A quick piece of trivia: Ben hit a walk-off homer in the first start of his career; the home run was his second career hit, the first coming earlier in the game. He's not your typical right-handed outfielder, as he's actually hit right handers better than left handers during his minor-league career. He can play all three outfield positions, so he'd be a good general-purpose fourth outfielder.

Ryan Garko (First Base)

PA	R	H	2B	3B	HR	RBI	SO	BB	SB	CS	BA	OBP	SLG	OPS	3 Yr	Fld	F$
530	68	126	26	1	19	71	95	40	0	1	.270	.344	.451	.795	.009	C	$6

Ryan has an aggressive yet compact swing, and his ability to get in the way of pitches (20 HBP) is an extra OBP bonus.

Franklin Gutierrez (Right Field)

PA	R	H	2B	3B	HR	RBI	SO	BB	SB	CS	BA	OBP	SLG	OPS	3 Yr	Fld	F$
465	55	107	24	2	12	54	100	33	9	3	.256	.314	.410	.724	.023	B	$1

An excellent defensive player, Gutierrez pushed aside Nixon to become the everyday right fielder. He'd be a center fielder on a lot of teams, but because Grady Sizemore isn't going anywhere, he'll need to continue to hit for power. A big concern for Franklin is plate discipline: He struck out 77 times and walked 21 times in 301 plate appearances. Gutierrez may be able to hit with power even with these rates, but he's had only 444 career plate appearances, still too small a sample for any conclusions.

Travis Hafner (Designated Hitter)

PA	R	H	2B	3B	HR	RBI	SO	BB	SB	CS	BA	OBP	SLG	OPS	3 Yr	F$
584	87	138	31	1	30	95	107	96	1	1	.290	.411	.548	.959	-.026	$22

Hafner hit "only" .266/.385/.451, a 118 OPS+ but a huge drop-off compared to his usual production. Though he still took his walks, Pronk hit a whopping 48 percent of balls in play on the ground; normally he's a line-drive machine. The Indians gave Hafner a four-year extension midway through the season; the projection says he'll be worth that deal.

Kenny Lofton (Center Field)

PA	R	H	2B	3B	HR	RBI	SO	BB	SB	CS	BA	OBP	SLG	OPS	Fld	F$
509	66	130	21	6	2	39	51	49	21	4	.291	.360	.379	.739	C	$1

For a player with his skill set, Lofton has aged remarkably well. When he joined the Indians at the trading deadline, he moved to left field not because of diminishing skills, but due to the presence of Grady Sizemore in center. Kenny talked of retirement during his stint with Cleveland, and it would be fitting for him to end his career where he had his greatest success.

Andy Marte (Third Base)

PA	R	H	2B	3B	HR	RBI	SO	BB	SB	CS	BA	OBP	SLG	OPS	3 Yr	Fld	F$
472	54	106	25	2	16	61	91	35	1	2	.247	.303	.427	.730	.024	D	$1

Last season was wasted for the third base prospect. He started the year as more or less the starting third basemen, but went on the DL in April. While Blake filled in for him, Marte hit an unimpressive .267/.309/.457 in

Buffalo. Because he's now out of options, the Indians have to carry him on their roster, which they should be able to do, but that roster inflexibility means that he can't have another bad stretch of at-bats. He has to perform now, or he'll be dealt.

Victor Martinez (Catcher)

PA	R	H	2B	3B	HR	RBI	SO	BB	SB	CS	BA	OBP	SLG	OPS	3 Yr	Fld	F$
594	78	154	33	0	19	81	76	65	1	1	.299	.379	.473	.852	-.030	C	$15

The major negative on Martinez going into last season was his inability to control the running game; he had allowed 100 stolen bases in 122 attempts in 2006. He worked on his throwing mechanics over the winter, and it showed . In 2007, he caught 32 percent of potential base stealers. That came as he had his most productive season at the plate. Martinez became the focal point of the offense, collecting 65 extra-base hits and creating 109 runs. In what became a nice three-way platoon, Martinez spent every Paul Byrd start at first base, allowing him to appear in 147 games without wearing down toward the end of the year.

Jason Michaels (Left Field)

PA	R	H	2B	3B	HR	RBI	SO	BB	SB	CS	BA	OBP	SLG	OPS	3 Yr	Fld	F$
386	44	93	20	1	7	41	65	33	3	2	.271	.336	.397	.733	-.032	B	$1

After getting an opportunity to start in 2006, Michaels returned to his familiar role of right-handed platoon outfielder. He continued to hit left handers well, and should stick with the team as long as Dellucci's the starting left fielder.

Jhonny Peralta (Shortstop)

PA	R	H	2B	3B	HR	RBI	SO	BB	SB	CS	BA	OBP	SLG	OPS	3 Yr	Fld	F$
582	73	142	29	2	19	76	126	58	3	2	.277	.350	.452	.802	.023	F	$10

He got a bit rangier in the field, and lot better at the plate in 2007. His bat is what justifies him staying at short; he has good power to all fields, especially to right center. As mentioned elsewhere in this section, a move to third makes sense on a number of levels.

Kelly Shoppach (Catcher)

PA	R	H	2B	3B	HR	RBI	SO	BB	SB	CS	BA	OBP	SLG	OPS	3 Yr	Fld	F$
281	35	64	14	0	13	43	77	23	0	1	.259	.328	.473	.801	-.006	B	$1

He was on a regular schedule last year, serving as Byrd's personal catcher. His offensive production all came before the All-Star break (.956 OPS before, .567 after), but as with any backup catcher, it's difficult to read too much of that into future results. The projections don't see the second-half drop-off as a problem, either.

Grady Sizemore (Center Field)

PA	R	H	2B	3B	HR	RBI	SO	BB	SB	CS	BA	OBP	SLG	OPS	3 Yr	Fld	F$
662	102	162	37	7	24	90	129	80	24	6	.288	.381	.506	.887	.025	F	$30

Sizemore is one of the few Cleveland core players with some upside left. That's promising, given that he posted a .852 OPS as a 24-year-old. The most interesting trend in Sizemore's recent stat lines is that his walks have spiked while his strikeouts have remained high. Obviously, the strikeouts haven't inhibited his offensive production, but the positive trend in walks should help him get more pitches to swing at in the strike zone.

Pitchers

Rafael Betancourt (Relief Pitcher)

W	L	ERA	TBF	IP	Hit	HR	SO	BB	HBP	3 Yr	F$
5	3	3.54	288	71	62	7	68	18	2	0.34	$5

If Borowski was the Indians' closer, Betancourt was the team's most valuable reliever, making multiple-inning appearances in high-leverage situations. Rafael relies overwhelmingly on his fastball, which he spots with laser-like accuracy. Hitters seem to have trouble picking up his pitches because of his short-armed delivery.

Joe Borowski (Relief Pitcher)

W	L	ERA	TBF	IP	Hit	HR	SO	BB	HBP	F$
4	3	4.41	290	68	66	8	51	27	2	$5

Joe saved a league-high 45 games in 2007, though he wasn't as dominating as his counting stats indicate. His stuff is pedestrian by closer standards, though he's not going to get rattled in a tough spot. Rafael Betancourt's the better reliever, but given Eric Wedge's bullpen usage patterns, I'm not so sure that switching the two would be a huge improvement.

Paul Byrd (Starting Pitcher)

W	L	ERA	TBF	IP	Hit	HR	SO	BB	HBP	F$
9	11	4.77	765	180	211	23	80	33	6	$1

His fastball tops out in the mid-80s, and he's a right hander to boot. Byrd somehow makes things work by using exceptional control of his pitches along with an ability to stay one pitch ahead of his opponent. But even with these compensations, each outing is a high-wire act, and even his successful performances last only five or six innings. The Indians picked up his 2008 option, a no-brainer considering how well he pitched throughout 2007.

Fausto Carmona (Starting Pitcher)

W	L	ERA	TBF	IP	Hit	HR	SO	BB	HBP	3 Yr	F$
10	9	4.08	749	177	187	14	111	57	9	-0.21	$4

Carmona got by early in 2007 with essentially his two-seamer, but as the season wore on, he began not only to integrate his secondary stuff into his game plan, but also to throw those pitches for strikes. He's still not a finished product, as his two ALCS starts showed, and all those 2007 innings may affect this year's effectiveness.

Aaron Fultz (Relief Pitcher)

W	L	ERA	TBF	IP	Hit	HR	SO	BB	HBP	3 Yr	F$
3	3	4.36	234	54	51	5	38	26	2	0.47	$1

As Rafael Perez rose to prominence in the Indians' bullpen, Fultz faded to a lesser role. The Indians picked up his 2008 option, so he'll be back as a match-up guy.

Masahide Kobayashi (Relief Pitcher)

W	L	ERA	TBF	IP	Hit	HR	SO	BB	HBP	F$
3	3	4.40	210	47	50	5	34	17	2	$1

Thus far the Indians' biggest addition of the winter, Kobayashi was an accomplished closer in Japan. The contract's not that bad (two years, $6.25 million), so the signing should give the Indians some relatively cheap setup depth.

Aaron Laffey (Starting Pitcher)

W	L	ERA	TBF	IP	Hit	HR	SO	BB	HBP	3 Yr	F$
7	10	5.07	692	155	183	15	64	63	10	-0.57	$1

Thanks to the ineffectiveness of Cliff Lee and Jeremy Sowers, Laffey joined the rotation in August and stayed in it the remainder of the season. He'd always been an intriguing prospect due to his extreme groundball rates, but in 2007 he started to miss bats in the minors, an improvement that transformed him from a fringe prospect to a potential major league starter. He'll battle Lee and Sowers for a rotation spot this spring.

Cliff Lee (Starting Pitcher)

W	L	ERA	TBF	IP	Hit	HR	SO	BB	HBP	3 Yr	F$
7	10	5.01	652	150	161	21	102	55	6	0.72	$1

Since a good 2005 season, Lee's had to deal with injuries, dead arm periods and a run-in with Victor Martinez, the latter being the biggest deal. He launched two careers in 2007: First, his spring training injury gave Carmona a spot in the rotation, and later, his ineffectiveness gave Laffey an opportunity to pitch in the big leagues. Because both Sabathia and Byrd are in the last years of their contracts and because Lee's contract is very reasonable, the Indians have decided to keep him around another season, though he'll have to win a spot in the rotation.

Jensen Lewis (Relief Pitcher)

W	L	ERA	TBF	IP	Hit	HR	SO	BB	HBP	3 Yr	F$
3	5	5.60	326	73	80	11	58	33	4	-0.27	$1

Lewis didn't start relieving until this past season, but took to it quickly. After just 10 appearances in Buffalo, the Indians brought him to the majors in July. By September, he was a key setup man, and saw considerable action down the stretch and in the playoffs.

Tom Mastny (Relief Pitcher)

W	L	ERA	TBF	IP	Hit	HR	SO	BB	HBP	3 Yr	F$
3	4	4.84	291	65	65	6	55	36	3	0.14	$1

If you've followed any bullpen for a couple of seasons, you know that the configuration going into the season won't look anything like the group at the end of the year, or even the at All-Star break. With that said, it doesn't look like Mastny has a spot in this season's Opening Day bullpen with the addition of Kobayashi. But, knowing bullpens, he'll be getting an opportunity sooner rather than later.

Rafael Perez (Relief Pitcher)

W	L	ERA	TBF	IP	Hit	HR	SO	BB	HBP	3 Yr	F$
6	5	4.48	444	103	105	11	72	42	5	-0.08	$1

Raffy Left filled a similar role as Raffy Right; they'd often alternate games, bridging the gap from the starter to the closer in a tight contest. Perez was effective against any type of hitter, though he was particularly good against left handers (.145/.209/.241).

C.C. Sabathia (Starting Pitcher)

W	L	ERA	TBF	IP	Hit	HR	SO	BB	HBP	3 Yr	F$
14	9	3.32	830	206	190	17	173	44	7	0.15	$28

Sabathia arrived in the majors at age 20 blessed with a strong, durable left arm. He's added to his natural gifts command, improved mechanics and a refined arsenal of off-speed pitches. C.C. was able to throw a league-high 241 innings last season because he allowed just 37 walks in those innings. The biggest question regarding Sabathia in 2008 won't be his pitching, but his contract status. He's a free agent after this season, and because of his age, ability and durability, a huge payday is coming his way.

Jeremy Sowers (Starting Pitcher)

W	L	ERA	TBF	IP	Hit	HR	SO	BB	HBP	3 Yr	F$
8	10	4.86	701	161	182	18	68	54	6	-0.45	$1

In 2006, Sowers threw 88.1 innings with a very nice 3.57 ERA. But there were warning signs behind that successful mark: a very low strikeout total (35), and a very high and virtually unsustainable Left on Base Percentage (76.3). In 2007, AL hitters hit .308/.360/.498 off him. The Indians sent him to Buffalo in June, and he wasn't brought back until the last week of the season. His minor-league numbers don't inspire confidence (112 hits in 96.2 Triple-A innings), so I think the projections are very optimistic.

Jake Westbrook (Starting Pitcher)

W	L	ERA	TBF	IP	Hit	HR	SO	BB	HBP	3 Yr	F$
9	9	4.24	687	160	179	12	89	52	5	0.34	$1

An innings-eater, Westbrook relies heavily on an excellent sinker to keep his pitch count low. After coming off the DL in late June, Westbrook quickly returned to form, sporting a 3.44 ERA after the All-Star break. The Indians signed him to a contract extension early last season, a deal that will pay Westbrook roughly $10 million over the next three seasons.

Colorado Rockies

by Brandi Griffin of Purple Row (purplerow.com)

2008 Projections

Record: 85-77
Division Rank: 2nd, one game back
Runs Scored: 845
Runs Allowed: 795

2007 in a Nutshell

All was ho-hum, slightly better than mediocre, through the middle of September. Then the rock quarry went *boom*! The team reeled off a comeback of historic proportions to force a play-in game with the Padres for the wild card spot. Matt Holliday slid close enough to home plate to give the Rockies the playoff berth, and they swept through the National League playoffs for their first pennant before getting their bell rung by the Red Sox in the World Series.

General Comments

Team Strengths

Colorado has standout defense and groundball-oriented pitchers who are adept at using it. The Rockies have a decent middle of the lineup (strong for the NL) and a solid bullpen.

Team Weaknesses

The bottom of the rotation was soft last season. It will be inexperienced this year. While the lineup's good for the National League, the sweep by Boston in the World Series shows that there's still a clear step to take before the Rockies are really ready to compete with the best AL teams. Catcher, second base and center field are particularly weak at the plate.

The General Manager is Known for...

Dan O'Dowd has atoned for past sins with a build-from-within strategy that came to fruition in 2007.

The Manager is Known for...

And Clint Hurdle atoned for past sins by navigating the team through those harrowing final days in September and guiding it to the World Series.

Ballpark Characteristics

Coors Field is a massive, altitude-enhanced edifice that can swallow other ballparks whole. It's still a hitters' park, but obviously Rockies pitchers seem to like what the humidor that treats baseballs has done.

The Minor League System is...

It's thinning from what it was two years ago, but there's still some impact talent percolating up. Franklin Morales projects as the top rookie for the team this season, but pitchers Greg Reynolds, Casey Weathers and Pedro Strop could all play significant roles by the time 2008 closes.

Favorite Team Blogs

Sparks of Dementia (http://sparksofdementia. blogspot.com/)

Up in the Rockies (http://mvn.com/mlb-rockies/)

Denver Sportszone (http://www.denversportszone. com/rox/)

Bad Altitude (http://badaltitude.baseballtoaster. com/)

Keys for 2008

Players Lost from Last Year's Team

Infielder Kazuo Matsui, Pitchers Josh Fogg, Jeremy Affeldt, LaTroy Hawkins, Rodrigo Lopez, Denny Bautista.

Players Acquired

Pitchers Luis Vizcaino, Kip Wells, Jose Capellan

Reasons to be Optimistic

Essentially the same team that won the National League last year returns. The starting pitching could get better with the maturing of young phenoms Ubaldo Jimenez and Morales.

Reasons to be Pessimistic

The NL West is tougher than ever, with both the Dodgers and Diamondbacks making significant acquisitions this winter while the Rockies more or less sat on their hands.

Due for a Better Season

Chris Iannetta certainly should improve, if he's given the playing time. Troy Tulowitzki has some room for growth as a hitter as well, which could make him one of the more valuable players in the league. Jimenez and Morales are due for a lot more MLB innings than they had in 2007, which will help the team tremendously, although Morales in particular likely won't produce in all of them the quality he gave in his short appearance with the Rockies last season. Jason Hirsh should have a stronger season, and more innings, in 2008.

Likely to Have a Worse Season

I figure Todd Helton will settle back down a bit after a big rebound last year. Garrett Atkins and Brad Hawpe may be due for a decline, but don't expect steep drops from any of them. Whoever wins the second base battle probably won't quite live up to the modest standard set by Matsui last season.

Still Left to Do

The opening left at second base by Matsui's departure has created a competition for the job in 2008, with homegrown players Jayson Nix, Ian Stewart, Jeff Baker, Clint Barmes and Omar Quintanilla being given a shot. Unless Stewart takes like a fish to water to the position switch, look for Nix to win the job by April.

By signing Wells, the team bought insurance in case Morales or Jimenez isn't ready to assume a starting role this spring, so both have just a little more proving to do before they are handed the reins of the Rockies' future.

Most Likely Team Outcome

Since they acquired Dan Haren, the Diamondbacks probably merit front-runner status in the NL West, but the Dodgers and Rockies look only slightly less strong, with the Padres just a hair behind those two. Any of these four teams could win the division with the right luck in 2008, but any also could finish fourth if things go sour. Therefore, I might as well root for my Rockies to win their first division crown this year.

Player Projections

Batters

Garrett Atkins (Third Base)

PA	R	H	2B	3B	HR	RBI	SO	BB	SB	CS	BA	OBP	SLG	OPS	3 Yr	Fld	F$
609	80	163	36	1	20	85	83	58	2	1	.303	.370	.484	.854	-.028	F	$17

Three things bode ill for Garrett's future with the Rox. First, Atkins is a talented hitter, but is already at his peak at 28 and is likely to decline over the next three seasons, perhaps significantly. Secondly, Garrett's a pretty bad defender at third, arguably the worst starter in the NL, assuming Ryan Braun moves to the outfield. Finally, the Rockies have a solid young replacement ready in Ian Stewart, whose superior glove probably evens these two out in value for 2008.

Rather than untangling the issue this winter, when A-Rod was floating out there for a minute or two, and Miguel Cabrera dominated the trade scene at the hot corner, the Rockies decided to go one more season with their current set-up at the infield corners. It seems clear that something has to give by April 2009, and Atkins still seems to be the most likely something.

Jeff Baker (Second Base)

PA	R	H	2B	3B	HR	RBI	SO	BB	SB	CS	BA	OBP	SLG	OPS	3 Yr	Fld	F$
323	41	82	17	2	12	45	69	23	1	1	.280	.335	.475	.810	-.003	D	$1

Baker started 2007 as the Rockies' primary right-handed bat off the bench, but Ryan Spilborghs usurped the role by midseason with what may have been his career year. Baker's got enough skills at the plate to get the title back with a solid season, but either way, the Rockies have quite the arsenal when it comes to dealing with the NL West's tough left handers.

Baker's trying out second base—this will add to his super-utility resume—and is a longshot to get that starting job in spring training. Depending on how things shake out at second and with Stewart, Baker could become available for trade to help shore up other areas by midseason.

Clint Barmes (Shortstop)

PA	R	H	2B	3B	HR	RBI	SO	BB	SB	CS	BA	OBP	SLG	OPS	3 Yr	Fld	F$
469	53	112	23	3	9	49	61	19	5	3	.263	.307	.394	.701	-.022	B	$1

Barmes will be trying to come back to the big club in the battle to replace Kazuo Matsui at second base. I'd give him long odds at that, but the team might be tempted to use him to replace Jamey Carroll as a utility infielder. This I worry about. While both are defensive standouts, Carroll added value on the basepaths and with his plate discipline that Barmes won't duplicate, and Clint's bat is a high altitude ghost.

Marcus Giles (Second Base)

PA	R	H	2B	3B	HR	RBI	SO	BB	SB	CS	BA	OBP	SLG	OPS	3 Yr	Fld	F$
507	62	124	28	3	7	50	77	45	10	3	.278	.345	.401	.746	-.026	C	$3

Brought in to San Diego to replace Josh Barfield at second base, Giles got off to a strong start (.327/.376/.459 in April) before stumbling badly (.199/.283/.273 from that point) and losing his job to Geoff Blum. Released following the season, Giles is still young enough (he turns 30 in May) to recover, but 2007 marked the second straight year his production plummeted, and right now, the future isn't looking real bright.

Brad Hawpe (Right Field)

PA	R	H	2B	3B	HR	RBI	SO	BB	SB	CS	BA	OBP	SLG	OPS	3 Yr	Fld	F$
539	73	129	27	4	21	75	114	71	1	2	.281	.375	.494	.869	-.024	D	$11

Hawpe has quietly ranked as one of the top right fielders in the National League the last two seasons. Projections for both years have underestimated his impact by quite a bit, and I wouldn't be surprised if he puts up slightly higher numbers than the line given here, but I think they might be closer this time.

Todd Helton (First Base)

PA	R	H	2B	3B	HR	RBI	SO	BB	SB	CS	BA	OBP	SLG	OPS	3 Yr	Fld	F$
612	84	151	36	3	13	70	70	102	1	1	.303	.420	.465	.885	-.047	B	$14

Helton's contract, because of its size, its duration, and its no-trade clause, virtually assures that the Rockies will be overpaying him for four more seasons. That written, he at least came close to giving the team its money's worth last season. His fist-pumping shout to the heavens as he clutched the last out in the NLCS will remain an iconic moment in Rockies history.

Note that, according to these three-year projections, Helton's OPS in 2010 (.838) at the age of 38 will still be higher than those of Atkins (.826) and Joe Koshansky (.828), his two possible replacements were the Rockies somehow able to get rid of Todd and his contract. If Colorado is going to throw money away, at least it picked an okay guy to do it with that time.

Matt Holliday (Left Field)

PA	R	H	2B	3B	HR	RBI	SO	BB	SB	CS	BA	OBP	SLG	OPS	3 Yr	Fld	F$
615	94	175	37	5	29	103	105	51	9	3	.319	.382	.563	.945	-.005	B	$35

I'm just going to go out on a limb and guess that nobody's going to come to this entry thinking: "Hmm … I've never heard of this Matt Holliday fellow. I wonder what my THT Preview says about the chap." So what do you want from me here? The guy's a beast, we all know that. As a Scott Boras client, his future with the Rockies once he reaches free agency after the 2009 season seems in doubt, but I don't want to give him up before then.

Chris Iannetta (Catcher)

PA	R	H	2B	3B	HR	RBI	SO	BB	SB	CS	BA	OBP	SLG	OPS	3 Yr	Fld	F$
376	46	86	17	3	10	42	70	41	1	1	.265	.353	.429	.782	.020	D	$1

The Rockies stumbled severely out of the gate in 2007, and Iannetta was the biggest victim of some early-season panic moves by management and the front office, which gave up too quickly on him. They threw the baby out with the Steve Finley and John Mabry soiled bathwater, you might say. Chris will start 2008 backing up Yorvit Torrealba again, but should finish it at the top of the depth chart.

Joe Koshansky (First Base)

PA	R	H	2B	3B	HR	RBI	SO	BB	SB	CS	BA	OBP	SLG	OPS	3 Yr	Fld	F$
533	68	122	24	2	24	78	125	51	2	2	.259	.332	.470	.802	.026	B	$1

He's not going to replace Helton, but he's a solid fill-in should Todd go down for any extended period this year. I feel for the player not getting the best opportunity for his career, but also for the team, which benefits from the depth he provides. Believe me, it's a moral quandary that keeps me up nights.

Jayson Nix (Second Base)

PA	R	H	2B	3B	HR	RBI	SO	BB	SB	CS	BA	OBP	SLG	OPS	3 Yr	Fld	F$
464	51	106	22	2	7	44	79	24	12	3	.249	.293	.360	.653	.016	C	$1

Nix could be considered my wishcast for 2008, the player for whom I'll plug my ears to your new-fangled projections and say will be decent anyway. He's a great defender with quick hands but an uninspiring record in the minor leagues. So the reason for my going fan-girl is a small-sample tournament in Taiwan for Team USA last fall, where he won the Most Outstanding Player honor over Evan Longoria, Colby Rasmus, Andy LaRoche and other better-known prospects.

There's plenty of reason to be confident that the SLG projection here is significantly low; he'll need only a bit of luck with his BABIP in the translation to MLB to be one of 2008's most surprising rookies.

Seth Smith (Right Field)

PA	R	H	2B	3B	HR	RBI	SO	BB	SB	CS	BA	OBP	SLG	OPS	3 Yr	Fld	F$
508	60	124	29	4	12	59	85	31	4	2	.267	.316	.424	.740	.025	C	$1

Smith likely will win the job of left-handed bench bat out of spring training over Cory Sullivan. He's not as good as his flukishly awesome performance at the end of 2007 would make it seem, but combined with the next guy, he gives the Rockies a virile and potent bench attack.

Ryan Spilborghs (Center Field)

PA	R	H	2B	3B	HR	RBI	SO	BB	SB	CS	BA	OBP	SLG	OPS	3 Yr	Fld	F$
463	59	122	25	3	10	54	77	41	6	3	.295	.360	.443	.803	-.022	C	$5

I don't know if Spilly can repeat the performance he had last season, but he's been somewhat surprisingly popping out the hits for the last three seasons (including one and a half in the minors), so by now his game seems legit.

Willy Taveras (Center Field)

PA	R	H	2B	3B	HR	RBI	SO	BB	SB	CS	BA	OBP	SLG	OPS	3 Yr	Fld	F$
467	60	127	16	4	2	38	66	23	28	6	.299	.340	.369	.709	-.015	A+	$1

Taveras as a starting center fielder is a decent value for a budget-minded team, particularly since he's not yet eligible for arbitration. The way the Rockies use him, however, frustrates me. He's a strong defender, he's fairly consistent at the plate both at home and away, but he shouldn't be the guy you give the most plate appearances to by batting leadoff.

Yorvit Torrealba (Catcher)

PA	R	H	2B	3B	HR	RBI	SO	BB	SB	CS	BA	OBP	SLG	OPS	3 Yr	Fld	F$
393	44	94	21	2	7	41	67	28	2	1	.267	.326	.397	.723	-.038	C	$1

After a strange free agency that had Torrealba go to he ..., well the Mets, and back, I'm not sure how to react. It's as if your kooky great aunt you never particularly liked passed away, you got all nostalgic anyway at her funeral, and three weeks later she suddenly showed as an undead and free-loading apparition at your doorstep. What do you do? I think what I'd do is live with the zombie one more season and then try and unload her on one of our unsuspecting siblings at the soonest possible convenience.

Troy Tulowitzki (Shortstop)

PA	R	H	2B	3B	HR	RBI	SO	BB	SB	CS	BA	OBP	SLG	OPS	3 Yr	Fld	F$
583	75	148	31	3	17	74	106	46	5	2	.285	.349	.455	.804	.049	B	$11

Let me be blunt: Troy Tulowitzki provided more value to his team than any MLB rookie in 2007, and I think you'd be hard-pressed to find a team that had more of a turnaround at any one position than the Rockies did at shortstop last season. The Rockies had somewhere between a seven-to-nine win swing from what Barmes provided the year before just by the exchange.

Pitchers

Taylor Buchholz (Relief Pitcher)

W	L	ERA	TBF	IP	Hit	HR	SO	BB	HBP	3 Yr	F$
5	6	4.69	408	95	101	12	61	31	3	0.05	$1

I don't have much to say about Taylor, which is probably a good sign for a middle reliever.

Aaron Cook (Starting Pitcher)

W	L	ERA	TBF	IP	Hit	HR	SO	BB	HBP	3 Yr	F$
9	9	4.43	692	159	184	13	63	50	6	0.37	$1

We sing his praises before every game. You know: "...the bombs bursting in air, the Rockies red glare..." He's all the proof I need that our flag is still there.

At any rate, I have a hard time expecting too much different from the projections when it comes to Cook this season. He still seems to get in trouble when he relies too heavily on his sinker, but it's still his one quality pitch. I might take a couple of tenths off his ERA, since he has a solid defense behind him to make that sinker look even better.

Manny Corpas (Relief Pitchers)

W	L	ERA	TBF	IP	Hit	HR	SO	BB	HBP	3 Yr	F$
4	4	4.24	299	69	76	6	51	22	3	-0.08	$5

The Rockies, more than most teams, develop most of their future MLB relievers in the minors as relievers, rather than starters. Because of this, there will often be insufficient innings to make accurate projections on players. That's particularly so if a pitcher has a spike in velocity and an accompanying performance epiphany more than mid-stream in his minor league rise, as Corpas did in the Venezuelan Winter League in the 2005-2006 offseason.

Before that, Corpas had racked up 230 innings. Since, he has 156, so the weight of these projections is still drawn mainly off the unspectacular numbers of his early unrefined career, rather than the stellar output of his later polished one. Ignore them: Barring injury, he should be just as good in 2008 as he was in 2007.

Josh Fogg (Starting Pitcher)

W	L	ERA	TBF	IP	Hit	HR	SO	BB	HBP	3 Yr	F$
8	10	5.39	710	159	185	22	83	61	7	0.47	$1

He's a gutsy, driven pitcher who's also level-headed and knows his significant limitations. There's no reason to think he's going to be much better than his projections, but he's highly unlikely to tank on you also. As we go to print, he's still a free agent. Now, the question is whether some team gets its money's worth when it signs him this offseason. It's doubtful, but he won't be the worst waste of dinero.

Jeff Francis (Starting Pitcher)

W	L	ERA	TBF	IP	Hit	HR	SO	BB	HBP	3 Yr	F$
11	10	4.48	809	186	200	20	131	65	8	0.10	$1

I have a feeling that Rockies fans might be expecting too much out of Jeff for 2008. The projection was much more generous last year, figuring him to come in with a 3.97 ERA, albeit with only 166 innings. I don't know why the numbers are suddenly so down on him, but there is a big red flag for me in that his 232 innings last year—including the playoffs—were more than 40 higher than his previous career high. I think the condition of his arm might become a bigger issue in the second half of the season.

Brian Fuentes (Relief Pitcher)

W	L	ERA	TBF	IP	Hit	HR	SO	BB	HBP	3 Yr	F$
4	3	3.77	277	65	56	7	65	27	3	0.34	$1

Even though he's likely to return for the start of 2008, the Rockies seem to be quietly trying to market Brian as the premier reliever available for trade midseason. He's a solid bullpen presence and left handed to boot, but is entering that phase of his career where his contract value is likely to far exceed his performance value, so I can't say I blame the team for attempting to move him.

Matt Herges (Relief Pitcher)

W	L	ERA	TBF	IP	Hit	HR	SO	BB	HBP	F$
4	4	4.51	308	70	75	7	45	28	3	$1

Being named in the Mitchell report for HGH purchases in 2004-2005 had to deflate what had probably been one of the high points of Herges' career, which had been seemingly given up for dead a year ago. Matt will likely face a suspension to open 2008, and after that the Rockies hope he shows 2007 wasn't a fluke. I've got my doubts.

Jason Hirsh (Starting Pitcher)

W	L	ERA	TBF	IP	Hit	HR	SO	BB	HBP	3 Yr	F$
8	8	4.80	614	140	139	19	93	62	7	-0.12	$1

Hirsh—along with Francis and Cook—needs to pick up some of the innings the Rockies are likely going to lose with Jimenez's five-inning act. Unfortunately, Jason's injury history suggests that probably won't happen. This is where Kip Wells and Mark Redman could become important. It's rolling the dice that one of the scrubs will be better in 2008 than the Rockies have any right to expect. As for Hirsh, he's a step or three better than Fogg in this slot and one place where the Rockies should be able to upgrade from 2007.

Ubaldo Jimenez (Starting Pitcher)

W	L	ERA	TBF	IP	Hit	HR	SO	BB	HBP	3 Yr	F$
8	10	5.45	733	160	166	21	121	97	9	-0.33	$1

With Jimenez and Franklin Morales, you're going to get wildly divergent prognostications for 2008 from statistics and scouting reports. For U-ball, I'm going to say ignore both.

As he did throughout September and the playoffs, Jimenez on most days will give the Rockies five or six innings of sometimes dominant, sometimes wildly nerve-wracking, traffic-congested baseball. A couple of runs might cross the plate, but he should usually leave the team in good position to win the game, although he'll regularly tax the bullpen. On a few days, he'll blow up and allow six or seven runs in an inning and get pulled earlier, and in a few others he'll have it all together and throw a complete game two hitter or something. In all, he's going to be more valuable than this projection suggests, but he's not going to live up to his potential this year, either.

Franklin Morales (Starting Pitcher)

W	L	ERA	TBF	IP	Hit	HR	SO	BB	HBP	3 Yr	F$
6	9	5.70	641	138	150	18	92	86	9	-0.60	$1

I differ more on Morales' projections than anybody else's on the team. For instance, I have no idea why he's projected to give up 18 MLB home runs in 2008. He gave up zero in 2004 in the Pioneer League (high altitude, homer friendly), six in 2005 at McCormick field in Asheville, a total of nine in 2006 in the California League, and 11 across three more hitter-friendly levels last season, including higher-altitude, humidor-deprived Colorado Springs. His pitches have induced some of the highest groundball rates in the minors and there's no reason to think that this will change. I'm going to suggest that Frankie Mo comes in a lot stronger than shown here.

Ramon Ramirez (Relief Pitcher)

W	L	ERA	TBF	IP	Hit	HR	SO	BB	HBP	3 Yr	F$
4	2	3.99	250	58	53	6	53	26	2	0.11	$1

Ramirez spent all but a handful of innings in Colorado Springs in 2007, but the Rockies' actions this offseason suggest that they still feel he's a part of their bullpen plans. I suspect he'll be battling Ryan Speier for a spot on the roster this spring.

Mark Redman (Relief Pitcher)

W	L	ERA	TBF	IP	Hit	HR	SO	BB	HBP	3 Yr	F$
7	9	5.30	630	140	167	17	67	55	6	0.44	$1

In just under 20 innings with the Rockies in 2007, Redman had an ERA+ of 150. These were crucial, end-of-season, we-need-to-win-every-single-game innings, too. The Rockies were 5-0 when he appeared in a game for them. So what am I supposed to do? Just ignore that and say that this is the same Redman who put up an ERA+ of just 37 in 2007 with Atlanta? That his full season numbers have gone the wrong direction—117, 96, 86, 82, 59—over the past five seasons?

Probably, but you don't understand. What I'm going to say is that Redman's shown glimpses of having what it takes to be a decent finesse lefty, but counting on him to be that is idiocy. Let's just say he'll be terrible and be pleasantly surprised if it turns out not to be true again.

Greg Reynolds (Starting Pitcher)

W	L	ERA	TBF	IP	Hit	HR	SO	BB	HBP	3 Yr	F$
5	5	4.79	388	89	100	10	42	30	5	-0.55	$1

The projection sees him as about as effective as Hirsh were he to pitch for Colorado this season, with a three-year progression that likes him a lot more than Jimenez or Morales, or any of the other Rockies starters, for that matter. It's going to be having my cake and eating it too if I ignore the projections of those two and take Reynolds' at face value, but that's exactly what I'm going to do, given the differences in their scouting profiles.

Reynolds should eventually be a right-handed version of Francis if things go right and he comes back healthy. He's not going to strike a lot of guys out, but he's got the stuff to do so if he has to. He's got a groundball rate that suggests to me—similarly to Cook and Morales—that these projections might actually be underestimating his real value when put in front of Colorado's defense. If Francis does get tired in the second half, having a replacement the quality of Reynolds could be invaluable to the Rockies getting back to the playoffs.

Josh Towers (Starting Pitcher)

W	L	ERA	TBF	IP	Hit	HR	SO	BB	HBP	3 Yr	F$
7	7	4.79	528	123	146	17	76	24	5	0.31	$1

Towers is known for impeccable control (1.5 walks per nine innings) and an inability to pitch from the stretch. Hitters slug about .350 when he throws from the windup and over .600 when he pitches from the stretch. Towers will go through odd streaks of striking out opposing hitters and those in which everything is up in the zone and is hammered. He relies on his defense to get outs and is improving in his ground ball/fly ball ratios (1.33 in 2007). He has the pinpoint control to come inside fearlessly, yet rarely does so. He needs everything to go right for him to succeed; he has zero margin for error since he lacks overpowering stuff (career strikeout per nine innings of 4.8).

Luis Vizcaino (Relief Pitcher)

W	L	ERA	TBF	IP	Hit	HR	SO	BB	HBP	3 Yr	F$
4	4	4.44	313	71	67	8	63	37	3	0.37	$1

From June through August in 2007, nobody beat the viz: He went 6-1 with a 1.31 ERA. Unfortunately, April, May and September also counted, and he was 2-1 with a 7.94 ERA in those months. Maybe it was just overwork that killed him down the stretch, in which case the Rockies may have gotten themselves a bargain. The most important factor in Vizcaino's success, as it is for most relievers, is his control.

Casey Weathers (Relief Pitcher)

The Rockies are indicating that their 2007 first-round draft pick could be ready for a big league call-up some time in 2008. Like many of the Rockies' young relievers, Weathers has upper-90s velocity and decent movement to his pitches.

Kip Wells (Starting Pitcher)

W	L	ERA	TBF	IP	Hit	HR	SO	BB	HBP	3 Yr	F$
7	9	5.29	633	140	156	17	92	70	6	0.33	$1

What a shame: a coulda/shoulda be a top-flight pitcher making eight figures a year. Wells throws hard and gets tremendous movement on his pitches, but he has never developed command and consistency. Coors Field is not likely to help him put things together.

Detroit Tigers

By Brian Borawski of The Hardball Times

2008 Projections

Record: 88-74
Division Rank: 2nd, two games back
Runs Scored: 871
Runs Allowed: 787

2007 in a Nutshell

The Tigers followed up a World Series appearance in 2006 with a solid but unspectacular season in 2007. Injuries were a primary cause for the decline in 2006 and if the team can stay healthy in 2008, there's no reason the Tigers shouldn't compete for the American League pennant. Despite not making the playoffs, the Tigers had some truly spectacular individual performances. Magglio Ordonez won the batting title, Curtis Granderson became the third player to have 20 doubles, triples, stolen bases and homers in a season and Justin Verlander threw the first no-hitter by a Tiger since 1984.

General Comments

Team Strengths

With the addition of Miguel Cabrera and Edgar Renteria, the Tigers have one of the toughest lineups in baseball. The Tigers will sport seven former All-Stars to go along with Granderson, who probably should have made the All-Star team in 2007. The Tigers' lineup is about as deep as they get.

Team Weaknesses

With no major additions to the bullpen, the Tigers will be relying on two erratic pitchers in Todd Jones and Fernando Rodney. The back end of the bullpen is also spotty, and while Tim Byrdak did a solid job as the Tigers' left-handed option, he doesn't have much of a track record to indicate whether he'll be able to repeat his solid 2007 season.

The General Manager is Known for...

Dave Dombrowski loves power arms. In three of the last four drafts, he's used his first-round pick to pick up a power pitcher. Dombrowski hasn't made any friends in the commissioner's office because he's helped rebuild the Tigers by ignoring MLB's slotting system. He's made a habit of picking up the best available player regardless of signability issues and he's done a good job of making sure he gets those draft picks into uniform.

The Manager is Known for...

Jim Leyland managed the Tigers to their first back-to-back winning seasons since the 1980s and he leveraged that into a contract extension. His lineup construction is a little suspect, but with the hitters he'll have in 2008, he shouldn't have a hard time throwing together one of the top offenses in baseball regardless of how he hits them.

Ballpark Characteristics

Comerica Park is known for triples. In the last three seasons, more triples have been hit in Comerica Park than in any other park in baseball. At one point, it was considered a pitchers' park, but this has been tempered a bit since the Tigers moved in their left field fences a few years ago.

The Minor League System is...

It's gutted. The Tigers traded several high level prospects to get better now and any prospect list thrown together before the winter meetings will have several guys now playing for the Marlins.

Favorite Team Blogs

Tiger Blog (http://www.tigerblog.net/)
The Detroit Tigers Weblog (http://www.detroit-tigersweblog.com/)
Bless You Boys (http://www.blessyouboys.com/)
Tiger Tales (http://detroittigertales.blogspot.com/)

Keys for 2008

Players Lost from Last Year's Team

The only significant player lost from the 2007 Tigers was Andrew Miller, the Tigers' first-round draft pick in 2006. Miller was a fill-in starter who was just going to compete for the fifth spot in the rotation, so his loss, at least in 2008, isn't a major one.

Players Acquired

The Tigers sold the farm to acquire Renteria, Cabrera and Dontrelle Willis. Jacque Jones, while somewhat of a secondary pickup, could also give the Tigers a big boost if he can get back to belting home runs.

Reasons to be Optimistic

The Tigers made a few big trades to significantly improve an already good offense. This team should score a ton of runs and it isn't out of the question that the Tigers lead the American League in offense in 2008.

Reasons to be Pessimistic

With the trades, the Tigers are quite a bit older. If some of their players regress, like Ivan Rodriguez, Renteria or even Ordonez, a great offense could look just decent.

Due for a Better Season

Nate Robertson is normally at the bottom of the league in run support; it seems like whenever he pitches well, the Tigers don't give him the runs to pick up the win. With the 2008 Tigers lineup and a full season, he could top 15 wins in a season for the first time.

Likely to Have a Worse Season

Ordonez will have a hard time topping his 2007 near-MVP season. In addition, 2007 was his first injury free season since 2004, so you wonder whether that hat will drop in 2008.

Still Left to Do

With the acquisition of Cabrera, Brandon Inge is the odd man out, so the Tigers will most likely move him; Inge said he wasn't happy about playing a utility role. His $6 million a year salary could prohibit the Tigers from getting too much for him, but some relief pitching help would be welcome.

Most Likely Team Outcome

With the trades the Tigers made, anything less then a World Series win will be viewed as a disappointment. The Tigers aren't a lock even to win the American League pennant, though, because the Yankees, Red Sox, Angels and Indians are all still great teams. But the Tigers put themselves into a position to seriously compete for a world title in 2008.

Player Projections

Batters

Miguel Cabrera (Third Base)

PA	R	H	2B	3B	HR	RBI	SO	BB	SB	CS	BA	OBP	SLG	OPS	3 Yr	Fld	F$
624	93	174	37	2	27	100	102	74	3	2	.324	.406	.551	.957	.040	F	$31

Cabrera is one the best hitters in the game today and changing leagues shouldn't have much effect on the mind-numbing numbers he puts up. Cabrera's problems come on the defensive side of the ledger. To put it nicely, he can be a liability in the field.

Curtis Granderson (Center Field)

PA	R	H	2B	3B	HR	RBI	SO	BB	SB	CS	BA	OBP	SLG	OPS	3 Yr	Fld	F$
612	89	152	30	13	21	78	135	55	15	2	.281	.348	.501	.849	.007	A+	$20

Like Ordonez, it's going to be tough for Granderson to replicate his 2007 season. He had a bunch of strikeouts again and while that's a concern, as long as he continues to hit the gaps and run like a madman, he should get his share of doubles and triples. Granderson's biggest knock is his inability to hit left-handed pitching. He had a paltry .494 OPS against lefties; his platoon split of .164 was the highest in the majors. If he can tackle those southpaws, another elite season isn't out of the question.

Carlos Guillen (First Base)

PA	R	H	2B	3B	HR	RBI	SO	BB	SB	CS	BA	OBP	SLG	OPS	3 Yr	Fld	F$
558	78	145	30	5	16	71	80	60	12	6	.297	.373	.477	.850	-.038	C	$18

Guillen has been one of the more reliable hitters for the Tigers the past few years and despite a nagging knee injury, he consistently belts 20 homers and drives in 80-90 runs. Guillen loses a little bit of value because he's moving to first base with the acquisition of Edgar Renteria, but he'll probably be hitting sixth in a stacked lineup, so RBI opportunities will be plentiful.

Brandon Inge (Third Base)

PA	R	H	2B	3B	HR	RBI	SO	BB	SB	CS	BA	OBP	SLG	OPS	3 Yr	Fld	F$
555	67	124	25	4	17	66	122	47	6	2	.254	.323	.425	.748	-.026	B	$1

While nothing has been decided, the speculation is that Inge is the odd man out after the Tigers acquired Miguel Cabrera. A Gold Glove caliber third baseman, Inge took a step back at the plate after three previous decent hitting seasons. If the Tigers can't figure out a way to trade him, Inge probably will see his plate appearances cut considerably, but he could provide some value because he'll see time at multiple positions.

Jacque Jones (Left Field)

PA	R	H	2B	3B	HR	RBI	SO	BB	SB	CS	BA	OBP	SLG	OPS	3 Yr	Fld	F$
505	59	123	24	3	11	55	83	41	5	2	.271	.333	.410	.743	-.036	B	$1

After burying himself deep inside the Cubs' doghouse early in the year, Jacque Jones responded to trade rumors by going on a tear to close out the season. That performance couldn't endear him to the fans and the team, and the Tigers acquired him in the offseason for relatively little. Jones can play all three outfield positions, but spent the majority of his time in the corner outfield role. His throwing arm is a tad weak for the right field spot and his range is below average. The Tigers should be able to hide him away at the bottom of the order and get more production from that spot than many around the league.

Magglio Ordonez (Right Field)

PA	R	H	2B	3B	HR	RBI	SO	BB	SB	CS	BA	OBP	SLG	OPS	3 Yr	Fld	F$
581	80	160	34	1	21	86	72	61	2	1	.314	.386	.508	.894	-.037	D	$21

It's hard to believe that Ordonez will be able to match his 2007 production, but, on the flip side, he will have a stronger lineup with Miguel Cabrera most likely batting behind him. If Gary Sheffield can stay healthy, he should get plenty of RBI opportunities even if he just hits his projected .894 OPS. One thing going against Ordonez is that he hit .429 with runners in scoring position in 2007. Even if he dips back down to his still respectable .335 career batting average with runners in scoring position, we will see a dropoff in production.

Placido Polanco (Second Base)

PA	R	H	2B	3B	HR	RBI	SO	BB	SB	CS	BA	OBP	SLG	OPS	3 Yr	Fld	F$
554	67	156	27	3	6	56	34	35	5	1	.311	.361	.413	.774	-.037	A	$10

Polanco is one of the Tigers' more underappreciated hitters. He led the team with a 24 percent line drive rate and he hit an unheard-of .402 after letting the count go to 0-2. Polanco struck out in just 5 percent of his plate appearances, leading the league, and while he's never going to belt a ton of homers, if he can get on base as projected, he's got the hitters behind him to drive him in.

Ryan Raburn (All Over)

PA	R	H	2B	3B	HR	RBI	SO	BB	SB	CS	BA	OBP	SLG	OPS	3 Yr	Fld	F$
500	65	115	23	4	19	67	107	45	8	3	.259	.329	.458	.787	.004	D	$1

Raburn's role on the team is a question mark until the Tigers figure out what to do with Brandon Inge. Raburn did a nice job in a utility role when he got called up in the second half. He played five positions in 2007, with his biggest role as a right-handed option in center field. If the Tigers can't deal Inge, then Raburn probably will spend most of his time on the bench. If Inge does get dealt, he should be able to find his way into the lineup two or three days a week at different positions.

Edgar Renteria (Shortstop)

PA	R	H	2B	3B	HR	RBI	SO	BB	SB	CS	BA	OBP	SLG	OPS	3 Yr	Fld	F$
549	66	140	28	3	9	57	79	47	10	3	.285	.346	.409	.755	-.032	B	$7

Renteria is a modern power shortstop. He's also not as bad as some make out with the leather. Although his range isn't as good as some of his contemporaries, he makes up for a lot of that with good old baseballing guile. He anticipates well and overall reckons to be an average shortstop—no Adam Everett, but certainly a lot better than Derek Jeter. There remain plenty of questions, though. How will Renteria adjust to going back to the American League, where he faltered badly? At 33, will he start to slide down the aging curve?

Ivan Rodriguez (Catcher)

PA	R	H	2B	3B	HR	RBI	SO	BB	SB	CS	BA	OBP	SLG	OPS	Fld	F$
507	57	134	27	4	10	57	83	21	2	2	.281	.311	.417	.728	A	$1

It's hard to tell whether age has caught up with Rodriguez, now 36. His 2007 season was one of the worst of his career at the plate, but it's just one year removed from a solid 2006 campaign. His inability to take walks (just nine in 515 plate appearances) is a liability, but the Tigers brought Rodriguez back to provide a veteran presence behind the plate. Pudge could surprise some people because he's playing for what probably will be his last contract before retirement.

Gary Sheffield (Designated Hitter)

PA	R	H	2B	3B	HR	RBI	SO	BB	SB	CS	BA	OBP	SLG	OPS	Fld	F$
488	70	116	20	1	20	69	59	64	13	2	.281	.381	.480	.861	C	$14

Health is the name of the game for Sheffield. If he can recover fully after shoulder surgery this offseason, there's no reason he shouldn't be a productive part of the lineup. After struggling in April 2007 as a full-time designated hitter (.675 OPS), he tore it up in May and June, posting an OPS above 1.000. His second half batting average of .203 was probably indicative of his injured shoulder, so if the injury continues to nag Sheffield, there's a good chance it'll sap some of his production.

Marcus Thames (Left Field)

PA	R	H	2B	3B	HR	RBI	SO	BB	SB	CS	BA	OBP	SLG	OPS	3 Yr	Fld	F$
362	51	87	18	2	23	66	82	30	2	1	.268	.332	.549	.881	-.036	D	$1

Thames is slotted to platoon in left field with the recently acquired Jacque Jones. so most of his at-bats will come against left- handed pitchers. On the one hand, he can rake left-handed pitching (.845 career OPS against lefties) but on the other, he's going to see just limited time, as he has the past couple of seasons. The Tigers are still rumored to be shopping him, so if he could catch on with a team that's willing to play him every day, 30-35 homers isn't out of the question.

Pitchers

Denny Bautista (Relief Pitcher)

W	L	ERA	TBF	IP	Hit	HR	SO	BB	HBP	3 Yr	F$
3	5	4.83	306	67	72	6	44	37	3	0.14	$1

Players with certain tools—in this case, a 95 mph fastball—seem to get an unfair number of opportunities with multiple teams to prove that they can't quite cut it in the majors, but at 28, you have to think that Bautista's chances to show otherwise are nearing their end point in Detroit.

Yorman Bazardo (Relief Pitcher)

W	L	ERA	TBF	IP	Hit	HR	SO	BB	HBP	3 Yr	F$
7	9	5.06	627	140	155	15	43	62	9	-0.59	$1

Bazardo came over from the Mariners in a trade prior to the 2007 season and had a decent season at Toledo before getting a call-up. He posted solid numbers (three-to-one strikeout-to-walk ratio and a 2.28 ERA in 23.2 innings) and he was virtually unhittable by right-handed batters (.420 OPS against). Bazardo would have competed for the fifth spot in the rotation, but unless someone goes down with an injury, he'll most likely be a vital cog out of the bullpen.

Jeremy Bonderman (Starting Pitcher)

W	L	ERA	TBF	IP	Hit	HR	SO	BB	HBP	3 Yr	F$
11	9	3.68	733	176	170	16	143	52	4	-0.05	$14

In 2007, Bonderman's OPS against was 1.130 in the first inning. His career mark in the first inning is .919, compared to only .762 overall. If Bonderman can get through the first inning, he's usually set for a solid start. He was shut down in September because of shoulder problems and his second half ERA (7.38) was almost a full four points higher then his first half ERA (3.48).

Throw in the fact that Bonderman has been on a lot of people's breakout lists the past three years and you have a pitcher who hasn't quite met expectations. This could be a defining year in Bonderman's career; there's just no guarantee what direction it could take.

Tim Byrdak (Relief Pitcher)

W	L	ERA	TBF	IP	Hit	HR	SO	BB	HBP	3 Yr	F$
5	3	3.85	307	71	62	7	63	36	2	0.37	$1

Byrdak was called up in mid-May and eventually filled the left-handed relief specialist role admirably. He held lefties to a .176 batting average against but he also did well against righties (.268 batting average against). He's a guy who can come in and throw multiple innings if needed. The Tigers haven't done much to shore up their pen this offseason, so Byrdak's job is probably pretty safe.

Jason Grilli (Relief Pitcher)

W	L	ERA	TBF	IP	Hit	HR	SO	BB	HBP	3 Yr	F$
4	5	4.70	346	78	83	9	48	34	4	0.40	$1

Grilli was the workhorse out of the pen and led Tigers relievers in innings pitched. You have to wonder why, because for most of the season, his ERA was well over the 5.00 mark. He pitched better in the second half, but all that did was make his numbers look a little more respectable. Still, he's only a year removed from a solid 2006 season and my bet is he bounces back as a back end option out of the pen in 2008.

Todd Jones (Relief Pitcher)

W	L	ERA	TBF	IP	Hit	HR	SO	BB	HBP	F$
4	3	3.73	281	66	66	4	37	23	2	$7

With Jones, you pretty much know what you're going to get: a high ERA for a closer, 30-35 saves, and, if you obsess about the Tigers, plenty of anxious moments. Jones doesn't strike out a lot of guys, he doesn't walk many, he doesn't let the ball leave the park too often. In fact, closing seems to be an ideal role for him. Coming in with nobody on and nobody out means the hit or two he gives up a lot of the time means he won't be hurting the team too much.

Macay McBride (Relief Pitcher)

W	L	ERA	TBF	IP	Hit	HR	SO	BB	HBP	3 Yr	F$
4	4	4.69	321	72	71	8	52	40	3	-0.08	$1

McBride faltered out of the gate last year and was sent back down to the minors in August. McBride could catch on as a second left-handed reliever, but he may be an odd man out in what's looking to be a pretty full bullpen.

Zach Miner (Relief Pitcher)

W	L	ERA	TBF	IP	Hit	HR	SO	BB	HBP	3 Yr	F$
6	6	4.62	465	105	111	10	58	50	4	-0.10	$1

Miner was one of the Tigers' more reliable relievers in 2007, although he seemed to live on borrowed time with a mediocre 1.45 WHIP despite the solid 3.02 ERA. Expect Miner to pitch mostly out of the pen, but a start or two isn't out of the question if a spot in the rotation needs filling.

Nate Robertson (Starting Pitcher)

W	L	ERA	TBF	IP	Hit	HR	SO	BB	HBP	3 Yr	F$
10	10	4.14	746	175	177	21	110	59	5	0.25	$5

In a lot of ways, Nate Robertson took a step back in 2007. After an impressive April, he hit the disabled list because of a tired arm. He did pitch a bit better over a higher number of innings in the second half, but his 177.2 innings was his lowest total since becoming a regular starter for the Tigers. His 155-strikeout season is now four years removed, so that's looking more and more like an anomaly as well. Robertson has done a solid job throughout his career without a lot of run support, so if he ever gets the hitters going during his starts, a 15-win season isn't out of the question.

Fernando Rodney (Relief Pitcher)

W	L	ERA	TBF	IP	Hit	HR	SO	BB	HBP	3 Yr	F$
4	3	3.37	258	61	52	5	55	25	3	0.23	$1

Rodney was another who spent a chunk of time on the disabled list in 2007, but what's encouraging to Tigers fans is that he was very effective when he came back. His second half ERA was 2.82 and he struck out 29 batters in 22.1 innings. When you combine that with an effective 2006 season where he was healthy, it's safe to say that Rodney should do a solid job as the Tigers' setup man in 2008.

Kenny Rogers (Starting Pitcher)

W	L	ERA	TBF	IP	Hit	HR	SO	BB	HBP	F$
7	6	4.05	503	118	122	12	56	37	4	$1

Rogers missed most of the 2007 season, but in six of 11 starts, he gave up two runs or fewer. Rogers doesn't rely on a power arm, so even though he's 43, his age shouldn't significantly detract from his performance. Of course there's the big IF, and that's whether he can stay healthy. He's had all offseason to get back into shape, so spring training should be a solid gauge as to how effective Rogers will be in 2008.

Justin Verlander (Starting Pitcher)

W	L	ERA	TBF	IP	Hit	HR	SO	BB	HBP	3 Yr	F$
12	8	3.75	762	180	170	18	146	59	10	-0.09	$13

Verlander followed up his 2006 Rookie of the Year campaign with an even better season in 2007. His walks per game stayed steady while he struck out two more batters a game, an encouraging trend. Verlander did have a mediocre second half compared to his first, but this was his first 200-inning season, so some wear was expected. It'll be interesting to see how all this work affects his performance in 2008, but I think his projection is relatively safe.

Dontrelle Willis (Starting Pitcher)

W	L	ERA	TBF	IP	Hit	HR	SO	BB	HBP	3 Yr	F$
11	10	4.26	835	191	201	18	100	73	10	-0.10	$1

During spring training, the then-pitching coach of the Marlins decided that the course of action for Willis was to slow his motion and throw his fast ball in 84-87 mph range instead of his natural 92-94. Slowing down Willis did produce the desired effect of producing more motion on his pitches. Unfortunately he couldn't control anything. If the Tigers let Dontrelle be Dontrelle, he could rebound this season.

Joel Zumaya (Relief Pitcher)

W	L	ERA	TBF	IP	Hit	HR	SO	BB	HBP	3 Yr	F$
4	2	3.54	244	57	45	5	54	30	2	-0.01	$1

In a freak accident, Zumaya injured his shoulder moving boxes when he felt his home might be threatened by the California forest fires this past fall. He's expected to come back in July, but the question will be how effective he is for the rest of 2008. When healthy, he's one of the more dominant pitchers out there, but in light of his injury in 2007 and what happened with his shoulder, he's definitely a wait-and-see kind of guy.

Florida Marlins

By Craig Strain of Fish Stripes (fishstripes.com)

2008 Projections

Record: 63-99
Division Rank: Last, 19 games back
Runs Scored: 721
Runs Allowed: 892

2007 in a Nutshell

The Florida Marlins finished last in the NL East for the first time since 1999, 18 games behind the Philadelphia Phillies.

The Marlins once again proved the baseball adage that good hitting cannot compensate for poor starting pitching and a lousy defense. The season was foreshadowed in spring training when Josh Johnson and Anibal Sanchez weren't ready due to lingering injuries and the defensive coach quit. The Marlins faced injuries throughout the season, especially affecting the previous season's starting staff. Three of the five were shut down early and two eventually required season-ending surgery.

The team led the league in errors (137) and finished last in almost every defensive metric. The Marlins also finished last in ERA (4.94) but managed a next-to-last finish in opponents' batting (.285).

General Comments

Team Strengths

The 2007 Marlins did a nice job of hitting for power; finishing the season with a team line of .267/.336/.448. The middle infielders combined for 60 home runs. The bullpen became a strength once the veteran closer idea was finally abandoned.

Team Weaknesses

The defense was awful. The Marlins finished last in the league in every category except errors—where they led the league. Another weakness was the young starting staff, which led to the inevitable injuries and inconsistency.

The General Manager is Known for...

Larry Beinfest and his team of scouts are considered among the best evaluators of young talent. They know each team's minor league system probably better than the other teams do. Beinfest also is known to value pitching and always insists that a pitcher by included in every return trade.

The Manager is Known for...

This will be Fredi Gonzalez's second season with the Marlins. He spent most of last season just trying to put his fingers in the holes of the dike that was the team. With the Marlins' many injuries, Gonzalez never had a chance to have a consistent lineup or starting staff. It's difficult to know how he manages strategically, but he is a player's manager. He does a good job of relating to the players and they seem to enjoy playing for him.

Ballpark Characteristics

Physically, the ballpark has two unique characteristics—the Teal Monster and the Bermuda Triangle. The Teal Monster is the 36-foot, six-inch high wall in left field. The Bermuda Triangle is the deepest area of the ballpark (434 feet).

Since the ballpark belongs to another team and the colors and signage depict this fact, it doesn't have a home park feel.

To quote a reader:
Depressing. I will revert to my favorite word, soul-stealing. Sterile and cavernous and deadening.

The Minor League System is...

The Marlins organization is stocked with young arms, but most of the top prospects are just now making it to Double-A. They are at least a couple of years away. In Cameron Maybin, the team acquired a possible impact position player who could be ready in a couple of years.

Favorite Team Blogs

Fish Chunks (http://fishchunks.blogspot.com/)
Future Fish (http://wwwmvn.com/milb-marlins/)
Fish @ Bat (http://www.fishatbat.com/)
Hook, Line Drive, & Sinker (http://gamefish.mlblogs.com/)

Keys for 2008

Players Lost from Last Year's Team

Pitchers Dontrelle Willis and Byung-Hyun Kim, infielders Miguel Cabrera and Aaron Boone, catcher Miguel Olivo.

Players Acquired

Pitchers Andrew Miller and Eulogio De La Cruz, outfielder Cameron Maybin, catcher Mike Rabelo, infielder Jose Castillo.

Reasons to be Optimistic

If some of the pitchers returning from injuries can give five or six good innings most starts, the bullpen can take it the rest of the way and the offense still should

77

score runs. On an individual level, if Hanley Ramirez can improve his defense and rebound from shoulder surgery, he could become the first Marlins player to win the MVP.

Reasons to be Pessimistic

It's hard to believe that the Marlins will have a better season without Willis and Cabrera. A lot of the pitchers are returning from surgery and who knows how they are going to perform. Also, even if the team defense makes some strides toward improving, it still could be the worst in the league.

Due for a Better Season

Scott Olsen. He went through the normal slump after the dramatic increase in innings the previous year.

Likely to Have a Worse Season

During the offseason, Ramirez had surgery to stop his shoulder from popping of socket. His recovery makes him a question mark.

Still Left to Do

The Marlins need an innings-eating starter, especially since they will have so many pitchers returning from injuries. And they must get the stadium deal lined out. The franchise always will be in flux until a stadium is built.

Most Likely Team Outcome

The Marlins finishing fifth in the National League East. Maybe they will have some things go their way and finish fourth, but fifth is the way to bet.

Player Projections

Batters

Alfredo Amezaga (Center Field)

PA	R	H	2B	3B	HR	RBI	SO	BB	SB	CS	BA	OBP	SLG	OPS	3 Yr	Fld	F$
417	46	99	16	5	1	29	54	31	9	5	.264	.322	.342	.664	-.029	A	$1

He's a switch hitter who is better as a left-handed hitter. Last season, he was forced into being the everyday center fielder by default. As the season went on, and when Cody Ross was healthy, the two would platoon in center field. Amezaga is not the first choice of the Marlins to play center this season and if the club has its way, he won't be a regular. That could help him be more productive in his limited times at the plate.

Jose Castillo (Second/Third Base)

PA	R	H	2B	3B	HR	RBI	SO	BB	SB	CS	BA	OBP	SLG	OPS	3 Yr	Fld	F$
363	39	86	18	2	7	38	67	22	1	1	.258	.306	.386	.692	.002	F-	$1

He's a nominee for one of the most frustrating Pirates of the last 15 years. After years of fans hearing about Castillo's potential, he ended May of 2006 with a .309/.361/.494 line to go with his eight homers. He's gone yard only six times in 598 plate appearances since then. His power completely disappeared in 2007, as he slugged only .335. That led the Pirates to cut him to make room for a Rule 5 pick in December. Somehow, all this qualifies him to be one of the highest-paid Marlins.

Alejandro De Aza (Center Field)

PA	R	H	2B	3B	HR	RBI	SO	BB	SB	CS	BA	OBP	SLG	OPS	3 Yr	Fld	F$
452	46	96	18	5	2	30	95	30	8	5	.241	.299	.326	.625	.031	B	$1

De Aza won the job as center fielder in spring training, but fractured his ankle in April and was on the DL until August. When he rejoined the team, he hit .207/.246/.270 in 111 at-bats, never regaining his stroke. De Aza probably won't be the team's starting center fielder in 2008 and may not figure into its plans at all.

Jeremy Hermida (Right Field)

PA	R	H	2B	3B	HR	RBI	SO	BB	SB	CS	BA	OBP	SLG	OPS	3 Yr	Fld	F$
533	70	126	29	2	16	67	111	63	5	3	.275	.367	.452	.819	.055	B	$7

Hermida missed the first month of the season recovering from a deep bone bruise in his right knee. When he finally rejoined the team, he got off to a slow start, hitting .231/.322/.422 before the All-Star break. In the second half, he started showing the promise expected of a a first-round draft pick and batted .340/.401/.555. If the second half Hermida is the real Hermida, his overall numbers should improve in 2008.

Mike Jacobs (First Base)

PA	R	H	2B	3B	HR	RBI	SO	BB	SB	CS	BA	OBP	SLG	OPS	3 Yr	Fld	F$
479	61	115	28	2	19	69	100	37	2	1	.266	.324	.471	795	.006	C	$0

After fracturing his thumb, he missed almost all of the month of June. At one point in early August, he went 31 at-bats without a hit, setting a dubious franchise record. The THT projections are probably correct for Jacobs, but in his defense, he hasn't had a healthy full season since he has been with the Marlins.

Cameron Maybin (Center Field)

PA	R	H	2B	3B	HR	RBI	SO	BB	SB	CS	BA	OBP	SLG	OPS	3 Yr	Fld	F$
461	58	106	18	4	11	49	119	44	11	4	.261	.337	.406	.743	.063	D	$1

After he tore up the minors, Maybin's debut in 2007 was a bit disappointing. It became clear rather quickly that the phenom center fielder wasn't quite ready to face big league pitching. If he makes the Marlins out of spring training, expect him to sputter to start the season, similar to the way Alex Gordon did with the Royals, but he should begin to show his promise in the second half.

Hanley Ramirez (Shortstop)

PA	R	H	2B	3B	HR	RBI	SO	BB	SB	CS	BA	OBP	SLG	OPS	3 Yr	Fld	F$
616	94	165	35	7	17	78	92	44	39	10	.296	.349	.476	.825	.024	F	$29

Ramirez followed his exceptional rookie year with an even better second season. With the trade of Miguel Cabrera, it is anticipated that Ramirez will hit third in the order instead of leading off. Hitting first last season, he hit .345/.405/.596 and when hitting third he produced .297/.331/.455. If he does move down in the order, his numbers could drop, at least until he becomes more comfortable in the slot.

Cody Ross (Center Field)

PA	R	H	2B	3B	HR	RBI	SO	BB	SB	CS	BA	OBP	SLG	OPS	3 Yr	Fld	F$
305	42	74	16	2	14	47	61	29	2	1	.275	.348	.505	.853	-.010	D	$1

The outfielder spent more than a month from early June to mid-July on the DL for a strained hamstring and wasn't able to finish the season after reinjuring the same hamstring. When Ross played, he did very well, batting .385/.474/.738 against left handers and hitting at a .306/.372/.602 clip against RHP. He has been getting shots in his hamstring during the offseason and may or may not be ready to go by spring training.

Matt Treanor (Catcher)

PA	R	H	2B	3B	HR	RBI	SO	BB	SB	CS	BA	OBP	SLG	OPS	3 Yr	Fld	F$
265	29	59	12	1	4	25	43	24	1	1	.256	.336	.369	.705	-.043	D	$1

Treanor had a breakout year last season. Well, a breakout year for a backup catcher hitting .269/.357/.392. He had the same problems at the plate as most catchers: They start the season stronger than they finish. The THT projections look spot-on since he will be seeing more time behind the plate than he did last season.

Dan Uggla (Second Base)

PA	R	H	2B	3B	HR	RBI	SO	BB	SB	CS	BA	OBP	SLG	OPS	3 Yr	Fld	F$
627	76	157	34	4	26	93	129	11	3	2	.265	.286	.467	.753	.001	C	$9

Last year, Uggla became the first second baseman in franchise history to hit 30-plus homers. He may be moved down in the lineup to the No. 4 to No. 6 spot to take better advantage of his power. If this does happen, he should be able to increase his RBI totals.

Josh Willingham (Left Field)

PA	R	H	2B	3B	HR	RBI	SO	BB	SB	CS	BA	OBP	SLG	OPS	3 Yr	Fld	F$
528	72	123	26	3	20	72	104	55	5	1	.270	.358	.472	.830	-.024	C	$7

He was shut down at the start of September because of a chronic herniated disc in his back. He is expected back in time for spring training, but given the problems he has had with his back the past two seasons, it wouldn't be surprising if at some point in the 2008 season he opts for back surgery. THT's projection of a slight dropoff looks about right if he is able to play all year.

Pitchers

Eulogio De La Cruz (Relief Pitcher)

W	L	ERA	TBF	IP	Hit	HR	SO	BB	HBP	3 Yr	F$
5	7	4.88	469	105	112	10	69	51	6	-0.40	$1

Another throw-in when the Tigers got Cabrera and Willis, De La Cruz has a surprisingly pedestrian minor league strikeout rate for a guy who can touch 100 mph on the gun. Like a lot of Double-A and Triple-A pitchers, De La Cruz got a look with the Tigers, but he was touched up in a handful of relief appearances. For the Marlins in 2008, he could catch on as a reliever but I'd think he gets another year in the minors to work on his control.

Lee Gardner (Relief Pitcher)

W	L	ERA	TBF	IP	Hit	HR	SO	BB	HBP	3 Yr	F$
4	4	4.01	297	70	68	6	48	25	3	0.39	$1

Gardner had the best year of his career in 2007, putting up a 1.94 ERA, 6.3 strikeouts, 2.2 walks, 8.7 hits per nine innings.

Kevin Gregg (Relief Pitcher)

W	L	ERA	TBF	IP	Hit	HR	SO	BB	HBP	3 Yr	F$
5	4	4.09	337	79	72	9	78	32	3	0.46	$1

Gregg became the Marlins closer in May, when Henry Owens went on the DL. He was a serviceable closer, putting up 32 saves. Gregg had one of the best years of his career in 2007, so a dropoff would be expected.

Josh Johnson (Starting Pitcher)

Johnson spent most of the 2006-07 offseason rehabbing an arm injury. By the time spring training broke, he still wasn't ready to go. In June, he made four starts only to be shut down, and ended up undergoing Tommy John surgery. His expected return date is 2009.

Logan Kensing (Relief Pitcher)

W	L	ERA	TBF	IP	Hit	HR	SO	BB	HBP	3 Yr	F$
2	3	4.00	174	41	36	4	38	18	2	-0.05	$1

Kensing spent most of last season recovering from Tommy John surgery. He re-joined the team in September and pitched very well, posting a 1.35 ERA, 8.8 strikeouts and 7.4 hits per nine innings. He probably will be used in late-inning situations.

Byung-Hyun Kim (Starting/Relief Pitcher)

W	L	ERA	TBF	IP	Hit	HR	SO	BB	HBP	3 Yr	F$
7	9	4.93	628	142	143	16	124	70	8	0.47	$1

Kim had two stints with the Marlins last season. When used as a reliever, he basically stunk. But as a starter, he was good for five-plus innings and kept the Marlins in the game. Whichever team he lands on, if he is used as a starter his rubber arm should be able to produce similar results in 2008.

Andrew Miller (Starting Pitcher)

W	L	ERA	TBF	IP	Hit	HR	SO	BB	HBP	3 Yr	F$
10	11	4.61	857	192	210	17	134	89	16	-0.36	$1

The Tigers' 2006 first-round draft pick, Miller got a cup of coffee and a major league contract to kick off his career. He threw six shutout innings in his 2007 debut and by June, he was in the Tigers' rotation for good ... until he got shut down at the end of August after a truly horrific second half. Miller's an extreme groundball pitcher, although this didn't really show up in 2007. The left hander was part of the deal for Cabrera and Dontrelle Willis, so instead of fighting for the fifth spot in the Tigers' rotation, he'll probably get a middle rotation spot with the Marlins.

Justin Miller (Relief Pitcher)

W	L	ERA	TBF	IP	Hit	HR	SO	BB	HBP	3 Yr	F$
6	5	3.72	420	99	87	8	111	44	4	0.28	$4

Miller was called up in May to help bolster the bullpen and he eventually became the team's set-up man. He had an excellent year for the Fish with a 3.65 ERA and 10.8 strikeouts per nine innings in his 61.2 innings with the club. Miller should do something similar this season.

Sergio Mitre (Starting Pitcher)

W	L	ERA	TBF	IP	Hit	HR	SO	BB	HBP	3 Yr	F$
7	9	4.56	616	142	161	13	80	47	8	0.03	$1

Mitre had a very good first half, posting a 2.85 ERA. Given that he had pitched 41 total innings the previous year, as the innings piled up, he began to wear down. In the second half, his ERA was 7.27. Mitre's overall numbers could improve as he develops arm strength and stamina. However, he did throw 108 more innings in 2007 than in 2006, so that could continue to take a toll.

Ricky Nolasco (Starting Pitcher)

W	L	ERA	TBF	IP	Hit	HR	SO	BB	HBP	3 Yr	F$
4	6	5.21	415	95	103	14	67	34	6	-0.13	$1

Nolasco made only four starts for the Marlins in 2007 before being shut down due to elbow tendinitis. He recently pitched in the Arizona Fall League, making seven starts and throwing a total of 23.2 innings. In those starts he allowed 22 hits and seven walks with 19 strikeouts and a 5.70 ERA. It remains to be seen if he can return to form and if his elbow can hold up over a 162-game season.

Scott Olsen (Starting Pitcher)

W	L	ERA	TBF	IP	Hit	HR	SO	BB	HBP	3 Yr	F$
8	11	4.86	738	169	176	22	130	74	5	-0.33	$1

Olsen experienced the expected down year last season after pitching a large number of innings for the first time in his career. His 2007 season was littered with control problems and breaking balls that didn't break. Olsen should rebound this season and easily could become the Marlins' No. 1 starter.

Henry Owens (Relief Pitcher)

W	L	ERA	TBF	IP	Hit	HR	SO	BB	HBP	3 Yr	F$
3	2	3.99	189	44	38	5	47	20	2	0.38	$1

Owens was having a good rookie season and was even the closer for the Marlins until he injured his shoulder. He had shoulder surgery in late August and isn't expected to rejoin the Marlins until after the All-Star break, if then.

Anibal Sanchez (Starting Pitcher)

W	L	ERA	TBF	IP	Hit	HR	SO	BB	HBP	3 Yr	F$
5	6	4.84	431	98	102	12	67	42	5	-0.39	$1

His shoulder problems continued in spring training and beyond. At the start of the season, his arm slot was wrong. He made six starts before undergoing shoulder surgery and he may be ready for spring training this year. It is hard to predict the response of pitchers coming off shoulder surgery.

Taylor Tankersley (Relief Pitcher)

W	L	ERA	TBF	IP	Hit	HR	SO	BB	HBP	3 Yr	F$
3	3	4.52	259	58	53	7	57	35	2	-0.11	$1

He spent April on the DL with shoulder inflammation, and when he returned he couldn't throw strikes and had a drop in velocity, producing a pre-All-Star 6.65 ERA and .279 BAA in 23 innings. After he worked on his troubles in the minors, he had a strong second half with a 1.48 ERA, .212 BAA. Tankersley should have a good 2008.

Rick VandenHurk (Starting Pitcher)

W	L	ERA	TBF	IP	Hit	HR	SO	BB	HBP	3 Yr	F$
9	14	5.28	943	209	213	32	199	113	10	-0.25	$1

The Marlins' pitching injuries got him a call-up in April. He was initially overmatched, but eventually made the necessary adjustments to the majors. When he was clicking, VandenHurk was an acceptable pitcher, but as the season progressed, he wore down and ended up throwing almost as many innings last season (147.1) as he had in the previous years (150). He easily could be in the Marlins starting rotation on Opening Day.

FEARLESS PREDICTIONS 2008 · ALL-STAR GAME

Houston Astros

by Lisa Gray of The Astros Dugout (mvn.com/mlb-astros)

2008 Projections

Record: 73-89
Division Rank: 4th, 15 games back
Runs Scored: 762
Runs Allowed: 858

2007 in a Nutshell

The Astros' 2007 season was an unmitigated disaster, and the team was saved from a last-place finish in the NL Central only by the sloppier play of the Reds and Pirates. The Astros were the worst baserunners in the league, had the second-worst team defense (ahead of only the Marlins), had two of the 10 worst starting pitchers in the NL, had a bullpen that blew leads in 27 games which were then lost, and had only five hitters with a positive Runs Created Above Average.

At season's end, fans used to many years of winning and several years of exciting last-minute surges were angry. Owner Drayton McLane appeared more interested in getting Craig Biggio 3,000 hits and guaranteeing his Hall of Fame induction than in securing a winning season for the Astros. Biggio was a hugely successful marketing draw despite the poor season, but since he retired at the end of the year, and since the fans therefore had no stimulus to return to the ballpark the next year, McLane decided that something needed to be done.

First, he fired Phil Garner, who was not a very good manager anyway. Then he fired Tim Purpura, whom the fans hated because he seemed incapable of making any trades or finding any reasonable players from the waiver wire or other teams' minor league rosters. The fans, rightly or wrongly, blamed Purpura for letting Andy Pettitte walk and for trading the immensely popular Willy Taveras for Jason Jennings, who ended his year as one of the 10 worst starting pitchers in the majors.

Finally, McLane decided to let Tal Smith essentially run the team, and he, in turn, hired Ed Wade, the former Phillies GM who had previously worked for him *and* who made it clear in his interview that he would agree to take orders from Smith.

To keep the fans coming to the stadium, Smith and Wade obviously decided to disassemble the previous year's team as much as possible, get rid of all the players the fans wanted gone (Jennings, Chad Qualls, Brad Lidge, Adam Everett and Chris Burke—they're still stuck with Woody Williams) and try to get the player the fans wanted most to acquire, Miguel Tejada.

This strategy worked: Season ticket sales have been brisk and, as Smith and Wade undoubtedly calculated, fans seem to care not a bit that Tejada was named in the Mitchell Report as a steroid user and wrote checks to his drug dealer for HGH or that Williams is still on the team.

General Comments

Team Strengths

Roy Oswalt is still an ace starter. Jose Valverde did a good job closing for a different team last year. Tejada and Carlos Lee will hit .300 and will not walk or strike out much (that's what counts in Houston). Michael Bourn and Kaz Matsui (if/when he's not hurt) will run fast and excite fans with their speed and defense. And Hunter Pence may repeat his last year's stats and excite fans with his aw-shucks-I'm-just-glad-to-be-here persona.

Team Weaknesses

They start with starting pitching (except for Oswalt), relief pitching (I'm more than a little worried about taking the Braves' castoffs), left-handed relief pitching, fielding (all fielders except Bourn and Matsui are among the worst in the majors and Pence is an unknown quantity in right) and a bench that has the strength of wet tissue.

The General Manager is Known for...

In Philadelphia, Wade was known for acquiring mediocre middle relievers, especially overly expensive ones. In Houston, he is known as a genius for getting rid of all the players the fans wanted gone, acquiring Tejada and completing the decimation of the farm that Purpura began.

The Manager is Known for...

Cecil Cooper had an excellent playing career as a Milwaukee Brewer.

Ballpark Characteristics

Minute Maid Park continues to have a reputation as a home run haven because of its inaugural season. It is true that too many pop flies end up as Crawford Box cheapies, but a greater number of well-hit fly balls die in the graveyard of the spacious center and right-center fields. Center field, of course, is infamous for its idiotic hill and in-play flagpole.

The Minor League System is...

It's the worst in organized baseball by a good margin. Drafts this decade have produced only two position players, Pence and the departed Chris Burke, and no starting pitchers. There are no minor leaguers above A-ball who could be called prospects or who could be expected to contribute to the major league team outside of a September cup of coffee.

I should also mention that the 2007 draft was, to put it mildly, bad: The Astros had neither a first- or second-round pick, and then failed to sign five of the next 11 picks, apparently because McLane refused to go over slot and the draftees chose to not sign at all. In view of the fact that the farm was already in poor condition, the failure to add any good prospects set the Astros' future back even further.

Favorite Team Blogs

Orangewhoopass (http://www.orangewhoopass.com/)
The Juice Box (http://thejuicebox.blogspot.com/)

Keys for 2008

Players Lost from Last Year's Team

Pitchers Brad Lidge, Chad Qualls, Dan Wheeler, Jason Jennings, Trever Miller, Juan Gutierrez, Brian Moehler, Dennis Sarfate and Troy Patton, infielders Morgan Ensberg, Chris Burke, Adam Everett, Eric Bruntlett, Craig Biggio and Mike Lamb, outfielders Luke Scott, Jason Lane, Orlando Palmeiro and Josh Anderson.

Players Acquired

Pitchers Jose Valverde, Doug Brocail, Chad Paronto, Geoff Geary, Jack Cassel, Oscar Villareal, Ryan Houston and Wesley Wright, infielders Kaz Matsui, Miguel Tejada and Geoff Blum, outfielders Michael Bourn and Reggie Abercrombie.

Reasons to be Optimistic

Watching the speed and defense of Bourn and Matsui (when he isn't injured) will be exciting. Tejada hitting .300 and grounding into 25 double plays will more than make up for the loss of Everett's glove. Lance Berkman's bat should rebound somewhat. Almost any starting pitcher *surely* must outpitch the gone and unlamented Jennings.

Lidge, Qualls and Wheeler won't be giving up any more home runs and losing games. Brocail will provide the leadership in the bullpen that had been sorely missing since Purpura foolishly refused to sign Russ Springer. And certainly Tejada and his Vitamin B-12 will provide the energy, or should I say, spark in the clubhouse that has been missing since Jeff Bagwell retired.

Reasons to be Pessimistic

1. Terrible defense on the left side with a righty groundball pitching staff
2. Only one good starting pitcher
3. No left-handed relief pitchers
4. Powerless bench consisting of three singles hitters
5. Significant discord in the clubhouse

Due for a Better Season

Lance Berkman

Likely to Have a Worse Season

Kazuo Matsui, Michale Bourn, Hunter Pence

Still Left to Do

The Astros must obtain better hitters for the bench, get a lefty reliever and sacrifice many live chickens to Jobu in hopes that he will see fit to help all starting pitchers not named Roy Oswalt throw 180 innings of 100 ERA+ pitching.

Most Likely Team Outcome

Fifth place with a record of 76-86.

Player Projections

Batters

Brad Ausmus (Catcher)

PA	R	H	2B	3B	HR	RBI	SO	BB	SB	CS	BA	OBP	SLG	OPS	Fld	F$
435	44	91	16	2	2	30	68	43	5	1	.241	.324	.310	.634	C	$1

Ausmus is a veteran, highly intelligent, well-spoken and good-looking. He has a reputation as a great defensive catcher with a limp bat. At 39, he was signed to back up Justin Towles and teach him the finer points of catching. He always hits the cover off the ball in spring training, then tires through the year. He may hit slightly better than terrible if he really catches only one day in five. I hope he will catch Wandy Rodriguez, who pitches much better when Ausmus is in the game, although Roy Oswalt, as ace, gets dibs.

Lance Berkman (First Base)

PA	R	H	2B	3B	HR	RBI	SO	BB	SB	CS	BA	OBP	SLG	OPS	3 Yr	Fld	F$
599	88	146	27	1	31	97	101	85	4	2	.291	.394	.534	.928	-.031	B	$21

At 32, he is one of the premier hitters in the NL. He had an unusually low batting average last year; he said he was healthy, but not seeing the ball well. He appeared to recover by the end of the year, so I would expect his usual .300/.400/.530 with his usual 30 homers and doubles and 100 walks and strikeouts. The new manager has vowed that he will not play Lance in the outfield. That's good, because he is a mediocre fielder at first base but an execrable one in the outfield.

Michael Bourn

PA	R	H	2B	3B	HR	RBI	SO	BB	SB	CS	BA	OBP	SLG	OPS	3 Yr	Fld	F$
331	38	72	8	5	2	21	64	29	13	3	.244	.314	.326	.640	-.011	A+	$1

Bourn can flat-out fly. This kid is instant damage if he gets on base, and he did so at a reasonably good clip for a rookie. He had long been considered a top trade chip, and the Phils finally moved him to his native Houston in the deal for Brad Lidge. If he can keep his on-base percentage in the .350 range, he could lead the league in steals as the Astros' leadoff man.

Darin Erstad (Center Field)

PA	R	H	2B	3B	HR	RBI	SO	BB	SB	CS	BA	OBP	SLG	OPS	3 Yr	Fld	F$
360	41	85	17	2	5	34	54	32	6	2	.267	.333	.380	.713	-.039	B	$1

His best days are far, far behind him. Erstad made two trips to the DL last season with left ankle problems and he wasn't efficient when he was healthy, hitting .248/.310/.335 in 310 at-bats. That line drive stroke we once saw from Erstad is almost nonexistent today and his ability to remain healthy is a huge question mark. He can, however play all three outfield positions and first base, which gives him a little value if he's not on the DL.

Carlos Lee (Left Field)

PA	R	H	2B	3B	HR	RBI	SO	BB	SB	CS	BA	OBP	SLG	OPS	3 Yr	Fld	F$
629	88	165	36	1	29	102	68	51	14	3	.292	.348	.513	.861	-.040	C	$26

He's what is aptly called a "professional hitter." His excellence at bat is mirrored by his ineptness in the field—only Manny Ramirez and Pat Burrell were less competent. He probably will hit around .300/.345/.500 with 25-30 doubles and 25-30 homers. He grounds into a substantial number of double plays, between 22-25 a year, and will continue to do so regardless of who is batting in front of him, as most are of the easy 6-4-3 variety. He will probably steal 10-12 bases, seldom getting caught, because he usually carefully picks a time when the pitcher is not looking.

Mark Loretta (Shortstop)

PA	R	H	2B	3B	HR	RBI	SO	BB	SB	CS	BA	OBP	SLG	OPS	Fld	F$
521	56	127	22	2	4	44	49	45	2	2	.276	.344	.358	.702	F	$1

He is a singles and doubles hitter who hits for high average and seldom walks or strikes out. He hit very well for the first half, but began tiring after the All-Star break when he became an everyday player after Adam Everett went down. If he has plenty of rest, which he should until Kaz Matsui, as usual, is injured and unable to play for part of the year, then I would expect his numbers to be at least as good as they were last year. His glove at short is Jeteresque and he's only slightly better at second.

Kazuo Matsui (Second Base)

PA	R	H	2B	3B	HR	RBI	SO	BB	SB	CS	BA	OBP	SLG	OPS	3 Yr	Fld	F$
428	51	101	18	4	4	36	70	29	17	2	.261	.313	.360	.673	-.030	C	$1

Was his new contract with the Astros an overreach? Yes, but go ahead and look really closely at the second basemen of the NL in 2007, adding (or in most cases subtracting) defensive and baserunning values to their offensive outputs (park-adjusted, even) and see where Kaz winds up ranking. Fluke or not, it surprised me, anyway.

Orlando Palmeiro (Pinch Hitter)

PA	R	H	2B	3B	HR	RBI	SO	BB	SB	CS	BA	OBP	SLG	OPS	F$
226	25	53	11	2	2	19	26	20	2	1	.267	.336	.372	.708	$1

Palmeiro is a lefty singles-hitting pinch hitter who seldom grounds into a double play or strikes out. Unfortunately, at 39, he doesn't even hit singles as often as he used to.

Hunter Pence (Right Field)

PA	R	H	2B	3B	HR	RBI	SO	BB	SB	CS	BA	OBP	SLG	OPS	3 Yr	Fld	F$
543	70	135	25	5	21	75	106	36	7	3	.270	.319	.466	.785	.027	C	$1

He had an outstanding rookie year with the bat, hitting .322/.369/.539 with 17 homers, 30 doubles and 17 steals. His fielding in center field was league average; now, with the acquisition of Michael Bourn and the removal of Luke Scott, Pence will be playing right. New manager Cecil Cooper doesn't intend to bat Pence second, which would take advantage of his speed and power, so he will most likely be batting sixth in front of Ty Wigginton. Pence is a high-strikeout, low-walk guy with a good deal of power and a reasonably high batting average. He may run more, if Tejada and Lee aren't on, to stay out of the double play.

Humberto Quintero (Catcher)

PA	R	H	2B	3B	HR	RBI	SO	BB	SB	CS	BA	OBP	SLG	OPS	3 Yr	Fld	F$
315	35	81	17	1	6	35	49	14	1	1	.281	.320	.409	.729	-.018	A	$1

He has a reputation of being a good defensive catcher and a reasonable bat, but actually, no evidence of either appeared in his 29 games last year. I see no evidence that he will surpass his career numbers of .233/.271/.309 and, in fact, I'm surprised he is still on the Astros' 40-man roster.

Cody Ransom (Third Base)

PA	R	H	2B	3B	HR	RBI	SO	BB	SB	CS	BA	OBP	SLG	OPS	3 Yr	Fld	F$
486	62	108	24	1	21	70	119	40	11	2	.248	.312	.452	.764	-.025	C	$1

The very definition of an excellent Triple-A hitter, he hits for average and power in the minors but neither in the majors. He has a very good glove at short and second.

Miguel Tejada (Shortstop)

PA	R	H	2B	3B	HR	RBI	SO	BB	SB	CS	BA	OBP	SLG	OPS	3 Yr	Fld	F$
572	77	160	30	2	20	82	64	43	2	1	.310	.367	.492	.859	-.032	C	$18

Last season wasn't kind to Tejada. He lost his consecutive-games streak, he lost 50 points of slugging, and his prediction that he'd bring a winner to Baltimore persisted in remaining fantasy. He ought to get a substantial boost from the friendly left field porch in Minute Maid, which will help him lead another team to the middle of the pack and put him in a better bargaining position when he goes back on the market in a couple of years. The bigger question mark is how he'll hold up at shortstop. Tejada has lost a step and was hardly a Gold Glover to begin with; left-field dingers or not, the Astros could be pining for Adam Everett by June.

Justin Towles (Catcher)

PA	R	H	2B	3B	HR	RBI	SO	BB	SB	CS	BA	OBP	SLG	OPS	3 Yr	Fld	F$
491	60	110	20	4	12	52	84	27	9	5	.253	.321	.400	.721	.040	D	$1

Towles did not appear to be in the Astros' future at the beginning of 2007, but was handed an opportunity to play in Double-A and made the best of it with a .976 OPS over 61 games. He was promoted to Triple-A midseason and to the majors in September, and so impressed the organization with his .375/.432/.575 over 14 games that he's supposed to be the starting catcher this year. He's played only 74 games above A-ball, but his minor league line reads .300/.393/.470. He reminds me a bit of the young Craig Biggio—runs well, doesn't walk or strike out much, seldom hits into double plays. So, for fun, here are the numbers Biggio produced his first full year, catching and batting eighth: .257/.336/.402.

Ty Wigginton (Third Base)

PA	R	H	2B	3B	HR	RBI	SO	BB	SB	CS	BA	OBP	SLG	OPS	3 Yr	Fld	F$
531	69	133	28	1	23	81	97	41	3	3	.279	.339	.486	.825	-.026	F	$12

He is expected to be the regular third baseman, for the first time in four years, though it's a job he was unable to keep with the Mets, Pirates or Devil Rays. He is a strict pull hitter with a bit of power (the Crawford Boxes are a powerful temptress). He doesn't walk much and strikes out a good 100 times a year. He is a Lead Glove fielder, too.

Pitchers

Brandon Backe (Starting Pitcher)

W	L	ERA	TBF	IP	Hit	HR	SO	BB	HBP	3 Yr	F$
4	6	5.45	415	93	102	15	53	41	5	0.76	$1

Backe had Tommy John surgery in September 2006 and returned a year later. He had pitched very well before he was injured, and he pitched reasonably well after his return. He definitely will be in the starting rotation. He was a decent strikeout pitcher before he was hurt with six or seven strikeouts per nine innings, but he gave up too many walks.

Dave Borkowski (Relief Pitcher)

W	L	ERA	TBF	IP	Hit	HR	SO	BB	HBP	3 Yr	F$
4	4	4.69	333	76	79	9	52	32	3	0.31	$1

He's a middle reliever/mop-up man who can throw more than one inning if need be. He's given the Astros an average 90 ERA+ over two seasons.

Doug Brocail (Relief Pitcher)

W	L	ERA	TBF	IP	Hit	HR	SO	BB	HBP	F$
4	4	4.16	291	69	67	8	42	24	2	$1

After missing much of 2006 due to heart problems, Brocail provided solid middle relief for the Padres last season. At age 40, he appeared in 67 games and finished with a tidy 3.05 ERA. Brocail also earned kudos for being the leader in the San Diego bullpen, keeping everyone loose during the game until called upon.

Paul Estrada (Relief Pitcher)

W	L	ERA	TBF	IP	Hit	HR	SO	BB	HBP	3 Yr	F$
4	4	4.67	319	72	68	9	66	42	3	-0.06	$1

This righty reliever has received a lot of hype but doesn't have the numbers to support it. His walk rate is high, at 5.4 per nine innings, and last year in Triple-A he had a 5.12 ERA and a 1.60 WHIP over 70 innings. I doubt it would improve in the majors.

Geoff Geary (Relief Pitcher)

W	L	ERA	TBF	IP	Hit	HR	SO	BB	HBP	3 Yr	F$
5	4	4.27	355	82	87	7	53	27	5	0.43	$1

No one demonstrated the up-and-down nature of relief pitching better than Geary, who went from being the team's most dependable reliever in '06 to being demoted twice in '07. He does not have the stuff to pitch the high-leverage innings. However, as a middle reliever, he will throw strikes and buy time.

Mark McLemore (Relief Pitcher)

W	L	ERA	TBF	IP	Hit	HR	SO	BB	HBP	3 Yr	F$
4	5	4.84	377	84	75	11	72	52	5	0.15	$1

Another lefty reliever, he, like Chris Sampson, has actually pitched better as a starter than a reliever. (In the minors, his ERA as a starter is 2.61 and his ERA as a reliever is 3.94.) He was injured a great part of the last four years, so lost his chance to start.

Trever Miller (Relief Pitcher)

W	L	ERA	TBF	IP	Hit	HR	SO	BB	HBP	3 Yr	F$
3	3	4.28	246	57	52	7	52	26	3	0.44	$1

He's a lefty reliever who is pretty league average. During his career, he's gotten right-handed hitters out reasonably well, but he struggled against them last year.

Brian Moehler (Relief Pitcher)

W	L	ERA	TBF	IP	Hit	HR	SO	BB	HBP	F$
4	4	4.60	320	74	83	9	39	22	3	$1

He's a right-handed middle relief/mop up pitcher who can pitch three or four innings if necessary.

Fernando Nieve (Relief Pitcher)

W	L	ERA	TBF	IP	Hit	HR	SO	BB	HBP	3 Yr	F$
4	5	5.26	379	85	89	14	59	41	4	-0.12	$1

He lost last year to Tommy John surgery, so it's uncertain when he will contribute to the team. I would expect him to start in the bullpen, pitching either in mop-up or middle relief. Before he was injured, he had a very lively fastball, but pitched much better in short relief than starting.

Roy Oswalt (Starting Pitcher)

W	L	ERA	TBF	IP	Hit	HR	SO	BB	HBP	3 Yr	F$
13	9	3.65	811	196	197	16	136	48	7	0.27	$14

Oswalt is the ace and the only good starter on the staff. Last year, he finished with a 14-7 record and a 3.18 ERA. I count three games the bullpen blew and 10 in which he gave up three or fewer runs over six innings or four runs over seven and received poor run support. He walked an uncharacteristically high 2.55 per nine innings, and his 212 innings were about 20 fewer than usual. He had to contend with both terrible fielding and mediocre run support.

Felipe Paulino (Starting Pitcher)

W	L	ERA	TBF	IP	Hit	HR	SO	BB	HBP	3 Yr	F$
5	9	5.87	571	125	140	21	80	64	7	-0.46	$1

He had a cup of coffee with the Astros in September, but has not thrown so much as a single pitch in Triple-A, yet many are predicting he'll be in the Astros' 2008 starting rotation. He had a 3.62 ERA and a 1.36 WHIP in Double-A, starting 22 games and throwing 112 innings with 0.5 home runs, four walks and 8.8 strikeouts per nine innings.

Stephen Randolph (Relief Pitcher)

W	L	ERA	TBF	IP	Hit	HR	SO	BB	HBP	3 Yr	F$
4	4	4.84	323	71	59	10	75	54	3	0.39	$1

He's a lefty reliever whose deficiencies were hidden in Triple-A because hitters there will swing at more pitches out of the strike zone than major leaguers will. He has no business in the majors, and if he is used as a LOOGY, he will give up a goodly number of walks and homers.

Wandy Rodriguez (Starting Pitcher)

W	L	ERA	TBF	IP	Hit	HR	SO	BB	HBP	3 Yr	F$
8	10	4.94	728	166	176	24	124	67	7	0.57	$1

At home last season, he pitched like Sandy Koufax 1968. On the road, he was mostly like a lousy No. 5 starter. He started his ML career as a nibbler resembling Kirk Rueter, but has gained confidence in his stuff and has become much more of a strikeout pitcher. His real problem is losing concentration when he gets emotional.

Chris Sampson (Starting Pitcher)

W	L	ERA	TBF	IP	Hit	HR	SO	BB	HBP	3 Yr	F$
7	7	4.77	561	131	147	19	55	34	7	0.47	$1

A sinker ball pitcher, Sampson, a much better starter than reliever, requires excellent infield defense to excel. He pitched like an ace (ERA was 3.29 and he lost four quality starts because of poor run support) until Everett went down for the year and Morgan Ensberg was replaced at third. Unfortunately, Wigginton and his lead glove are still at third and Tejada isn't much of an improvement over Loretta. So don't expect much from Sampson, even if his arm has fully healed from the elbow injury that shut him down last season.

Jose Valverde (Relief Pitcher)

W	L	ERA	TBF	IP	Hit	HR	SO	BB	HBP	3 Yr	F$
5	3	3.21	282	69	52	6	78	28	2	0.27	$15

Valverde bounced back from a 2006 season that saw him lose his roster spot to lead the majors in saves with 47. He held opposing batters to a .196 average, with left- and right-handed batters struggling almost equally. However, Arizona fans never felt fully confident: Perhaps they remembered his prior struggles, or maybe it was just the number of one-run games, where there was no room for error. He will likely be good in 2008, though repeating his 2.66 ERA might be a stretch.

Oscar Villarreal (Relief Pitcher)

W	L	ERA	TBF	IP	Hit	HR	SO	BB	HBP	3 Yr	F$
4	4	4.16	321	75	73	8	52	28	3	0.07	$1

Villarreal is pretty much a dictionary definition of mediocre: He strikes out a few, walks a few, and when the beancounters hibernate for the winter they'll tell you his ERA is around league average. Moving from what is ostensibly a pitcher's park to a band box (Minute Maid) won't do much for his raw statistics, but he'll no doubt remain effective. A 4.15 forecast ERA may be a little on the low side.

Woody Williams (Starting Pitcher)

W	L	ERA	TBF	IP	Hit	HR	SO	BB	HBP	F$
8	11	5.18	733	169	191	30	83	49	8	$1

Houston-born and raised, Williams always wanted to pitch for his hometown team and couldn't get his phone calls returned until he was too old to be any good any more. He's in the second year of a two-year contract and will most likely be the No. 4 or No. 5 starter. Last year, he always seemed to do fine except for one inning in which he'd give up three to five runs, costing himself (and the team) the game.

Kansas City Royals

by Bradford Doolittle of the Kansas City Star (kansascity.com)

2008 Projections

Record: 73-89
Division Rank: Last, 17 games back
Runs Scored: 784
Runs Allowed: 879

2007 in a Nutshell

Last season marked the Royals' first full campaign under general manager Dayton Moore and KC displayed an air of competence that had been lacking during the previous Allard Baird administration. Kansas City won 69 games, a seven-game improvement over the season before and 13 games better than the 106-loss debacle of 2005. Despite the improvement, though, the Royals finished last for the fourth season in a row.

Moore dipped into the free-agent market last offseason, inking starter Gil Meche to a much-maligned five-year, $55 million deal to head up the Royals rotation. Meche posted a fine season (ERA+ of 128). Moore also shored up a run-prevention group that finished in the middle of the American League—the best showing in a decade—by snagging Mets control specialist Brian Bannister in a trade, picking up Rule 5 revelation Joakim Soria, who ended the season as the Royals closer, and dealing for Braves shortstop prospect Tony Pena Jr., who contributed a fine season with the glove.

The offense was disappointing, finishing next-to-last in the AL in runs scored. However, the jewels of the Royals player development system, third baseman Alex Gordon and hitter-without-a-position Billy Butler, arrived in the big leagues. KC hopes the pair can serve as the Royals' offensive catalysts for the next decade.

Manager Buddy Bell called it a career, completing a track record of hard luck and ineptitude that left him as the man who managed and played in more games without experiencing the postseason than any other figure in baseball history. Moore replaced him with hot managerial prospect and successful Japanese skipper Trey Hillman. While the Royals snapped their string of three straight 100-loss seasons, Moore was unsatisfied with the incremental improvement and spent his winter waving cash at several big name free agents, most of whom refused to bite.

General Comments

Team Strengths

The Royals trimmed over a full run off their per-game runs against average of 2006, finishing with their fewest runs allowed in a full season since 1993. Led by Meche, the starters shone in the early part of the season but it was the bullpen that emerged as the strength of the pitching staff. Soria finished with 17 saves and a 2.48 ERA in 69 relief innings. Octavio Dotel was decent as the closer before Moore flipped him in a deadline deal for Braves prospect Kyle Davies.

And Zack Greinke, after being demoted from the rotation, turned into a dominating set-up guy before returning to the starter's role toward the end of the season. Meanwhile, the pitching was bolstered by a much-improved defense. Sparked by Pena, who led AL shortstops in both revised zone rating and out-of-zone plays, the Royals led the league in RZR and were above the league average in OOZ.

Team Weaknesses

If the Royals had only repeated their offensive performance of 2006, they might have made a run at .500, which is saying something in the tough AL. Alas, KC featured only three players able to post an OPS+ of 100 or better and that includes the cup-of-coffee types. Mark Grudzielanek's .302/.346/.426 performance in 116 games was the only solid performance by a Royals hitter once position is taken into account. Incredibly, Emil Brown led the Royals in RBIs for the third straight season—with 62. The hitters finished last in the league in home runs (102), 13th in walks and ahead of only three sabermetrically slanted teams (Oakland, Toronto and Cleveland) in stolen bases.

And it wasn't the park—the Royals scored almost the same number of runs at home (355) as on the road (351). The starting rotation was thin despite nice seasons from Meche and Bannister. The other slots were a hodgepodge of incompetence, with too many starts going to the likes of Scott Elarton, Odalis Perez and Jorge de la Rosa. The Royals finished 13th in the AL with 64 quality starts.

The General Manager is Known for...

Moore has cleaned house since taking over for Allard Baird during the 2006 season. Among mainline fans in

Kansas City, Moore is still enjoying a sort of honeymoon: He's the guy that's going to lead the team out of the shadows.

Nationally, it's likely he's best known for overspending on the likes of Meche and, most recently, Jose Guillen. Moore's top priority is to build a state-of-the-art player development machine. He's got a ways to go in that regard, but most observers think the lower rungs of the Royals system are in better shape than in the recent past. The jury is still out on Moore, but it's pretty evident that he's a capable executive, has a plan for building the organization and is implementing that plan with the full support (in terms of resource allocation) of ownership.

The expectations of Royals fans have diminished so severely that most viewed last season's moderate improvement as a victory. Moore didn't and, if anything, he at least has created an atmosphere of accountability that bodes well for the franchise's direction.

The Manager is Known for...

Hillman was a successful minor-league manager in the Yankees system, then went to Japan and led the Nippon Ham Fighters to their first championship in a quarter century. That team scored a lot of runs via the home run and, indeed, Hillman is considered to be somewhat of the Earl Weaver mold in terms of preference for the three-run homer. However, his next Ham Fighters squad lacked power so he turned into the Pacific Rim version of Mike Scioscia, bunting and stealing his way into another Japan Series appearance.

That kind of versatility attracted Moore's attention as well as that of other teams, including the Yankees. Hillman's presence may eventually help the Royals in the Japanese free-agent market. KC did land reliever Yasuhiko Yabuta in the offseason, but lost out on pitcher Hiroki Kuroda and outfielder Kosuke Fukudome. No problem as long as someday Hillman helps the Royals land Japanese wunderkind Yu Darvish—one of his starters with the Ham Fighters.

Ballpark Characteristics

Kauffman Stadium played as a neutral park in 2007 after being quite hitter-friendly the previous season (park factor of 100 vs. 105). The park still features distant fences and spacious alleys that cut down on home runs and inflate batting average, doubles and triples. Overall, it's a very fair (and beautiful, I might add) playing venue. The stadium is undergoing a $250 million renovation that will be done in phases, with the 2010 season targeted for completion. That's a lot of money to be pumped into a 34-year old stadium that isn't in an ideal location.

In addition, there is talk of moving the fences back in a few feet to improve the home run numbers. When the fences were last moved in at "The K," the stadium was one of the most offensive-friendly parks in the majors. That wouldn't seem to jibe with Moore's Braves-inspired blueprint.

The Minor League System is...

The Royals graduated the best the system had last season when Gordon and Butler assumed everyday roles in the lineup. That's a pretty good rookie class right there. In 2008, the pipeline is likely to be a little dry. Starter Luke Hochevar, the top pick of the 2006 draft, may win a rotation spot or pitch out of the big-league bullpen. He looked good in a cup-of-coffee stint with the Royals in September but had been inconsistent with Triple-A Omaha. No rookie position players are likely to get significant time with the Royals this season, though a slew of pitchers may contribute.

The upper minors are pretty barren. The lower-level teams are where the action is, especially on whichever team last year's top pick, infielder Mike Moustakas, plays. He looks like a keeper. And with another 90-plus loss season, the Royals have one more early first-round pick to look forward to next June.

Favorite Team Blogs

In Dayton We Trust (http://www.indaytonwetrust.blogspot.com/)

Doolittle Brothers (http://doolittlebrothers.com/)

Keys for 2008

Players Lost from Last Year's Team

The Royals are one of the few teams that can sincerely claim that losing their RBI leader, Brown, improves their fortunes. Longtime Royal Mike Sweeney is a free agent and his return to KC is questionable. Jason LaRue was chased out of town with pitchforks and torches. He's the Cardinals' problem now. Perez, Elarton and Reggie Sanders are all nice enough guys, but they're all gone, too. The only departure of any significance is reliever David Riske, who posted a 2.45 ERA in 65 appearances last season. He signed with the Brewers.

Players Acquired

The Royals lost out on free-agent targets like Kuroda, Torii Hunter, Carlos Silva and Andruw Jones. But Hillman won't be arriving at his first big-league camp empty handed. Moore over-committed to the mercurial Guillen, but he's an upgrade over Brown. Alberto Callaspo, acquired from Arizona, may be a steal. He'll team with Esteban German in sort of a super utility combo. Miguel Olivo was brought in to emulate the lack of plate discipline by shortstop Pena, provide terrible defense and back up John Buck behind the plate. Moore, hoping to continue last season's success in the pen, signed an expensive pair of setup men, righty Yabuta and journeyman lefty Ron Mahay.

Reasons to be Optimistic

The Royals' improvement last season was heartening because not only did they win more games, but they did so because of a core group of players—Gordon, Butler, David DeJesus, Mark Teahen, Greinke, Buck and Soria—who are on the upswing of the career arc. Moore has done a nice job of upgrading the big-league roster and replenishing the talent in the lower minors. The addition of Hillman as the manager (combined with the subtraction of Bell) could net an extra few wins for the Royals as well.

Reasons to be Pessimistic

Moore has plenty of work left to do. As well as Pena played defensively last season, a contending team cannot have a bat of his caliber in the lineup every day. The starting rotation has question marks: Did Meche and Bannister have career seasons? Can Greinke perform well as a big-league starter for a full season? Who fits in beyond that?

In addition, much of last season's improvement was due to a solid bullpen. With a mostly new crew in 2008, there is no guarantee of repeating that performance. The putrid offense of last season really only added Guillen, which doesn't seem like nearly enough. On top of all that, the Royals play in a mercilessly difficult division.

Due for a Better Season

John Buck improved both his power and patience last season, but saw his overall line dragged down by a .222 batting average. Part of the problem was his inability to make consistent contact. Bell's bizarre use of players may have hurt Buck. His .243 average on balls in play wasn't too surprising given his low rate of line drives, but Buck will be 27 this season and with a little luck and regular time could have a big season.

Gordon fell well short of expectations and projections, hitting .247/.314/.411 as a 23-year-old rookie. Look for a big-time improvement in Gordon's sophomore campaign.

Likely to Have a Worse Season

Grudzielanek is a rarity—a 37-year-old second baseman who posted one of his best offensive seasons. He's still a Royal, still penciled in at the keystone spot and due to tumble off a cliff. The Royals are well-positioned for that with Callaspo and German around. On the pitching staff, Bannister had a .739 Defense Efficiency Ratio behind him—the highest of all qualifying starters in the AL. He got lucky in terms of keeping fly balls in the park, has a low strikeout rate and has a poor ground ball rate. Look out.

Still Left to Do

The Royals had a fistful of dollars to unload this offseason but were unable to attract the marquee names on the free agent market. That actually should bode well long term, because it's unlikely that any of those free agents would have made much of a difference on a team still in development. Moore should have plenty of fiscal flexibility going forward, not a bad position to be in.

All that's left before the season is to shake out the last two spots in the rotation. The candidates include Hochevar, Neal Musser, John Bale, Kyle Davies, de la Rosa, Leo Nunez and, possibly a yet-to-be-determined rehabbing veteran. The Royals also may sign another outfielder with some pop for a reserve role.

Most Likely Team Outcome

Hopes for further improvement really lay at the feet of Gordon and Butler. If the pair can become the star-caliber hitters that most think they will eventually, the Royals could add to last season's win total. Hillman is a more likely candidate to squeeze whatever is there from the Royals roster than was Bell. But the bullpen probably will regress a bit and the Royals are playing in the wrong division of the wrong league at the wrong time. Any improvement over last season's 69 wins would be a victory for the 2008 Royals.

Player Projections

Batters

John Buck (Catcher)

PA	R	H	2B	3B	HR	RBI	SO	BB	SB	CS	BA	OBP	SLG	OPS	3 Yr	Fld	F$
417	51	94	21	1	16	57	88	34	1	2	.254	.324	.445	.769	-.001	C	$1

Buck, entering his fifth season with the Royals, is a pretty solid catcher and has some real positive attributes with the stick. However, his negative attributes (striking out, low batting average) could lead a non-thinking manager to park Buck on the bench. Let's hope Trey Hillman isn't one of those managers because Buck has a chance of being an above-average catcher. The .769 OPS he's projected for would be well above last season's AL average for catchers (.713).

Billy Butler (Designated Hitter)

PA	R	H	2B	3B	HR	RBI	SO	BB	SB	CS	BA	OBP	SLG	OPS	3 Yr	Fld	F$
536	69	141	32	2	17	73	77	47	1	1	.296	.361	.478	.839	.077	C	$10

A .794 OPS at 21 is nothing to sneeze at. In fact, it's the best ever for a Royals player that young. Butler's debut was pretty much in line with what you'd have expected given his minor-league record. Butler's OPS is projected to swell from .839 this season to .916 in 2010 and it's easy to imagine him doing even better. Butler has a quick bat, generates a lot of power without over-swinging and makes consistent contact. While Alex Gordon may be the Royals' best overall player over the next few years, Butler is likely to be a better hitter.

Alberto Callaspo (Shortstop)

PA	R	H	2B	3B	HR	RBI	SO	BB	SB	CS	BA	OBP	SLG	OPS	3 Yr	Fld	F$
465	50	117	23	4	3	39	43	32	3	3	.276	.326	.370	.696	.010	D	$1

Callaspo became the latest in a line of Arizona prospects who raked in the minors (.317 career batting average) but flopped in the majors. His situation was not helped by a domestic violence arrest, though no charges resulted. However, his eventual departure for Kansas City in a trade probably had less to do with that, than with Callaspo batting only .215 in 56 games for the D-backs.

David DeJesus (Center Field)

PA	R	H	2B	3B	HR	RBI	SO	BB	SB	CS	BA	OBP	SLG	OPS	3 Yr	Fld	F$
592	75	144	32	6	8	57	75	55	7	3	.281	.363	.414	.777	-.029	C	$6

DeJesus is entering the dangerous territory of the "tweener". He's a solid player, normally above league average in both offense and defense. But his bat doesn't play well at a corner outfield spot and he's at the age when his range may not hold up enough for him to be an everyday center fielder. DeJesus had a subpar year at the plate in 2007 even though he was at that magical age of 27. His power numbers were down and he got unlucky on balls in play. He should bounce back and, in fact, our projections have him again finishing with an above-average OPS. His revised zone rating numbers in center field were strong last season, which should be enough to justify his continuing as the Royals leadoff hitter and starting center fielder.

Joey Gathright (Center Field)

PA	R	H	2B	3B	HR	RBI	SO	BB	SB	CS	BA	OBP	SLG	OPS	3 Yr	Fld	F$
491	64	120	19	5	0	33	69	48	30	11	.283	.363	.351	.714	-.008	B	$1

Gathright hit so well last season that many were clamoring for him to become a fixture in the Royals lineup. Gathright is a uniquely talented player, but he probably is not going to be a regular on a winning team. The Royals will attempt to maximize Gathright's value as a bench player who can get on base and is slowly learning how to use his speed on the basepaths. He hits with zero power, but is pretty solid with the glove. If he can continue to hit over .300, Gathright can start. But who can maintain a .365 average on balls in play?

Esteban German (Second Base)

PA	R	H	2B	3B	HR	RBI	SO	BB	SB	CS	BA	OBP	SLG	OPS	3 Yr	Fld	F$
417	53	102	20	5	3	34	61	43	12	3	.284	.365	.393	.758	-.039	C	$1

After a 2006 season in which he was arguably baseball's most valuable utility player, German's offensive numbers sagged to below league average in 2007. German's power numbers and plate discipline ratios were steady, but his average on balls in play dropped from an unrealistic .388 all the way to .307. If he can get back up to a sustainable .320 or so, he'll be fine. If German doesn't produce, his playing time will suffer since the Royals traded for Alberto Callaspo and re-signed Jason Smith, both for utility roles.

Ross Gload (First Base)

PA	R	H	2B	3B	HR	RBI	SO	BB	SB	CS	BA	OBP	SLG	OPS	3 Yr	Fld	F$
340	43	93	21	3	8	42	43	20	3	2	.297	.339	.459	.798	-.031	B	$1

When the Royals signed Ross Gload last season, you just knew Buddy Bell would overexpose the prototypical "steady veteran." Indeed, that's just what happened as Gload chewed up quite a bit of Ryan Shealy's playing time. Sure, Shealy struggled, but at least he's got upside. The lefty-hitting Gload has generally been platooned, but he may actually possess counter-platoon tendencies. He can help a team, but is far too limited to be given the 346 plate appearances he received last season.

Alex Gordon (Third Base)

PA	R	H	2B	3B	HR	RBI	SO	BB	SB	CS	BA	OBP	SLG	OPS	3 Yr	Fld	F$
581	79	140	36	3	20	79	119	51	8	3	.275	.350	.475	.825	.059	C	$14

Okay, so he didn't set the baseball world on fire. There is still plenty to like about Gordon. After a dreadful start, he hit .272/.321/.458 after May 15 and projects to an .825 OPS in 2008. The ball jumps off Gordon's bat.

Big-league pitchers exploited Gordon with low-and-inside breaking pitches early in the season and found that they could jump in front of him by throwing fastball strikes early in the count; Gordon would invariably take a pitch or two. He got more aggressive and had some success, but his walk rate dropped and soon pitchers jumped on that. That's life in the big leagues. As a rookie, Gordon was reacting to what the pitcher was trying to do. At some point, pitchers are going to be dancing to Gordon's tune.

Mark Grudzielanek (Second Base)

PA	R	H	2B	3B	HR	RBI	SO	BB	SB	CS	BA	OBP	SLG	OPS	Fld	F$
499	56	131	28	3	5	48	65	29	2	2	.286	.333	.393	.726	B	$1

Grudzielanek was named the Royals player of the year in the offseason, which says more about the team than it does about Grudzielanek. He's been better than anyone could have hoped for during his two seasons in KC, and has been a .300 hitter, give or take a few points, for five seasons now, the first of which was his age-33 season. That's an odd career path; one wouldn't want to wager significant money that Grudzielanek can keep it going.

Jose Guillen (Right Field)

PA	R	H	2B	3B	HR	RBI	SO	BB	SB	CS	BA	OBP	SLG	OPS	3 Yr	Fld	F$
530	69	135	29	2	17	71	86	32	4	1	.282	.340	.458	.798	-.031	B	$7

Seattle plucked Guillen from the scrap heap for a few million dollars last year and he went on to have a strong offensive season. He wasn't even close to being a distraction or cancer, and while his defense was bad, much of that stems from leg injuries from which he recovered over the course of the summer. For Kansas City, he should basically be Emil Brown all over again. The good Emil Brown.

Miguel Olivo (Catcher)

PA	R	H	2B	3B	HR	RBI	SO	BB	SB	CS	BA	OBP	SLG	OPS	3 Yr	Fld	F$
454	50	107	23	2	13	55	104	17	3	3	.250	.282	.405	.687	-.025	B	$1

The catcher has some power, but really isn't a very good hitter. He tees off on a first-pitch fastball, but has trouble with the breaking stuff. He probably will do about the same as last season's .237/.262/.405.

Tony Pena (Shortstop)

PA	R	H	2B	3B	HR	RBI	SO	BB	SB	CS	BA	OBP	SLG	OPS	3 Yr	Fld	F$
466	47	117	22	5	2	37	73	15	5	3	.268	.296	.355	.651	-.007	A	$1

Pena was almost guaranteed a warm reception in Kansas City based on the sheer fact that he's not Angel Berroa. Or is he? Pena drew 10 walks in 536 plate appearances. That's very Berroa-like. In terms of Gross Production Average, Pena was the third-worst hitter in the American League. But he was one of the best defensive players in the league. That's a tradeoff the Royals are willing to make for the time being.

Ryan Shealy (First Base)

PA	R	H	2B	3B	HR	RBI	SO	BB	SB	CS	BA	OBP	SLG	OPS	3 Yr	Fld	F$
404	50	94	23	1	15	56	89	33	1	0	.260	.327	.454	.781	-.020	A	$1

Shealy showed enough after being acquired from Colorado in 2006 that the Royals hoped he could become their everyday first baseman. That didn't really work out—three home runs in 189 plate appearances. Shealy will be 28 this season and isn't thought of as the answer to much of anything these days. If Shealy can turn things around, there is an opening at first base for the Royals with Butler likely to DH.

Jason Smith (Shortstop)

PA	R	H	2B	3B	HR	RBI	SO	BB	SB	CS	BA	OBP	SLG	OPS	3 Yr	Fld	F$
297	36	69	14	3	10	37	77	19	2	1	.254	.307	.439	.746	-.034	C	$1

Talk about all or nothing: Smith hit six homers in 149 plate appearances last season but struck out more than a third of the time. The Royals are bringing him back, however, mostly because he can play shortstop somewhat capably.

Mark Teahen (Right Field)

PA	R	H	2B	3B	HR	RBI	SO	BB	SB	CS	BA	OBP	SLG	OPS	3 Yr	Fld	F$
544	73	133	30	6	12	60	107	57	11	2	.280	.357	.444	.801	.009	C	$1

Teahen was once again one of the Royals' most surprising players. This time, it was for the wrong reasons. Teahen's power all but disappeared. He lost more than 100 points in slugging percentage despite posting almost identical batting- and on-base averages as the season before. The projection of an .801 OPS seems about right for Teahen, providing he recovers at least some power in his golden "age 27" season.

The problem is that an .801 OPS as a left or right fielder is a net loser. With Gordon at third base, why not try Teahen at second? As it is, the Royals have actually discussed playing Teahen at first base, where his bat has even less value.

Pitchers

John Bale (Starting/Relief Pitcher)

In his first season after coming over from Japan, Bale struck out more than one batter an inning, limited his walks, allowed only one home run in 40 innings and posted a decent 4.05 ERA despite getting unlucky on balls in play. Bale is lefty who doesn't seem to have any real mastery of lefties and the Royals are going to try him as a starter. Bale is a sleeper, but we don't have a projection for him due to his limited recent experience.

Brian Bannister (Starting Pitcher)

W	L	ERA	TBF	IP	Hit	HR	SO	BB	HBP	3 Yr	F$
8	9	4.62	677	156	167	19	79	53	8	0.08	$1

Only a terrible final start prevented Bannister from finishing in the top 10 in AL ERA, and he finished third in the voting for AL rookie of the year. He attracted much attention for his "feel for pitching" and other such touchy-feely qualities. Bannister does possess excellent control. The Royals are counting on him to be their No. 2 starter entering the season, but when looking a measures like average on balls in play, groundball percentage and homers/fly ball, it's pretty apparent that he was a beneficiary of good fortune last season. His list of comps isn't encouraging, either. He's the most likely player on the Royals to suffer a collapse in 2008.

Kyle Davies (Starting Pitcher)

W	L	ERA	TBF	IP	Hit	HR	SO	BB	HBP	3 Yr	F$
6	9	5.42	628	138	153	18	81	70	6	-0.34	$1

Davies was part of the swag the Royals got when they flipped Octavio Dotel to the Braves. Davies may be evidence of a blind spot GM Moore has for the prospects of his former employer. Davies has excellent stuff and no real idea of where it's going. He has an unsightly 6.24 ERA in 287 big-league innings. He'll be only 24 this season, so there's still time for him. A few pitchers of Davies' description do eventually emerge, though few were as bad for as many innings as Davies has been in The Show. Davies won't be shoehorned into the rotation if he doesn't show improvement.

Jorge de la Rosa (Starting Pitcher)

W	L	ERA	TBF	IP	Hit	HR	SO	BB	HBP	3 Yr	F$
6	8	5.27	575	127	141	17	83	63	5	0.12	$1

De la Rosa is a lefty version of Davies–good stuff, poor control. His ERA (5.85) is a little better than Davies', though he's logged fewer innings (274). But he's two years older than Davies and that makes a lot of difference. Solid velocity aside, de la Rosa's poor command and lack of movement make it unlikely that he'll ever become a league-average pitcher. His 130 innings in 2007 probably will be the most he'll ever throw in a season.

Brandon Duckworth (Relief Pitcher)

W	L	ERA	TBF	IP	Hit	HR	SO	BB	HRP	3 Yr	F$
4	5	5.35	360	79	92	9	43	38	3	0.45	$1

Does anyone remember a guy named Brandon Duckworth who struck out 167 batters in 2002? That was a long time ago, and Duckworth's strikeout rates have declined to the point where they're about one to one with his walks. Injuries have something to do with that.

Jimmy Gobble (Relief Pitcher)

W	L	ERA	TBF	IP	Hit	HR	SO	BB	HBP	3 Yr	F$
4	3	4.47	284	65	65	7	55	28	2	0.11	$1

Once a promising starter, Gobble doesn't look like he is ever going to make it in anyone's rotation. Nevertheless, his strikeout rate as a reliever is exponentially better than it was when he started, and, last season, he looked like he was finding his stride as a lefty killer. Men have made millions with that skill set.

Zack Greinke (Starting Pitcher)

W	L	ERA	TBF	IP	Hit	HR	SO	BB	HBP	3 Yr	F$
6	6	4.48	472	109	113	13	82	37	4	-0.18	$1

Greinke is THE pitcher to watch on the Royals this season and, perhaps, THE pitcher to watch in all the American League. Something really clicked in Greinke last season as he went from tentative to ultra-aggressive without sacrificing command. He cultivated a nasty demeanor as a reliever, one he brought with him as he returned to the rotation later in the season. His velocity, which now touches the upper 90s, stayed with him, as did the strikeouts. The Greinke that generated the tepid projections you'll see this spring is no more. Greinke will be one of the AL's 10 best starters in 2008.

Luke Hochevar (Starting Pitcher)

Hochevar pitched well in a late-season call-up, salvaging a little from a disappointing year from baseball's top draft pick in 2006. With the Royals, he displayed good command and sported a wicked groundball percentage that belied what he did in the minors. As right-hander Hochevar moved up the ladder, he seemed to have more problems with left-handed hitters. The Royals will take a long look at him as a rotation candidate. The bullpen is also a possibility. Most likely, he'll begin the season as a starter at Triple-A Omaha.

Gil Meche (Starting Pitcher)

W	L	ERA	TBF	IP	Hit	HR	SO	BB	HBP	3 Yr	F$
10	10	4.29	790	183	187	20	128	69	6	0.48	$2

With the market for starting pitchers as it is, Meche may grow into that $55 million deal after all. If he pitches four more seasons like he did in 2007, the contract will be a bargain for the Royals. Meche posted the best season of his career, a fact that may have been missed by anyone who still pays attention to won-loss records. His groundball rate (46.8 percent) was his best in recent seasons, and he maintained most of his improved strikeout rate of 2006 while taking his command to a new level. Perhaps most importantly, the oft-injured Meche logged a career-best 216 innings.

Leo Nunez (Relief Pitcher)

W	L	ERA	TBF	IP	Hit	HR	SO	BB	HBP	3 Yr	F$
4	6	5.16	413	93	103	14	62	35	5	-0.29	$1

"Li'l Leo," as he's called by some in KC, generates big radar readings with what appears to be a 12-year-old's body. Nunez had struggled before last season after being rushed into his big league career by Baird. Then he got hurt in the minors, so last season has to be considered a pleasant surprise.

Once considered a power arm for a short relief role, he was shifted to the rotation in the minors before last season. He then did pretty well in six starts with the Royals (3.99 ERA, 21 strikeouts in 29-plus innings). But he was even better out of the bullpen: 16 strikeouts and two walks in 14-plus innings. He's considered a prime candidate for the back of the rotation entering 2008. However he's used, he's going to have to solve his propensity for giving up the long ball.

Joel Peralta (Relief Pitcher)

W	L	ERA	TBF	IP	Hit	HR	SO	BB	HBP	3 Yr	F$
5	4	4.10	328	77	76	9	58	25	3	0.37	$1

Peralta was a valuable member of last year's bullpen. His 87.2 relief innings were just one-third of an inning off the AL lead. He's now logged over 160 innings over the last two seasons. As such, you shouldn't consider Peralta a likely candidate to repeat his 3.80 ERA. Peralta seems to pitch better in low-leverage situations.

Odalis Perez (Starting Pitcher)

W	L	ERA	TBF	IP	Hit	HR	SO	BB	HBP	3 Yr	F$
7	9	4.89	631	143	166	16	71	49	5	0.30	$1

Perez is looking for a new home. His time in Kansas City wasn't very successful and his strikeout rate has become unsightly. The Royals have been so desperate for starting pitchers that, despite his troubles, Perez never was tried as a reliever. For any team interested in Perez, that might be a thought. Perez does pitch a little better against lefties, but that's not to say he pitches well against them.

Joakim Soria (Relief Pitcher)

W	L	ERA	TBF	IP	Hit	HR	SO	BB	HBP	3 Yr	F$
5	3	3.52	292	70	63	6	66	24	3	-0.02	$11

Soria was quite a catch off the Rule 5 circuit. The Royals had planned to carry him through the season, spotting him in low-leverage situations. But they soon figured out that Soria was their best bullpen pitcher. Soria has terrific command of a versatile array and has good, if not overwhelming, stuff. Soria's best feature is his delivery—it's smooth and easy-looking, but hitters seem to have trouble picking up the ball out of his hand. We'll see if that deceptiveness holds up after batters have seen him a few times, but his future certainly seems bright. Just 23, he may add velocity as his wiry frame fills out. He has the arsenal and the background to be an excellent starting pitcher, but the Royals are planning to use him as their primary closer in 2008.

Los Angeles Angels of Anaheim

by Sean Smith of Anaheim Angels All the Way (lanaheimangelfan.blogspot.com)

2008 Projections

Record: 89-73
Division Rank: 1st, by ten games
Runs Scored: 783
Runs Allowed: 706

2007 in a Nutshell

The Angels came into 2007 as the favorites and did not disappoint. On April 25, they were tied for first, and never trailed after that, spending 153 days in first place. While the Mariners gave the Angels a good race for most of the year, the Angels crushed their hopes with a three-game sweep in late August, and were able to coast their way through September. Their playoffs were over much too quickly, with a frustrating three-game sweep at the hands of the Red Sox.

General Comments

Team Strengths

The front line pitching was tremendous, with John Lackey and Kelvim Escobar having the best seasons of their careers and combining for 37 wins. The Angels got a lot of people on base, which led to 822 runs, fourth in the league. As usual, the Angels hit for a high average: .284. This team is not known for drawing walks, but did have five players take 50 or more, enough to push the team on-base percentage to .345, third in the league. The Angels stole 139 bases, second most in the league, and took every extra base they could.

The Angels had their typical large share of injuries in 2007, but they were saved by depth. Maicer Izturis filled in capably at second and third when Chone Figgins and Howie Kendrick were hurt. Reggie Willits filled in at all three outfield spots and surprised everyone by doing a great Brett Butler impression with a .391 OBP and 27 steals.

Team Weaknesses

First was a lack of power. The Angels ranked 12th in home runs, and only Vladimir Guerrero topped 20. From May through July, the Angels had no power at all as Guerrero went into a homer drought, hitting only seven during those three months; his power returned in August and September, with 13 homers.

The back end of the rotation was terrible. Ervin Santana struggled every time he pitched away from Anaheim, and Bartolo Colon, after a few promising early-season starts, was ineffective and/or hurt for most of the season.

The General Manager is Known for ...

He caused the downfall of the Soviet Union. Just kidding—Tony Reagins' name is close to that of our 40th president and he is clearly not afraid of deficit spending. One of his first moves was to give Torii Hunter $90 million over the next five seasons.

Reagins is a rookie general manager, replacing Bill Stoneman, who remains in the organization as a consultant, so it's too early to evaluate him. While Stoneman often seemed reluctant to make trades, Reagins got off to a quick start, trading popular shortstop Orlando Cabrera to the Chicago White Sox for Jon Garland. Then, while Hunter was rumored to be headed elsewhere, Reagins jumped in, met Hunter's agent at a Del Taco in Corona, and quickly hammered out a deal the day before Thanksgiving. The story should be good enough to get Hunter some kind of endorsement deal for Del Taco.

The Manager is Known for...

Mike Scioscia takes things one day at a time. He's a strong leader who never panics or overreacts to short-term player fluctuations. When Scot Shields had a string of bad outings, Scioscia left it to people like us, on the Internet boards and radio talk shows, to do the panicking. He stuck with his player and let him work through his struggles. Good thing, because this team once again will count on Shields as an important part of the bullpen.

Scioscia appears to be a confident leader, and players enjoy playing for him. An exception to this would be Jose Guillen, and it appears the solution to a player who doesn't like Scioscia's way is to show him the highway. Most players seem to be fine doing things Scioscia's way.

Ballpark Characteristics

Historically it has been a pitchers' park, though for 2007, baseball-reference.com shows it had a 105 park factor, favoring hitters. Last year, the Angels hit .305 at home and .263 on the road, scoring almost 100 more runs at home. That says more about the hitters and the season they had than the park. Angels pitchers were better at home, too, though not to the same extent as the hitters. The dimensions are standard, about 330 down the lines and 406 in center. The right-center field wall is an 18-foot-high scoreboard.

The Minor League System is...

The farm system now probably ranks in the bottom half of MLB clubs, but that is mostly because the system did its job and graduated an excellent group of young players to the big leagues. For years, Baseball America ranked the Angels among the top organizations in baseball, and in its 2005 Prospect Handbook ranked the Angels first, ahead of the Dodgers, Brewers, Twins and Braves.

So the Angels were judged as a top farm club three years ago. Have they produced tangible results at the major league level? Looking back on that top 30 prospect list, I find 12 players who contributed to the 2007 Western Division champs (including Jered Weaver, mentioned in the book but not ranked as he was unsigned at the time). These players accounted for 97 Win Shares in 2007.

Among the other highly ranked farm systems from three years ago, the Brewers prospects contributed 101 Win Shares (not including Ryan Braun, who had yet to be drafted), followed by the Angels and Braves (97), Dodgers (87) and Twins (64). The farm system has lived up to expectations. The Angels haven't been quite as productive as the Brewers, but they have brought plenty of good young talent to Orange County.

Favorite Team Blogs

Halos Heaven (http://www.halosheaven.com/)

6-4-2 (http://6-4-2.blogspot.com/)

Chronicles of the Lads (http://anaheimangelsblog.blogspot.com/)

Keys for 2008

Players Lost from Last Year's Team

Orlando Cabrera, pitcher Bartolo Colon.

Cabrera had a great year, hitting over .300, scoring 100 runs and winning a Gold Glove. His trade was a surprise. While I like the idea of selling high (Cabrera will be 33 and unlikely to match his 2007 season), it doesn't look so great now that the Angels were not able to trade extra pitching for an impact bat. Colon has been unable to stay healthy and pitch effectively for two years now. The Angels have better options and have to move on.

Players Acquired

Jon Garland, Torii Hunter

Garland is a solid, unspectacular pitcher; he should give the team 200 innings of a league-average ERA at the back of the rotation.

Hunter turned out to be the big catch of the 2007-08 free agent class. While the Angels signed Gary Matthews Jr. as a center fielder last season, the $50 million due him did not prevent them from getting a better one. Hunter's power will be welcome, and he

and Matthews will cover a lot of ground in the outfield. Hunter's weakness is that he's not a patient hitter. He'll fit right in on this team.

Reasons to be Optimistic

The Angels are a strong team and should have no trouble repeating in the AL West. The A's have traded their ace, Dan Haren, and while it's too early to say how much the players they received will help in the future, they are unlikely to contribute as much as Haren in 2008. The Mariners played over their heads in 2007, and it still wasn't good enough. The Rangers once again are rebuilding.

Reasons to be Pessimistic

The big hitter to help out Vlad in the middle of the order? The Angels still don't have him. The Angels targeted Miguel Cabrera in trade talks, but it did not work out. It doesn't seem like the Angels tried for the second best Miguel on the market, Tejada. Perhaps Arte Moreno didn't want another star of the Mitchell report on his team. So, the big bat behind Vlad is Hunter. He's is a fine player, but if he's your second-best hitter, you don't have a great offense.

Due for a Better Season

Ervin Santana. He's the hardest thrower on the team. His control is good, he has three quality pitches, and he gets enough strikeouts. One of these days he's going to learn to deal with his homesickness (3.14 career ERA at home, 7.14 on the road).

Santana was a good pitcher in 2005-06, is only 25, and has nothing physically wrong with him, so he's a safe bet to bounce back. If Mike Napoli and Kendrick can stay healthy, they should be ready for big seasons, Kendrick will hit for a huge average and Napoli will bring the power and walks.

Likely to Have a Worse Season

Last year, I mentioned Figgins as "likely to have a better year." He did. Now he's likely to have a worse season. Just as he wasn't really a .260 hitter in 2006, he's not really a .330 hitter either. He should hit around .290. It's hard to imagine Lackey and Escobar having better seasons, so they probably will drop off a bit, too.

Still Left to Do

Preferably, nothing. They need to avoid making mistakes: The rumor that they want Paul Konerko or the possibility that they'd go for Joe Crede raise specters ranging from harmful to pointless. This is a 90-win team for 2008. The only thing left to do is to go out and win it on the field.

Most Likely Team Outcome

Another West Division title.

Player Projections

Batters

Garret Anderson (Left Field)

PA	R	H	2B	3B	HR	RBI	SO	BB	SB	CS	BA	OBP	SLG	OPS	Fld	F$
489	59	125	28	1	14	63	70	39	1	1	.282	.338	.445	.783	C	$1

Anderson had his best season since he signed his current contract in 2004. In the second half, he hit as well as he ever has, .305/.361/.530. He even drew 26 walks in 266 at bats. For the previous 3.5 years, he was a marginal ballplayer being paid a premium salary. This likely will be his last season as an Angel; even if he plays well, the team already has large salary commitments to three outfielders.

Erick Aybar (Second Base)

PA	R	H	2B	3B	HR	RBI	SO	BB	SB	CS	BA	OBP	SLG	OPS	3 Yr	Fld	F$
474	49	112	21	5	2	35	65	20	11	7	.256	.294	.340	.634	.031	A	$1

Aybar may get more playing time than he deserves in 2008: Manager Mike Scioscia went out of his way last year to get him playing time despite a terrible bat. He was even used 26 times as a pinch hitter, an incredible amount for a league that uses the DH. Aybar hit only .237 last year but, given his minor league record and youth, he could hit .270-.290. With no power, no walks, and a tendency to get thrown out on the bases, it would be an empty batting average. If he were a stronger hitter batting right handed, he would make the perfect platoon complement to Izturis.

Chone Figgins (Third Base)

PA	R	H	2B	3B	HR	RBI	SO	BB	SB	CS	BA	OBP	SLG	OPS	3 Yr	Fld	F$
534	75	136	23	6	5	46	79	52	38	11	.288	.356	.394	.750	-.034	C	$18

He totaled 17 homers in 2005-2006, and only three last year, By avoiding the uppercut, he hit line drives 26 percent of the time, and ground balls 47 percent. It was worth the tradeoff, but don't expect to see it again. For 2008, expect something closer to his normal line, .290 with about eight homers.

Vladimir Guerrero (Right Field)

PA	R	H	2B	3B	HR	RBI	SO	BB	SB	CS	BA	OBP	SLG	OPS	3 Yr	Fld	F$
609	90	165	35	1	27	98	64	71	7	4	.315	.398	.539	.937	-.042	D	$28

He's aggressive—at the plate, in the field, on the bases. Sometimes he's aggressive to a fault, but you can't criticize the whole package. He plays the game with pure joy, and may have the biggest smile in baseball. Guerrero may not be the absolute best player in baseball, but he's certainly in a top-20 discussion and I can't think of any player I'd rather watch on the field.

Torii Hunter (Center Field)

PA	R	H	2B	3B	HR	RBI	SO	BB	SB	CS	BA	OBP	SLG	OPS	3 Yr	Fld	F$
571	80	144	31	1	24	86	90	50	16	6	.283	.349	.489	.838	-.030	C	$20

Hunter spent last season telling every journalist from New York to New Zealand that he would love to play in their hometown in 2008, and Bill Plaschke in Los Angeles ended up the lucky winner. Hunter still struggles with plate discipline and has yet to adjust his routes to admit that he does not cover the same range as he did in 2002. In his final Metrodome plate appearance, he walked to the plate to a standing ovation. Ozzie Guillen promptly ordered his intentional walk and a camera angle showed him laughing in the dugout as he ruined the moment.

Maicer Izturis (Shortstop)

PA	R	H	2B	3B	HR	RBI	SO	BB	SB	CS	BA	OBP	SLG	OPS	3 Yr	Fld	F$
387	48	97	18	3	5	37	40	34	10	3	.282	.345	.395	.740	-.008	B	$1

He's probably going to get most of the time at shortstop this year. As a hitter, he's probably a slight upgrade over Cabrera, at least against right handers. Izturis, a switch hitter, has not hit lefties at all. As a defender, it's hard to tell because Cabrera rarely missed games during his three years as an Angel.

Howie Kendrick (Second Base)

PA	R	H	2B	3B	HR	RBI	SO	BB	SB	CS	BA	OBP	SLG	OPS	3 Yr	Fld	F$
434	55	123	28	4	10	55	70	14	5	3	.302	.333	.464	.797	.028	B	$5

The AK-47 is considered by many to be the finest assault rifle ever produced due to its durability and ease of use. While the HK-47 sprayed base hits at a fully automatic rate, he was able to play only 88 games due to hand and wrist injuries. We don't know if Howie was just unlucky last year, or if he's one of those injury-prone players. Kendrick played solid defense, and, if healthy, should develop 15-20 home run power.

Casey Kotchman (First Base)

PA	R	H	2B	3B	HR	RBI	SO	BB	SB	CS	BA	OBP	SLG	OPS	3 Yr	Fld	F$
425	52	105	25	2	10	50	47	42	2	3	.281	.355	.440	.795	.036	A	$1

Kotchman was worth the wait. His first full season would have fit right in the prime of Mark Grace or Wally Joyner's career. While he didn't hit a lot of home runs, his slugging percentage was more than acceptable at .467 thanks to 37 doubles. His defense was Gold Glove quality. He didn't play much against lefties. He's shown little platoon split as far as batting and on base averages, though all his power has come against right handers.

Jeff Mathis (Catcher)

PA	R	H	2B	3B	HR	RBI	SO	BB	SB	CS	BA	OBP	SLG	OPS	3 Yr	Fld	F$
465	51	102	27	2	9	48	93	30	7	1	.242	.292	.379	.671	.029	C	$1

Mathis has gone backwards as a hitter. In 2005, he hit 21 homers with a .499 slugging percentage in Triple-A. Even in an extreme hitting environment, that's pretty good for a 22-year-old catcher. He hit only .244 there last year, with little power, and his major league numbers, .211 with a 64 OPS+, are about what you'd expect from such poor Triple-A numbers. Toward the end of the season, the Angels gave Mathis and Napoli equal time. I hope that trend will not continue—Mathis should be no more than the backup.

Gary Matthews Jr. (Left Field?)

PA	R	H	2B	3B	HR	RBI	SO	BB	SB	CS	BA	OBP	SLG	OPS	3 Yr	Fld	F$
558	72	134	29	3	15	67	93	57	12	4	.272	.346	.434	.780	-.037	C	$9

Matthews can go from the best center fielder in baseball to the worst in the span of just one play. In the first game of the season, he crashed against the wall to end the first inning and save a run. In the third. he dropped an easy fly ball with two out. John Lackey then loaded the bases, and Matthews made a spectacular diving catch on a Hank Blalock liner to end the inning. He'll play a corner in 2008, and if healthy should be well above average there, at least on defense.

Kendry Morales (First Base)

PA	R	H	2B	3B	HR	RBI	SO	BB	SB	CS	BA	OBP	SLG	OPS	3 Yr	Fld	F$
431	49	110	23	1	12	54	65	23	0	2	.276	.318	.429	.747	.026	A	$1

He's got some ability, but his power has been inconsistent (only five homers in 64 games at Salt Lake City) and he doesn't walk much. Unless he shows rapid improvement, it's hard to see a starting spot for him on the Angels. His playing abilities are very similar to Robb Quinlan, which is not good news for the original Quinlan, especially since Morales adds the benefit of being a switch hitter.

Mike Napoli (Catcher)

PA	R	H	2B	3B	HR	RBI	SO	BB	SB	CS	BA	OBP	SLG	OPS	3 Yr	Fld	F$
365	49	73	16	1	16	50	90	48	5	2	.239	.349	.454	.803	.006	C	$1

Napoli is different from the typical Angels hitter, a power and walks guy. Last year, the question on whether he would stick centered on his batting average. Hitting .240 as a catcher, Napoli is a tremendously valuable offensive player, but could he?

Napoli answered those concerns by hitting .247 and cutting his strikeout rate from 34 percent to 29 percent. Unfortunately, two new questions surfaced: Is he durable enough? Will his defense be acceptable? Napoli played only 75 games last year and threw out only 21 percent of basestealers. In 588 plate appearances over two years, Napoli has 26 homers and 84 walks, so the Angels will be best off if he can catch 120-130 games.

Robb Quinlan (First Base)

PA	R	H	2B	3B	HR	RBI	SO	BB	SB	CS	BA	OBP	SLG	OPS	3 Yr	Fld	F$
277	32	71	15	1	7	34	40	16	2	2	.278	.322	.426	.748	-.038	C	$1

One more reason that signing Shea Hillenbrand was foolish last year: Quinlan gives you the same skills without the price tag or the delusion that he's some kind of All-Star.

Quinlan's career totals seem to do a reasonable job of expressing his ability: a .290 hitter with moderate power. He's a useful bench guy, a good bat against lefties and capable of handling four positions without embarrassing himself, but he may be traded or released due to the Angels' roster crunch.

Juan Rivera (Right Field)

PA	R	H	2B	3B	HR	RBI	SO	BB	SB	CS	BA	OBP	SLG	OPS	3 Yr	Fld	F$
272	34	71	15	1	10	39	37	19	1	2	.286	.339	.476	.815	-.032	C	$1

After returning from a broken leg, Rivera had almost no mobility; anything hit on the ground was pretty much an automatic double play (five in only 14 games). The Torii Hunter signing puts him out of a job; he may have had a shot at DH duties otherwise. Rivera probably won't be with the Angels this year unless they carry six outfielders. Reggie Willits is cheaper. He's a fine right-handed slugger as long as a team is willing to give him regular time—he doesn't seem to hit to his potential when used erratically.

Reggie Willits (Left Field)

PA	R	H	2B	3B	HR	RBI	SO	BB	SB	CS	BA	OBP	SLG	OPS	3 Yr	Fld	F$
486	57	112	19	3	0	32	75	58	16	6	.272	.363	.332	.695	-.001	C	$1

What a pleasant surprise he was. He looks kind of like David Eckstein, and despite being no power threat whatsoever drew a ton of walks. His on-base percentage was .391, and once on he stole 27 bases in 35 chances. The bad news is that his strikeout percentage was almost 20 percent.

It's unlikely he can sustain a .290 average without making more contact. And to make more contact, he'll have to swing earlier in the count than he does. Willits will have to make a choice—he can keep a super high walk rate and hit .260, or he can hit .290 by taking fewer pitches. As a defender, he was outstanding in left but looked shaky in center or right. With Torii Hunter's signing. Willits probably will have a vastly reduced role in 2008.

Brandon Wood (Shortstop/Third Base)

PA	R	H	2B	3B	HR	RBI	SO	BB	SB	CS	BA	OBP	SLG	OPS	3 Yr	Fld	F$
533	68	123	31	3	24	80	136	37	6	1	.254	.308	.478	.786	.071	C	$1

He hasn't progressed since hitting more than 40 home runs in the California League as a 20-year-old. While he has power, at this point he's well below average as a major league hitter. He did cut his strikeout rate from 33 percent to 28 percent while moving up a level, but his batting, on-base, and slugging percentages all fell. With the trade of Cabrera, he might be the solution at shortstop, but he will likely head back to Salt Lake City to start the 2008 season.

Pitchers

Chris Bootcheck (Relief Pitcher)

W	L	ERA	TBF	IP	Hit	HR	SO	BB	HBP	3 Yr	F$
3	5	5.60	334	73	85	9	46	35	4	0.66	$1

In 2006, he pitched at Triple-A, mostly in relief, and posted a 6.68 ERA. The former first-round draft pick didn't appear to have much of a future, but he earned a spot in the Angels bullpen and pitched somewhat effectively. His FIP ERA was 4.12, much better than his actual ERA of 4.77. He struck out more than two for every walk and threw in the mid 90s, so he could turn out to be an important part of the bullpen for the next few years.

Bartolo Colon (Starting Pitcher)

W	L	ERA	TBF	IP	Hit	HR	SO	BB	HBP	3 Yr	F$
8	7	4.19	559	134	136	17	86	33	5	0.41	$1

The Angels signed him for four expensive seasons and received only a season and a half of great pitching. The effort was never lacking. At times last year, Colon looked as good as in his Cy Young 2005. In his second start of the season, he struck out 11 Devil Rays in seven innings, regularly throwing in the high 90s. He won his first five decisions, but the more he pitched, the more he seemed to be pitching in pain. For 2008, he probably would be best off on a team that can give him long rests as often as possible.

Kelvim Escobar (Starting Pitcher)

W	L	ERA	TBF	IP	Hit	HR	SO	BB	HBP	3 Yr	F$
11	8	3.78	729	174	165	15	143	57	4	0.37	$12

Escobar had a breakout year, jumping to an 18-7 record from 11-14. Well, no, actually it might not have been a breakout year. Escobar pitched slightly better in 2007, but his run support jumped from 3.78 per game to 6.30. Escobar still has a great fastball, and mixes it with a nasty splitter. He's not quite the horse that Lackey is, making 30 starts each of the last two years and missing a few months in 2005. His elbow will always be a concern.

Jon Garland (Starting Pitcher)

W	L	ERA	TBF	IP	Hit	HR	SO	BB	HBP	3 Yr	F$
11	10	4.11	798	189	199	18	96	50	5	0.39	$6

For the second year in a row, Garland was your typical No. 3 starter, logging 200 innings while posting an ERA in the low to mid-fours. This, however, may have been a bit of an aberration. Garland's strikeout rate continues to drop to dangerously low levels and, more importantly, he's getting the ball more up in the zone: His groundball rate declined for the second year in a row. Interestingly, Garland posted the lowest home run rate of his career, but his sinker isn't sinking as much as it used to and that should draw a few red flags.

John Lackey (Starting Pitcher)

W	L	ERA	TBF	IP	Hit	HR	SO	BB	HBP	3 Yr	F$
13	9	3.70	822	196	188	16	164	59	7	0.47	$17

In 2007, Lackey put it all together. Since 2005, he has been one of the better pitchers in baseball, but last year he was just a little bit better and more consistent. He won 19 games, beating his previous best of 14. His run support, 4.49 per game, was actually a bit less than he received in 2005 or 2006. He entered his final start trailing Fausto Carmona in ERA, and was neck and neck with that day's opponent, Haren. He came through with seven shutout innings in a 2-0 Angels victory and won the ERA title, the first Angel to do so since Frank Tanana 30 years ago.

Dustin Moseley (Starting/Relief Pitcher)

W	L	ERA	TBF	IP	Hit	HR	SO	BB	HBP	3 Yr	F$
4	6	5.12	407	91	105	11	52	36	4	0.06	$1

Moseley doesn't throw especially hard, but gets a good number of ground balls (48 percent last year) and doesn't walk many. He pitched well both as a starter and reliever. He'll probably be in long relief in 2008. If the Angels trade one of their starters, Moseley would be the swingman/emergency starter.

Darren Oliver (Relief Pitcher)

W	L	ERA	TBF	IP	Hit	HR	SO	BB	HBP	F$
4	3	4.46	284	66	69	8	46	24	2	$1

He's listed as the only left hander in the Angel bullpen, but that's not quite accurate. He's a right-handed pitcher who just happens to throw with his left hand. Oliver allowed a .553 OPS against right-handed hitters, but was hit hard (.810) by lefties. Oliver got off to a slow start as the Angels tried to use him in a LOOGY role, but as the season went on he was used for longer outings against all kinds of batters, and was perhaps the team's most reliable reliever in the second half.

Francisco Rodriguez (Relief Pitcher)

W	L	ERA	TBF	IP	Hit	HR	SO	BB	HBP	3 Yr	F$
5	3	3.09	292	71	54	5	86	30	2	0.15	$16

K-Rod heads into his final season before free agency. Obviously, he's an outstanding pitcher, striking out 12 per nine innings, but a K-Rod save is no sure thing. He'll put his fair share of baserunners on, throw a few wild pitches, and make us sweat a bit. Then, with the tying run in scoring position and a big slugger up, he'll get strike three and point to the sky.

Ervin Santana (Starting Pitcher)

W	L	ERA	TBF	IP	Hit	HR	SO	BB	HBP	3 Yr	F$
9	10	4.79	751	173	179	23	133	62	8	-0.08	$1

Santana easily has the best arm on the team, with a fastball that can reach 97, 98 mph at times out of the bullpen. He'll usually top out at 95-96 as a starter. His troubles on the road continued: a 3.27 ERA at home and 8.38 on the road. At this point, he probably doesn't have a starting job due to the trade for Garland. He might become an outstanding reliever, with a fastball good enough to close, but he certainly has the talent to rebound and be a successful starter.

Joe Saunders (Starting Pitcher)

W	L	ERA	TBF	IP	Hit	HR	SO	BB	HBP	3 Yr	F$
10	10	4.60	764	176	187	21	114	65	5	0.09	$1

Over the last three years, Saunders has accumulated a full season's workload in the majors—33 starts and 187 innings. He was pitching well until September, when he seemed to run out of gas: His ERA was 6.83 and he gave up six homers in 27 innings. Saunders is the only lefty starter on the team, so he'll be very important against teams, like the A's, with predominantly left-handed hitting.

Scot Shields (Relief Pitcher)

W	L	ERA	TBF	IP	Hit	HR	SO	BB	HBP	3 Yr	F$
5	3	3.54	317	76	67	6	74	29	3	0.32	$5

Shields had a terrible second half last year, with a 7.36 ERA after a 1.70 first half. It was mostly due to an awful August. In September, the ERA still looked bad, but he struck out 17 in 11 innings. The Angels need to trust other relievers and avoid overworking Shields to keep him fresh for the whole season.

Justin Speier (Relief Pitcher)

W	L	ERA	TBF	IP	Hit	HR	SO	BB	HBP	3 Yr	F$
4	2	3.84	243	58	53	7	52	19	2	0.37	$1

Despite missing 2.5 months to illness, Speier was everything the Angels could have expected after signing him to a four-year deal. He has excellent control, is tough to hit, and has shown a very small platoon split, especially important for a bullpen without a typical lefty. Speier gets the job done without exceptional velocity; his fastball is mostly in the high 80s. He has a very good slider and some deception in his delivery.

Jered Weaver (Starting Pitcher)

W	L	ERA	TBF	IP	Hit	HR	SO	BB	HBP	3 Yr	F$
9	9	4.28	674	159	161	20	126	47	5	-0.08	$6

I'm not sure if Weaver was ever completely healthy in 2007. He began the season on the disabled list with biceps and shoulder issues. When he came back, his stuff was unimpressive: He was pitching mostly in the upper 80s instead of the low 90s of 2006. He seemed to lack the stuff to put away batters, yet he managed an ERA of 3.91, 17 percent better than league average, and struck out 6.4 per nine innings.

If he's 100 percent physically in 2008, he's still probably not as good as he looked in 2006, but should be one of the top 10 pitchers in the league.

Los Angeles Dodgers

by Aaron Sapiro of Rockin' the Ravine (mvn.com/mlb-dodgers)

2008 Projections

Record: 82-80
Division Rank: 4th, 4 games back
Runs Scored: 764
Runs Allowed: 764

2007 in a Nutshell

A team with World Series potential managed to finish fourth in its division. There was a very obvious identity crisis last year under former manager Grady Little, and a team that wasn't supposed to score many runs stayed true to its billing, as management flip-flopped on whether to go with the vets or embrace the popular LA youth movement.

There was turmoil in the locker room, and the Dodgers completely faded down the stretch. After .500 or better records in the first four months of the season, the Dodgers went 25-32 in the last two months and watched their playoff hopes crumble as everyone pointed fingers.

Injuries to the pitching staff didn't help; $15 million man Jason Schmidt was lost for the season early, as were Randy Wolf, Yhency Brazoban, Hong-Chih Kuo and Chin-Hui Tsao. For Dodgers fans, an overall 82-80 record doesn't begin to explain the disappointment of watching division foes Arizona and Colorado compete for a chance to get swept in the World Series.

General Comments

Team Strengths

It's pretty hard to ignore the back of the bullpen. Led by National League ERA leader Takashi Saito (1.40), the Dodgers' biggest struggle was finding starters who could get the ball to their back four.

Saito is the closer, with 39 saves last season, but everyone knows all about 23-year-old, 290-pound, Jonathan Broxton, who had 99 strikeouts to go along with only 25 walks. Getting the ball to Brox and Takashi is reliable left-hander Joe Beimel, who had a 3.88 ERA and gave up only one home run last season. On the other side, workhorse right-hander Scott Proctor, acquired from the Yankees for Wilson Betemit last year, has thrown in 83 games in both of the past two seasons.

Look for yet another return of The Artist formerly known as Yhency Brazoban, a Jim Tracy staple. "Brazo" has thrown a total of only 6.2 innings over the last two seasons because of recurring elbow trouble.

Team Weaknesses

The Dodgers finished second to last in NL homers last season, just in front of the Washington Nationals, with 129. Jeff Kent, at 39, led the team with 20. Sure, the Dodgers got Andruw Jones, and that helps tremendously, but he hit only 26 last season, certainly an off year by his standards. Matt Kemp, James Loney and Andre Ethier are all a year older and stronger, but if the Dodgers want to scare anyone, they need to start hitting some balls over the fence.

The team's biggest problem has been finding that ever-elusive extra base hit. The team was last in the NL with a .395 slugging average with runners in scoring position, and dead last in the majors with a .327 SLG with RISP and two out.

The General Manager is Known for...

He loves the kids.

As he enters his third year as the Dodgers general manager, many organizations have thrown tons of big names across Ned Colletti's desk hoping he might budge. He hasn't.

Miguel Cabrera, Johan Santana, Miguel Tejada— the Dodgers thought about making a move for all, but in the end Colletti refused to part with any of the young kids he feels will make a difference right now and in the future.

Kemp, Loney, Chad Billingsley, Broxton, LaRoche, Jonathan Meloan and Clayton Kershaw. If any of these guys end up making a huge impact in the future of the game, it's going to be in a Dodgers uniform, and it's going to be for no other reason than the stubbornness of Ned Colletti.

The Manager is Known for...

Take your pick: Twelve postseason appearances in 12 years, 10 AL East titles, six American League pennants, four World Series titles including three in a row, two Manager of The Year awards. He's Joe Torre.

Those who know him say his best attribute is the way he can manage personalities and keep an entire team in check. It was all pretty obvious in New York, and I can't think of a team that is more in need of an ego check than the Dodgers, after the charade they put on at the end of last season.

At his news conference in Dodger Stadium just after he was announced as the new manager, he made a point to make sure that every member of the media knew to address him as "Joe," rather than "Mr. Torre."

That's fine by me, Joe.

Ballpark Characteristics

Though it's probably the most beautiful and scenic park in baseball, there really isn't anything special about the field after the Dodgers moved the seats forward for field boxes, and the infamous acres of foul room were cut to almost nothing. For only $35 a person, sit with everyone you know and enjoy All-You-Can-Eat in the right field pavilion.

Dodger Stadium has 56,000 seats, and from the top of the park, the views of downtown LA, the Elysian Hills, and the San Gabriel mountains make the atmosphere at Chavez Ravine unmatched by any other ballpark in the country.

Also used as a major concert venue, Dodger Stadium has played host to the likes of the Beatles, the Rolling Stones, Elton John, Michael Jackson, Bruce Springsteen, Dave Matthews Band, and many more

The Minor League System is...

It's an interesting question for the Dodgers organization as a whole. It was long considered one of the best farm systems in baseball, but Dodgers prospects have now turned into Dodgers starters. That being said, there is still a lot to look forward to, especially on the mound, with 19-year-old Kershaw rated the top left-handed prospect in baseball. Kershaw had a 2.29 ERA in 122 innings in 2007 between Single-A and Double-A, while collecting 163 strikeouts and giving up only nine homers.

Reliever Meloan spent some time in the bigs at the end of 2007, striking out seven in seven innings. He excelled in both Double-A and Triple-A, boasting an ERA of 2.03 and notching 20 saves, a 7-2 record and 91 strikeouts in over 66 innings.

In the field, Delwyn Young swings a hot stick, although he struggles defensively. Tony Abreu and All-Star Futures Game MVP Chin-Lung Hu seem to be the future major league middle infield. All three hit over .325 in the minors. Young led the three with a SLG of .571 and 97 RBIs.

Favorite Team Blogs

MVN.com (http://mvn.com/mlb-dodgers/)

Dodger Thoughts (http://dodgerthoughts.baseball-toaster.com/)

Dodger Dugout (http://www.dodgerdugout.com/)

The 6-4-2 Double Play Guys (http://6-2-4.blogspot.com/)

Sons of Steve Garvey (http://www.sonsofstevegarvey.com/)

Blue Heaven (http://dodgersblueheaven.blogspot.com/)

Dem Bums (http://www.la-dodgersblog.com/)

Dodger Junkie (http://blog.dodgerjunkie.com/)

The Trolley Dodger (http://www.trolleydodger.com/)

Keys for 2008

Players Lost from Last Year's Team

I don't know if I would consider Luis Gonzalez a "key" loss, but he won't be a Dodger any longer. The team didn't lose any extremely valuable assets or any longtime Dodgers. Ramon Martinez is gone after two years. Mike Lieberthal got a career-low 77 at-bats last year; he's gone.

Wolf pitched only about half a year for the Dodgers, and David Wells pitched even less; they'll both be somewhere else this year. Rudy Seanez and Roberto Hernandez may no longer have jobs in the bullpen.

For Dodgers fans, the two losses that will be most noticeable are 6-foot-11 lefty Mark Hendrickson, and fan favorite Olmedo Saenz, although he hit only .191 last season. Hendrickson wasn't insanely effective by any means, but he pitched more innings last year than anyone not named Penny, Lowe or Billingsley. Plus, if things went wrong, he was always a fun scapegoat.

Players Acquired

Andruw Jones. Hiroki Kuroda. Joe Torre.

Yes, I know Torre is the manager and doesn't actually play anymore, but can you think of a bigger off-season acquisition than the move the Dodgers made to snag Joe Torre?

That all looks pretty good. Jones, arguably the best defensive center fielder of this decade, will be in Dodger Blue. He had a rough year in 2007, hitting .222, but his 26 home runs and 94 RBIs would both have been tops on the Dodgers. He's a superstar, and Los Angeles loves that. Look for Jones to bounce back from a rough year, especially because he's signed to only a two-year deal, and he'll be looking for an even bigger one when he's done with that. He won't be back.

Japanese import Kuroda was signed in hopes he'll be solid in the starting rotation. Esteban Loaiza, acquired late in the season last year, will be given a chance to compete for the fifth starter's spot. The Mitchell report's own Gary Bennett was signed as the backup catcher.

Reasons to be Optimistic

Russell Martin. He's absolutely the cornerstone of the Dodgers franchise; this is Russell Martin's team. He works his butt off every time he steps on the field, he makes the right decisions, manages the pitching staff and is still coachable and learning. Last year, in his first full MLB season, he was the NL's starting catcher at the All-Star game, won the Gold Glove for best defensive catcher, and locked up the Silver Slugger as the best offensive catcher in the NL just for fun.

Reasons to be Pessimistic

The NL West is going to be unbelievable again. After all the talk two years ago that it might be the worst division in the history of baseball, it might be the best this year. The Dodgers have made some serious moves after finishing fourth. The Rockies went to the World Series with probably the best offensive bunch in the National League. The Diamondbacks are super-young, getting more talented, and probably have the best pitching staff in the NL. If they don't, the Padres certainly do, behind Cy Young winner and Dodger-killer Jake Peavy. The Giants spent another offseason overspending, hoping to compete.

The biggest problem inside the Dodgers clubhouse is the outfield. Ethier, Kemp, Jones and Juan Pierre are all guys who deserve to start in this league. Why is that a problem? One of them won't be starting, and one of them isn't going to be happy about it. It's not going to be Jones riding the bench, so look for Torre to try to find a way to manage the three other egos at once. He doesn't have a DH this time around.

Due for a Better Season

Rafael Furcal is heading into the final year of his three-year deal, and you have to believe that he doesn't want this to be his last season in LA. After injuring his ankle in spring training, Furcal was never himself the entire year.

Counting from his breakout year in 2003 (five seasons ago), Furcal in 2007 had lows in games played, runs, hits, doubles, triples, home runs, RBIs, walks, stolen bases, batting average, slugging percentage, on-base percentage and double plays turned. Go ahead and read that back again. If you think a player of Rafael Furcal's caliber is going to have a season like that again, you're crazy.

Likely to Have a Worse Season

If I had to pick someone, I would say Jeff Kent. Not that his numbers from last year jumped out of the page at you or anything, but he did manage to lead eligible Dodgers in batting average at .302, home runs with 20 and SLG with .500.

He had 79 RBIs, so it isn't like his numbers (other than his batting average) are going to drop drastically. It's just that with the addition of Jones, and the continuing growth of Kemp, Loney and Martin, the Dodgers aren't going to be asking as much from Kent. His days as the cleanup hitter and most feared bat in the lineup are over, he's going to be turning 40, and he's probably going to share some time at the two-bag with Tony Abreu. He got tired at the end of last season; it could happen again, and possibly earlier this time around.

Still Left to Do

There's still no answer at third base, after eight different guys played there last year. Nomar Garciaparra's health doesn't exactly give you the highest amount of confidence, and LaRoche has only 93 major league at-bats.

Brad Penny is a beast, Derek Lowe is either the most underrated or underachieving pitcher in the league, Billingsley is easily the most talented pitcher on the staff, and Kuroda could be solid or get Kei Igawa'd. Even if all goes well, that's still only four starters. Schmidt and Loaiza might bounce back from injuries—doubtful—or the team could go with some combination of D.J. Houlton, Eric Stults and Eric Hull to fill that fifth starter's spot.

Most Likely Team Outcome

This is an organization that brought in Joe Torre for only three years, and overpaid for Andruw Jones for only two. The talent level of this team is certainly comparable to, if not better than, the cream of the National League.

Frank McCourt and Co. are trying to win a World Championship right now, and they aren't going to be happy with anything less. The fans of LA are getting restless; the Dodgers have won only one playoff game since the '88 title. I don't know where exactly the Dodgers are going to end up, but I'd say anything short of a Word Series appearance would be a letdown.

Player Projections

Batters

Tony Abreu (Shortstop)

PA	R	H	2B	3B	HR	RBI	SO	BB	SB	CS	BA	OBP	SLG	OPS	3 Yr	Fld	F$
533	62	142	35	4	5	53	75	27	4	1	.288	.331	.406	.737	.052	C	$1

Twenty-three year old and a Jack-of-all-trades, Abreu started games at second, short and third. He proved that he can be more than adequate, and there are rumblings through Dodger World that he should be getting more time at second over Kent and hitting second in the lineup instead of Juan Pierre. He's consistently been an effective bunter. If he isn't handed the second-base job, he'll be useful off the bench, especially for a team that probably will start two injury-prone vets in its infield.

Andre Ethier (Right Field)

PA	R	H	2B	3B	HR	RBI	SO	BB	SB	CS	BA	OBP	SLG	OPS	3 Yr	Fld	F$
506	63	128	26	4	13	60	79	46	1	3	.286	.356	.449	.805	.016	C	$1

He's been the most consistent of the Dodgers prospects. He knows how to hit the ball to the other field. He's fantastic defensively; he'll probably be best suited as a right fielder later on in his career thanks to his fine arm. He might be the odd man out after the acquisition of Andruw Jones, but it isn't because he hasn't proven anything. In the games he starts, look for him to provide some pop from the back of the lineup.

Rafael Furcal (Shortstop)

PA	R	H	2B	3B	HR	RBI	SO	BB	SB	CS	BA	OBP	SLG	OPS	3 Yr	Fld	F$
606	77	152	26	5	7	55	72	52	26	7	.281	.342	.386	.728	-.030	C	$13

In his two years as a Dodger, he's had a tendency to show up to spring training overweight and out of shape, the most likely cause of both injuries that ended up lingering all year. He's playing winter ball in the Dominican this offseason, and it might be the best thing he can do for himself. If he finds his inner Rafael Furcal, and shows up to spring training healthy and ready to play, this could be a big return to glory season for the shortstop.

Nomar Garciaparra (First/Third Base)

PA	R	H	2B	3B	HR	RBI	SO	BB	SB	CS	BA	OBP	SLG	OPS	3 Yr	Fld	F$
454	52	115	22	1	10	52	43	34	2	1	.280	.335	.411	.746	-.050	C	$1

Every year that he's been healthy, he's put up terrific numbers. People want to pretend that he was healthy in 2006, but injured all year in 2007. Truth is, he played in 122 games in '06, and 121 games in '07. He hit .303 with 93 RBIs and 20 homers in his first year as a Dodger, and the city embraced him. He came back in his second year and managed a .283 average, seven homers, 59 RBI, and a career-low .371 SLG.

Andruw Jones (Center Field)

PA	R	H	2B	3B	HR	RBI	SO	BB	SB	CS	BA	OBP	SLG	OPS	3 Yr	Fld	F$
603	80	132	26	1	32	95	118	65	3	2	.253	.342	.491	.833	-.034	A	$14

Coming into a contract year and having hit 92 home runs in the previous two seasons, most expected Jones to put up more stellar numbers before waltzing off into the Georgia sunset with Scott Boras and his newly minted bank vault. But Jones was terrible for Atlanta in 2007. He swung for the fences every at-bat. He had no rhythm, was often getting ahead of the ball, wasn't working the count properly. If you watched him day in, day out, it was no surprise that he could muster only a .222/.311/.413 batting line.

Beneath the statistical veneer, Jones was actually unlucky. Although he has taken a step back, it isn't as large as the numbers suggest. Very rarely does a potential Hall-of-Fame hitter become a bad player overnight, and his projected line looks a little light, even though he'll be playing in the generous confines of Dodger Stadium. Even if he does suffer, he's still a legend with the glove and is worth at least a win in the field. He'll be back to par soon enough.

Matt Kemp (Left Field)

PA	R	H	2B	3B	HR	RBI	SO	BB	SB	CS	BA	OBP	SLG	OPS	3 Yr	Fld	F$
551	76	155	32	5	18	77	108	30	11	3	.304	.345	.493	.838	.054	C	$18

Matt Kemp has every single tool available to him on lockdown. There's a reason the Dodgers wouldn't trade him and Clay Kershaw to Minnesota for Johan Santana. He hits the ball as hard as Gary Sheffield or Vlad Guerrero, and he runs the bases like a young Ken Griffey Jr. However, he cannot hit a curveball to save his life, and teams started to realize that after a while.

Jeff Kent (Second Base)

PA	R	H	2B	3B	HR	RBI	SO	BB	SB	CS	BA	OBP	SLG	OPS	Fld	F$
522	68	129	30	1	17	70	69	58	2	2	.286	.370	.470	.840	F	$9

This could be the last lap for one of the greatest offensive second basemen ever. He led the team offensively last year, but he also ignited the spark that caused the rift between the vets and the kids late in the season. He's had problems catching up to the fastball in his older years (especially the high ones), but if you make a mistake and hang a curveball, you'd better watch out. If, at 40, he can play 136 games again, he can probably still be effective. The question is the same though, for him and Nomar: Can they last another full season?

Andy LaRoche (Third Base)

PA	R	H	2B	3B	HR	RBI	SO	BB	SB	CS	BA	OBP	SLG	OPS	3 Yr	Fld	F$
457	59	108	22	1	18	64	76	50	3	2	.271	.355	.467	.822	.018	C	$3

Even though Nomar is going to get the first look at third base, LaRoche is the main reason the Dodgers settled on the Andruw Jones contract, and didn't look to trade for or sign an established third baseman. LaRoche's minor league numbers are off the charts, but during his two brief major league stints, he showed a bad-ball tendency and looked nervous at the plate.

James Loney (First Base)

PA	R	H	2B	3B	HR	RBI	SO	BB	SB	CS	BA	OBP	SLG	OPS	3 Yr	Fld	F$
586	72	154	34	4	13	69	90	49	2	2	.292	.350	.445	.795	.054	B	$1

For the first time in his three spring camps, he knows he will be the starting first baseman. He struggles to hit for power, but he has a knack for coming up big in pressure situations. His glove at first base might be the most special part about him: At 23, the kid can pick it.

Russell Martin (Catcher)

PA	R	H	2B	3B	HR	RBI	SO	BB	SB	CS	BA	OBP	SLG	OPS	3 Yr	Fld	F$
551	73	136	28	2	12	62	77	58	15	6	.283	.363	.424	.787	.022	B	$7

Last year, he led all NL catchers in games, at-bats, runs, hits, home runs, total bases, stolen bases, batting average, slugging percentage and on-base percentage. His homers and stolen bases are projected to drop, but with 19 home runs and 21 steals last year, you have to believe he has a shot to become the first 20-20 Dodger since Shawn Green in 2001.

Juan Pierre (Left Field)

PA	R	H	2B	3B	HR	RBI	SO	BB	SB	CS	BA	OBP	SLG	OPS	3 Yr	Fld	F$
648	85	172	24	8	2	49	43	28	48	13	.290	.326	.368	.694	-.036	B	$23

Poor, poor Juan Pierre. Between the 2006 and 2007 seasons, the Dodgers knew they needed a big power bat. They didn't get one, panicked and signed Pierre to a huge five-year deal. He played up to expectations last year, leading the team in at-bats, runs, hits, triples and, obviously, stolen bases, while playing in all 162 games.

The thing is, everyone hates him now. No one wants to stunt the growth of Ethier or Kemp. Pierre turned into the odd man out in this giant wheel-of-popularity contest. His deal has four more years, but people don't think the Dodgers can keep the other two until the Jones deal is done. Until then, Pierre's going to want to play all 162 games again, even after being asked to move to left for the new guy. Get ready.

Pitchers

Joe Beimel (Relief Pitcher)

W	L	ERA	TBF	IP	Hit	HR	SO	BB	HBP	3 Yr	F$
4	3	4.10	290	67	68	6	37	28	2	0.29	$1

The best situation for Beimel is a runner on first. He has the best pickoff move on the squad, and if he isn't pickin' fools off at first, chances are he's getting a comebacker and turning it around for a double play. This team stands a much better shot at winning if Beimel doesn't have to do much more than get lefties out—he's been holding them to a .188 average.

Chad Billingsley (Starting Pitcher)

W	L	ERA	TBF	IP	Hit	HR	SO	BB	HBP	3 Yr	F$
8	7	3.79	568	133	115	14	116	64	5	-0.16	$5

One of the most talented pitchers to put on a Dodgers uniform in the last two decades, Bills is only 23 years old and has four pitches he can throw for a strike. The key for him is going to be keeping his nasty curveball down in the zone, and improving upon the 15 homers he gave up last year. He went through a stretch when he was absolutely unhittable. He had 141 strikeouts in 147 innings.

Jonathan Broxton (Relief Pitcher)

W	L	ERA	TBF	IP	Hit	HR	SO	BB	HBP	3 Yr	F$
6	3	3.05	325	79	61	7	88	32	2	0.01	$8

Big Jon Broxton—290 pounds, 23 years old, future closer, future All-Star. What he lacks in personality he makes up for in velocity. Jon Broxton is human; he can't throw every day. Last year he was in 83 games and pitched 82 innings. He's an incredible setup man, but there is a reason that he broke down at the end of the last two seasons.

Eric Hull (Relief Pitcher)

W	L	ERA	TBF	IP	Hit	HR	SO	BB	HBP	3 Yr	F$
4	3	4.39	297	67	61	7	68	38	4	0.37	$1

Hull came out of nowhere to make five appearances in relief, all in games that were blown apart by three runs or more. He did show good stuff, major league poise, and a swooping change in his first big league innings at 27 years old.

Hong-Chih Kuo (Starting Pitcher)

W	L	ERA	TBF	IP	Hit	HR	SO	BB	HBP	3 Yr	F$
5	5	4.00	382	89	78	10	91	43	4	0.14	$1

He's had two Tommy John surgeries in three years, and has a career 5.38 ERA and a 2-10 record. There is still something about Hong-Chih Kuo, though. He doesn't freak under pressure, and he made only his sixth career start in the 2006 playoffs, on the road, against the Mets. The Dodgers had him slated in as the fifth starter leaving spring training last year, but he broke down and went into surgery again.

Hiroki Kuroda (Starting Pitcher)

W	L	ERA	TBF	IP	Hit	HR	SO	BB	HBP	F$
11	9	3.78	773	181	174	21	137	49	7	$13

Kuroda is probably the wild card of the season. He was 103-89 with a 3.69 ERA in his 11-year career in Japan. The signing was a big deal because it meant the Dodgers didn't have to deal any of their young talent to get that fourth pitcher they needed.

Esteban Loaiza (Starting Pitcher)

W	L	ERA	TBF	IP	Hit	HR	SO	BB	HBP	F$
6	7	4.62	495	116	123	17	77	34	4	$1

It was a desperation move to pick up his $7.5 million deal late last year, and it didn't work out. He threw an average fastball, an average curve and an average change-up in five starts for the Dodgers, walked 18 and gave up nine homers. He has back, shoulder and adrenaline problems; he'll be given a chance to compete for the fifth starter's spot, but there's reason to believe he won't grasp it.

Derek Lowe (Starting Pitcher)

W	L	ERA	TBF	IP	Hit	HR	SO	BB	HBP	3 Yr	F$
12	9	3.56	772	187	188	16	116	51	5	0.31	$12

Everyone knows Derek Lowe throws a great sinker. What they might not know is that Lowe had four games in which he pitched eight innings or more (including three complete games), and found a way to lose three of them. Sometimes Lowe shows signs of brilliance, but he also had eight starts of five innings or fewer. Consistency and focus are two serious questions.

Jonathan Meloan (Relief Pitcher)

W	L	ERA	TBF	IP	Hit	HR	SO	BB	HBP	3 Yr	F$
4	3	3.45	269	64	51	7	71	29	3	-0.01	$1

He's projected to get 71 strikeouts in 64 innings this year, but at only 23 years old, he could be a bit of an adventure. He blasted through the minor league system as a reliever, but he still swears he can start and be as effective as he was in college at Arizona. The sooner he can slow down and mature, the sooner he can make an impact.

Brad Penny (Starting Pitcher)

W	L	ERA	TBF	IP	Hit	HR	SO	BB	HBP	3 Yr	F$
11	9	3.98	775	182	184	18	123	61	6	0.58	$6

Penny's game is about heart and the pursuit of victory. For him, it's a matter of finding the appropriate channel for that energy. If he can control his emotions and put it all together, he's one of the most dominant and intimidating pitchers in the National League. By the way: career low 3.03 ERA last year to go with a career high .246 batting average.

Scott Proctor (Relief Pitcher)

W	L	ERA	TBF	IP	Hit	HR	SO	BB	HBP	3 Yr	F$
5	4	4.27	354	82	76	11	73	34	3	0.27	$1

Scott Proctor doesn't stop throwing the baseball. He wants to toe the rubber every single day. And guess what? That manager who threw him for 102 innings in 2006 is back running his team, and all signs say he's ready to do the same thing again.

Takashi Saito (Relief Pitcher)

W	L	ERA	TBF	IP	Hit	HR	SO	BB	HBP	F$
5	2	2.92	269	67	53	6	79	20	3	$16

Saito's been a gift to Dodgers fans. He's a pleasure to watch, and his postgame celebration is perhaps the best we've ever seen. Since coming to the states, he's compiled a 1.77 ERA, converted 63 saves in 69 opportunities, and struck out 185 in 142 total innings. His fastball and slider continue to be deceptive. He also doesn't walk anyone; that's important in a closer.

Jason Schmidt (Starting Pitcher)

W	L	ERA	TBF	IP	Hit	HR	SO	BB	HBP	3 Yr	F$
5	6	4.49	433	100	96	13	84	44	4	0.47	$1

Hell, I don't know. Ask a Giants fan. He's making close to $16 million this year, and it would be surprising if he ever touched a baseball again wearing a Dodgers uniform. Darren Dreifort? Kevin Brown? Carlos Perez?

If it weren't for that Andruw Jones contract, Schmidt would be the highest-paid player on the roster again, and it's almost a guarantee that he makes more millions than he pitches games. Strong piece of advice: Don't ever mention his name in the greater Los Angeles area.

Milwaukee Brewers

by Eric Johnson of Brew Crew Ball (brewcrewball.com/)

Team Projections

Record: 88-74
Division Rank: 1st, by one game
Runs Scored: 826
Runs Allowed: 752

2007 in a Nutshell

The Brewers finished with their first winning record in 15 years, but the milestone was overshadowed somewhat by a second-place finish in the NL Central after the team spent most of the year leading the division.

The Brewers ripped off a 22-7 run early to open up a 6.5-game lead over the Cubs on May 9, the largest of any division leader at the time; their 24-10 record was the best in baseball. The lead would grow as large as 8.5 games on June 23, but Brewers fans watched in dismay as Chicago went 51-38 over the remainder of the reason, catching them for good on Sept. 19. Two games behind the Cubs on Sept. 26, the Brewers failed on consecutive days to capitalize on Chicago losses, falling later in the day at home each time.

General Comments

Team Strengths

The Brewers led the league in home runs with 231, en route to finishing fifth in the league with 4.94 runs per game. Closer Francisco Cordero was dominant, racking up 44 saves and an 86/18 strikeout-to-walk ratio (K/BB) in 63.1 innings while allowing only four home runs. Depth was also a strength: The Brewers' second-best hitter, Rookie of the Year Ryan Braun, and best starting pitcher down the stretch, Yovani Gallardo, both started the season in the minor leagues.

Team Weaknesses

The rotation was a mess. Ben Sheets was less good than usual, and about as injured. Jeff Suppan pitched a lot of mediocre innings, and Chris Capuano and Dave Bush both imploded, posting ERAs over 5.00. Capuano suffered (or inflicted) such abject misery that he was relegated to the bullpen, which behind Cordero was shaky, with regular appearances by the Bad Turnbow, Matt Wise's crumbling psyche, and memorable misadventures by the likes of Greg Aquino and Grant Balfour. That problem perhaps forced Doug Melvin into overpaying for Scott Linebrink at the trade deadline.

Infield defense also was an issue, with Braun, Prince Fielder, and Rickie Weeks all being below average at their positions; Braun's defense was so problematic that the team has moved him to left field to begin 2008.

The General Manager is Known for...

Melvin made his name in Milwaukee with shrewd moves like the Richie Sexson deal. His reputation as a trader may have suffered recently as he has shifted from rebuilding to contending mode and made a few dubious swaps like the one for Linebrink. He does seem to have a fondness for former Rangers, liking Gabe Kapler so much that he recused himself from Kapler's evaluation process so as not to taint it.

The Manager is Known for...

Ned Yost is famous for poor bullpen management due inflexibility and intransigence. He obviously prefers some players to others for unknown reasons, though there is not a particular pattern to note. He also has a reputation of being skilled at handling young players.

Ballpark Characteristics

The roof, the only fan-shaped retractable one in baseball, has suffered repeated malfunctions of its pivot system, as well as many leaks during rainstorms. The park's cathedral-like arches cast an odd shadow that falls between home plate and the pitcher's mound during day games, making the ball hard to pick up as it moves between the two lighting conditions.

The Minor League System is...

...surprisingly well-stocked. Slugging outfielder Matt LaPorta (if that's where he plays) should be ready by 2009. Manny Parra reemerged as a pitching prospect, tossing a perfect game at Triple-A and pitching well for the Brewers until a broken finger ended his season.

In Matt Gamel, the Brewers have a mini-Braun: not quite as good a hitter and, incredibly, perhaps a worse defender at third. Catcher Angel Salome and fireballing starter Jeremy Jeffress are both promising prospects, but were also both suspended last year for substance violations. It will be interesting to see what the Brewers do with the compensatory picks they got for Cordero and Linebrink; player personnel guy Jack Zduriencik has never had extra choices to work with before.

Favorite Team Blogs

Brew Crew Ball (http://www.brewcrewball.com/)

Al's Ramblings (http://albethke.blogspot.com/)

Fire Ned Yost (http://www.firenedyost.com/)

Brewers Bar (http://mvn.com/mlb-brewers/)

The Wisconsin Sports Bar (http://thewisconsinsportsbar.blogspot.com/)

Keys for 2008

Players Lost from Last Year's Team

Pitchers Francisco Cordero, Ray King, Linebrink and Wise, infielders Tony Graffanino and Corey Koskie, outfielders Geoff Jenkins and Kevin Mench, catcher Damian Miller.

Players Acquired

Pitchers Randy Choate, Eric Gagne, Guillermo Mota and David Riske and Salomon Torres, catcher Jason Kendall and Eric Munson, outfielders Gabe Kapler and Mike Cameron.

Reasons to be Optimistic

The Brewers' phenomenal young core should continue to develop, and the slew of bullpen signings should more than compensate for the loss of Cordero. Just as important, the signings should prevent people like Chris Spurling from pitching meaningful innings. Sheets could envision a free agent plunder in his future, improve his conditioning, and stay healthy for the whole season.

Reasons to be Pessimistic

Sheets also could get injured again, and Gallardo, at only 22 years old, also has to be considered an injury risk. If they both go down, the starting rotation could be in for more tough times. Defense is also still an issue, as Weeks and (especially) Fielder will probably remain below average on the right side of the infield, Ryan Braun will be learning a new position, and no one knows how well Bill Hall will readjust to third base after a year spent in the outfield.

Due for a Better Season

At least one of them will likely be gone by Opening Day, but both Bush and Capuano should rebound to post at least league-average seasons. Weeks looked very good in the last two months of the year, and if his wrist problems are behind him, could ride the resulting confidence to a breakout season.

Likely to Have a Worse Season

Braun will be hard-pressed to duplicate his astonishing debut, but fortunately he's set the bar so high that he'll still be a valuable hitter even if he suffers a dramatic loss in production. J.J. Hardy is probably due for a regression in slugging.

Still Left to Do

Trade some of the surplus starting pitching and, depending on what the team decides to do with Braun, acquire either a left fielder or third baseman.

Most Likely Team Outcome

An improvement over last year's record, approaching 90 wins; whether that will be enough to top the Cubs is hard to say.

Player Projections

Batters

Ryan Braun (Third Base/Left Field)

PA	R	H	2B	3B	HR	RBI	SO	BB	SB	CS	BA	OBP	SLG	OPS	3 Yr	Fld	F$
519	77	137	28	4	29	91	101	33	11	4	.289	.338	.549	.887	.041	F-	$22

The public perception of Braun is pretty much right on: He hits like he knows what's coming and plays defense like he's blindfolded. Now, the Brewers have decided to cut their losses and move him to left field. In addition to his skill at the plate, he can run, though he looks like Crazy Legs Hirsch doing it. Speaking of nicknames, they don't get much better than "The Hebrew Hammer," but it turns out Braun isn't actually a practicing Jew.

Mike Cameron (Center Field)

PA	R	H	2B	3B	HR	RBI	SO	BB	SB	CS	BA	OBP	SLG	OPS	3 Yr	Fld	F$
565	76	125	30	5	18	69	129	59	16	5	.254	.337	.445	.782	-.041	C	$6

As he did the previous season, Cameron got off to a poor start in 2007 before rebounding. He didn't bounce back as far this time, and it's hard to say how much he'll bounce back in the future. Cameron is 35 years old and will miss the first 25 games of 2008 due to a violation of the league's drug policy. He is still a plus defender in center field but he's a risky pickup.

Craig Counsell (Infield)

PA	R	H	2B	3B	HR	RBI	SO	BB	SB	CS	BA	OBP	SLG	OPS	Fld	F$
410	46	85	17	3	3	30	55	45	9	4	.244	.335	.335	.670	A+	$1

Hometown hero Counsell is still a very good defender all around the infield, and his batting eye is intact. Other than that, he doesn't offer much, but he's a fine backup to have around for a young, defensively challenged infield.

Joe Dillon (Third Base)

PA	R	H	2B	3B	HR	RBI	SO	BB	SB	CS	BA	OBP	SLG	OPS	3 Yr	Fld	F$
468	65	115	29	2	18	68	67	51	5	2	.282	.361	.495	.856	-.024	C	$1

Dillon finally got a chance to play major league baseball on a semi-regular basis late in the season and rewarded the Brewers with fine stats. His bat makes him a more valuable backup second baseman/third baseman than Tony Graffanino, and he also can play in the outfield corners and at first.

Prince Fielder (First Base)

PA	R	H	2B	3B	HR	RBI	SO	BB	SB	CS	BA	OBP	SLG	OPS	3 Yr	Fld	F$
608	94	155	34	1	37	112	102	76	2	3	.301	.397	.587	.984	.076	D	$29

It's pretty hard not to like a guy with his combination of fire and fuzziness. Oh, and he hit 50 homers. I would have felt slightly guilty if he won the MVP, because his defense at first is mediocre at best, but he's already the leader of the team and hits the ball really far. Given his age (not yet 24), I think the Brewers can count on getting a few monstrous, perhaps Ortiz-esque, seasons out of him before he gets expensive and they have to trade him for half the Diamondbacks organization.

Gabe Gross (Left Field)

PA	R	H	2B	3B	HR	RBI	SO	BB	SB	CS	BA	OBP	SLG	OPS	3 Yr	Fld	F$
356	45	80	18	2	10	42	71	43	5	1	.260	.349	.429	.778	-.015	A	$1

Despite lacking Geoff Jenkins' resemblance to Brett Favre, Gross is more than capable of replacing Jenkins' production from the left side of the plate and in left field, but the team decided to keep him in the role of fourth outfielder and move Braun to left instead.

Tony Gwynn Jr. (Center Field)

PA	R	H	2B	3B	HR	RBI	SO	BB	SB	CS	BA	OBP	SLG	OPS	3 Yr	Fld	F$
401	43	92	14	4	2	29	66	33	9	5	.253	.314	.330	.644	.009	C	$1

Gwynn did more for the Rockies with his game-tying triple off Trevor Hoffman in the last game of the season than he did for the Brewers the rest of the year. Maybe fans (and executives) will get past his last name and accept that he is what he is: a slap-hitting fast guy who plays pretty good defense and has no power.

Bill Hall (Third Base)

PA	R	H	2B	3B	HR	RBI	SO	BB	SB	CS	BA	OBP	SLG	OPS	3 Yr	Fld	F$
509	65	120	31	2	19	71	120	45	5	2	.265	.330	.467	.797	-.021	C	$6

I bet a six-pack last offseason that Hall would have a higher OPS than Prince Fielder in 2007. Whoops. In addition to his generally anemic hitting in 2007, Hall looked lost in center field at the beginning of the year and developed a bad habit of flipping the ball up to his hand out of his glove rather than reaching in for it, leading to a few embarrassing errors. Nevertheless, he's still easy to cheer for because of his affability, humility, and his flair for the dramatic. He'll be moving back to third base after the team decided to cut bait on Ryan Braun there.

J.J. Hardy (Shortstop)

PA	R	H	2B	3B	HR	RBI	SO	BB	SB	CS	BA	OBP	SLG	OPS	3 Yr	Fld	F$
484	58	120	24	2	16	64	62	35	3	1	.273	.324	.446	.770	.016	C	$2

Hardy was possessed by the spirit of Alex Rodriguez early in the year, when he found himself dueling with teammate Fielder for the NL home run lead, but fell off a cliff in June and July. Despite a respectable August and September, he somewhat amazingly ended up with worse overall numbers than Weeks. He's probably not going to hit 25 homers again, because he pulls everything and has mediocre plate discipline, but he's still a good hitter for a shortstop. He plays above-average defense despite his lack of foot speed, gliding around out there like Cal Ripken.

Corey Hart (Right Field)

PA	R	H	2B	3B	HR	RBI	SO	BB	SB	CS	BA	OBP	SLG	OPS	3 Yr	Fld	F$
499	73	127	29	6	20	72	96	37	15	4	.285	.343	.511	.854	.022	C	$15

Ned Yost finally forgave Hart for whatever grievous sin Hart had committed, and lo and behold, the lad can play a little. Taking over the leadoff spot from Weeks, Hart thawed his manager's heart by hitting for power and average, playing surprisingly good defense both in the corners and in center, and running the bases with aplomb. He'll hit like a right-handed Jenkins for awhile, I think.

Jason Kendall (Catcher)

PA	R	H	2B	3B	HR	RBI	SO	BB	SB	CS	BA	OBP	SLG	OPS	3 Yr	Fld	F$
527	58	125	22	1	4	44	50	46	5	3	.271	.347	.350	.697	-.044	C	$1

At 34, Kendall no longer possesses the stealing ability he once had. His throwing arm is suspect, but he still can call a game and lead a team.

Rickie Weeks (Second Base)

PA	R	H	2B	3B	HR	RBI	SO	BB	SB	CS	BA	OBP	SLG	OPS	3 Yr	Fld	F$
488	72	107	21	5	15	57	105	57	20	2	.261	.367	.447	.814	.014	D	$8

Weeks hit well in April, displaying the power that was lacking for most of last year, before scar tissue in his wrist began giving him problems. It got in his head, and he spent the summer swinging awkwardly at breaking balls low and away. Come August, he found himself in Triple-A, leaving Brewers fans wondering if he ever was going to be anything more than a tease, but he hit like a man on fire after being recalled on Aug. 10. The power was back, the plate discipline was several levels above anything he'd displayed previously, and he was a terror on the bases.

Defensively, the story is similar: He's still below average overall, but shows flashes of brilliance and definitely has the athletic ability to play at least a competent second base.

Pitchers

Dave Bush (Starting Pitcher)

W	L	ERA	TBF	IP	Hit	HR	SO	BB	HBP	3 Yr	F$
10	10	4.40	748	179	186	24	124	41	9	0.49	$6

After he posted a 4.02 FIP and xFIP in 2006, many people had Bush pegged as a breakout candidate last year, but Bush went backward in most regards, in particular his skyrocketing hit rate. He has a frustrating tendency to cruise for several innings, pitching very efficiently, before falling prey to the big inning. The hit rate is projected to regress a bit, and he has a sunnier projection than you might expect.

Chris Capuano (Starting Pitcher)

W	L	ERA	TBF	IP	Hit	HR	SO	BB	HBP	3 Yr	F$
9	9	4.53	682	160	162	22	126	54	6	0.66	$2

Capuano had an outstanding 2006, in which he basically duplicated his 18-win 2005, only with half the walks, and like Bush seemed primed for a quality 2007. Also like Bush, he failed to deliver, and in fact was moved to the bullpen. Additionally, he seemed to lose the magic of his secret weapon, his pickoff move.

Eric Gagne (Relief Pitcher)

W	L	ERA	TBF	IP	Hit	HR	SO	BB	HBP	3 Yr	F$
4	2	3.35	226	55	44	5	55	21	2	0.36	$9

Gagne was very effective with the Rangers, and then he fell apart when the Red Sox traded for him. He still struck batters out regularly (22 in 18.2 innings), but he also issued nine walks and struggled mightily when batters made contact. During his time with the Red Sox, batters making contact and not fouling the pitch off hit an astounding .448. Even if Gagne was throwing meatballs when he fell behind to avoid walking another batter, that's a nearly impossible number to achieve.

Yovani Gallardo (Starting Pitcher)

W	L	ERA	TBF	IP	Hit	HR	SO	BB	HBP	3 Yr	F$
10	8	3.88	694	165	142	17	159	70	5	-0.20	$13

The pitching version of Ryan Braun, Gallardo performed as well as possibly could be expected from a 21-year-old and pretty much assumed the ace role after Ben Sheets' hamstring injury. He also hit an RBI double in his first major league at-bat, and two homers as the year went on. After years of watching Sheets and Doug Davis "hit," it's a pleasure having a pitcher who can handle the bat this competently. The projection system loves him, and so do the scouts; as long as he doesn't get injured, he's going to be good.

Seth McClung (Relief Pitcher)

W	L	ERA	TBF	IP	Hit	HR	SO	BB	HBP	3 Yr	F$
5	5	4.43	390	89	81	10	82	50	3	0.08	$1

McClung pitched well at Triple-A after being acquired from Tampa Bay for Grant Balfour and didn't embarrass himself after getting called up. He's got good stuff, but it's going to be hard for him to get a chance after the Brewers signed half of the available free agent relievers.

Guillermo Mota (Relief Pitcher)

W	L	ERA	TBF	IP	Hit	HR	SO	BB	HBP	3 Yr	F$
4	3	4.48	276	65	63	8	52	25	2	0.46	$1

By trading Johnny Estrada for Mota, then losing Matt Wise to the Mets (who released Estrada) as a free agent, the Brewers effectively traded Wise and $2 million for Mota. The good news is that Mota is a more versatile pitcher than Wise, with a power arm. The bad news is that he's probably off steroids for good.

Manny Parra (Starting Pitcher)

W	L	ERA	TBF	IP	Hit	HR	SO	BB	HBP	3 Yr	F$
6	8	4.80	549	124	128	14	98	58	7	-0.07	$1

Finally healthy, Parra threw a perfect game at Nashville before filling in ably in Milwaukee. Lefties with his stuff are always prized possessions, and he's now the system's best pitching prospect after Gallardo's graduation and Will Inman's trade. He'll likely be competing with three more established pitchers in Capuano, Bush and Vargas for the last rotation spot, so he could either end up back in Triple-A or in the bullpen.

David Riske (Relief Pitcher)

W	L	ERA	TBF	IP	Hit	HR	SO	BB	HBP	3 Yr	F$
4	3	4.05	281	67	61	8	57	25	2	0.41	$1

Riske tossed up a 2.45 ERA for a couple of million bucks and cashed in with a new three-year, $13 million contract from the Brewers. He's dependable, but generally has faltered closing out games.

Ben Sheets (Starting Pitcher)

W	L	ERA	TBF	IP	Hit	HR	SO	BB	HBP	3 Yr	F$
9	8	3.91	612	150	141	19	124	36	3	0.57	$12

As opposed to Geoff Jenkins, who merely looks like Favre, Sheets could actually be Favre, if he could shed his malingerer image. He's an affable, quotable good ol' boy, who, if he could stay healthy, would be the figurehead of the team. Last season featured both finger and hamstring injuries, as well as concerns about his shoulder when he saw a marked drop in his strikeout rate over the first couple of months of the season. He rebounded with a vintage June, followed shortly thereafter by the finger injury, after which he pitched only 22 more innings.

He's rather renowned for his junk food diet and less-than-stellar conditioning; being in his walk year may motivate him to change those things somewhat.

Brian Shouse (Relief Pitcher)

W	L	ERA	TBF	IP	Hit	HR	SO	BB	HBP	F$
3	3	3.94	237	56	54	4	38	23	3	$1

Every time Shouse throws a pitch, I cringe, because it looks like there's no way he could possibly get a major league hitter out throwing the ball 73 mph over and over. Yet somehow he manages it, though there is absolutely no reason Shouse, a left hander, should have more innings vs. righties than lefties. At some point every year, it is a given that Ned Yost will extrapolate Shouse's success against lefties as some sort of overall relief genius.

Jeff Suppan (Starting Pitcher)

W	L	ERA	TBF	IP	Hit	HR	SO	BB	HBP	3 Yr	F$
10	11	4.68	807	187	200	21	103	68	7	0.43	$1

As long as the $35 million the Brewers owe Suppan over the next three years (including a $2 million buyout in 2011) doesn't hamstring them from making other moves, he's a useful, durable fourth/fifth starter. Since he pitched the most innings on the team and doesn't strike anyone out, there's no doubt the Brewers' porous defense hurt him more than anyone else on the staff.

Derrick Turnbow (Relief Pitcher)

W	L	ERA	TBF	IP	Hit	HR	SO	BB	HBP	3 Yr	F$
4	4	3.76	292	68	55	6	74	38	2	0.40	$2

Alternately excellent and execrable, but always frustrating, Turnbow walked 23 batters in his last 21 innings to end the year on a sour note. It's usually apparent early on, by about pitch three, if Turnbow has his stuff—apparent to everyone but Yost, anyway. I wonder if losing his best friend on the team, Matt Wise, will affect his performance.

Claudio Vargas (Starting Pitcher)

W	L	ERA	TBF	IP	Hit	HR	SO	BB	HBP	3 Yr	F$
7	9	5.05	614	142	148	24	106	53	4	0.65	$1

Vargas acquired a Houdini reputation early on by doing things like walking the bases loaded and escaping unscathed, which was frustrating enough without his super slo-mo routine. For the most part, Vargas was effective as a fifth starter, but Bush, Capuano and Parra are all better bets going forward.

Carlos Villanueva (Starting Pitcher)

W	L	ERA	TBF	IP	Hit	HR	SO	BB	HBP	3 Yr	F$
6	6	4.39	453	106	98	14	86	44	4	-0.21	$1

You know who the Brewers traded for this guy? Leo Estrella and Wayne Franklin. Villanueva is preternaturally poised on the mound and uses his change-up very effectively, racking up more strikeouts than you'd predict given his raw stuff. Among the logjam of starters vying for the fourth and fifth slots, Villanueva is probably the closest to a guaranteed job.

Minnesota Twins

by Will Young of Will's Title is Too Long (wyoung.net/twins)

2008 Projections

Record: 79-83
Division Rank: 3rd, 11 games back
Runs Scored: 733
Runs Allowed: 756

2007 in a Nutshell

For the first time since 2000, the Twins finished a season below .500. The Twins played exactly like one would expect from a .500 team. They never reached more than five games below .500 and they reached six games above .500 just once (on July 15). The team never had a winning streak longer than five games or a losing streak longer than six.

An offense driven by singles created problems: The team was shut out 14 times. By July, most fans knew the playoffs were out of reach and the Twins traded Luis Castillo for prospects. If not for sentimentality, Torii Hunter would likely also have been sent packing.

General Comments

Team Strengths

The Twins have as much, if not more, young starting pitching as any other team. Scott Baker finally put questions about his future to rest. Kevin Slowey experienced growing pains, but looks very valuable. Most teams would love to have a cheap, young innings-eater like Boof Bonser around, but he is about to get lost in the organizational shuffle. Glen Perkins could not even get a sniff of a spot start. Of course, Francisco Liriano will be returning from Tommy John surgery.

Team Weaknesses

Scoring runs is the big problem. The Twins could not hit home runs. They could not hit doubles. They could not draw walks. Their baserunning has regressed from a peak a few years ago (no one trips between bases more than Michael Cuddyer, for instance).

The General Manager is Known for...

He'll be remembered for botching his first transaction. Bill Smith traded a player to be named later to the Cubs for Craig Monroe, hoping that Monroe would accept a large cut in pay. If Smith had checked the collective bargaining agreement, he would have noticed that the percentage of Monroe's salary that he was offering was not allowed unless the player was non-tendered (in which case, any team could sign him for any amount). Get all that?

Monroe ended up signing a one-year contract for just under $4 million, which means he cost the Twins about double what they had hoped to pay him. Plus, with Cuddyer and Delmon Young in the corner outfield spots, Monroe seems to be an expensive platoon designated hitter.

On the bright side, Smith also has recognized that a team cannot win a pennant with a 12-man pitching rotation and a Little League offense: He pulled the trigger on a six-player trade centered on Matt Garza and Delmon Young.

The Manager is Known for...

Ron Gardenhire does a very good job annually with his pitching staff. He never abuses his starting pitchers and he typically does a great job leveraging the bullpen. (Last season featured his least effective bullpen, yet it still was above average). When the team is struggling, Gardenhire will occasionally pick an incredibly stupid fight with an umpire and make a fool out of himself in the hopes that it will motivate the squad. On the other hand, when things are going well, he usually stays out of the way.

Ballpark Characteristics

The Metrodome has only two seasons left, but with each passing year and the opening of more new ballparks, it has furthered its transition from the Homerdome to a pitchers' park. Two or three times a year, a fielder will lose a ball in the gray roof, leading to hilarious moments such as Prince Fielder hitting a 250-foot home run. The FieldTurf that was added a few seasons ago has slowed the speed of ground balls tremendously.

The Minor League System is...

It's full of good pitching prospects, but devoid of hitting prospects above the lowest levels. None of the minor leaguers should be expected to make much of an impact in 2008.

Ben Revere was the team's first round pick in 2007 and was widely mocked as a signability selection as well as an overdraft. However, he hit .325/.388/.461 in the Gulf Coast League and displayed excellent speed with 10 triples and 21 stolen bases. He is a long way from the major leagues but could develop into anything from Kenny Lofton to Denard Span. (Never heard of Span? Exactly.).

Favorite Team Blogs

The Twins Geek (http://twinsgeek.blogspot.com/)
Aaron Gleeman (http://www.aarongleeman.com)
SBG Nation (http://stickandballguy.com/blog/)

Keys for 2008

Players Lost from Last Year's Team

Hunter and Johan Santana are gone. Garza and Jason Bartlett went to Tampa Bay in a challenge trade that could look idiotic or fantastic in a year or two. Carlos Silva will not be back and RonDL White finally, mercifully, decided to retire.

Players Acquired

Just four years after being the No. 1 pick in the amateur draft, and just one year after being Baseball America's No. 3 prospect, Delmon Young was traded from Tampa Bay to Minnesota. Young has superstar potential and the Twins hope his right-handed bat develops enough to compensate for Hunter's loss. Brendan Harris, acquired in the same trade, should be the utility infielder. He will back up Mike Lamb, who should finally end Punto's reign as one of the worst regulars in baseball, and Adam Everett, who will provide Gold Glove defense at short.

The Santana trade brought in four prospects: outfielder Carlos Gomez and right-handers Philip Humber, Kevin Mulvey and Deolis Guerra. Gomez is young, athletic and full of potential, but his performance has yet to reflect it. Guerra, 19, is much in the same position. Humber and Mulvey are ready to make an immediate impact, but the question is whether it will be meaningful. Humber was the No. 3 overall pick in the 2005 draft, but his ceiling now looks like the back of the rotation. Mulvey keeps the ball n the park, but his low strikeout rate means he has no margin for error.

Long-time Twins killer Monroe (.322/.356/.544 in his career against Minnesota) was acquired from the Cubs, but may be too expensive to stick. Howie Clark and Jason Pridie could compete for spots on the bench.

Reasons to be Optimistic

Few teams possess as many elite players as the Twins with Joe Mauer, Justin Morneau, Joe Nathan and, the Twins hope, Francisco Liriano. If those four combine to be as dominant together as their record shows they can be, and a few young players step up, the Twins could contend for a playoff spot even without Santana.

Reasons to be Pessimistic

Santana and Hunter are gone, and Nathan could be next. Liriano may need a few months to rediscover himself after missing all of last season for Tommy John surgery. Also, as great as those four elite players can be, if the others produce below replacement level (like Punto), the offense will get ugly.

Due for a Better Season

Punto had the second-worst season in the history of the franchise according to Value Over Replacement Player calculations, so one would hope that he can bounce back. Of course, there is a huge divide between him having a better year and him actually being useful with the bat. After struggling for consistent playing time during the first half of the season, Jason Kubel was arguably the team's best hitter after the All-Star break and might consolidate his gains over the course of the entire season.

Likely to Have a Worse Season

Matt Guerrier is unlikely to improve his ERA+ for the fifth consecutive season, but he still will be an asset for the Twins, bridging the gap from the starters to Pat Neshek and Nathan.

Still Left to Do

There is still no clear starter at second base. Gardenhire and Smith will need to sift through Punto, Harris, Alexi Casilla and Brian Buscher.

The Twins have many internal candidates to fill out the rotation spots behind Baker. Slowey and Bonser are likely candidates, and ultimately Liriano will grab a spot. Still, there is plenty of time for Nick Blackburn, Perkins, Humber, Mulvey, or even Brian Duensing or Jeff Manship to try to grab one of those places.

Most Likely Team Outcome

It will take a lot of luck and some major improvement to the offense for the team to hang with Cleveland and Detroit in 2008. Instead, look for the Twins to duke it out with Kansas City and Chicago for third place in the Central. Aiming to return to above .500 seems like a reasonable expectation, but injuries and a failure to improve from some of the young bats could have the team trying to avoid 90 losses.

Player Projections
Batters

Alexi Casilla (Second Base)

PA	R	H	2B	3B	HR	RBI	SO	BB	SB	CS	BA	OBP	SLG	OPS	3 Yr	Fld	F$
563	59	130	19	4	0	36	84	30	22	8	.253	.299	.306	.605	.032	D	$1

Rarely has a player turned from such a pleasant surprise to such a huge disappointment as quickly as Casilla. Most Twins fans were shocked they could receive a living person in exchange for J.C. Romero, let alone a decent prospect. However, the excitement of 2006 was short-lived as Casilla proved horribly overmatched, and worse, lackadaisical after replacing Luis Castillo at second base in August. Showing how disgusted he was with Casilla's effort, Gardenhire routinely sat him in September despite the month being an open audition for the future.

Michael Cuddyer (Right Field)

PA	R	H	2B	3B	HR	RBI	SO	BB	SB	CS	BA	OBP	SLG	OPS	3 Yr	Fld	F$
563	72	134	30	3	17	70	105	58	3	2	.272	.354	.449	.803	-.021	C	$6

Cuddyer possesses a cannon for a right arm and punishes anyone trying to take the extra base. On the other hand, he gets poor jumps on balls down the line. Finally, no one trips and falls over their own feet while running the bases more often than he does.

Adam Everett (Shortstop)

PA	R	H	2B	3B	HR	RBI	SO	BB	SB	CS	BA	OBP	SLG	OPS	3 Yr	Fld	F$
381	37	84	18	3	2	28	57	17	6	2	.238	.276	.324	.600	-.027	A+	$1

Everett's the absolute best fielding shortstop since Ozzie Smith, not arguably. Roy Oswalt said he never bothered to see what happened to any ground ball hit to the left side or up the middle when Everett was there because he knew it would be an out. That's confidence. Everett is also an excellent bunter, basestealer and baserunner, but seldom had a chance to bunt or steal over the past few years. He's not a great hitter, but he isn't as bad as last year's .232/.281/.318 over 66 games.

Carlos Gomez (Center Field)

PA	R	H	2B	3B	HR	RBI	SO	BB	SB	CS	BA	OBP	SLG	OPS	3 Yr	Fld	F$
483	58	111	21	5	4	39	86	22	22	7	.251	.300	.348	.648	.050	A	$1

Carlos Gomez may eventually turn into an outfield version of Jose Reyes. He is already an above-average fielder and may be faster than Reyes. His bat lacks punch, though scouts say he has the potential to develop into a hitter capable of 20 home runs in a season. The best thing for Gomez would be to spend time developing that bat in Triple-A, but he may not get that luxury.

Brendan Harris (Shortstop)

PA	R	H	2B	3B	HR	RBI	SO	BB	SB	CS	BA	OBP	SLG	OPS	3 Yr	Fld	F$
509	59	123	27	3	11	56	92	37	3	2	.270	.328	.414	.742	-.004	D	$1

The only thing keeping Brendan Harris from becoming one of the better hitting shortstops in baseball is his glove. He often plays the position as if he were wearing cement shoes, routinely letting routine ground balls get by him. And while he is capable of playing second base or third base, his glove is still a liability at second and his bat is not good enough to play third. He has 15-20 home run power and can hit .300, but will struggle to find regular playing time again in the big leagues.

Jason Kubel (Left Field)

PA	R	H	2B	3B	HR	RBI	SO	BB	SB	CS	BA	OBP	SLG	OPS	3 Yr	Fld	F$
444	56	111	24	2	14	58	74	37	4	1	.278	.339	.454	.793	.028	C	$2

A season and a half into his recovery from major knee surgery, Kubel was the Twins' best hitter during the second half of 2007. Unfortunately his warts are very noticeable. He has no foot speed (despite that, he has deceptively good range, though he may be the DH in 2008) and has a propensity to strike out looking at fastballs right down the pipe.

Despite giving Jacque Jones more than 700 plate appearances against southpaws, Gardenhire has shown no willingness to discover whether Kubel can be more than a platoon player. With the acquisitions of Craig Monroe and Delmon Young, it looks like it will be even longer before Kubel gets that shot.

Mike Lamb (Third Base)

PA	R	H	2B	3B	HR	RBI	SO	BB	SB	CS	BA	OBP	SLG	OPS	3 Yr	Fld	F$
394	46	95	18	3	9	43	59	35	1	1	.271	.336	.416	.752	-.031	C	$1

He's a lefty who hits for average and has some power. Lamb hits lefties very well and doesn't need to be platooned. He can play third, although he is not a good fielder because he gets late jumps on balls and has poor range, but he does have a strong and accurate arm. He is somewhat better fielding at first.

Joe Mauer (Catcher)

PA	R	H	2B	3B	HR	RBI	SO	BB	SB	CS	BA	OBP	SLG	OPS	3 Yr	Fld	F$
500	68	132	28	3	11	59	58	65	6	1	.310	.399	.467	.866	.023	A+	$10

Like Morneau, Mauer failed to live up to the high standards he had set in 2006. Of course, by becoming the first catcher in history to win the AL batting title, he had set some very high standards. With each passing season, it seems less likely that he will ever develop into the 20-home run threat many hoped he could be. Still, there is absolutely nothing wrong with having a line drive machine with excellent plate discipline and Gold Glove-worthy defense behind the plate.

Unfortunately, locals are slowly turning against him—he is underappreciated for being so consistently good but blamed for never quite being good enough. Despite missing two parts of last season to injury, there is no talk (and should not be) of moving him out from behind the plate. Any rumor to the contrary is coming from a bored reporter or an idiotic fan.

Justin Morneau (First Base)

PA	R	H	2B	3B	HR	RBI	SO	BB	SB	CS	BA	OBP	SLG	OPS	3 Yr	Fld	F$
597	82	151	31	3	29	96	90	60	1	1	.287	.360	.524	.884	-.007	C	$20

One of the many moves that indicated Terry Ryan's withdrawal from the demands of being a GM was his inability to reach a long-term deal with Morneau. While he took a step back from his MVP campaign, he is still the best power threat the organization has had since Harmon Killebrew. There is nothing more fun than watching him get ahead in the count and sit on a fastball. Plus, he has become a very underrated defensive player with soft hands around the bag.

Trevor Plouffe (Shortstop)

PA	R	H	2B	3B	HR	RBI	SO	BB	SB	CS	BA	OBP	SLG	OPS	3 Yr	Fld	F$
517	47	105	26	3	4	40	99	25	6	3	.222	.263	.316	.579	.058	C	$1

The former first-round pick has always played impressive defense, but last year his bat finally picked up. The Twins have promoted him aggressively, so his subpar offensive numbers always came against older players. Last year, he further solidified his claim as the team's shortstop of the future, making Bartlett and Everett merely stop-gaps until he becomes ready.

Nick Punto (Third Base)

PA	R	H	2B	3B	HR	RBI	SO	BB	SB	CS	BA	OBP	SLG	OPS	3 Yr	Fld	F$
500	55	110	21	4	2	35	78	46	16	5	.250	.318	.329	.647	-.020	B	$1

Somehow, Ryan talked himself into a two-year extension for Punto, based on a couple of decent months in the middle of 2006. It is hard to decide what is more mind-boggling: that he managed to *slug* (!!!) .155 during the month of August or that he managed to get 84 plate appearances that month. Even the casual fans finally turned on him by the end of the season: His every move was met by a chorus of boos during September.

Mike Redmond (Catcher)

PA	R	H	2B	3B	HR	RBI	SO	BB	SB	CS	BA	OBP	SLG	OPS	Fld	F$
313	34	82	17	1	2	28	33	20	1	1	.289	.342	.377	.719	A	$1

If you could draw up the perfect complementary player to Joe Mauer, you would end up with a person nearly identical to Mike Redmond. In his career against southpaws, he has hit .332/.389/.436; he will play through nearly any malady; and he manages to get hit by something (player, bat, foul ball, etc.) in just about every game he plays. Of course, because expectations are lower, some Twins fans are always clamoring for more Redmond than Mauer.

Delmon Young (Right Field)

PA	R	H	2B	3B	HR	RBI	SO	BB	SB	CS	BA	OBP	SLG	OPS	3 Yr	Fld	F$
577	71	161	34	4	13	71	105	22	8	4	.296	.326	.445	.771	.071	C	$11

Young is a five-tool talent who has yet to demonstrate three of those tools at any level. While Young will be a perennial .300 hitter, he is a pure line drive hitter and there are serious doubts that he will ever be a consistent power threat. In the minors, DY hit a home run once every 24 at-bats, a rate that has fallen to once every 48 at-bats since his call-up in late 2006. He has speed, but stole only 10 bases in 2007 despite 135 singles.

Defensively, he has established himself as having one of the best arms in baseball, but often looks uncomfortable in right field, playing too deep and often taking poor angles on fly balls. While he fancies himself a Vlad Guerrero-type hitter, until he learns even a little patience at the plate (26 walks) his ceiling is .330 with 20 home runs and 20 stolen bases. Any team would be happy to have numbers like that from a 22-year-old, but they would be a little disappointing for a player with Young's talent.

Pitchers

Scott Baker (Starting Pitcher)

W	L	ERA	TBF	IP	Hit	HR	SO	BB	HBP	3 Yr	F$
10	9	4.30	714	168	178	21	118	42	7	0.07	$4

It took a year for Baker to recover mentally from being jerked around in May 2006, but he proved to be effective after finally receiving a vote of confidence from his manager in June 2007. His season culminated in a one-hit shutout of the Kansas City Royals in which he took a perfect game into the ninth inning. After Ron Gardenhire showed some support, Baker finished the year with a 3.55 ERA in his final 19 appearances.

Boof Bonser (Starting Pitcher)

W	L	ERA	TBF	IP	Hit	HR	SO	BB	HBP	3 Yr	F$
9	10	4.53	721	167	171	23	132	61	6	0.08	$1

Weight and fatigue problems conspired to prevent Bonser from building upon his 2006 season. Instead, he has found himself falling down the totem pole and may have lost his spot in the starting rotation. He throws both a slider and a curveball ("the Booferdoodle"), but does not mix his pitches well. Instead, the slider will be used the first few innings and then, around the third inning, the Booferdoodle will come and dazzle the opposition for two innings.

A refocused and svelte Bonser is talented enough to claim a spot in most starting rotations, but this is a critical year for him: He could find himself heading back to Triple-A again.

Jesse Crain (Relief Pitcher)

W	L	ERA	TBF	IP	Hit	HR	SO	BB	HBP	3 Yr	F$
3	2	3.63	195	47	46	4	31	13	2	0.02	$1

A torn labrum and rotator cuff mercifully ended a season of Crain-wrecks in May. Pitching coach Rick Anderson completely overhauled his approach, and with each passing year, Crain was striking out more batters and becoming more of a groundball pitcher. It remains to be seen if he can pick up where he was in 2006 or if he will reinvent himself again.

Brian Duensing (Starting Pitcher)

W	L	ERA	TBF	IP	Hit	HR	SO	BB	HBP	3 Yr	F$
8	9	4.79	677	155	174	19	78	51	7	-0.40	$1

Now four years removed from Tommy John surgery, this lefty has visited and succeeded at every minor league level. He admits to trying to emulate Tom Glavine and throws five different pitches, with the slider serving as his out pitch. He was the starting pitcher for the United States in its victory against Cuba in the Baseball World Cup championship game last November.

Matt Guerrier (Relief Pitcher)

W	L	ERA	TBF	IP	Hit	HR	SO	BB	HBP	3 Yr	F$
5	4	3.98	325	76	78	8	54	23	3	0.40	$1

In 2005 and 2006, Guerrier contributed consecutive excellent seasons, picking up the middle innings and bridging the gap between the starters and the elite members of the back of the bullpen. Last year, he hopped several people in the pecking order and hiked up his strikeout rate considerably. Perhaps the prototypical Twins pitcher, Guerrier relies much more on control and command than velocity. To complement his mediocre fastball, he throws a big, bending curveball that occasionally ends up over the fence or at the backstop.

Philip Humber (Starting Pitcher)

W	L	ERA	TBF	IP	Hit	HR	SO	BB	HBP	3 Yr	F$
6	9	4.96	578	133	137	22	94	49	8	-0.12	$1

Humber had Tommy John surgery and hasn't fully regained the zip on his fastball. At this stage, he doesn't project to be better than a No. 4 starter.

Francisco Liriano (Starting Pitcher)

W	L	ERA	TBF	IP	Hit	HR	SO	BB	HBP	3 Yr	F$
6	3	3.27	337	82	71	8	88	26	3	0.05	$6

He was handled with kid gloves during his 2006 season, so expect more of the same in 2008 as he returns from Tommy John surgery. It would not be surprising to see him start the year in Triple-A or the bullpen as the Twins try to work him slowly back into the rotation. Sadly, Twins fans are very pessimistic about his return simply because their only experience with the surgery was with Joe Mays—a player who never would have repeated his 2001 season even if healthy.

Joe Nathan (Relief Pitcher)

W	L	ERA	TBF	IP	Hit	HR	SO	BB	HBP	3 Yr	F$
6	2	2.82	287	71	55	6	82	22	2	0.27	$17

Nathan declined last year from amazing to merely excellent. His performance fell across the board: His strikeout, walk and home run rates were all worse than in 2006. Still, it is hard to find fault with a guy who has a 1.88 ERA during an off year. He got a late start as a reliever because of a position change and arm surgery, so there is not as much mileage on his arm as most 33-year-olds have. Since he'll be a free agent after the season, do not be surprised to see Nathan flipped to a contender if the Twins falter early.

Pat Neshek (Relief Pitcher)

W	L	ERA	TBF	IP	Hit	HR	SO	BB	HBP	3 Yr	F$
5	3	3.66	298	71	60	8	79	27	3	0.11	$3

A player who "gets it," Neshek blogs, loves to interact with the fans, collects autographs, handles fame with aplomb and likes to track his game-by-game performance through Win Probability Added. Plus, he has a funky style, delivering pitches from the side and finishing many with "the salute" as he whips his pitching arm backwards with the pointer finger out. Do yourself a favor and try to watch him pitch. You'll quickly become a fan. The projection does not like his stated goals for 2008: a WHIP under 1.00 and 100-plus strikeouts.

Glen Perkins (Relief Pitcher)

W	L	ERA	TBF	IP	Hit	HR	SO	BB	HBP	3 Yr	F$
3	3	4.92	242	54	56	7	40	26	3	-0.22	$1

As a Minnesotan, the hype surrounding Perkins has seemingly always been greater than the performance since he was drafted in the first round in 2004. He is an extreme flyball pitcher with subpar command. If he returns to starting pitching, he seems a good bet to be a horrible disappointment unless he can learn to either keep the ball in the park or stop putting guys on base.

Yohan Pino (Relief Pitcher)

W	L	ERA	TBF	IP	Hit	HR	SO	BB	HBP	3 Yr	F$
6	6	4.87	488	112	122	15	74	37	5	-0.30	$1

Another extreme control pitcher, Pino has the added bonus of racking up nearly a strikeout per inning throughout his minor league career. On the other hand, he does not possess a blazing fastball, so he may eventually reach a level at which his subpar natural stuff gets lit up by opposing hitters. He may become a cheap choice for those old Matt Guerrier innings in which the game is not completely out of hand, but the elite relievers need more rest.

Dennys Reyes (Relief Pitcher)

W	L	ERA	TBF	IP	Hit	HR	SO	BB	HBP	3 Yr	F$
3	3	3.79	217	50	49	3	38	24	2	0.26	$1

Last year was the first since 2001 in which Reyes played for the same team as the previous year. Two different stints on the disabled list disrupted his season, but his time on the roster was mostly forgettable. While his ERA of 3.99 is respectable, Reyes had a WHIP of 1.88 and he had eight games in which he failed to retire even a batter. Even more frightening, right-handed batters hit .364/.509/.500 against him.

Juan Rincon (Relief Pitcher)

W	L	ERA	TBF	IP	Hit	HR	SO	BB	HBP	3 Yr	F$
4	4	3.66	289	68	63	5	58	27	3	0.29	$1

With each passing year, his outstanding 2004 season gets further away. His strikeout rate, opponents' batting average and strikeout-to-walk ratio have declined in three straight seasons. Plus, while he was initially included in the Matt Garza-Delmon Young swap, the Rays evidently balked after examining his medical records. Rincon allowed more home runs in June and July last season than in all of 2005-06 combined.

Kevin Slowey (Starting Pitcher)

W	L	ERA	TBF	IP	Hit	HR	SO	BB	HBP	3 Yr	F$
10	9	4.23	702	167	170	22	107	40	7	-0.32	$6

Slowey throws two different types of fastball with excellent control. He does an excellent job of spotting his cutter on the outside corner and turning it into a pitch that is hard to hit solidly. Still, he has a hard time putting away batters and half the home runs he allowed came with two strikes. An absurdly low 29 percent of balls in play against him were ground balls. If he can work on those two red flags, he can be an effective starter.

New York Mets

by Dave Studenmund of The Hardball Times

2008 Projections

Record: 92-70
Division Rank: 1st, by two games
Runs Scored: 802
Runs Allowed: 700

2007 in a Nutshell

I can't talk about it.

General Comments

Team Strengths

The Mets have three outstanding players in their prime and under contract for a long time. Barring injury, Carlos Beltran, David Wright, Jose Reyes and Johan Santana should form the core of a solid Mets team for many years to come. The trick for the Mets is to effectively fill in other star and role players around them.

The Mets are also a very good fielding team. Beltran may be the best center fielder in the league and only Alou is below average among their other outfielders. Reyes is among the best at shortstop and Luis Castillo still provides solid defense at second. David Wright is somewhat inconsistent at third, but very good overall. Brian Schneider has lost some skills with age, but he's still one of the best backstops in the game.

Team Weaknesses

Prior to the Santana deal, the Mets' starting pitching was pretty thin. Every starter other than the new ace has issues: Pedro Martinez (injury, age), John Maine (stuff), Oliver Perez (inconsistency, wildness) and Orlando Hernandez (age) could all be fine, but probably won't be. It won't be a major surprise if everyone of them finishes with an ERA over 4.00.

Although the Santana deal makes the rotation immensely stronger, it still has potential holes. And the deal has rendered the Mets' minor league system virtually barren.

The General Manager is Known for...

Nabbing Santana against all odds. Seriously, Omar Minaya has shown a talent for making relatively minor pickups that pay big dividends. In 2006, he looked like a genius by pulling off a series of minor moves (such as signing Endy Chavez, Jose Valentin and Chad Bradford) that helped propel the Mets into the finals of the National League playoffs. His touch wasn't quite as magical in 2007, but he did manage to unearth a Ruben Gotay and a Jorge Sosa.

On the trade front, his results have been more mixed. Minaya pulled off some steals in Maine and Perez, but he didn't show an appreciation of how rare young star talent is when he traded Lastings Milledge to the Nationals for two good but known quantities, Church and Schneider. Trading Heath Bell to the Padres was a clunker.

Minaya also has to take a big hit for the poor state of the Mets' minor league system. Though he's tried to make splashes in international signings, Fernando Martinez and Deolis Guerra have been the only major fruits of that labor. And he has taken a low-key approach to the draft, losing top draft picks because of free agent signings and subsequently refusing to take chances on high-dollar talent that is available in the later rounds of the draft.

He's been accused of showing a preference for Latin American players, and the composition of the Mets' roster seems to bear that out. However, that may simply be a matter of finding the best value.

The Manager is Known for...

Being solid. Willie Randolph is a solid guy who doesn't show a lot of emotion or imagination. Pretty much the opposite of Bobby Valentine.

Ballpark Characteristics

Shea Stadium has consistently been a pitcher's park since it opened in 1964. Strikeout and flyball pitchers, in particular, have found Shea to their liking. Think Tom Seaver. Sid Fernandez may be the archetypal Shea Stadium pitcher. An extreme flyball pitcher, Fernandez had a career 2.52 ERA at Shea, 4.01 everywhere else.

Shea is also one of the ugliest ballparks in the majors and will be replaced in 2009 by Citi Field, which has been modeled on Brooklyn's old Ebbets Field. Reportedly, the Home Run Apple won't be transported to the new stadium. If this upsets you, express your displeasure at http://www.savetheapple.com/.

The Minor League System is...

It was weak; it is now destitute. Since promoting Wright and Reyes to the majors in 2003 and 2004, the Mets' system had been bare in all positions except outfield. With Milledge now traded to the Nationals and four of their top ten prospects off to the Twins, outfielder Fernando Martinez is now the only minor leaguer close to being a Grade A propect.

Favorite Team Blogs

Mets Blog (http://www.metsblog.com/)

Amazin Avenue (http://www.amazinavenue.com/)

Faith and Fear in Flushing (http://faithandfear. blogharbor.com/blog/)

Take the 7 Train (http://mvn.com/mlb-mets/)

Keys for 2008

Players Lost from Last Year's Team

Catcher Paul Lo Duca, starting pitchers Tom Glavine, Phil Humber and Dave Williams, reliever Guillermo Mota, outfielders Lastings Milledge, Carlos Gomez and Shawn Green and second baseman Jose Valentin. Johnny Estrada, we hardly knew ye.

Players Acquired

Ryan Church, Brian Schneider and relief pitcher Matt Wise. The Mets essentially swapped Lo Duca for Schneider, Green/Milledge for Church and Mota for Wise. And Carlos Gomez and three prospects for Johan Santana.

Reasons to be Optimistic

Any team with Wright, Reyes, Beltran and Santana and a strong supporting cast is going to compete. Plus, the Mets are a major-market team and can afford to make critical moves during the season.

Reasons to be Pessimistic

It's true that all pitching staffs carry risks and issues, but the Mets carry more than most. First baseman Carlos Delgado, a key bat in the middle of the lineup, may be on the cusp of a critical career decline, but maybe not...

Due for a Better Season

Perhaps no everyday player is as critical to the Mets' chances in 2008 as Delgado. He had a disappointing year in 2007, posting the lowest home run total of any full season in his career. He's likely to bounce back to some extent, but he won't match the production of his younger years. A bigger comeback from Delgado would do a lot to cement the Mets' pennant chances.

I'm looking for Reyes to overcome his late season slump and have a fine year.

Likely to Have a Worse Season

Age is going to take the bloom off last year's production from Alou and Hernandez.

Still Left to Do

The pieces of a fine bullpen are there, but they don't yet fit together.

Most Likely Team Outcome

With Santana on board, it will be a disappointment if the Mets don't win the division.

Player Projections
Batters

Moises Alou (Left Field)

PA	R	H	2B	3B	HR	RBI	SO	BB	SB	CS	BA	OBP	SLG	OPS	Fld	F$
401	54	108	21	1	15	59	42	37	2	1	.304	.369	.495	.864	C	$5

When Alou takes his stance in left field, he spreads his legs so far apart that it hurts to watch him. I have never understood how he moves from that position. Don't blame the Mets' fall on Moises—he batted .402 in September.

Marlon Anderson (Left Field)

PA	R	H	2B	3B	HR	RBI	SO	BB	SB	CS	BA	OBP	SLG	OPS	3 Yr	Fld	F$
238	30	60	12	1	7	30	37	20	3	1	.284	.345	.449	.794	-.037	B	$1

Marlon Anderson has been a late-season hero for both the Dodgers and Mets in recent years, but he's not a regular player. He's a left-handed bat off the bench who can't really play the infield any longer.

Carlos Beltran (Center Field)

PA	R	H	2B	3B	HR	RBI	SO	BB	SB	CS	BA	OBP	SLG	OPS	3 Yr	Fld	F$
584	85	138	31	2	27	90	96	66	20	3	.272	.355	.501	.856	-.032	C	$25

One of the game's truly gifted talents, Beltran appears to be hobbled by minor injuries much of the time. He'll almost certainly hit more than the projected 27 home runs this year, but the exact number will probably depend on those bumps and bruises.

Luis Castillo (Second Base)

PA	R	H	2B	3B	HR	RBI	SO	BB	SB	CS	BA	OBP	SLG	OPS	3 Yr	Fld	F$
564	66	144	19	4	2	43	45	56	16	7	.293	.365	.360	.725	-.036	B	$1

Castillo doesn't have the speed he once had, and that's a concern because speed is pretty much his entire game. When the legs go completely, so will Castillo's value. That's why I was surprised Minaya signed him to a four-year deal this offseason.

According to Baseball Reference, the most similar batter to Castillo through the age of 31 is Willie Randolph.

Ramon Castro (Catcher)

PA	R	H	2B	3B	HR	RBI	SO	BB	SB	CS	BA	OBP	SLG	OPS	3 Yr	Fld	F$
246	31	58	13	0	11	37	56	21	0	1	.264	.330	.473	.803	-.016	D	$1

Castro had a good year at bat, but in limited action. Plus, he threw out only 7 percent of baserunners. It would be nice to see him get more action, but it might not be a good sign for the Mets.

Endy Chavez (Center Field)

PA	R	H	2B	3B	HR	RBI	SO	BB	SB	CS	BA	OBP	SLG	OPS	3 Yr	Fld	F$
288	33	71	13	3	1	22	35	18	8	2	.275	.321	.360	.681	-.030	A+	$1

Endy Chavez is Carlos Beltran without the bat. Thanks to one spectacular play in the postseason, Mets fans will always adore Endy. You could call him the anti-Timo.

Ryan Church (Right Field)

PA	R	H	2B	3B	HR	RBI	SO	BB	SB	CS	BA	OBP	SLG	OPS	3 Yr	Fld	F$
474	60	111	28	2	14	59	98	48	3	2	.268	.349	.446	.795	-.025	C	$1

Decent eye, decent mid-range power, solid corner defense and a low salary … those are the strengths. But there's the complacent attitude that rubs some the wrong way, the strikeouts, and the inability to do anything with a quality breaking pitch that drive others batty. Never as good as his biggest fans thought nor as terrible as the detractors, if he's your worst outfielder, you've got a pretty good team. While nobody does well on an 0-2 count, he's helpless, hitting just .116 for his career with boatloads of strikeouts, especially on middling junk—the kind of performance that's likely to bring out the boo birds.

Carlos Delgado (First Base)

PA	R	H	2B	3B	HR	RBI	SO	BB	SB	CS	BA	OBP	SLG	OPS	Fld	F$
569	77	131	30	1	25	84	108	65	2	1	.269	.362	.488	.850	D	$13

There's hope for Delgado. He batted only .188/.262/.260 in April but .274/.348/.489 the rest of the year. Unfortunately, Citi Field isn't opening until 2009—Delgado has batted only .226 at Shea the past two years.

Damion Easley (Second Base)

PA	R	H	2B	3B	HR	RBI	SO	BB	SB	CS	BA	OBP	SLG	OPS	Fld	F$
292	36	67	13	1	10	37	44	26	2	1	.261	.337	.437	.774	D	$1

Easley was an All-Star second baseman in the late 1990s and showed signs of solving the Mets' second base hole last year, but he's just a useful bench player at this stage of his career.

Ruben Gotay (Second Base)

PA	R	H	2B	3B	HR	RBI	SO	BB	SB	CS	BA	OBP	SLG	OPS	3 Yr	Fld	F$
399	44	91	21	2	8	42	70	29	4	2	.255	.314	.392	.706	.013	D	$1

Gotay is a patient hitter who managed to bang out a lot of line drives for the Mets last year, but his range is limited and he has trouble turning the double play. He's a switch hitter, which makes him useful as a pinch hitter, but he batted only .194 against lefties in 2007.

Jose Reyes (Shortstop)

PA	R	H	2B	3B	HR	RBI	SO	BB	SB	CS	BA	OBP	SLG	OPS	3 Yr	Fld	F$
666	102	170	29	11	10	63	74	53	60	14	.284	.340	.419	.759	.009	B	$34

Remember when we were worried that Reyes didn't know how to take a walk? Not anymore. He increased his walk total to 77 last year, up from 27 two years ago. Reyes slumped horribly in September, when he batted .205. When Reyes' stroke is off, he hits lots of pop flies and can't seem to buy a line drive. Let's hope he can recover his stroke this year, the same way he learned to take a walk.

Brian Schneider (Catcher)

PA	R	H	2B	3B	HR	RBI	SO	BB	SB	CS	BA	OBP	SLG	OPS	3 Yr	Fld	F$
463	49	104	21	1	6	42	61	46	1	1	.256	.333	.357	.690	-.033	B	$1

As his ability with the bat backslid, the talk of his defensive prowess grew. While Schneider received much too much credit for his work with the Nats' beleaguered staff, there's little doubt that he's a solid receiver, and he's quite good at controlling the opposing running game. He really shouldn't face left-handed pitching, and his line against righties isn't anything to write home about, but given the sorry state of catching, and factoring in his defense, he's clearly middle-of-the-pack, far from the back-up he's often portrayed as by people who didn't like the Milledge trade.

David Wright (Third Base)

PA	R	H	2B	3B	HR	RBI	SO	BB	SB	CS	BA	OBP	SLG	OPS	3 Yr	Fld	F$
625	98	169	37	2	25	95	100	71	25	4	.313	.394	.528	.922	.030	B	$36

If the Mets had won their division last year, Wright might have won the league MVP. And he can be better; Wright slumped in the first month and was sometimes susceptible to the outside slider. Though he's no Ryan Zimmerman in the field, he's an above-average fielder.

Pitchers

Pedro Feliciano (Relief Pitcher)

W	L	ERA	TBF	IP	Hit	HR	SO	BB	HBP	3 Yr	F$
5	2	3.37	285	67	59	4	58	29	3	0.36	$2

Feliciano is an outstanding lefty reliever for the Mets, very effective against lefty batters and not too shabby against righties, either. He was superb in 2006, with a 2.09 ERA, and he was also productive the first half of 2007 (2.59 ERA). He didn't have a strong second half, however, posting a 3.69 ERA during that time. Turns out he had a newborn daughter in the middle of the year who had a congenital heart condition (and who eventually required open heart surgery). His daughter is reportedly in good health now, and we might see an ERA under 3.00 once again for Feliciano.

Aaron Heilman (Relief Pitcher)

W	L	ERA	TBF	IP	Hit	HR	SO	BB	HBP	3 Yr	F$
6	3	3.22	336	81	72	6	65	26	3	0.36	$6

Heilman is the Mets' primary setup man, often pitching in more critical situations than Wagner. He's adapted well to the role, and you no longer hear fans discuss whether Heilman would be more valuable as a starter. The irony is that Heilman should probably be a closer, only entering the game at the begining of an inning. Batters have hit only .218 against him with the bases empty but .273 with men on.

Orlando Hernandez (Starting Pitcher)

W	L	ERA	TBF	IP	Hit	HR	SO	BB	HBP	F$
8	8	4.25	620	146	132	20	125	58	7	$6

El Duque was very, very hard to hit last year; his line drive rate of only 12 percent was incredibly low, totally out of character with previous years. It was a late burst of youth from the ultimate craftsman, but not likely to be a sustained one.

John Maine (Starting Pitcher)

W	L	ERA	TBF	IP	Hit	HR	SO	BB	HBP	3 Yr	F$
10	9	4.03	730	173	158	21	146	67	6	0.09	$10

Maine had a great first half last year, when he was 10-4/2.71, and a terrible second half (5-6/5.53). In fact, his second-half performance was one of the key reasons the Mets didn't hold onto first place, though he partially redeemed himself with a spectacular outing in the next-to-last game of the year. Did he tire, or did hitters catch up with his relatively straight fastball? Personally, I think it was a little of both, and I'll be happy with an ERA just a little over 4.00 this year.

Maine is a fastball/flyball pitcher, tailor-made for Shea Stadium. In fact, his ERA was 3.44 at home and 4.39 on the road. I'd expect that split to continue in 2008.

Pedro Martinez (Starting Pitcher)

W	L	ERA	TBF	IP	Hit	HR	SO	BB	HBP	F$
7	5	3.74	438	107	94	13	96	28	5	$9

At this stage, there is no reason to think that Pedro won't pitch over 150 innings this year. If he does, and he posts an ERA between 3.50 and 4.00, this will be a successful season for the Mets' pitching leader. Just don't expect anything better than that, despite his 2.57 ERA at the end of last year.

Mike Pelfrey (Starting Pitcher)

W	L	ERA	TBF	IP	Hit	HR	SO	BB	HBP	3 Yr	F$
7	9	4.57	631	142	152	13	91	62	10	-0.37	$1

Pelfrey doesn't seem to be quite the same pitcher the Mets drafted. A year ago, Pelfrey was considered the top prospect in the organization and Baseball America said, "He should be in the Mets rotation for years to come and has the potential to be a legitimate No. 1 starter." Unfortunately, Pelfrey lost something off his stuff last year and posted only a 4.26 ERA in Triple-A New Orleans.

Oliver Perez (Starting Pitcher)

W	L	ERA	TBF	IP	Hit	HR	SO	BB	HBP	3 Yr	F$
8	10	4.79	713	163	154	25	150	80	7	0.09	$1

Which Oliver Perez will show up in 2008? The 3.56 Perez of 2007, or the 6.55 Perez of 2006? For the Mets to win it all, he'll have to perform better than THT's projection.

Duaner Sanchez (Relief Pitcher)

W	L	ERA	TBF	IP	Hit	HR	SO	BB	HBP	3 Yr	F$
2	2	3.69	36	154	33	3	29	16	2	0.33	$1

Sanchez didn't pitch at all last year, and it's pretty hard to predict how he'll do in 2008. But a return the health and effectiveness would be a huge boost to the bullpen and the Mets' prospects. Offseason reports have been optimistic about his health; only time will tell about his effectiveness.

Johan Santana (Starting Pitcher)

W	L	ERA	TBF	IP	Hit	HR	SO	BB	HBP	3 Yr	F$
15	8	2.83	798	204	157	23	223	41	5	0.31	$40

Last year was his worst season as a starting pitcher, yet he was still able to finish fifth in the Cy Young voting. Always a flyball pitcher, Santana allowed a few too many to end up in the seats last season. The explanation is simple: A much smaller percentage of his fly balls were pop-ups in 2007 and a much higher percentage of his fly balls went over the fence. Both percentages were way out of line with the rest of his career, so it was likely a one-year fluke. As long as he stays healthy, there is no way he is not topping his strikeout projection.

Scott Schoeneweis (Relief Pitcher)

W	L	ERA	TBF	IP	Hit	HR	SO	BB	HBP	3 Yr	F$
4	3	3.89	274	63	60	5	42	30	3	0.35	$1

Granted, Schoeneweis was a bit unlucky last year, but I have no idea why the THT system thinks he'll lower his ERA over a run. I'll be happy with something in the mid 4's. Left-handed batters batted only .204 against him last year, when he was paid $3.6 million. In other words, he was one well-paid LOOGY.

Joe Smith (Relief Pitcher)

W	L	ERA	TBF	IP	Hit	HR	SO	BB	HBP	3 Yr	F$
3	3	3.58	230	54	49	3	45	24	3	-0.16	$1

Joe Smith is just plain baseball fun, a sidearming righty in the mold of Chad Bradford and a draft pick out of college who has spent very little time in the minors. Right-handed batters have a tough time against the sidearmer, but lefties hit him hard. Smith and Feliciano make a nice pair of bullpen weapons for manager Willie Randolph.

Jorge Sosa (Relief Pitcher)

W	L	ERA	TBF	IP	Hit	HR	SO	BB	HBP	3 Yr	F$
7	7	4.45	547	127	129	16	79	46	4	0.30	$1

The Mets were pleasantly surprised when Sosa provided a real boost to the starting rotation in May. The bloom came off that rose in June and July, so Sosa was moved to the bullpen where he provided some quality innings. He's a fastball/slider pitcher with a very strong platoon differential (lefty batters hit .326 against him last year) so it's best if he sticks to the bullpen where he will hopefully be deployed judiciously by Randolph.

Billy Wagner (Relief Pitcher)

W	L	ERA	TBF	IP	Hit	HR	SO	BB	HBP	F$
5	3	2.91	291	72	56	6	78	24	2	$18

He may have a lost a little bit off his fastball, but Wagner is still one of the best closers in the game. Unfortunately, he picked a key stretch in late August to become vulnerable, allowing runs in five consecutive appearances and increasing his ERA a full run.

They say that opposites attract. Wagner's agent is a former Mets minor leaguer named Bean Stringfellow. Wagner is generously listed at 5-foot-10.

Matt Wise (Relief Pitcher)

W	L	ERA	TBF	IP	Hit	HR	SO	BB	HBP	3 Yr	F$
4	3	3.96	261	62	59	7	46	21	2	0.35	$1

Wise collapsed down the stretch after hitting Pedro Lopez in the face on July 25, which cost him his job. If he's recovered, he's a valuable reliever with a wicked change-up.

New York Yankees

by Larry Mahnken of The Hardball Times

2008 Projections

Record: 93-69
Division Rank: 2nd, four games back
Runs Scored: 919
Runs Allowed: 778

2007 in a Nutshell

More bombshells than nutshells since last we looked back on a Yankees season. The team started poorly despite a spectacular Alex Rodriguez April, had another horrid streak that put it hopelessly behind Boston, got hot with the weather, and almost caught the Red Sox in a comeback from 14.5 games behind that would have been the greatest in American League history.

The Yanks wound up in the wild card spot and got skunked in four by Cleveland.

Then the big news began: Manager Joe Torre was dissed and quit, A-Rod said he wanted out, too. So did Mariano Rivera and Jorge Posada and Andy Pettitte.

In the end, the team overpaid to keep Posada and Rivera, knowing that without those two it would be relegated to also-ran status, an unacceptable option in New York, particularly in the final season of Yankee Stadium. Then, in mid-November, Rodriguez reached out personally to senior vice president Hank Steinbrenner, bypassing agent Scott Boras, and signed a new contract.

General Comments

Team Strengths

The team's one true strength is the lineup. The Yanks scored half a run more per game than the Tigers, who were second in that category, and led the league in most important offensive categories. In a tremendously balanced lineup, only two players with more than 200 at-bats finished with a below-average OPS. Despite leading the league in homers, they are not really a power-hitting team. Their strength lies in their ability to get on base—only one regular, Melky Cabrera, had a below-average OBP. Bench depth was a strength, particularly in the second half, but on a star-filled team like the Yankees, it's less important than it normally would be.

Team Weaknesses

While a subject of frequent criticism, pitching wasn't really a weakness for the Yankees—they were just slightly below average on the mound. However, compared to the offense, and the pitching of the rival Red Sox, the pitch-ing looked bad. They lacked (and lack) a dominant ace, and struggled to find a reliever other than Rivera until Joba Chamberlain came along late in the season.

Despite the addition of several younger players over the last couple of seasons, age is still an issue. The Yankees had the second-oldest lineup and oldest pitching staff in the league, though they were younger than the 2006 team in both categories.

The General Manager is Known for...

With the Yanks, it's not being in charge. Other teams are built to fit the vision of their GM, with the owner usually entering only to set payroll limits with only secondary consideration of the players involved.

Under George Steinbrenner, the general manager was one of several advisers, and his opinions often would be dismissed if The Boss were more inclined to listen to one of his other "baseball people." GM Brian Cashman was temporarily able to wrest control after the 2005 season, and began to craft the team in his own way. But with the new direction of Hank and Hal Steinbrenner, Cashman's role has been reduced to adviser again. It remains to be seen how much influence he has with his new bosses, and whether the course he put the team on will be changed.

It is Cashman's apparent desire that the Yankees build from within, usually using their fortune to supplement their homegrown players and retain them through their prime seasons, rather than buying the team's core on the free agent market.

The Manager is Known for...

He's reputed to be a control freak.

Joe Girardi will have to measure up to his ultra-successful predecessor in his first season as Yankees manager, but his style is more likely to be compared to that of Torre's predecessor, Buck Showalter. Like Showalter, Girardi is strict with his players and tries to be prepared for every situation. That seemed to work with the young players in Florida, but it remains to be seen how it will play with the Yankees veterans, who are accustomed to Torre's generally laid-back attitude.

Girardi's history with the team may help him, as his players probably already had respect for him as a former coach and (for a few of them) teammate. However, Girardi's controlling personality led to clashes with his previous boss, Florida's Jeffrey Loria.

Ballpark Characteristics

One of the most famous sports arenas in the world, Yankee Stadium is entering its last season as the home of the Bronx Bombers, who will move across the street in 2009.

While the skeleton remains the same, Yankee Stadium is hardly the same ballpark that Babe Ruth played in. The right field porch is deeper, the left-center field gap is shallower, the roof is gone. Still, Yankee Stadium has a history that even players feel when they come there. Many ballparks are glitzier, have more fan amenities, and showcase their home city more than Yankee Stadium, but Yankee Stadium feels like a place where championship baseball is played—probably because it has been played there so many times.

The new stadium will try to capture the look of the classic, but that "mystique and aura" probably won't translate.

The Minor League System is...

Greatly improved, and now one of the better ones in baseball.

The minor league system had the best winning percentage in baseball, for what that's worth. Cashman finally convinced the team that it should start paying attention to the draft, and the Yankees have flexed their financial muscle there, drafting players who fell only because of signability issues and frequently paying over slot to get what they want. They've also aggressively pursued international talent, and now their top prospects are no longer just the best in their system, but genuine top prospects.

At the moment, however, most of their best prospects are in the low minors, and unlikely to have an impact in the majors for the next couple of seasons. Their best (excluding Chamberlain) is either Austin Jackson or Jose Tabata, and neither has played above A-ball.

Favorite Team Blogs

Peter Abraham's LoHud Yankees Blog (http://yankees.lhblogs.com/)

Bronx Banter (http://bronxbanter.baseballtoaster.com/)

NoMaas (http://nomaas.org/)

The Replacement Level Yankees Weblog (http://www.replacementlevel.com/)

Keys for 2008

Players Lost from Last Year's Team

Roger Clemens retired ... again ... maybe. Either way, Hank Steinbrenner has shown little interest in bringing Clemens back. First baseman Doug Mientkiewicz was hurt most of the year, but was pretty good when he played. At press time, he was still a free agent, but unlikely to return. Among pitchers, Luis Vizcaino signed with the Rockies and Ron Villone remains unsigned. Infielder Andy Phillips was released and signed with the Reds.

Players Acquired

Reliever LaTroy Hawkins was the only player the Yankees had acquired at press time. He'll replace Vizcaino in the bullpen.

Reasons to be Optimistic

With Rodriguez's return, the lineup remains one of the best in baseball. The team didn't lose a single key player from last year's team, which was one of the best in baseball. Phil Hughes and Chamberlain have the talent to develop into aces right now.

Reasons to be Pessimistic

Hughes and Chamberlain could just as easily be busts. While Chien-Ming Wang and Pettitte can be relied on for 400 good innings, the rest of the rotation is more up in the air. Mike Mussina looks like toast, Ian Kennedy was good in his first pro season but has unexceptional stuff.

The offense also is likely to be less powerful than 2007, with Rodriguez and Posada unlikely to repeat their performances, and many other key players getting older. In the bullpen, Rivera looked shaky at times in '07, and while the overall results were good, at 38 he could lose it at any time.

Due for a Better Season

Not a single player on the roster did worse than expected in 2007. Some of the younger players may improve.

Likely to Have a Worse Season

Rodriguez, Posada and Chamberlain figure to do worse because they were so much better than expected last year, but all should still be good in 2008—probably very good.

Still Left to Do

The most immediate need is reliable relief pitching, followed by a reliable starter. It is unlikely that the team will make significant moves toward filling these needs—that would require sacrificing a great deal of potential in the Yanks' young players.

Most Likely Team Outcome

To win the division, the Yankees will have to be the best team in baseball—a goal they can reach if they play the way they did in the second half last year, or if Hughes and Chamberlain develop into good starters. If their rotation struggles, however, they'll find themselves in a tough battle just to make the playoffs again.

Player Projections
Batters

Bobby Abreu (Right Field)

PA	R	H	2B	3B	HR	RBI	SO	BB	SB	CS	BA	OBP	SLG	OPS	3 Yr	Fld	F$
626	86	146	33	2	14	70	111	93	20	6	.280	.389	.431	.820	-.035	D	$19

Abreu's power dropped suddenly after he won the Home Run Derby at the 2005 All-Star Game, but the severity of that dropoff was partly an illusion stemming from a better-than-expected first half power-wise and the fact that he'd hit 30 home runs rather than, say, 29, in 2004. Still, Abreu's power dropoff was very real: He lost doubles power as well as homers. But Abreu still has a great eye, still can hit it out when he gets the right pitch, and was an offensive force for the Yankees from the beginning of June until the end of the season.

Wilson Betemit (Third Base)

PA	R	H	2B	3B	HR	RBI	SO	BB	SB	CS	BA	OBP	SLG	OPS	3 Yr	Fld	F$
352	43	81	16	1	14	49	86	34	1	1	.260	.331	.453	.784	.004	D	$1

Why does a team needing middle relief trade away one of its few moderately effective relievers for a backup infielder? Well, Scott Proctor wasn't that reliable, and at 26 entering 2008, Betemit still has upside. The Yankees might look to trade Betemit to fill a more pressing need—like middle relief help (wait a second…)—but at this point he looks to be spending 2008 splitting first base duties with Shelley Duncan and filling in for Jeter, Cano and A-Rod.

Melky Cabrera (Center Field)

PA	R	H	2B	3B	HR	RBI	SO	BB	SB	CS	BA	OBP	SLG	OPS	3 Yr	Fld	F$
590	72	151	26	5	10	60	67	44	13	4	.286	.342	.411	.753	.036	D	$1

A nice surprise in 2006, Cabrera was really great for about two months in the middle of 2007, but he disappeared for the last month and a half. That finish makes the Yankees willing to part with him for pitching—and the two months before that make teams willing to give up those players for him.

Cabrera's defense is controversial among statheads—some numbers make it look great, some make it look awful. Like Bernie Williams, he appears to take some bad routes that he makes up for with his speed. Unlike Williams, he has a great arm. If Cabrera ends up being like Williams with the bat, too, the Yankees will either regret trading him or be thankful they didn't. There's potentially more to this kid than we've seen so far.

Robinson Cano (Second Base)

PA	R	H	2B	3B	HR	RBI	SO	BB	SB	CS	BA	OBP	SLG	OPS	3 Yr	Fld	F$
580	77	168	36	4	18	82	71	33	3	3	.313	.354	.496	.850	.030	D	$19

The Alfonso Soriano/Alex Rodriguez deal in the 2003-04 offseason looked pretty good for the Yankees—they got the best player in baseball at a discount. But it looks even better with the development of Robinson Cano. Cano is almost as good offensively as Soriano, better defensively, and several years younger. Cano might get even better over the next few seasons—developing a little more power, drawing a few more walks. He's already one of the best second basemen in baseball.

Johnny Damon (Left Field)

PA	R	H	2B	3B	HR	RBI	SO	BB	SB	CS	BA	OBP	SLG	OPS	3 Yr	Fld	F$
578	77	142	26	3	14	66	76	62	20	4	.281	.359	.427	.786	-.050	B	$15

Good contract or bad contract? This season can't secure the former, but it certainly can confirm the latter. Damon filled a vital need for the Yankees in 2006, but fell off severely last season and was pushed out of center by Melky Cabrera. If the Yankees end up trading Cabrera, then Damon could continue to be a valuable asset to the team if his OPS stays above .800. If instead he's playing mostly left field and DH, he'll need a career year at 34 to be a positive contributor.

Shelley Duncan (First Base)

PA	R	H	2B	3B	HR	RBI	SO	BB	SB	CS	BA	OBP	SLG	OPS	3 Yr	F$
464	58	99	19	1	25	73	107	38	1	2	.239	.307	.470	.777	-.021	$1

He's big, he's powerful, he's fun in the dugout, and he's a fan favorite. Duncan will get his chance as a first baseman/backup outfielder for the Yankees this season, but don't expect great things from him. An occasional long homer, and probably a couple of curtain calls, but this is no long-term solution to an inexplicable hole for the highest-paid team in baseball.

Jason Giambi (Designated Hitter)

PA	R	H	2B	3B	HR	RBI	SO	BB	SB	CS	BA	OBP	SLG	OPS	F$
411	61	86	16	0	23	66	81	71	1	0	.265	.407	.526	.933	$6

Giambi only provided what the Yankees expected out of him for two seasons, and is so injury-prone the team is afraid to use him at first base. But he's still a dangerous bat, and while this is almost certainly his last season in pinstripes, if he can match his projected numbers and stay healthy in October, he might bring the Yankees what they wanted out of him when they gave him the big contract—a ring.

Derek Jeter (Shortstop)

PA	R	H	2B	3B	HR	RBI	SO	BB	SB	CS	BA	OBP	SLG	OPS	3 Yr	Fld	F$
641	87	174	30	3	12	71	95	62	17	4	.310	.386	.439	.825	-.042	F-	$22

It was inexcusable ever to have given Derek Jeter a Gold Glove, let alone three, given his defensive range—especially at this point in his career. That being said, Jeter has still been a valuable player for the Yankees year in and year out, because his contributions with his bat and on the basepaths have been superior for a shortstop. He's never matched the promise of his 1999 season, but he's been a very consistent performer. He's reached the age where many similar players have suddenly lost all offensive value, and recent nagging injuries may foreshadow a similar fate for him.

Hideki Matsui (Left Field)

PA	R	H	2B	3B	HR	RBI	SO	BB	SB	CS	BA	OBP	SLG	OPS	3 Yr	Fld	F$
513	70	130	27	2	19	72	64	60	2	1	.292	.374	.490	.864	-.036	C	$13

New York toyed with trading Matsui during the offseason—and may do so after we go to press. But while Matsui has never been the super-slugger he was in Japan, he's been a good player for the Yankees since an up-and-down first season in New York. People have already forgotten that before Matsui, the Yankees struggled to find even league-average offensive production from left field.

Doug Mientkiewicz (First Base)

PA	R	H	2B	3B	HR	RBI	SO	BB	SB	CS	BA	OBP	SLG	OPS	3 Yr	Fld	F$
304	36	70	16	1	7	34	44	31	1	1	.269	.349	.419	.768	-.037	A+	$1

It probably wasn't a very smart idea for the Yankees to bring in Mientkiewicz in the first place, but it worked out for them about as well as could be expected. Mientkiewicz got hurt early in the season after a hot streak, then got hot again shortly after returning to the lineup. He skipped three months of completely sucking, which made his overall numbers pretty good. He's probably done as a Yankee, but he'll end up somewhere in 2008—someone always overvalues defense at first.

Jose Molina (Catcher)

PA	R	H	2B	3B	HR	RBI	SO	BB	SB	CS	BA	OBP	SLG	OPS	3 Yr	Fld	F$
280	29	64	15	0	5	29	55	16	2	1	.253	.299	.372	.671	-.013	B	$1

He may not be much, but compared to the dreck the Yankees have trotted out as backup catcher the past few seasons, Molina is Mike Freaking Piazza. He'll do just fine in the role, and if Posada goes down … well, the Yankees hope that doesn't happen.

Jorge Posada (Catcher)

PA	R	H	2B	3B	HR	RBI	SO	BB	SB	CS	BA	OBP	SLG	OPS	Fld	F$
540	73	131	28	1	19	73	92	70	1	1	.286	.383	.476	.859	C	$11

Good timing for Jorge, who put together his best offensive season just in time to make his last contract a big one. Posada will be overpaid, and he'll probably be a liability before this contract expires, but there are no alternatives for the Yankees behind the plate right now.

Alex Rodriguez (Third Base)

PA	R	H	2B	3B	HR	RBI	SO	BB	SB	CS	BA	OBP	SLG	OPS	3 Yr	Fld	F$
633	107	161	27	1	41	118	116	90	17	4	.308	.417	.598	1.015	-.037	C	$46

It took four seasons for Rodriguez to finally be accepted by Yankees fans—and one statement by Scott Boras during Game Four of the World Series for him to blow it. The way Rodriguez came back should heal some of the damage, but not all of it. Fact is, it took the best year of his career to meet the fans' expectations. A-Rod probably won't repeat his 2007, but he's probably going to remain the best player in the game for a few years, which means the difference between the Yankees making the playoffs and staying home in October. That might be worth $30 million to them right there.

Pitchers

Chris Britton (Relief Pitcher)

W	L	ERA	TBF	IP	Hit	HR	SO	BB	HBP	3 Yr	F$
4	4	4.06	292	69	63	8	55	26	2	-0.06	$1

It really is inexplicable that Britton didn't get more time in the majors for the Yankees in 2007. Sure, he's a fatty fatty fat fat, but he's one who's pitched well in the majors—including for the Yankees in very limited time. Considering how desperate the team was for middle relief help, you'd think he'd have gotten a closer look.

Brian Bruney (Relief Pitcher)

W	L	ERA	TBF	IP	Hit	HR	SO	BB	HBP	3 Yr	F$
3	3	4.35	251	58	50	6	47	32	2	-0.05	$1

Bruney's got great stuff, awful command of it, and a tendency to throw a fit when he's pulled from a game or assigned to the minors. It's not that Paul O'Neill-style "I expect better out of myself" kind of tantrum, but the "don't you realize how great I am?" kind. If Bruney ever finds command of his stuff, he could be a dominant reliever, but he might end up running himself out of the game with his attitude first.

Joba Chamberlain (Starting/Relief Pitcher)

W	L	ERA	TBF	IP	Hit	HR	SO	BB	HBP	3 Yr	F$
7	6	4.19	494	116	108	14	119	46	5	-0.07	$4

The Yankees brought Chamberlain up in August to help the bullpen while limiting his innings pitched for the year. They had high hopes, but couldn't have expected what they got. Chamberlain's 1,192 ERA+ was the highest in MLB history for a pitcher who'd given up an earned run. He made great hitters look foolish with his 100-mph fastball and slider, both of which he threw with great control.

The Yankees appear ready to start Chamberlain in the bullpen in 2008, if only to keep his innings count under control in his second professional season. While he does fill a major hole there, Chamberlain likely will have more long-term value as a starter, where he can use his good third and fourth pitches. Look for him to be in the rotation by the All-Star break.

Roger Clemens (Starting Pitcher)

W	L	ERA	TBF	IP	Hit	HR	SO	BB	HBP	F$
8	6	3.80	528	127	121	12	89	38	5	$1

The verdict on Clemens the accused is still out, but Clemens the pitcher is likely done. The Yankees overpaid him hoping they'd get a real ace, but instead they got an average pitcher with injury problems. That probably helped them make the playoffs, but even that didn't likely make it a worthwhile contract. Still, he might match his projections should he pitch in 2008, especially if he goes back to Houston.

Kyle Farnsworth (Relief Pitcher)

W	L	ERA	TBF	IP	Hit	HR	SO	BB	HBP	3 Yr	F$
4	3	4.18	280	66	60	8	61	28	2	0.41	$1

Farnsworth came to New York in yet another desperate attempt by the Yankees to buy bullpen help. Not surprisingly, it's failed. Farnsworth has a great fastball and a big slider. Unfortunately, he has trouble throwing either pitch over the plate without serving it up for the batter, making him terribly unreliable as a late-innings reliever. At times, he'll command his pitches well enough to be dominant for a stretch, but that's just a tease that fools his manager into putting him back into a vital spot, which he'll inevitably blow.

The Yankees were fairly desperate to move him last season but found no takers. He won't start the season as the Yankees' top setup man, but if and when Chamberlain is moved into the rotation and LaTroy Hawkins pitches like he's LaTroy Hawkins, he'll get his shot to blow some games. And he will.

LaTroy Hawkins (Relief Pitcher)

W	L	ERA	TBF	IP	Hit	HR	SO	BB	HBP	F$
3	4	4.75	259	59	68	6	31	21	2	$1

If you ever wonder why fringe players seem to find it so important to sign with a contending team, look no further than what a playoff appearance for Colorado did to LaTroy Hawkins' bank account this winter.

Philip Hughes (Starting Pitcher)

W	L	ERA	TBF	IP	Hit	HR	SO	BB	HBP	3 Yr	F$
7	7	4.12	520	123	115	14	95	46	5	-0.28	$4

Though overshadowed by Joba Chamberlain at season's end, Hughes came into 2007 as possibly the best pitching prospect in baseball. Injuries wiped out half his season, but there was a lot of promise in those 73 MLB innings. He was dominant in September, took a no-hitter into the seventh against Texas in May (before getting injured), and was spectacular in the postseason.

What stood out most was Hughes' use of the change-up, which the Yankees have tried to get all their young pitchers to master. Hughes struggled to command his excellent curve at times, and his fastball never reached the mid-90s levels it had in the minors (probably due to a change in mechanics the Yankees hoped to correct in the offseason).

Ian Kennedy (Starting Pitcher)

W	L	ERA	TBF	IP	Hit	HR	SO	BB	HBP	3 Yr	F$
7	9	5.19	655	149	151	23	118	68	8	-0.24	$1

Kennedy doesn't have much of a fastball, and his other pitches are good but not great. If everything goes right, and he has good control, he could be a pretty good pitcher, but he also could turn out to be nothing. So far, professional baseball has been a spectacular success for Kennedy—he posted a 1.87 ERA in 149 minor league innings and a 1.89 ERA in three MLB starts—but the sample size is still so small and his stuff so unimpressive that it'll take a while before anyone really believes he's got ace potential.

Mike Mussina (Starting Pitcher)

W	L	ERA	TBF	IP	Hit	HR	SO	BB	HBP	F$
9	9	4.46	671	159	175	20	108	34	5	$3

If Mussina is going to remain effective, he's going to have to reinvent himself. His fastball isn't going to get by anyone's bat nowadays, forcing him to have nearly pinpoint control with it and his other pitches. Sometimes he does, and he looks very good. But usually he won't, and it's just a matter of time before he gets pounded.

Ross Ohlendorf (Relief Pitcher)

W	L	ERA	TBF	IP	Hit	HR	SO	BB	HBP	3 Yr	F$
3	7	6.53	415	89	118	14	42	38	5	-0.16	$1

Part of the swag the Yankees got in return for Randy Johnson, Ohlendorf isn't much of a prospect, though he could find himself a place in the Yankees' bullpen this season. He impressed Joe Torre in that role last season, and Joe Girardi is sure to give him a shot early on, especially considering how weak the relief options are.

Andy Pettitte (Starting Pitcher)

W	L	ERA	TBF	IP	Hit	HR	SO	BB	HBP	F$
11	10	4.35	807	189	204	20	121	59	4	$3

As one of the most prominent players named in the Mitchell report, Pettitte will get his share of jeers on the road this season, but Yankees fans have already accepted his confession, so there'll be no awkward period at home for him like there was for Giambi. His borderline Hall of Fame chance is likely gone, but he's a pretty good pitcher who'll give the Yankees around 200 above-average innings with the occasional gem (and occasional clunker).

Edwar Ramirez (Relief Pitcher)

W	L	ERA	TBF	IP	Hit	HR	SO	BB	HBP	3 Yr	F$
4	4	3.93	292	69	58	7	85	31	4	0.16	$1

Ramirez has a great change-up and some delightful minor league numbers, but major league hitters appeared to be able to sit on that change-up and take it out far too often for Ramirez to be effective. Still, he's done well enough in the minors that some team should give him a full season to prove himself. It just shouldn't be a team trying to make the playoffs this year.

Mariano Rivera (Relief Pitcher)

W	L	ERA	TBF	IP	Hit	HR	SO	BB	HBP	F$
5	3	3.12	289	72	66	5	62	15	3	$16

Think about what this says about Mariano Rivera: He posted a 3.15 ERA, had a 142 ERA+, and saved 30 games in 2007 … and it was the worst season of his career as a reliever. By a lot.

Rivera's final contract makes him the highest-paid reliever in history, and the Yankees hope that 2007 was more a blip than a sign of things to come. Rivera still throws hard, still has great control, and is still as cool as ever … but every now and then he just doesn't seem to quite have it. It's at this point, if you're a Yankees fan, to head over to Baseball Reference and appreciate how very, very lucky your team has been the last decade to have had this guy.

Chien-Ming Wang (Starting Pitcher)

W	L	ERA	TBF	IP	Hit	HR	SO	BB	HBP	3 Yr	F$
11	9	3.75	746	178	190	11	81	48	5	0.12	$6

Wang was never a strikeout artist in the minors, but in the majors it's gotten a bit ridiculous. Wang has struck out fewer than four men per nine innings, leaving some overzealous statheads to label him a fluke. Well, he's not a fluke. He's not particularly hit-lucky and he's not particularly homer-lucky. He just doesn't strike guys out.

Well, the Yankees are pretty sure they know what they've got in Wang, so don't look for him to get demoted after a couple of lousy outings. Even in October. Wang was the single biggest reason the Yankees didn't play Boston in the ALCS last year instead of Cleveland, but that'll happen with him sometimes. His overall numbers are perfectly fine for a No. 1 pitcher in a deep rotation. If he were a No. 2 or No. 3 pitcher, few would find fault with him.

Oakland Athletics

by Sal Baxamusa of The Hardball Times

2008 Projections

Record: 77-85
Division Rank: Tied for Last, 12 games back
Runs Scored: 748
Runs Allowed: 803

2007 in a Nutshell

Rich Harden got hurt and missed a huge chunk of the season, Eric Chavez struggled with injuries, and Milton Bradley kept tweaking various body parts. Wait, isn't that what happened in 2006? But without the depth of the 2006 team, the 2007 version stumbled its way to a sub-.500 finish.

For the second consecutive year, the A's were decimated by injuries, causing many to call for the head of trainer Larry Davis. That's not totally fair; with so much player movement (and so much money on the table), players are increasingly independent about their workout regimens and the team can only hope to serve them in an advisory role. Furthermore, general manager Billy Beane took a calculated risk in assembling a team of players with known injury histories.

As noted in the *THT Annual*, the A's lost 1,200 player days to the disabled list and more than 50 players rotated through the 25-man roster. Regulars Dan Johnson, Bobby Crosby, Chavez, Travis Buck, Bradley, Mark Kotsay and Bobby Kielty all missed significant time. Starters Esteban Loaiza and Harden combined for 30 innings. And the troika of top relievers, Huston Street, Justin Duchscherer and Kiko Calero, all sat out large chunks of the year.

Whether they could have competed at full health is not the point; the team as assembled was a collection of known injury risks. It's a decent gamble to take for a mid-market team, but one that ultimately didn't work out.

Once it became clear that Oakland would not compete for the AL West last year, Beane rid the team of Bradley, Jason Kendall, Kielty, Joe Kennedy and Loaiza, receiving mostly salary relief and roster flexibility in return. The Angels' aggressive (though ultimately unsuccessful) overtures on the market and their young talent forced Beane's hand in the winter: Go for broke in 2008 or blow it up and start over. One week after a December pow-wow to assess the team health, Beane chose the rebuilding route and started by trading Dan Haren and Nick Swisher.

General Comments

Team Strengths

A complete lack of expectations and a management team successful enough to be given the benefit of the doubt. As far as on-field performance, the position players at the bottom of the defensive spectrum might not be awful. The offense might even be average if everything breaks right. More likely, however, is that everything will just break.

Team Weaknesses

Black holes at shortstop and center field. Crosby deserves another season to show what he can do at shortstop, but Chris Denorifa is an unknown after missing last year rehabilitating his throwing arm from ligament surgery. Outside of Joe Blanton, the rotation will struggle to log innings, which could overtax a bullpen whose top talents have significant injury histories.

The General Manager is Known for...

After trading Swisher, Billy Beane recounted a conversation he had with assistant GM David Forst: "We can't let hope be our strategy here … if this needs to be done, it needs to be done." Beane's greatest strength as an executive is that he identifies his team's needs and position relative to the league and acts accordingly. For the past few years, that meant taking risks on Loaiza, Mike Piazza and Frank Thomas, with varying degrees of success. For the next few years, it means stockpiling talent, evaluating prospects, and sucking up a few losses along the way.

Do you remember when Kenny Williams was crowned "Bestest GM Ever!" after the White Sox won the World Series? That same guy is now handing out four-year contracts to the likes of Scott Linebrink. General managers are like players: There are good ones and bad ones and the good ones have good and bad years and the bad ones have bad and good years.

Still, it wasn't surprising that, when a Beane-constructed team finally floundered, the yahoos came out of the woodwork proclaiming "We knew it! Billy's s--- don't work!" The most obnoxious of these was former infielder Mike Pagliarulo, who opined "this is MONEY HAUL, the worst-spent dollars in major league baseball" and "Forst uses OPS, OBP, LLBean, FYI and SOB as a system of analysis."

The FYI system worked when Beane and his management staff—yes, that includes his scouts—guided the A's to four division championships, one wild card and eight consecutive winning seasons. Payroll limitation or no, that's a pretty good history.

The Manager is Known for...

Relentless optimism. He'll need it, too, to captain the A's through the next few years. In his first year at the helm, Bob Geren didn't do much on the field to distinguish himself from his predecessors Ken Macha and Art Howe. Fans traumatized by Ricardo Rincon and Jim Mecir will swear that Geren's bullpen management was superior, but it's too early to draw any conclusions. While Beane's iron fist theory of field management is probably overblown, it suffices to say that he probably won't ever hire a manager hellbent on putting his own imprimatur on the team. And why not? Middle managers should implement the organizational philosophy, not buck it.

Ballpark Characteristics

The McAfee Coliseum has by far the most foul territory in the league, which depresses batting average on balls in play. While it has played as a fairly neutral park this decade, the Coliseum played as the most pitcher-friendly park in the AL last year. Flyball pitchers tend to get a little help in the evening, as the thick air tends to kill balls at the warning track.

The Minor League System is...

Restocked, thanks to the booty from the Haren and Swisher trades and a promising 2007 draft class. The minors don't boast any future superstars, but feature a number of players who are likely to contribute at the major league level. Daric Barton and Carlos Gonzalez are the front line position player talents, with Barton likely to open the year in the majors and Gonzalez following later this season and early next season. Barton and Gonzalez are corner players, however, and the A's addressed some up-the-middle concerns by buying low on the struggling Ryan Sweeney. Watch for Matt Sulentic and Javier Herrera, two highly talented players without the matching results.

Trevor Cahill and the newly acquired Brett Anderson and Gio Gonzalez are the top pitching prospects, but all are a few years away and of course there's that nastily high attrition rate for young pitchers. Faustino de los Santos has the highest ceiling of any of the pitching prospects, but he has several years before the majors. Guys like Jason Windsor, Shane Komine, Dan Meyer and Dallas Braden have succeeded in the high minors, but none profile to be much more than back-of-the-rotation starters, if that.

Favorite Team Blogs

Athletics Nation (http://www.athleticsnation.com/)

Catfish Stew (http://www.catfishstew.baseballtoaster.com/)

San Francisco Chronicle (http://www.sfgate.com/sports/)

New A's ballpark (http://www.newballpark.blogspot.com/)

Keys for 2008

Players Lost from Last Year's Team

Last year, the A's lost their most valuable pitcher and hitter (Barry Zito and Frank Thomas) to free agency. This year, Beane traded the team's most valuable pitcher and hitter in Haren and Swisher. Bradley, Kennedy, Loaiza, Kielty and Kendall were all dealt midseason, while Piazza, Stewart, Mark Kotsay, Marco Scutaro and Connor Robertson will all have new digs in 2008.

Players Acquired

Carlos Gonzalez, Anderson, Aaron Cunningham, Chris Carter, Greg Smith and Dana Eveland came over in the Dan Haren trade; Gio Gonzalez, Sweeney and De Los Santos were the haul for Nick Swisher. Only Eveland and Sweeney are likely to see much time in the majors in 2008. Jack Hannahan, Jack Cust, Jerry Blevins, Rob Bowen and Andrew Brown were acquired in mid-2007. Chris Denorfia was also acquired last year but sat out the season recovering from Tommy John surgery; he should be ready for 2008.

Reasons to be Optimistic

Watching young players blossom for a contender is more fun than watching them blossom for an also-ran, but watching a young team struggle is far preferable to watching an old team tank. Tracking the development of Travis Buck, Barton and Eveland this year and Carlos Gonzalez, Sweeney, Javier Herrera, Cunningham, Gio Gonzalez and Anderson in the coming years should at least be entertaining.

The opening of Cisco Field in 2011 should allow the A's to cap their rebuilding project with a few top-shelf free agents—that is, if the new stadium is the cash cow fans were promised and ownership decides not to pocket all that extra scratch. Managing partner Lew Wolff sounds like he wants to win, but the proof will be in the proverbial pudding come 2011.

Reasons to be Pessimistic

The attrition rate for prospects is high, particularly for pitchers. There's a non-zero probability that, despite best efforts and due diligence, this rebuilding project ends a few years down the line with a mulligan.

As good as the A's baseball operations department has been, their marketing has left something to be desired. That a team in such a good media market can have such poor television and radio contracts is beyond belief. With the A's targeting 2010-2012 for contention, they could stand to raise their profile in the Bay Area, especially with the Giants facing an extended period of suckitude.

Due for a Better Season

If I choose Harden, does that guarantee that he will end up having Tommy John surgery? I'm always optimistic about Chavez putting it back together, and if the offseason surgeries cured what ailed him, he could be quite good this year. And then traded.

Likely to Have a Worse Season

Like Chad Gaudin last year, Lenny DiNardo needs to cut his walks and up his strikeouts. Unfortunately, DiNardo doesn't sport nearly the stuff that Gaudin does. If DiNardo puts up the same peripherals next year as he did last year, he likely will see an increase in his ERA.

Still Left to Do

Complete the rebuilding project, which may include trading Blanton, Street and Mark Ellis, among others. Look for the A's to target young middle infielders in their next batch of trades.

Most Likely Team Outcome

The A's aren't nearly good enough to compete for the Wild Card. Where Oakland finishes among the stunningly mediocre AL West is a moot point, but last place isn't out of the question. Look for 70-75 wins and an eye toward the future.

Player Projections

Batters

Daric Barton (First Base)

PA	R	H	2B	3B	HR	RBI	SO	BB	SB	CS	BA	OBP	SLG	OPS	3 Yr	Fld	F$
551	70	136	37	4	9	59	70	65	2	3	.286	.372	.438	.810	.076	B	$2

Only one hitter 24 years old or younger is projected to have a higher OBP, and that's Prince Fielder. Barton will never have that kind of power, but he's not exactly a groundball-hitting machine either. At Triple-A, about 21 percent of his balls in play were line drives and only 37 percent were ground balls. In a few years, he could be a .400 OBP/40 doubles kind of player—and since he looks like a mediocre defensive first baseman, he'll have to do that in order to be valuable.

Rob Bowen (Catcher)

PA	R	H	2B	3B	HR	RBI	SO	BB	SB	CS	BA	OBP	SLG	OPS	3 Yr	Fld	F$
219	25	47	11	1	5	23	48	25	1	2	.250	.341	.399	.740	.026	D	$1

He's a backup catcher, and since he can hit a little, he also serves as a bat off the bench. It's hard to believe that the Cubs traded him for the ghost of Jason Kendall.

Emil Brown (Left Field)

PA	R	H	2B	3B	HR	RBI	SO	BB	SB	CS	BA	OBP	SLG	OPS	3 Yr	Fld	F$
463	55	109	23	2	10	50	78	41	7	1	.264	.333	.402	.735	-.037	C	$1

Brown is not the headiest of players, which probably earns him much more criticism than he deserves. While he slumped last season at the plate, his previous two seasons were capable enough. As a fourth or fifth outfielder, Brown can help a team.

Travis Buck (Right Field)

PA	R	H	2B	3B	HR	RBI	SO	BB	SB	CS	BA	OBP	SLG	OPS	3 Yr	Fld	F$
360	43	83	22	3	6	36	66	34	3	1	.262	.335	.407	.742	.033	A	$1

Buck's got the speed to play an acceptable center field, but some of his routes and his first-step instincts are ... well, unfortunate. He's limited to the corners, where he is an average defender. Many of his 2007 homers just cleared the fence, according to Greg Rybarczyk's Hit Tracker. Unless he develops significantly—possible, since he's just 24—he may never hit 20 home runs in a season.

Eric Chavez (Third Base)

PA	R	H	2B	3B	HR	RBI	SO	BB	SB	CS	BA	OBP	SLG	OPS	3 Yr	Fld	F$
459	58	103	24	2	18	63	84	51	3	1	.256	.338	.461	.799	-.038	C	$2

You think I'm going to say something bad about my favorite player? I'm rooting hard for him to get back to where he was just a few years ago. Three offseason surgeries later, he may do just that.

Bobby Crosby (Shortstop)

PA	R	H	2B	3B	HR	RBI	SO	BB	SB	CS	BA	OBP	SLG	OPS	3 Yr	Fld	F$
399	47	90	19	1	10	45	69	34	7	1	.251	.317	.394	.711	-.009	C	$1

Think we have a pessimistic projection? A .711 OPS would be an 80-point upgrade over his 2006-2007 seasons. Crosby has accumulated enough terrible major league plate appearances to overshadow his fine minor-league career. Since he once was a future MVP, A's fans should be thrilled if he turns into even an average shortstop. His biggest wart is that he can't make contact. That wouldn't be so bad if he still had the power that he flashed early in his career, but over the past two years his power has completely evaporated.

Jack Cust (Designated Hitter)

PA	R	H	2B	3B	HR	RBI	SO	BB	SB	CS	BA	OBP	SLG	OPS	3 Yr	F$
559	78	114	24	1	25	78	148	110	0	3	.258	.404	.486	.890	-.016	$9

It could be the bottom of the ninth of Game Seven of the World Series with a man on third and one out, and Cust wouldn't choke up on the handle. A hulking, left-handed monster, he has a swing designed for power, and nothing else. His huge uppercut generates tons of power to all fields: His homers last year were distributed equally. That's remarkable for a guy who hits so many home runs. When he made contact, the result was disastrous for opposing pitchers: .437 average/.861 SLG. A third of his fly balls went over the fence.

The problem is, he doesn't make contact very often. Almost a third of his plate appearances ended in a strikeout, including an embarrassing number of called third strikes, and he would shatter the single-season strikeout record given a full season of plate appearances.

Mark Ellis (Second Base)

PA	R	H	2B	3B	HR	RBI	SO	BB	SB	CS	BA	OBP	SLG	OPS	3 Yr	Fld	F$
550	67	135	28	3	15	67	77	42	5	3	.275	.336	.436	.772	-.034	B	$5

That he hasn't won a Gold Glove isn't a crime of Everettian proportions, but he's the finest defensive second baseman in the league by both THT's ratings and my eyes. David Pinto's Probabilistic Model of Range puts him near the top and Mitchel Lichtman's Ultimate Zone Rating rates him as +20 runs/season between 2003 and mid-2007. That kind of defense, along with a league-average bat, makes him very valuable.

Jack Hannahan (Third Base)

PA	R	H	2B	3B	HR	RBI	SO	BB	SB	CS	BA	OBP	SLG	OPS	3 Yr	Fld	F$
505	60	111	24	1	11	53	113	64	4	3	.257	.353	.393	.746	.004	C	$1

The power he flashed last year wasn't real. He could be a decent stopgap at second if Ellis is dealt.

Dan Johnson (First Base)

PA	R	H	2B	3B	HR	RBI	SO	BB	SB	CS	BA	OBP	SLG	OPS	3 Yr	Fld	F$
502	63	112	25	1	16	63	74	68	0	1	.263	.363	.438	.801	-.020	C	$1

Another year, another projected .800 OPS. His strikeout-to-walk ratios have always been encouraging, and he at least gets on base a little. If Cust gets pressed into outfield duty, Johnson may see some time at DH.

Shannon Stewart (Left Field)

PA	R	H	2B	3B	HR	RBI	SO	BB	SB	CS	BA	OBP	SLG	OPS	3 Yr	Fld	F$
501	58	127	22	2	8	51	53	39	6	3	.281	.340	.392	.732	-.045	C	$1

Stewart recovered nicely from the plantar fasciitis that limited him between 2004-2006, but he wasn't able to escape the effects of aging. It's worth considering how history would view Stewart had he had played center field rather than the corners. In Toronto and Minnesota, he was blocked by superior defenders Jose Cruz Jr., Vernon Wells and Torii Hunter, but Stewart had the reputation of a could-be center fielder. Now age and injury have sapped him of his speed, making a corner spot his only option, and his gap power is all but gone, making him well below average as a corner outfielder.

Kurt Suzuki (Catcher)

PA	R	H	2B	3B	HR	RBI	SO	BB	SB	CS	BA	OBP	SLG	OPS	3 Yr	Fld	F$
472	48	98	21	2	6	40	75	41	1	1	.236	.311	.339	.650	.015	C	$1

For A's fans still working off the Kendall hangover, a full year of Kurt Suzuki will be a breath of fresh air. He'll be valuable during his cost-controlled years but that doesn't mean that he'll be good. The OBP projection looks a little bit low—he reached base at a .376 clip in the minors—but the power looks about right.

Pitchers

Joe Blanton (Starting Pitcher)

W	L	ERA	TBF	IP	Hit	HR	SO	BB	HBP	3 Yr	F$
13	9	3.73	823	198	203	17	120	46	5	0.12	$12

His strikeout rates aren't sexy, but Kentucky Joe has decreased his walk and home run rate every year since becoming a fixture in the A's rotation. Over the past three years, he has hurled 625.2 innings (6.4 per start) with a 4.04 Fielding Independent Pitching. Over that same time, Player A has hurled 662.2 innings (6.5 per start) with a 3.94 FIP. Both Player A and Blanton will be 27 next year. Player A, otherwise known as Dan Haren, recently fetched a major haul of prospects on the trade market.

Dealing Blanton now doesn't make sense. Even rebuilding teams need somebody to pitch, and Blanton is as good a bet as any to hurl 200 innings. His peripheral numbers are good and improving, and he's under club control until 2010. He is one of the 30 best starters in the majors, and yet he doesn't seem to be valued as such, either by the A's (who have not offered him a long-term contract) or by … well, anybody.

Dallas Braden (Starting Pitcher)

W	L	ERA	TBF	IP	Hit	HR	SO	BB	HBP	3 Yr	F$
7	7	4.28	539	125	124	14	92	46	5	-0.17	$1

Braden sported an ugly ERA last year, but his fielding-independent numbers were pretty decent. The Oakland defense, a pretty good unit, allowed a .343 Batting Average on Balls in Play behind him. So was his poor debut a matter of luck? Perhaps, but it is worth mentioning that Braden was seen as a trick pitcher in the minors. Despite an unimpressive repertoire, Braden struck out loads of batters in the minors with an outstanding screwball. But when he arrived in the majors, he rarely, if ever, threw it.

The rumor was that management put the kibosh on the screwgie due to concerns about his health. If he is allowed to throw the screwball, he may yet turn out to be a useful pitcher.

Andrew Brown (Relief Pitcher)

W	L	ERA	TBF	IP	Hit	HR	SO	BB	HBP	3 Yr	F$
5	3	3.83	309	72	63	6	63	34	3	0.08	$1

The most notable thing about Brown is that he has been traded for Milton Bradley twice. Otherwise, he's a middle reliever with strikeout tendencies but a propensity for the walk.

Kiko Calero (Relief Pitcher)

W	L	ERA	TBF	IP	Hit	HR	SO	BB	HBP	3 Yr	F$
3	3	3.89	237	56	50	5	49	24	2	0.33	$1

It's unclear whether his shoulder instability is a chronic or traumatic injury, but, like Justin Duchscherer, his ability to contribute this year is a question. Also like Duchscherer, he is nasty when on, throwing a slider that is death on righties.

Santiago Casilla (Relief Pitcher)

W	L	ERA	TBF	IP	Hit	HR	SO	BB	HBP	3 Yr	F$
4	4	4.28	294	67	62	7	59	34	3	0.14	$1

The pitcher formerly known as Jairo Garcia finally stuck in the majors. He's no great shakes, but he's good to have around while he makes the league minimum. He's your generic hard-throwing middle reliever with a good slider and control problems.

Joey Devine (Relief Pitcher)

W	L	ERA	TBF	IP	Hit	HR	SO	BB	HBP	3 Yr	F$
3	3	3.94	239	56	48	5	52	27	3	-0.01	$1

Is he ready for the bigs yet? Since bursting onto the scene in 2005 as the new Mariano Rivera, Devine has logged only 53 innings. He is famous for giving up grand slams at the most inopportune moments. Last year, he was reasonably effective though used only in low-leverage situations. This could be the year he is given a regular slot in the pen. If he is, we'll see if he deserves the badge of a first-round draftee.

Lenny DiNardo (Relief Pitcher)

W	L	ERA	TBF	IP	Hit	HR	SO	BB	HBP	3 Yr	F$
6	7	4.80	503	113	130	11	58	48	4	0.42	$1

DiNardo wins the Kirk Saarloos memorial award for achieving good results with awful peripherals. Last year's 1.2 strikeout-to-walk ratio was not a result of not throwing enough strikes. DiNardo simply doesn't have the stuff to strike guys out. Like Saarloos, he's a junkballer who lives off grounders; had he qualified he would have been in the top five in the AL last year. He'll see significant time in Oakland this year—hey, somebody's got to pitch, right?

Justin Duchscherer (Relief Pitcher)

W	L	ERA	TBF	IP	Hit	HR	SO	BB	HBP	3 Yr	F$
3	2	3.50	189	46	42	4	39	13	1	0.24	$1

Word out of Oakland is that Duke is being considered for a spot in the rotation. While he started in the minors, the conventional wisdom is that he doesn't have the stuff or endurance to succeed as a starter in the majors. He relies on two pitches, but they are both beauties: a very good cut fastball and tremendous looping curve, both of which he throws for strikes. He racks up strikeouts and rarely offers the free pass. A bigger question is his health. A hip injury and subsequent surgery ended his season in May, and he already has a history of back troubles.

Alan Embree (Relief Pitcher)

W	L	ERA	TBF	IP	Hit	HR	SO	BB	HBP	F$
4	3	4.02	283	66	64	7	49	23	2	$1

It would be shocking if he finished 2008 in Oakland. A solid lefty reliever who owns lefties and controls righties should be able to fetch something shiny (if unspectacular) on the summer trade market.

Chad Gaudin (Starting Pitcher)

W	L	ERA	TBF	IP	Hit	HR	SO	BB	HBP	3 Yr	F$
9	10	4.39	744	170	170	16	123	78	7	-0.17	$1

Designated for assignment by the Blue Jays before the 2006 season, Gaudin was acquired on the cheap. Moved to the rotation in 2007, he made 34 starts, pitched nearly 200 innings and sported a 95 ERA+. He upped his strikeouts, reduced his walks and generally kept the batted balls on the ground. Of concern are offseason surgeries on his hip and foot, but he's expected to be ready for the season.

Rich Harden (Starting Pitcher)

W	L	ERA	TBF	IP	Hit	HR	SO	BB	HBP	3 Yr	F$
5	3	3.41	287	69	57	6	67	27	2	0.10	$1

In the AL, only C.C Sabathia and Erik Bedard project to have a lower ERA than Harden. But who actually believes he can stay healthy enough to make 30 starts—or 15? It's not that he's necessarily injury prone—although he's had all manner of shoulder, elbow, oblique and biceps ailments. It's the terrifying possibility that the whole shebang could give out and he'll end up on Dr. Lewis Yocum's operating table. Given his filthy stuff and his inability to stay healthy, the legend of what he could do if only he were healthy will continue to grow with each injury.

Colby Lewis (Relief Pitcher)

W	L	ERA	TBF	IP	Hit	HR	SO	BB	HBP	3 Yr	F$
7	7	4.70	559	128	135	17	80	48	5	0.41	$1

At one point, Lewis retired 24 consecutive batters over eight appearances. But he's still a terrible pitcher.

Jay Marshall (Relief Pitcher)

W	L	ERA	TBF	IP	Hit	HR	SO	BB	HBP	3 Yr	F$
3	3	4.40	246	55	61	4	26	25	3	-0.33	$1

The last submariner the A's got from the White Sox was Chad Bradford, and that seemed to work out pretty well. A Rule 5 pick, Marshall was used as a groundball specialist rather than a LOOGY. While 58 percent of opponents' batted balls were grounders, he struggled in this role and may yet end up as a left-handed specialist.

Huston Street (Relief Pitcher)

W	L	ERA	TBF	IP	Hit	HR	SO	BB	HBP	3 Yr	F$
5	2	2.92	252	63	50	5	64	17	2	0.08	$15

Street's FIPs from 2005-2007: 2.62, 2.61, 2.70. Among relievers during that time period, he ranks 10th in WHIP, 10th in K/BB and 12th in ERA. And he's only 24 years old. In other words, he's an elite reliever at a very young age. We don't know a lot about how relievers age, so it's hard to say whether his youth is a mark in his favor. Along with Chad Cordero, he will be an interesting case study in pitchers who were groomed and used as ace relievers from day one.

Philadelphia Phillies

by Jason Weitzel of Beer Leaguer (beerleaguer.com)

2008 Projections

Record: 90-72
Division Rank: 2nd, two games back
Runs Scored: 867
Runs Allowed: 772

2007 in a Nutshell

A strong finish, coupled with the Mets' collapse, helped the Phillies clinch the NL East on the season's final day and return to the postseason for the first time since 1993. The joy was short-lived: They were swept in three by the Rockies.

Shortstop Jimmy Rollins won National League Most Valuable Player, while the club got MVP-caliber support from Chase Utley, Ryan Howard and Aaron Rowand. Cole Hamels asserted himself as the team's ace, a bright spot in an otherwise lackluster pitching staff. Forced to take desperate measures, the team converted Opening Day starter Brett Myers into a closer.

The club passed 10,000 all-time losses midway through the season. Howard set a major league record by striking out 199 times. Able to overcome a rough start, the team battled through many setbacks, earning the city's respect for its gritty play.

General Comments

Team Strengths

Power and speed. One could say the Phillies were a team of MVPs, but more to the point, they were a team of overlapping MVPs at various segments over the six-month season. Rollins won it for a great campaign from start to finish. Rowand had that kind of season, too, staying consistent and exceeding expectations. Utley was better than both for about two-thirds of the season. Howard needed time on the disabled list before putting up MVP-caliber numbers. And don't forget Pat Burrell, who ruled over July and August.

Under the guidance of coach Davey Lopes, the team stole 138 bags—second in the NL—and had a league-best 87.9 percent success rate. Lopes also oversaw the outfield defense. The Phillies notched 39 outfield assists, tops in the NL. On the pitching front, bright spots included Hamels up front and Myers in the back.

Team Weaknesses

The team had too many pitchers with no business on a major league roster. The Phils used 28 pitchers in '07; more than half didn't belong. Ineffective starts by Adam Eaton, Freddy Garcia and others murdered the patchwork bullpen. Marginal pitchers like Geoff Geary and Antonio Alfonseca were forced into high-leverage innings. Tom Gordon started the season hurt. Ryan Madson was lost by July.

The Phils tested about a half-dozen Triple-A nobodies. In their most desperate hour, they re-signed Jose Mesa. Committing Myers to the pen meant J.D. Durbin and others pitched every fifth day. Run ragged, they somehow held it together and took the East by a nose.

The General Manager Is Known for...

He's into making "small splashes," as Pat Gillick famously stated this winter. The GM will be the first to admit the core players were already in place when he took over the team before the 2006 season, leaving room to work around the perimeter mostly. Even his scouting and development directors are largely the same as they were under the man he replaced, Ed Wade.

Results have been mixed. He's had some success picking through the bargain bin (Greg Dobbs, Jayson Werth), but almost none when it comes to high-priced inventory (Eaton, Garcia). He short-changed the bullpen in each of his first two seasons, which basically cost the Phillies a trip to the postseason in '06. Many trades, such as the Bobby Abreu deal, were of the salary dump variety, netting nothing. His best success has come at the trade deadline.

To some degree, his hands are tied. Although payroll is expected to be near $105 million, added wiggle room would go a long way. The park isn't doing him favors, either. Enticing the few quality, available pitching arms becomes a challenge.

Gillick, 70, is expected to step down when his contract expires after the season, and unless Brad Lidge, Geoff Jenkins and his other acquisitions set the world on fire, his legacy will be that of a stop-gap figurehead between Wade and the next guy. Although he is in no danger of leaving this club in disarray, the last two seasons have seen little to improve the team's future.

The Manager is Known for...

Charlie Manuel shows folksy dialect and aw-shucks gesticulation to outsiders. He's an unflappable guru and steadfast believer to those who actually count (players and management). After steering the ship through rocky chop, Manuel's Phillies arrived one win shy of

90, which would have led the league with Arizona and Colorado. For that, and the up-beat attitude management says rubs off on players, he was given a two-year extension in October with a club option for a third.

Under Manuel, the NL East champs never quit and played hard despite one of the league's worst pitching staffs. He knows hitting. He's overseen the growth of several superstars and the team's second MVP in as many seasons. He handles all types of players with finesse, from high-motor guys like Shane Victorino and Rollins to stubborn veterans. He keeps the spotlight shining on the field instead of in the clubhouse—possibly his most underrated trait.

He's tough. Philadelphia has not broken him, despite his facing machine gun fire since the day he was hired. He saw worse heat in Japan, the kind that shatters jaws.

His shortcomings are obvious. He's not the guy you want pulling the strings in a best-of-five playoff series. He doesn't have a great feel for pitching. His teams have started cold and put themselves in early April holes in all three of his seasons as skipper.

Ballpark Characteristics

Citizens Bank Park is a phone booth. Pitchers obsess over it. Even the hitters must feel guilty about it. There is a short window in April when it plays like a normal ballpark, but as soon as the weather heats up, it becomes a launching pad. The cheapest shots land in the flowers above the left field fence. Balls hit high and hard have a great chance of leaving.

Otherwise, it's a nice, retro-style park with a good selection of food and beverages. Besides the Mets games and dollar dog nights, the crowd has adopted a pleasant Wrigley Field vibe. It's getting harder to purchase good seats, but there are plenty of spots to stand and watch the action.

The Minor League System is...

The Phillies are without many prospects who project as major league players. Most of the the best are pitchers, and the best of the bunch—righty Carlos Carrasco and lefty Josh Outman—best resemble middle-rotation starters. Nevertheless, it's early, especially with Carrasco, who's 20 and considered to have the highest ceiling. Outman is 23 and may be closest to the majors.

2007 first-round pick Joe Savery is a big left hander who's barely gotten his feet wet; it's hard to know where he stands, but the early indication is he has the stuff to make it. The same goes for Class-A second baseman Adrian Cardenas, who looks like the organization's best position talent and was named Baseball America's high school player of the year in 2006. The team is also quite high on switch-hitting catcher Jason Jaramillo, who could be up with the club as early as this season.

Fans tend to blame the shallow pool on Wade, for signing free agents and relinquishing high draft choices in the process. Better reasons would include poor scouting and an over-emphasis on raw, toolsy players like 2004 first rounder Greg Golson, who does everything right except make contact with a baseball. Golson, an outfielder, struck out 173 times last season, 16 more than 2005 second-round choice Mike Costanzo, who was packaged to Houston in the Lidge deal (then re-gifted to the Orioles for Miguel Tejada).

Favorite Team Blogs

Swing and a Miss (http://swingandmiss.blogspot.com/)

Balls, Sticks & Stuff (http://www.ballssticksstuff.com/)

Phuture Phillies (http://www.phuturephillies.com/)

Phillies Flow (http://www.philliesflow/)

We Should Be GMs (http://pabaseball.blogspot.com/)

Keys for 2008

Players Lost From Last Year's Team

Rowand received the five-year deal he was seeking and will be a nice fit for the Giants. As of this writing, the Phillies were still talking with agent Scott Boras about right-hander Kyle Lohse. Outfielder Michael Bourn will have an opportunity to become an everyday player and leadoff hitter in Houston. Reliever Geary devoured the middle innings; the Phillies will need to find someone else to do it. Tadahito Iguchi filled in admirably at second base when Utley broke his hand. The Phils offered him third base; he took a job at his natural position in San Diego instead.

Players Acquired

You won't find a more pivotal player going into next season than newly acquired closer Brad Lidge, who's hoping a change of scenery will help restore his shattered confidence. A right field platoon of free agents Werth and Jenkins will make the loss of Rowand more palatable.

In addition, right-hander Chad Durbin will be used as a swing man, having held the same role for the Tigers last season. Eric Bruntlett, part of the Lidge deal, replaces Abraham Nunez as the utility infielder. So Taguchi figures to replace Burrell late in games and occasionally spot Shane Victorino in center field. If healthy, perpetually injured outfielder Chris Snelling could figure into the plans. Left-hander Shane Youman was claimed off waivers from Pittsburgh.

Reasons to be Optimistic

Rollins, Utley and Howard weren't built to sit at home in October. Hamels' curveball came along nicely. At 24, he may already be the league's best lefty. Signing Lidge means Brett Myers moves back into the rotation, setting up a formidable one-two punch with Hamels.

Reasons to be Pessimistic

In the bullpen, the Phillies are asking Gordon to pitch 70-80 innings of high-pressure relief through a torn labrum. Madson, who will likely work the seventh, missed the final two months with shoulder problems. Should Lidge fail, the bullpen is sunk.

Their off-season pursuit of a fifth starter suggests a vote of no confidence in Eaton.

Due for a Better Season

Helms will improve his .246/.297/.368 line, but will have to do so from the bench.

Likely to Have a Worse Season

The Phillies may have gotten lucky with Kyle Kendrick (10-4, 3.87 ERA). They'll find out whether he has stuff to avoid a sophomore slump.

Still Left to Do

The team continues to pursue help at third base, the rotation and bullpen, though officials have suggested the roster, as it stands today, will be the same when they arrive at Clearwater.

Most Likely Team Outcome

The road to the postseason will again go through the division, where 89 wins was good enough to edge the Mets. The Phils won the East despite having a boatload of issues with their pitching, and they're in danger of having history repeat itself in 2008. They're very thin in the rotation and bullpen; one bad break would set off a chain reaction and would be tough to overcome. Once again, they'll try to run and slug their way to the top and hope the pitching sorts itself out.

Player Projections
Batters

Pat Burrell (Left Field)

PA	R	H	2B	3B	HR	RBI	SO	BB	SB	CS	BA	OBP	SLG	OPS	3 Yr	Fld	F$
556	77	123	25	1	27	84	119	90	0	1	.270	.390	.508	.898	-.028	F	$13

In a season filled with many offensive heroes, Burrell regained his swagger after a brutal start and set a career high in OBP (.400), thanks in large part to 114 walks and a more aggressive approach at the plate. Burrell is entering the final year of his contract. He must prove he can still rake, and also field, or else he limits his future to being a designated hitter. The projections expect another standard-issue season, including a high on-base percentage, albeit with fewer walks, and good power totals.

Chris Coste (Catcher)

PA	R	H	2B	3B	HR	RBI	SO	BB	SB	CS	BA	OBP	SLG	OPS	3 Yr	Fld	F$
403	44	96	17	1	11	47	63	22	1	1	.261	.310	.402	.712	-.047	C	$1

For the first time in his career, Coste enters the season with job security, as the team's backup catcher. If anything, he runs the risk of being caught from behind by a prospect (Jason Jaramillo) instead of being blocked by a lousy veteran like Barajas, but for the most part, he's safe.

Coste went from having a 119 OPS+ in 2006 to an 83 in 2007, struggling badly toward the end. Unfortunately, '07 may be the better indicator. His flaws may no longer be a secret to opposing pitchers. Age and irregular action may also work against him.

Greg Dobbs (Third Base)

PA	R	H	2B	3B	HR	RBI	SO	BB	SB	CS	BA	OBP	SLG	OPS	3 Yr	Fld	F$
397	48	99	20	3	9	45	66	31	3	1	.276	.333	.423	.756	-.030	D	$1

"Dobber" can't field or hit the target, but the Phillies sure win when he plays. They were 49-29 in games he started. Dobbs, who was claimed off waivers from Seattle before the season, came out of the blue to start 56 games at third base; the rest were in the outfield and at first base. Expect modest or no improvements defensively, and there's reason to be skeptical of his bat. He appears to be a pure fastball hitter who can't hit lefties or breaking stuff, and will be exposed.

Pedro Feliz (Third Base)

PA	R	H	2B	3B	HR	RBI	SO	BB	SB	CS	BA	OBP	SLG	OPS	3 Yr	Fld	F$
560	65	135	28	3	20	75	83	32	1	1	.260	.302	.442	.744	-0.035	A	$1

Provides outstanding third base glove work and is defensively versatile, but his bat doesn't justify full-time status. Grade-B power is his only offensive asset.

Wes Helms (Third Base)

PA	R	H	2B	3B	HR	RBI	SO	BB	SB	CS	BA	OBP	SLG	OPS	3 Yr	Fld	F$
334	40	83	21	2	9	42	64	23	0	1	.277	.332	.450	.782	-.032	D	$1

His poor hitting in 2007 was a shock. Some people were expecting upwards of 70-75 RBIs. His previous two seasons suggested he'd figured out how to hit for high average and Charlie Manuel lauded his ability to hit to the opposite field. Instead, he looked sluggish. Nevertheless, Helms is a prime candidate for a comeback season, but no telling where now that the Phillies have Pedro Feliz for third base.

Ryan Howard (First Base)

PA	R	H	2B	3B	HR	RBI	SO	BB	SB	CS	BA	OBP	SLG	OPS	3 Yr	Fld	F$
612	98	146	27	1	43	118	165	103	1	1	.294	.417	.612	1.029	-.023	C	$34

The most impressive stretch of the 2007 season by any Phillie may have been Howard's final four months. After returning from the disabled list May 25, he was baseball's best power hitter, with 41 homers and 113 RBIs to finish with 47 and 136.

Since entering the league, he leads all players in home runs (125) and RBIs (344). No player has ever reached 100 home runs faster. In a time when blinding power—natural or otherwise—is drying up, the Phillies are sitting on the best in the biz. He also entered the history books with the dubious distinction of setting the single-season strikeout mark with 199. To achieve the kind of numbers we're projecting, he'll need to recognize when he's being pitched around and lay off the garbage. Unfortunately, it's likely that pitchers will avoid him more than ever.

Geoff Jenkins (Right Field)

PA	R	H	2B	3B	HR	RBI	SO	BB	SB	CS	BA	OBP	SLG	OPS	3 Yr	Fld	F$
492	65	119	26	2	19	69	109	46	2	1	.276	.356	.478	.834	-.044	C	$7

A Brewer going all the way back to 1995, Jenkins wore out his welcome in Milwaukee a bit with his streaky play and public grousing about being benched in '06, but always played hard and was a defensive gem in left field. He's younger than you think (33 starting the season) and kills righties; he'll make a good platoon player in Philly.

Jimmy Rollins (Shortstop)

PA	R	H	2B	3B	HR	RBI	SO	BB	SB	CS	BA	OBP	SLG	OPS	3 Yr	Fld	F$
677	100	177	35	11	19	83	75	44	35	4	.286	.334	.470	.804	-.037	D	$29

Not surprisingly, the reigning MVP faces a sizable drop from his career year, including a pedestrian OPS and home run total.

Not that stat guys felt he had the numbers to outpoll Matt Holliday and David Wright in the first place. Though his numbers look shallow compared to Holliday and Wright, his season was not without historical merit. Rollins became the first player to produce 200 hits (212) and 20 doubles (38), triples (20), home runs (30) and stolen bases (41). He set a league record for shortstops with 380 total bases, breaking Ernie Banks' mark set in 1958. His 139 runs and 88 extra-base hits were league records for a shortstop. He also set a major league record with 716 at-bats.

Carlos Ruiz (Catcher)

PA	R	H	2B	3B	HR	RBI	SO	BB	SB	CS	BA	OBP	SLG	OPS	3 Yr	Fld	F$
447	55	109	24	3	10	50	58	39	4	2	.278	.349	.432	.781	-.036	C	$1

"Chooch" contributed a .259/.340/.396 line with six homers and 54 RBIs, rounding out the bottom of the lineup with better-than-expected production and excellent gap power, smacking 29 doubles and two triples in 374 at-bats. Above all, he turned out to be a fine catcher. Ruiz needs to be kept under 400-425 at bats again to stay fresh.

So Taguchi (Center Field)

PA	R	H	2B	3B	HR	RBI	SO	BB	SB	CS	BA	OBP	SLG	OPS	Fld	F$
381	44	96	18	2	4	35	47	26	8	3	.290	.335	.393	.728	C	$1

To be charitable to Taguchi, he's a perfectly good fifth outfielder with a well-rounded skill set: a little speed, a little D, some on-base ability. As long as he doesn't have to take more than 200 at-bats for your team, he's an asset.

Chase Utley (Second Base)

PA	R	H	2B	3B	HR	RBI	SO	BB	SB	CS	BA	OBP	SLG	OPS	3 Yr	Fld	F$
588	87	156	36	4	22	86	97	51	10	2	.303	.376	.517	.893	-.033	A	$24

One joy of watching the Phillies reach the postseason was to see how Utley, a great competitor, would perform on the big stage. After one go-round, the answer was "wretchedly." Utley went 3-for-11 with five strikeouts, picking the worst possible time to become invisible. He was kept off-balance by Game One starter Jeff Francis and never regained his footing.

Forget that. Utley probably would have won the National League MVP if his hand hadn't been broken one of the 25 times he was hit by a pitch. Despite missing a month, he set a club record with 49 doubles. The NL record is 64.

Shane Victorino (Center Field)

PA	R	H	2B	3B	HR	RBI	SO	BB	SB	CS	BA	OBP	SLG	OPS	3 Yr	Fld	F$
488	68	125	21	7	11	53	62	31	19	4	.286	.342	.441	.783	-.014	A	$11

The Phillies' most overrated player is an average everyday outfielder when you factor in his overall contribution, perhaps a little below. Vic is beloved for his arm, speed and charm, but there are serious concerns whether he can withstand an entire season as Rowand's replacement in center field. He has an awful swing. His game depends a great deal on speed, especially to leg out hits. The slightest ding would make him a burden to the lineup.

That said, he's a magnificent defender with a laser beam for an arm. He will be asked to put in overtime playing next to Pat Burrell in left.

Jayson Werth (Right Field)

PA	R	H	2B	3B	HR	RBI	SO	BB	SB	CS	BA	OBP	SLG	OPS	3 Yr	Fld	F$
377	49	87	18	2	12	47	83	45	6	2	.269	.360	.449	.809	-.017	A	$1

Werth figures to split time in right field with Geoff Jenkins. The recipient of a new one-year, $1.7 million deal, he's still a pretty good value. He's a much better hitter against left handers.

Pitchers

Chad Durbin (Starting/Relief Pitcher)

W	L	ERA	TBF	IP	Hit	HR	SO	BB	HBP	3 Yr	F$
6	8	5.22	550	125	136	22	84	46	7	-0.37	$1

Durbin would have gotten a shot as the Tigers' fifth starter had the they not picked up Dontrelle Willis. He filled in admirably when Kenny Rogers started the season on the disabled list with blood clots in his arm.

Adam Eaton (Starting Pitcher)

W	L	ERA	TBF	IP	Hit	HR	SO	BB	HBP	3 Yr	F$
6	10	5.66	656	146	168	25	87	59	8	0.35	$1

Statistically, Eaton was one of the worst NL starters. Some felt he was pitching hurt, but injury can't explain myriad mental impairments, such as his chronic problems in the first inning and inability to put away hitters when he was ahead in the count. Throw in lousy command and the results speak for themselves. Eaton underwent an off-season MRI and the results were negative. However, the team's steady pursuit of an extra starter this winter, along with the addition of Chad Durbin, suggest the Phils have little faith in his ability to recover.

Tom Gordon (Relief Pitcher)

W	L	ERA	TBF	IP	Hit	HR	SO	BB	HBP	F$
4	2	3.90	236	56	52	7	49	19	2	$1

The sorest spot on the roster will be the eighth inning, where Gordon, age 40, holds the key after two seasons cut short with shoulder problems. Flash no longer has the same snap to his curveball, but remarkably, the right hander pitched well down the stretch. The Phillies are walking a tightrope here. If Gordon fails, it could set off a chain of events that leads to another bullpen call for Myers.

Cole Hamels (Starting Pitcher)

W	L	ERA	TBF	IP	Hit	HR	SO	BB	HBP	3 Yr	F$
10	8	3.92	683	165	152	22	158	50	5	-0.09	$14

Hamels' name rarely comes up in Phillie-fandom. The reason: Fans are legitimately scared about his elbow and his injured past. They don't want to get their hopes up on a 24-year-old. They've taken a "too good to be true" approach.

It's a shame, because he's the next Steve Carlton. His curveball came along nicely. His change-up is second to none. The report on his elbow is favorable. An MRI revealed no structural damage, just soreness. If he stays healthy, masters the breaking ball and maintains his competitive edge, Hamels will be a dominant major league pitcher for years.

Kyle Kendrick (Starting Pitcher)

W	L	ERA	TBF	IP	Hit	HR	SO	BB	HBP	3 Yr	F$
7	11	5.41	726	163	194	23	67	56	8	-0.64	$1

Kendrick survived his rookie season by pitching smart and keeping the ball down. Plenty of pitchers can make a living this way. An out pitch would help, and he needs to figure out how to handle left-handed hitters. As it stands, he's the Phillies' fourth starter. It may be asking too much.

Brad Lidge (Relief Pitcher)

W	L	ERA	TBF	IP	Hit	HR	SO	BB	HBP	3 Yr	F$
4	4	3.85	297	70	60	8	84	30	3	0.36	$9

He was one of the three best closers in the NL until September 2005, when he lost control of slider, fastball, Albert Pujols (in the NLCS) and two World Series games. Over the next two seasons, he lost and regained his closer job several times. He still throws a 97 mph fastball and a 91 mph slider that's unhittable when he's right. And he still strikes out a dozen per nine innings, but walks almost four. He isn't injured and should do well in Philly, though he'll give up more homers there.

Kyle Lohse (Starting Pitcher)

W	L	ERA	TBF	IP	Hit	HR	SO	BB	HBP	3 Yr	F$
9	10	4.85	739	170	187	23	105	52	9	0.66	$1

The asking price for Lohse, a free agent, had been shrinking as of this writing as teams realize he's a middle-to-back-end starter on a good team and nothing more. The right hander went 9-12 with a 4.62 ERA with the Reds and

Phillies, who acquired him last season at the trade deadline. He provided quality starts during the stretch drive. At 29, he's the rare free agent starter with upside.

Ryan Madson (Relief Pitcher)

W	L	ERA	TBF	IP	Hit	HR	SO	BB	HBP	3 Yr	F$
4	4	4.54	301	69	73	8	51	26	3	0.14	$1

When things go badly for Madson, he suffers from equal parts bad command and limited repertoire (his lack of a third pitch hurts him more as a starter). That said, his numbers compared favorably with previous seasons. He seems to be at his best when he's assigned a low-pressure inning. A healthy "Mad Dog" would go a long way in setting an early tempo in the bullpen. However, due to the shoulder injury last year, the chances of that happening are no better than 50-50.

Jamie Moyer (Starting Pitcher)

W	L	ERA	TBF	IP	Hit	HR	SO	BB	HBP	F$
10	11	4.71	788	185	200	28	106	51	6	$1

Moyer says he's ready for another round, but at 45, he's a candidate for decline. Although he's the picture of fitness, and he still knows how to feast on young hitters like those in Florida, one assumes the downward slope must arrive sooner or later. By July and August, the grind appeared to be taking a toll. Another 200 innings seems unlikely.

Brett Myers (Starting Pitcher)

W	L	ERA	TBF	IP	Hit	HR	SO	BB	HBP	3 Yr	F$
6	4	3.72	378	91	83	11	89	30	3	0.10	$4

Myers is moving back into the rotation against his wishes, but, at 27, certainly has the stuff to reassert himself as one of the league's top right-handed starters. We'll see how Myers transitions back after making only three starts in '07, and whether he gained a helpful perspective in relief. As a starter, he had been tinkering with a cut fastball to go with a hammer curve and steady command. He's at his worst when he lets his emotions get the best of him.

Nevertheless, don't get your heart set on Myers as a starter. He and the team agree he's got the makeup to become an elite closer, plus he's a strike thrower. Some felt that keeping Myers as the closer, moving Lidge to the eighth inning and acquiring another starter would have been the best plan.

J.C. Romero (Relief Pitcher)

W	L	ERA	TBF	IP	Hit	HR	SO	BB	HBP	3 Yr	F$
3	4	4.40	262	59	56	5	48	36	2	0.42	$1

Romero, who was designated for assignment by the Red Sox midway through the season, shored up the Phillies' greatest need: left-handed relief. In 51 games with the Phils, Romero posted a 1.24 ERA and held opponents to a .130 average. Left handers were just 5-for-40 (.125) against him, including 1-for-18 (.056) to finish the season.

Over his career, he's been a solid, but never elite, reliever due to inconsistency due to lack of command and a traditionally wide difference in splits. A three-year, $12 million extension was a show of faith by the Phillies, but it would be unwise to expect the same level of dominance this season.

Mike Zagurski (Relief Pitcher)

W	L	ERA	TBF	IP	Hit	HR	SO	BB	HBP	3 Yr	F$
3	3	3.90	228	53	46	6	53	25	2	-0.05	$1

Zagurski made the greatest strides of any Phillies minor leaguer last season. A total unknown before 2007, all he did was smoke three levels of the farm system and earn a call-up to the big club before a bad hammy ended his season. There's still time for Zagurski to hone his craft. He's likely to start the season in Triple-A.

Pittsburgh Pirates

by Pat Lackey of Where Have You Gone, Andy Van Slyke? (whereisvanslyke.blogspot.com)

2008 Projections

Record: 70-92
Division Rank: Last, 18 games back
Runs Scored: 720
Runs Allowed: 837

2007 in a Nutshell

The Pirates added Adam LaRoche and Tony Armas to a team that won 67 games in 2006 and got about what they should have expected: a 68-win team. On the bright side for Pirates fans, this was bad enough to get Dave Littlefield fired after six disastrous years as general manager and with him went scouting director Ed Creech and director of player development Brian Graham, who were equally bad.

General Comments

Team Strengths

The Pirates gave up 846 runs last year, but their offense is so dreadful that pitching has to be the team strong point. Ian Snell and Tom Gorzelanny are promising young starters who broke out in 2006 and Paul Maholm showed flashes of why he was a first-round draft pick. Still, everyone beyond that in the rotation is an adventure. Matt Capps has been solid out of the pen for two straight years and sometimes the other guys in the bullpen can hold a lead long enough for him to get into the game.

Team Weaknesses

There are either gaping holes or serious questions about every position on the diamond. Will Ronny Paulino ever seem competent again? Will LaRoche hit for a whole season? Will Jason Bay rebound and return to form? Is Nate McLouth any good? Can Jack Wilson actually hit? The list could go on forever.

The General Manager is Known for...

Currently, Neal Huntington is known for not being Dave Littlefield and very little else. Like his predecessor, he talks a good game, but beyond that all he's really done is cut some dead weight from the Pirates' 40-man roster and replace it with pitchers who throw hard and in the general vicinity of the plate. Still, it's early in his tenure to judge him because he's been dealt an ugly hand in Pittsburgh and has been on the job only since September.

The Manager is Known for...

The cynic would say, "losing 88 games in Triple-A last year, then somehow getting a major league job." Really, that wouldn't be too cynical because that's what happened. John Russell, who managed the Phillies' Triple-A affiliate from 2006-2007 and functioned as Lloyd McClendon's third base coach in Pittsburgh before that, is charged with reining in a clubhouse that walked all over Jim Tracy last year. He's the typical "we need to play defense and work on fundamentals" guy, the type that always seems to manage teams like the Pirates and never seems to have much success. Still, he's not Jim Tracy, and that's a relief to a lot of people in Pittsburgh.

Ballpark Characteristics

Lots of people say that PNC Park is one of the best places to watch baseball in the country and they're right. It sits on the banks of the Allegheny River, providing a great view of the Pittsburgh skyline. The food is great and not terribly expensive (at least not relative to other parks), and just about everything about the park is aesthetically pleasing. It really is the best part (and often the only good part) about seeing the Pirates play.

The Minor League System is...

Calling it "barren" isn't completely fair, but that's pretty close to the truth. In the whole system, Neil Walker and Andrew McCutchen are by far the best prospects, and there are serious questions about both. Walker has yet to hit consistently after a wrist injury and struggled a bit with his transition from catcher to third base, while McCutchen never found any sort of groove at Double-A Altoona last year.

The team's last two No. 1 picks, Brad Lincoln and Daniel Moskos, function as the top two pitching prospects. Lincoln had Tommy John surgery and missed all of 2007 while Moskos was a reliever in college and struggled in the New York-Penn League last year.

Steven Pearce was the one breakout hitter in the system last year, killing the ball from high-level A-ball to a September call-up, and Dave Davidson was a pleasant surprise on the mound, though he's only a reliever.

Favorite Team Blogs

Bucs Dugout (http://www.bucsdugout.com/)
Honest Wagner (http://honestwagner.blogspot.com/)

Pittsburgh Lumber Company (http://mvn.com/mlb-pirates/)

Bucs Trade Winds (http://www.bucstradewinds.net/)

Pirate Player Profiles (http://users.rcn.com/wtmiller/pirateprofiles.htm/)

Keys for 2008

Players Lost from Last Year's Team

Pitchers Shawn Chacon and Salomon Torres, first baseman Josh Phelps. The fact that the Pirates will probably miss all of them should tell you what kind of team they're fielding in 2008.

Players Acquired

Evan Meek? Ty Taubenheim? Josh Wilson? T.J. Beam? Wilson's a middle infielder; the others are pitchers. Pretty close to "no one," but not quite.

Reasons to be Optimistic

In the history of baseball, something stranger than a team like the 2008 Pirates having a winning record must have happened. Littlefield, Creech, Graham and Tracy are all gone and that's a good thing. At the very least, Pirates fans might be able to look back at 2008 as the year things started to turn around.

Reasons to be Pessimistic

The Pirates are almost certainly locked in on their 16th consecutive losing season and it will take a heroic effort by the entire organization to avoid the 17th in 2009. To date, Huntington hasn't shown much of a plan to get the team there and Greg Smith, the new scouting director, is one of the people known for ruining the Tigers before Dave Dombrowski got there. And one can't forget that the team is still owned by the penny-pinching Nutting family.

Due for a Better Season

Jason Bay, maybe, only because he can't get worse. Besides that, I wouldn't bet on anyone on this team having a better season in 2008 than he did in 2007.

Likely to Have a Worse Season

It's really hard to single out players on the Pirates who can get worse in 2008, though statistically Freddy Sanchez and Jack Wilson are probably the top two candidates to drop off. Pirates fans will probably have a worse 2008, as their favorite team will be tying the all-time record for consecutive losing seasons by any sports franchise in America.

Still Left to Do

Firing Littlefield was a good first step, but now the team has to prove there's actually a vision and plan for rebuilding the franchise from the bottom of the minors on up. By this time next year, the picture on Huntington should be much clearer.

Most Likely Team Outcome

Barring a late fire sale before the season, the 2008 Pirates will be a lot like the 2007 Pirates: flashes of potential and some exciting baseball eventually outweighed by their lack of talent and a final result of 67-72 wins.

Player Projections

Batters

Jason Bay (Left Field)

PA	R	H	2B	3B	HR	RBI	SO	BB	SB	CS	BA	OBP	SLG	OPS	3 Yr	Fld	F$
588	81	137	29	3	23	81	128	71	8	1	.272	.366	.479	.845	-.031	B	$13

Watching a guy go from a yearly OPS of .900+ to .745 is alarming. On June 3, Bay was hitting .312/.382/.540. From June 4 on, he went .204/.291/.337 in 368 plate appearances. Many people attributed Bay's slump to a knee injury suffered at the end of 2006 that necessitated arthroscopic surgery that winter. He missed a lot of time in September to rest the knee, but there were also whispers suggesting that he may be losing bat speed.

These projections suggest an in-between explanation: that the injury may have affected him, but he's probably never again going to be the hitter he once was. That's likely why Huntington has been shopping Bay pretty aggressively this offseason. If Bay gets off to a good start like he did last year, it would be surprising to see him in a Pirates uniform at the All-Star break.

Jose Bautista (Third Base)

PA	R	H	2B	3B	HR	RBI	SO	BB	SB	CS	BA	OBP	SLG	OPS	3 Yr	Fld	F$
556	66	122	28	2	16	66	104	53	4	2	.251	.329	.416	.745	-.006	F-	$1

Bautista can play all over the field and is a pretty solid utility guy. He can also get on base, and even has a little pop. As a regular third baseman, however, he's a butcher with the glove. Unfortunately, the Pirates have him starting at third base and not in a utility role.

Ryan Doumit (Right Field)

PA	R	H	2B	3B	HR	RBI	SO	BB	SB	CS	BA	OBP	SLG	OPS	3 Yr	Fld	F$
357	48	88	20	1	13	50	71	29	3	2	.279	.353	.473	.826	.014	F	$1

Doumit is good at two things: hitting and getting injured. In an ideal world, he'd be the Pirates' starting catcher, but the former management's love of Ronny Paulino and Doumit's repeated hamstring injuries have prevented that from happening. He's since been switched to the outfield, where his fielding has been decent and he's shown a pretty good arm from right field. Still, that's where Xavier Nady and probably Steven Pearce will likely roam, so Doumit probably will fill the "backup catcher/fourth outfielder/emergency first baseman" role.

Chris Duffy (Center Field)

PA	R	H	2B	3B	HR	RBI	SO	BB	SB	CS	BA	OBP	SLG	OPS	3 Yr	Fld	F$
371	48	93	16	4	3	31	61	23	18	4	.277	.332	.376	.708	-.003	A	$1

At the age of 28, Duffy will likely be starting 2008 in Triple-A. He's never demonstrated the ability to hit consistently at a major league level.

Adam LaRoche (First Base)

PA	R	H	2B	3B	HR	RBI	SO	BB	SB	CS	BA	OBP	SLG	OPS	3 Yr	Fld	F$
558	71	134	34	1	21	80	114	53	1	1	.271	.341	.471	.812	-.026	C	$8

Last year, LaRoche had a .498 OPS on May 4, then went .299/.365/.498 the rest of the way. While that's not bad, it's also not what the Pirates had hoped for when they traded for him last January. His power didn't play to PNC Park's short right field fence as they had hoped, mostly because he sprays line drives around the field. If he can avoid another slow start, he should have a solid year. He's a good hitter, but he's still not the middle-of-the-lineup power lefty the Pirates seem to be perpetually in search of.

Nate McLouth (Center Field)

PA	R	H	2B	3B	HR	RBI	SO	BB	SB	CS	BA	OBP	SLG	OPS	3 Yr	Fld	F$
403	55	93	20	3	10	45	72	33	18	2	.262	.333	.420	.753	-.006	C	$2

The Pirates gave extended trials in center field to Chris Duffy, Rajai Davis and Nyjer Morgan, but have often seemed reluctant to play McLouth, even though he looks like the one guy of the four who might be a decent outfielder. He killed the ball in the second half of the year and had arguably the best offensive numbers of any Pirate with more than 300 plate appearances. I hope the new management will give him a longer look.

Xavier Nady (Right Field)

PA	R	H	2B	3B	HR	RBI	SO	BB	SB	CS	BA	OBP	SLG	OPS	3 Yr	Fld	F$
462	57	115	24	1	16	63	89	27	2	1	.274	.327	.450	.777	-.026	D	$4

Nady finally managed to figure out right-handed pitching last year, putting up a respectable .802 OPS against righties. Unfortunately, he slipped against lefties and hit only .278/.330/.476 overall. He also missed a bunch of time due to various lingering injuries. He's not an everyday player, but the Pirates are forced to use him as one.

Ronny Paulino (Catcher)

PA	R	H	2B	3B	HR	RBI	SO	BB	SB	CS	BA	OBP	SLG	OPS	3 Yr	Fld	F$
478	53	122	24	1	10	54	79	34	1	2	.280	.331	.408	.739	-.001	C	$1

After he hit .310 in his rookie year, everyone expected Paulino to drop off a little bit in 2007. In that regard, he was one of the few Pirates who met expectations as he flirted with the Mendoza line until July. This year's projection sees a middle-of-the-road path for him, more along the lines of what people expected from him in 2007. The Pirates' new front office seems determined to acquire some competition for him behind the plate, likely because he was pretty awful at catching baseballs and throwing runners out last year.

Steven Pearce (Right Field)

PA	R	H	2B	3B	HR	RBI	SO	BB	SB	CS	BA	OBP	SLG	OPS	3 Yr	Fld	F$
556	71	133	31	3	22	70	90	33	7	2	.262	.313	.464	.777	.027	B	$1

Pearce is the rare Pirates minor leaguer who has found a way to exceed expectations. He started last year in Lynchburg (High-A) and killed the ball all the way to a September call-up with the Bucs. He even showed a bit of patience at the plate to go with his 31 homers, a rarity for anyone in the Pirates system. If he can keep hitting at the big league level, he makes Nady expendable.

Freddy Sanchez (Second Base)

PA	R	H	2B	3B	HR	RBI	SO	BB	SB	CS	BA	OBP	SLG	OPS	3 Yr	Fld	F$
578	66	163	38	3	5	59	61	27	1	1	.304	.340	.415	.755	-.031	C	$4

After he won the batting title in 2006, Sanchez' average dropped 40 points last year and his OBP and SLG dropped an according 30 points. He's truly an empty .300 hitter, as there's very little on-base ability or power to go with his high batting average. The projection sees a big drop in slugging percentage in 2008. If that happens, Sanchez will be nearly worthless as an offensive player, high batting average or not.

Jack Wilson (Shortstop)

PA	R	H	2B	3B	HR	RBI	SO	BB	SB	CS	BA	OBP	SLG	OPS	3 Yr	Fld	F$
532	58	134	26	3	7	52	54	33	3	3	.279	.328	.389	.717	-.042	C	$1

Over the seven seasons of his big league career, Jack Wilson has managed to hit well for approximately four months. Two of those months were his torrid August and September last year, which brought most of his seasonal stats to career highs. The projection sees a return to the old Jack Wilson in 2008 and that seems like a good bet, since the better part of the past seven years certainly agrees with it.

Pitchers

Jonah Bayliss (Relief Pitcher)

W	L	ERA	TBF	IP	Hit	HR	SO	BB	HBP	3 Yr	F$
3	4	5.02	287	64	63	8	53	34	3	0.16	$1

He's not so affectionately nicknamed "The Gas Can" by Pirates fans for throwing gas onto fires instead of putting them out, like a good reliever should. But hey, he throws hard!

Matt Capps (Relief Pitcher)

W	L	ERA	TBF	IP	Hit	HR	SO	BB	HBP	3 Yr	F$
5	3	3.63	309	75	68	7	57	21	3	-0.18	$9

Capps did a nice job after taking over the closer role for the Pirates in May. His career is actually quite mystifying. His out pitch is a relatively straight 94 mph fastball that is remarkable only because he throws it over the plate again and again (he's walked only 28 hitters in 163.2 career big league innings). One would assume that he would get pounded, but he's actually been a very effective reliever the past two years.

Shawn Chacon (Relief Pitcher)

W	L	ERA	TBF	IP	Hit	HR	SO	BB	HBP	3 Yr	F$
5	5	4.71	406	92	91	10	63	46	4	0.32	$1

Chacon was solid out of the pen last year for the Pirates, striking out a very not-Chacon-like 62 hitters in 76.2 innings and providing good middle and long relief. The Pirates chose not to negotiate with him and he filed for free agency. They're interested in bringing him back, but they're not alone because he's marketing himself as a potential starter and that seems to be raising his value on the market. He was quite bad as a starting pitcher last year, and signing him for that purpose would probably be a mistake given his recent history (a baffling 2005 stint with the Yankees aside).

Dave Davidson (Relief Pitcher)

W	L	ERA	TBF	IP	Hit	HR	SO	BB	HBP	3 Yr	F$
3	4	4.94	269	59	60	6	45	36	3	-0.30	$1

Davidson had a semi-breakout year by pitching well in both Double-A and Triple-A last year. He's quite good at keeping the ball in the park, allowing only three homers in 67.1 minor league innings. He made a brief cameo with the Bucs in September and may get a longer look if Marte is traded, though he's probably not quite ready for prime time yet (and the projection agrees).

Zach Duke (Starting Pitcher)

W	L	ERA	TBF	IP	Hit	HR	SO	BB	HBP	3 Yr	F$
7	8	4.46	600	139	161	11	66	40	5	-0.46	$1

The reigning "most frustrating pitcher on the Pirates" (a mantle inherited from Kip Wells, who got it from Kris Benson, who got it from Jason Schmidt), Duke missed a good chunk of 2007 with arm troubles. Maybe those arm troubles explain the .359 batting average opponents put up against Duke in 2007. One tends to blame the Pirates' awful defense for Duke's troubles (he's had one of the worst batting averages on balls in play against him in either league for each of the last two years), but last year Duke struck out only 41 hitters in 107.1 innings. If he's ever going to right the ship, that's the first thing that has to change.

Tom Gorzelanny (Starting Pitcher)

W	L	ERA	TBF	IP	Hit	HR	SO	BB	HBP	3 Yr	F$
10	9	4.23	756	176	176	16	120	67	9	-0.07	$2

He's a highly touted young pitcher who made it through the Pirates minor league system and managed to meet expectations in the big leagues. The most interesting part of his projection is innings pitched. He threw more than 200 for the Bucs last year, and in one seven-start span in May and June threw 110, 118, 120, 97, 117, 97 and 123 pitches. He's got a bit of a history with arm problems and so seeing him projected to throw almost 30 fewer innings in 2008 isn't much of a surprise.

John Grabow (Relief Pitcher)

W	L	ERA	TBF	IP	Hit	HR	SO	BB	HBP	3 Yr	F$
4	3	4.07	263	61	60	5	50	26	2	0.45	$1

Before last year, Grabow was a decent left-handed reliever with almost no lefty/righty split. In 2007, Grabow had what was widely viewed as a bad year, but held lefties to an OPS more than 200 points lower than righties. One would think that a team like the Pirates wouldn't need him and Marte, but hardly any movement has been made to trade either.

Paul Maholm (Starting Pitcher)

W	L	ERA	TBF	IP	Hit	HR	SO	BB	HBP	3 Yr	F$
9	9	4.48	722	166	183	16	100	60	8	-0.11	$1

From May 25 to Aug. 28, Maholm had a nice run of 18 starts where he put up a WHIP of 1.28 and a 3.69 ERA. It was definitely the best stretch of his career, though his relatively low number of strikeouts in that stretch (5.4 per nine innings) suggests that at least some of it was probably smoke and mirrors. Still, he can be a solid bottom-of-the-rotation guy if he can approximate those numbers over a full season. He'll be 26 in 2008, so that still seems possible.

Damaso Marte (Relief Pitcher)

W	L	ERA	TBF	IP	Hit	HR	SO	BB	HBP	3 Yr	F$
3	3	3.78	237	55	48	4	58	27	2	0.36	$1

Last year, lefties were 6-for-64 against Marte with four singles and two doubles. That's one of the most insanely dominant splits in recent memory. Marte was also half-decent against righties, making him an incredible steal at $2 million in 2008 and a very likely trade target for a lot of teams.

Matt Morris (Starting Pitcher)

W	L	ERA	TBF	IP	Hit	HR	SO	BB	HBP	3 Yr	F$
10	10	4.60	795	185	205	18	96	55	8	0.42	$1

Dave Littlefield's final mistake. Why would a team on the Pirates' budget that constantly complains about financial restraints go out and pick up a washed-up starter and his entire $10 million salary for 2008? If Morris even approaches the hot start he had with the Giants last year, he'll probably be on the first plane out of Pittsburgh.

Franquelis Osoria (Relief Pitcher)

W	L	ERA	TBF	IP	Hit	HR	SO	BB	HBP	3 Yr	F$
4	4	4.87	337	75	87	6	39	32	5	0.04	$1

He's managed to survive Huntington's winter bullpen remodeling, so he'll probably have a good shot at a spot in Pittsburgh this spring, especially with Salomon Torres having been traded. He's absolutely useless against lefties, who have a .409/.458/.655 career line against him.

Romulo Sanchez (Relief Pitcher)

W	L	ERA	TBF	IP	Hit	HR	SO	BB	HBP	3 Yr	F$
3	4	5.70	293	64	74	9	38	31	4	-0.52	$1

Sadly, Sanchez is the best Latin American signing of the Dave Littlefield era. There is some upside here: He's a huge guy and he throws smoke. After struggling with his control early in his career, something seemed to click last year in Double-A and he earned a late call-up to the Pirates. He probably won't compete for a bullpen spot out of the gate in 2007, but a strong showing in Triple-A could get him a midseason call-up.

Ian Snell (Starting Pitcher)

W	L	ERA	TBF	IP	Hit	HR	SO	BB	HBP	3 Yr	F$
10	10	4.40	770	181	183	22	151	62	6	0.10	$4

In 2006, when Snell first emerged as a reliable pitcher, he had two huge problems: left-handed hitters (.912 OPS against!) and home runs (29 allowed in 186 innings). In the first half of 2007 he held lefties to a .670 OPS against and gave up only nine homers in 116.2 innings. He went into the break with a 2.97 ERA and a 1.17 WHIP.

In the second half, lefties started clocking him again (.963 OPS against) and he gave up 13 homers in 91.1 innings. His ERA jumped to 4.83 in that span and his WHIP jumped to 1.54. If he can keep lefties in check and the ball in the park for a larger part of 2008, he might be better than anyone thinks. If not, then what we see is what we get.

John Van Benschoten (Starting Pitcher)

W	L	ERA	TBF	IP	Hit	HR	SO	BB	HBP	3 Yr	F$
6	8	5.42	587	129	142	15	84	69	7	0.17	$1

Last year was his first significant action since 2004. The Pirates were fooled by his deceivingly low Triple-A ERA and gave him nine big league starts. He got thrashed in all nine, in every single way possible. The projection doesn't see much of a future for him and it's hard to disagree with that.

San Diego Padres

by Geoff Young of The Hardball Times

2008 Projections

Record: 86-76
Division Rank: 1st, by one game
Runs Scored: 754
Runs Allowed: 708

2007 in a Nutshell

The Padres played about as well as they had in 2006, when they won the NL West, but the rest of the division improved. Colorado finished the season on a torrid streak that culminated in a 13-inning victory over the Padres in a one-game playoff at Coors Field to determine which team would earn the final spot in the postseason.

General Comments

Team Strengths

The Padres have good young power, a strong front of the rotation, and a strong bullpen. It didn't get much play, but among all big-league teams, only the Brewers (110) hit more home runs on the road than the Padres did (99) in 2007. Adrian Gonzalez, Kevin Kouzmanoff and Khalil Greene form a strong nucleus, while Hairston and prospect Chase Headley could supply additional power in 2008. Jake Peavy bounced back from a substandard showing (by his standards) and won the Cy Young Award, while Chris Young built on his strong 2007 performance before being slowed by injuries toward season's end.

Team Weaknesses

The Padres struggled to get on base. Only the Diamondbacks and White Sox had lower OBPs. The back end of the rotation, "led" by Justin Germano, Clay Hensley and David Wells, was a disaster. The team, because of to the departures of Josh Barfield and Dave Roberts, also featured less speed than version 2006.

The General Manager Is Known for...

Kevin Towers is known for generally getting good value in trades, especially where pitchers are involved, finding creative ways to build an organization on a tight budget, and being candid with the media.

The Manager Is Known for...

This was Bud Black's first managerial stint at any level so it's tough to say, but in his rookie season, Black called more pitchouts than any other manager in baseball and had a very quick hook with his starters. He also stuck with Kouzmanoff, his rookie third baseman, whose early-season struggles could have gotten him sent to Triple-A under Black's predecessor, Bruce Bochy.

Ballpark Characteristics

Petco Park was the most difficult place to score runs in baseball in 2007, as it was each of the previous two seasons. In 2004, its first year of existence, only Seattle's Safeco Field was less conducive to offense, and even then, not by much. Visiting right fielders often have trouble negotiating the irksome Petco Porch that juts out along the foul line, as well as the visitors' bullpen.

The Minor League System is...

Improving. It's not as bad as last year, but it's still not where it needs to be. For the first time in a long time, the Padres have two legitimate future everyday players who have experience in the high minors (Matt Antonelli, Headley), and in right hander Mat Latos, they have a rare high-ceiling power arm. Grady Fuson and company have done a nice job of building depth in the system, but the Padres could use a few more impact-type prospects to complement the B- and C-level guys that currently inhabit the organization.

Favorite Team Blogs

Duck Snorts (http://ducksnorts.com/blog/)
Friar Forecast (http://friarforecast.com/)
Gass Lamp Ball (http://www.gaslampball.com/)
San Diego Spotlight (http://mvn.com/mlb-padres/)

Keys for 2008

Players Lost from Last Year's Team

Infielders Geoff Blum, Morgan Ensberg and Marcus Giles, outfielders Milton Bradley, Mike Cameron, Brady Clark, Jason Lane and Rob Mackowiak, pitchers Brett Tomko and Doug Brocail.

Players Acquired

Infielders Tadahito Iguchi, Luis Rodriguez and Callix Crabbe, outfielder Jim Edmonds, pitchers Michael Gardner, Carlos Guevara, Randy Wolf and Mauro Zarate.

Reasons to be Optimistic

Gonzalez, Peavy and Young have played together for two seasons now. They're still young and they've got long-term contracts. This is the nucleus of the club, and it's a strong one. The Padres are as good as anyone in terms of getting value from their bullpen, and if Black's rookie campaign is any indication, he's capable of handling himself as a big-league manager.

Reasons to be Pessimistic

The NL West has gone from baseball's laughingstock to arguably its toughest division in a few short years. The Diamondbacks and Rockies are loaded with young talent, while the two other California teams have cash to burn. If the Dodgers and Giants start investing more wisely, things could get even tighter. It's probably going to take 90 wins to claim the division. Not many Padres figure to improve on last year's numbers.

Due for a Better Season

Maybe Brian Giles and Kouzmanoff, although not by much. Young if he stays healthy. Possibly Barrett, but mainly because he was dreadful in 2007.

Likely to Have a Worse Season

Age could catch up to Greg Maddux, although it hasn't yet. Bell likely will slip some. We don't know how Edmonds and Iguchi will respond to playing half their games at Petco Park.

Still Left to Do

The Padres need depth at the back of their rotation and someone to step in when Edmonds inevitably lands on the DL.

Most Likely Team Outcome

I said 85 wins last year, and they ended up with 89. I'll say 87 this time around—good enough for second place in the NL West and possibly a wild card berth.

Player Projections

Batters

Matt Antonelli (Second Base)

PA	R	H	2B	3B	HR	RBI	SO	BB	SB	CS	BA	OBP	SLG	OPS	3 Yr	Fld	F$
569	69	128	19	4	15	61	104	52	13	6	.254	.327	.396	.723	.064	D	$1

Before the Padres signed Iguchi, there was talk that Antonelli might break camp as the club's starting second baseman. Antonelli, a former third baseman at Wake Forest, took to second nicely in 2007 but has spent less than half a season above A-ball, so there's no hurry here. Eventually he'll settle in as a solid top-of-the-order option. Think along the lines of former Astros second baseman Bill Doran, or maybe Tony Bernazard.

Josh Bard (Catcher)

PA	R	H	2B	3B	HR	RBI	SO	BB	SB	CS	BA	OBP	SLG	OPS	3 Yr	Fld	F$
388	46	93	21	1	6	39	59	41	6	2	.273	.351	.394	.745	-.039	F-	$1

Bard followed his "breakout" 2006 season with a less exciting but still impressive effort. The home run power disappeared, but the switch-hitting catcher maintained a high batting average, knocked a ton of doubles, and controlled the strike zone well. Bard hit .330/.386/.456 away from Petco Park, .376/.452/.514 against left handers, and .406/.496/.584 with runners in scoring position. On the defensive side, he threw out just 8 percent of base stealers, although much of his futility can be explained by the fact that two of his starting pitchers, Greg Maddux and Chris Young, do not hold runners.

Michael Barrett (Catcher)

PA	R	H	2B	3B	HR	RBI	SO	BB	SB	CS	BA	OBP	SLG	OPS	3 Yr	Fld	F$
409	46	97	21	2	10	47	60	28	1	2	.261	.316	.409	.725	-.040	F-	$1

Barrett came to San Diego in June and promptly saw his game fall apart. He hit .226/.235/.286 for the Padres. At 31 years old, a rebound isn't out of the question, although he looked lost down the stretch in 2007. If Barrett comes anywhere near the projection given, the Padres and their fans should be ecstatic. He accepted arbitration and is expected to back up Bard behind the dish.

Jim Edmonds (Center Field)

PA	R	H	2B	3B	HR	RBI	SO	BB	SB	CS	BA	OBP	SLG	OPS	Fld	F$
435	53	94	20	2	15	54	94	55	1	2	.253	.348	.439	.787	C	$1

He was always a streak hitter, but the hot streaks are shorter now and the cold streaks represent Edmonds' default setting. He just can't pull the ball consistently anymore. To give Edmonds the benefit of the doubt, he was coming back from foot and back surgeries last spring, took only a few spring training at-bats, and probably shouldn't have been activated until May 1 or so. A full spring of preparation in 2008 might help Edmonds enjoy one final hurrah, but don't count on it—at Petco Park, he's not a sure bet to break double digits in homers

Brian Giles (Right Field)

PA	R	H	2B	3B	HR	RBI	SO	BB	SB	CS	BA	OBP	SLG	OPS	Fld	F$
562	69	128	27	3	9	54	59	79	4	3	.271	.376	.399	.775	B	$1

Giles played the entire 2007 season on a bad knee. He had microfracture surgery in October and doctors "found it hard to believe he was able to go out there every day with very little cartilage in the knee." Giles is good for no more than 12-15 homers these days, but if he's healthy, expect a slight rebound from the veteran.

Adrian Gonzalez (First Base)

PA	R	H	2B	3B	HR	RBI	SO	BB	SB	CS	BA	OBP	SLG	OPS	3 Yr	Fld	F$
615	81	159	34	2	25	92	112	55	1	1	.290	.353	.495	.848	.035	B	$17

Gonzalez followed up his fine 2006 campaign with another that proved it was no fluke. His batting average dropped 22 points, but his walk rate and isolated power both improved, which would seem to bode well for the future. Gonzalez will be 26 this season, and although Petco Park suppresses his overall numbers somewhat (he hit just .266/.335/.424 there in 2007 vs. .295/.358/.570 on the road), he should continue to provide solid production at first base for the Padres now and into the foreseeable future.

Khalil Greene (Shortstop)

PA	R	H	2B	3B	HR	RBI	SO	BB	SB	CS	BA	OBP	SLG	OPS	3 Yr	Fld	F$
550	66	127	32	3	18	71	104	34	3	1	.253	.304	.436	.740	-.023	C	$1

Greene has terrific power for a shortstop, and poor plate discipline for anyone. He is hurt by Petco Park more than most. Since the Padres moved downtown in 2004, Greene has hit .228/.288/.370 there, while hitting .280/.335/.515 on the road. In 2007, he became one of 10 shortstops in big-league history to hit 40 doubles and 20 homers in the same season. He'll hit for more power than his projection indicates.

Scott Hairston (Left Field)

PA	R	H	2B	3B	HR	RBI	SO	BB	SB	CS	BA	OBP	SLG	OPS	3 Yr	Fld	F$
358	47	84	16	2	16	52	70	32	2	1	.266	.335	.481	.816	-.001	B	$1

In the first-ever trade between San Diego and Arizona, Hairston came to the Padres and provided a serious shot in the arm as his new team chased his old team in the NL West. In 31 games for the Padres, Hairston hit .287/.337/.644 and darned near was the hero of the season (his two-run homer off Jorge Julio gave San Diego an 8-6 lead in the top of the 13th inning at Colorado in Game No. 163). Hairston, who turns 28 at the end of May, is expected to at least share left field duties in 2008.

Chase Headley (Third Base)

PA	R	H	2B	3B	HR	RBI	SO	BB	SB	CS	BA	OBP	SLG	OPS	3 Yr	Fld	F$
563	67	123	25	3	15	63	125	59	1	1	.251	.336	.407	.743	.054	C	$1

Arguably the best prospect in the Padres system, Headley destroyed the Texas League (.330/.437/.580) in 2007. A third baseman by trade, the switch-hitting Headley may get some looks in left field this spring. He doesn't have much to prove in the minor leagues, but he is blocked at the hot corner in San Diego. Long-term, expect Jeff Cirillo type production out of Headley.

Tadahito Iguchi (Second Base)

PA	R	H	2B	3B	HR	RBI	SO	BB	SB	CS	BA	OBP	SLG	OPS	3 Yr	Fld	F$
528	64	122	22	3	10	53	92	55	11	3	.265	.345	.391	.736	-.043	C	$2

Iguchi split time between the White Sox and Phillies in 2007. He's 33 years old and owns a career line of .276/.347/.421. Although his power slipped a tad (pun partially intended) last year, the rest of his offensive skills appear to have remained intact. No single part of Iguchi's game stands out, but he's a capable stopgap until Matt Antonelli is ready. At the very least, he represents an upgrade over the disaster that was Marcus Giles. Most defensive metrics I've seen indicate that Iguchi is an above-average second baseman.

Kevin Kouzmanoff (Third Base)

PA	R	H	2B	3B	HR	RBI	SO	BB	SB	CS	BA	OBP	SLG	OPS	3 Yr	Fld	F$
476	65	119	24	2	18	67	84	30	15	1	.276	.329	.465	.794	.003	B	$1

Through May 7, the rookie third baseman was hitting an abysmal .108/.172/.193. Kouzmanoff hit .309/.362/.511 the rest of the way. Depending on whom you ask, his defense at the hot corner ranges somewhere between awful and slightly below average. With that bat, his glove shouldn't be an issue. Like many of his teammates, Kouzmanoff performed better on the road (.273/.327/.496) than at home (.276/.331/.412). He hit .371/.431/.571 in September and October. The projection listed is conservative.

Paul McAnulty (Left Field)

PA	R	H	2B	3B	HR	RBI	SO	BB	SB	CS	BA	OBP	SLG	OPS	3 Yr	Fld	F$
386	45	90	19	2	9	43	71	38	1	2	.265	.340	.412	.752	-.001	B	$1

McAnulty missed a lot of time in 2007 due to problems with his right quad and never got on track. He's a 27-year-old who hits when healthy but who doesn't have a position. Time is running out for him.

Pitchers

Heath Bell (Relief Pitcher)

W	L	ERA	TBF	IP	Hit	HR	SO	BB	HBP	3 Yr	F$
6	3	2.84	331	81	68	5	85	27	3	0.24	$9

Acquired before the 2007 season, Bell became Bud Black's most trusted setup man by year's end. He throws hard and throws strikes, and somehow the Mets didn't have a use for that combination. Bell could see some save opportunities when Trevor Hoffman needs a day off, and could eventually transition into Hoffman's replacement.

Kevin Cameron (Relief Pitcher)

W	L	ERA	TBF	IP	Hit	HR	SO	BB	HBP	3 Yr	F$
4	3	3.96	282	65	59	5	51	34	3	0.32	$1

The Padres snagged Cameron from Minnesota in the 2006 Rule 5 draft. He stuck with the big club and finished with a sparkling 2.79 ERA, although it was a tale of two seasons: He posted a 0.31 ERA in the first half, and 5.34 in the second. Cameron's cutter bores in on left-handed batters and is difficult to drive (he allowed five extra-base hits, all doubles, on the season). His command is spotty (5.58 walks per nine innings), and occasionally Black seemed to forget about him—Cameron once went 17 days without pitching, and had 10 days rest on three other occasions.

Justin Germano (Starting/Relief Pitcher)

W	L	ERA	TBF	IP	Hit	HR	SO	BB	HBP	3 Yr	F$
9	8	4.09	661	157	161	16	93	43	8	-0.09	$4

In a typical Kevin Towers move, Germano was claimed off waivers from Philadelphia at the end of spring training and made 23 starts for the Padres. His first-half performance (5-3, 3.90 ERA) provided a shot in the arm when Clay Hensley got hurt, but eventually Germano's below-average stuff caught up with him and he faded (2-7, 4.98) in the second half. Germano is an extreme finesse pitcher who relies heavily on command. If he's got it, he can be effective; if not, things get ugly fast. He could slot in at the back end of a rotation or as a swingman.

Justin Hampson (Relief Pitcher)

W	L	ERA	TBF	IP	Hit	HR	SO	BB	HBP	3 Yr	F$
4	4	4.32	330	76	74	8	52	34	3	0.11	$1

Hampson, another waiver wire pickup, did a nice job out of the bullpen for San Diego. He worked in fairly low-leverage situations and posted a 2.70 ERA over 39 appearances. Hampson has extensive starting experience in the minors, and there's been talk of returning him to the rotation, although no timetable exists. He'll probably be one of Black's long relievers again in 2008.

Clay Hensley (Starting Pitcher)

W	L	ERA	TBF	IP	Hit	HR	SO	BB	HBP	3 Yr	F$
6	9	4.73	612	139	146	15	84	65	5	0.49	$1

Hensley's 2007 season was derailed by a series of injuries that limited him to 50 innings and a stratospheric 6.84 ERA. It's easy to forget that he finished 10th in the NL in ERA back in 2006. If Hensley is healthy, his projection is low. Unfortunately, he's coming off September labrum surgery, which means all bets are off. Hensley expects to be ready for spring training, but the smarter money says not to expect much before the All-Star break.

Trevor Hoffman (Relief Pitcher)

W	L	ERA	TBF	IP	Hit	HR	SO	BB	HBP	F$
4	3	3.48	262	64	55	6	50	19	2	$12

Two crucial late meltdowns notwithstanding, Hoffman enjoyed yet another fine season and extended his big-league saves record to 524. The strikeout rate continues to decline, which makes watching him a little more nerve-wracking than it used to be, but by and large he still gets the job done. Opponents batted .181/.241/.268 against Hoffman at Petco Park in 2007, as compared to .295/.326/.489 on the road. Hoffman hasn't faced more than seven batters in a game since Sept. 12, 2002, against the Giants. He hasn't worked more than a single inning since Sept. 29, 2004, also against the Giants.

Wilfredo Ledezma (Relief Pitcher)

W	L	ERA	TBF	IP	Hit	HR	SO	BB	HBP	3 Yr	F$
4	4	4.00	303	70	64	7	58	33	3	0.07	$1

The left hander looked a lot like a guy with a 5.28 career ERA. Ledezma's role headed into 2008 is uncertain, but if he stays in San Diego, pitching coach Darren Balsley will have himself quite the challenge.

Greg Maddux (Starting Pitcher)

W	L	ERA	TBF	IP	Hit	HR	SO	BB	HBP	F$
11	10	3.61	771	189	194	17	97	31	6	$14

Maddux won 14 games in 2007, marking the 20th consecutive season he'd recorded 13 or more victories. He didn't walk a batter in six August starts. On May 14, at home against the Reds, Maddux tossed the Padres' only complete game of the year. In short, he did what he always does: made his full complement of starts and kept his club in the game. Maddux turns 42 in April and hasn't had an ERA below 3.96 since 2002.

Cla Meredith (Relief Pitcher)

W	L	ERA	TBF	IP	Hit	HR	SO	BB	HBP	3 Yr	F$
5	4	3.22	325	79	78	4	56	21	3	-0.20	$6

Meredith is durable (he worked in 80 games last year) and induces a ridiculous number of ground balls (5.78 ground ball/fly ball ratio in 2007, 4.70 for his career). Like most sidearming right handers, Meredith is more effective against his own kind (.232/.268/.305 over his career) than against southpaws (.293/.347/.424). He'll continue to help bridge the gap between the starters and Hoffman in 2008.

Jake Peavy (Starting Pitcher)

W	L	ERA	TBF	IP	Hit	HR	SO	BB	HBP	3 Yr	F$
13	9	3.31	797	196	164	18	200	59	6	0.13	$27

Peavy won the NL Cy Young Award in 2007 and then signed a contract extension that will keep him in San Diego through 2012. Peavy sometimes is portrayed as a product of Petco Park, but since the Padres moved downtown, his numbers at home (2.86 ERA) have been only a little better than those on the road (3.10). For the most part, Peavy is the same pitcher regardless of where he performs. Assuming good health, he should remain one of the elite pitchers in baseball in 2008 and through the reminder of his current contract.

Mark Prior (Starting Pitcher)

W	L	ERA	TBF	IP	Hit	HR	SO	BB	HBP	3 Yr	F$
4	4	4.07	70	295	62	9	67	27	4	0.13	$1

Prior once again will begin the season injured, recovering from surgery on his shoulder. He is scheduled to return in June or July, but what the Padres can expect from him remains to be seen. If he returns, do not expect him to instantly return to his form of 2003, when he won 18 games. The Padres will need to proceed with caution and slowly work him into the mix with an eye on using him most down the stretch if they're in a run for the playoffs.

Tim Stauffer (Starting Pitcher)

W	L	ERA	TBF	IP	Hit	HR	SO	BB	HBP	3 Yr	F$
6	9	4.97	596	136	152	17	84	48	6	-0.11	$1

It's difficult to watch a guy like Stauffer struggle. The Padres took him with the fourth overall pick in the 2003 draft. After he was drafted but before he signed, he admitted to experiencing some shoulder weakness and saw his bonus knocked from $2.6 million to $750,000. You'd like to see that sort of honesty rewarded, but in this case, he just hasn't been the pitcher the Padres thought he'd be, having posted a 6.37 ERA over 94.2 innings in the big leagues. Stauffer turns 26 in June and is a longshot to have a career in San Diego.

Joe Thatcher (Relief Pitcher)

W	L	ERA	TBF	IP	Hit	HR	SO	BB	HBP	3 Yr	F$
4	3	3.33	266	64	55	5	61	24	3	0.09	$1

Thatcher came over from Milwaukee as part of the Scott Linebrink trade. Thatcher posted goofy numbers (1.35 ERA, 6.40 strikeout-to-walk ratio) in Double- and Triple-A before becoming a key member of the Padres bullpen down the stretch. He formerly played in the independent Frontier League and provides another data point in favor of scouring unusual sources for talent, particularly relief pitchers.

Randy Wolf (Starting Pitcher)

W	L	ERA	TBF	IP	Hit	HR	SO	BB	HBP	3 Yr	F$
6	7	4.37	522	121	118	14	95	49	5	0.42	$1

In his 18 starts in a Dodger uniform, Wolf lasted past six innings only three times. You can attribute that to the shoulder trouble that flared up late in the season, but regardless, the Randy Wolf project didn't go as planned. He signed a smart contract with San Diego that should pay completely based off incentives. He's a good pitcher, and can be effective when healthy. He threw only 102.2 innings last season.

Chris Young (Starting Pitcher)

W	L	ERA	TBF	IP	Hit	HR	SO	BB	HBP	3 Yr	F$
10	9	3.68	690	167	136	19	152	63	6	0.33	$16

Young is big but doesn't throw hard. He relies instead on intelligence and a deceptive delivery for success. In his two seasons with the Padres, Young has been among the toughest pitchers to hit in the big leagues. An extreme flyball pitcher, he cut way down on his home runs allowed last year (10, down from 28 in 2006). Young left his July 24 start at Coors Field after two innings due to a strained oblique. At the time, he led MLB with a 1.82 ERA. After a brief stint on the DL, he returned and posted a 5.96 ERA over his final 10 starts.

San Francisco Giants

by Steve Treder of The Hardball Times

2008 Projections

Record: 70-92
Division Rank: Last, 16 games back
Runs Scored: 654
Runs Allowed: 765

2007 in a Nutshell

Barry B. hit it, Barry Z. bit it, and except for Matt'n Tim, the team never got wit' it.

Preseason projections suggested Bonds' reaching 756 home runs would be a close call, but he started hot and had 17 homers by the All-Star break, removing the drama from the will-he-or-won't-he question. The Giants' offense surrounding their superannuated cleanup hitter was atrocious. The only remaining entertainment was watching big-bucks free agent ace Zito struggle while youngsters Matt Cain and Tim Lincecum dazzled. Overall, the '07 Giants weren't terrible, but neither were they anything close to competitive.

General Comments

Team Strengths

The starting pitching is at least solid, and could be tremendous. Zito was a major disappointment in 2007, but he showed improvement over the season's final weeks and overall his results weren't disastrous. He could clearly do better in 2008, and he's joined by perhaps the most impressive one-two punch of very young starters in the game in Cain and Lincecum.

The team has lots of alternatives to fill out the rotation. Noah Lowry has been iffy the past two years, but he's still only 27 and was excellent in 2004-05. Plus, 27-year-old Kevin Correia looks ready to step forward as a starter, 25-year-old Jonathan Sanchez could be right behind him, and 26-year-old Patrick Misch is a dark horse who could surprise.

Questions abound regarding the rest of the roster, but with Omar Vizquel at shortstop and Aaron Rowand in center field, key elements are in place for a solid defense.

Team Weaknesses

Well, basically, everything else. The hitting in 2007 was pitiful even including Bonds' 170 OPS+; in 2008

runs will be as rare in San Francisco as moments of candor in the presidential campaign. Indeed this team potentially presents a historically impotent offense.

The bullpen was a scramble in '07, and with Correia likely shifting to the rotation, the relief pitching shapes up as a problem in '08.

The General Manager is Known for...

He has a truly fanatical predilection for filling holes with extreme-veteran, short-term fixes. Thus Brian Sabean's posture as the post-Bonds Giants face a daunting rebuilding task will be—well, interesting to watch. Given that his first move this offseason was to re-sign shortstop Vizquel, who had a poor year with the bat in 2007 and will be 41 in '08, one is left in somewhat horrified wonder. Owner Peter Magowan's July 2007 decision to re-sign Sabean to a two-year deal with an option for 2010 is, to say the least, puzzling.

The Manager is Known for...

Bruce Bochy is calm and steady. He isn't one to panic when things get rough, but Bochy's critics imply that his stoicism fostered a listlessness in the '07 Giants. Like Sabean, he's faced with a distinctly different charter as the team enters 2008, and Bochy's track record doesn't provide encouragement that he'll come up with bold and creative approaches.

Ballpark Characteristics

For the fifth straight season, AT&T Park in 2008 played as a neutral run environment, adding to the evidence that the extreme pitcher-friendly mode it manifested in its initial three years was an aberration. It's a very difficult home run park for left-handed hitters (rendering Bonds' achievements all the more remarkable), but not so for right handers, and the foul territory is minimal.

The Minor League System is...

It's not quite a barren wasteland, but pretty close, especially for a team with as many holes to fill as this one. Over the years the organization has demonstrated a fine ability to produce pitchers, but almost none at producing position players. The current ready-to-harvest crop of position-player features a few modestly talented utilityman types, but nothing resembling a potential star, while the young pitching is exceptionally strong.

Favorite Team Blogs

Only Baseball Matters (http://www.onlybaseball-matters.com/)

The Giants Baseball Blog (http://www.giantsbase-ballblog.blogspot.com/)

Baycityball (http://www.baycityball.com/)

McCovey Chronicles (http://www.mccoveychronicles.com/)

Keys for 2008

Players Lost from Last Year's Team

Bonds is gone, leaving a vast crater in the middle of the order. Pedro Feliz signed with the Phillies, leaving the Giants with few third base alternatives. Ryan Klesko is also unsigned; he wasn't good in 2007. First base was a hole then and so it remains.

Players Acquired

Rowand is the new center fielder, bringing a track record of good defense and up-and-down offense. He's no star, but will be helpful.

That's it as of this writing, suggesting that there are significant moves yet to come.

Reasons to be Optimistic

Lincecum and Cain,
And why not Spahn and Sain?
Else it's pray for rain
To drown the bone-deep pain.

Reasons to be Pessimistic

Start with the first through eighth slots in the batting order. Seriously, this will almost certainly be an appallingly weak-hitting lineup. The starting pitching will likely get assistance from the defense, but beyond that it will carry a crushing load.

Due for a Better Season

Zito could bounce back to some degree, and most of the young pitchers are ascendant. Ray Durham might climb partway back up the cliff he fell off in 2007.

Likely to Have a Worse Season

Rowand won't likely be repeating his 123 OPS+ of 2007. Bengie Molina turns 33 in July, and probably won't match his 2007 career highs of 19 homers and 81 RBIs.

The really sad news is that disappointing performances won't be required for this team to do poorly. And if the team encounters unusually bad fortune—say, serious injuries to one or more of the young pitchers, hardly an extreme long shot—the 2008 Giants could be horrific.

Still Left to Do

There's plenty. As of this writing, first base and third base remain utterly unaddressed, and the bullpen could use some attention as well.

Most Likely Team Outcome

Last place is a certainty. The only question is just how deeply buried they'll be. A 100-loss season wouldn't be at all surprising; anything fewer than low-90s would be a good performance. The plausible worst-case scenario is a 110-loss meltdown.

Player Projections

Batters

Eliezer Alfonzo (Catcher)

PA	R	H	2B	3B	HR	RBI	SO	BB	SB	CS	BA	OBP	SLG	OPS	3 Yr	Fld	F$
303	35	74	15	1	9	38	66	13	1	1	.266	.310	.425	.735	-.021	C	$1

Alfonzo surprised Giants fans by holding his own as a stopgap regular in 2006, then spent most of '07 on the DL with a knee injury. Solitary asset is nice pop in his bat. Devoid of strike zone judgment, and a poor defensive catcher.

Rich Aurilia (Infield)

PA	R	H	2B	3B	HR	RBI	SO	BB	SB	CS	BA	OBP	SLG	OPS	Fld	F$
414	47	102	21	2	8	45	53	29	1	1	.270	.322	.400	.722	A	$1

Nagged by injuries, didn't hit well as an infield supersub in 2007. Might still be useful in a utility role.

Barry Bonds (Left Field)

PA	R	H	2B	3B	HR	RBI	SO	BB	SB	CS	BA	OBP	SLG	OPS	Fld	F$
493	79	102	20	1	24	72	59	127	3	2	.287	.475	.551	1.026	C	$1

Obvious and enormous questions pervade as to whether he'll play, with whom he would play, and whether he'd be healthy. But if, if, and if, Bonds' performance over the past couple of years indicates that he can still be a first-rate offensive force.

Rajai Davis (Center Field)

PA	R	H	2B	3B	HR	RBI	SO	BB	SB	CS	BA	OBP	SLG	OPS	3 Yr	Fld	F$
430	51	99	17	3	2	32	65	29	24	7	.255	.312	.330	.642	-.008	C	$1

Splendid speed and nice center field defense. If he can build upon 2007's .361 OBP, then we'll have something here. Far more likely he won't, and what we have is just another utility outfielder.

Ray Durham (Second Base)

PA	R	H	2B	3B	HR	RBI	SO	BB	SB	CS	BA	OBP	SLG	OPS	Fld	F$
515	62	121	25	3	12	57	64	50	7	2	.266	.338	.413	.751	D	$2

One of the game's overlooked gems over the past decade, he suddenly fell off a cliff in the second half of 2007, hitting a ridiculous .165/.256/.247. Durham's career is at a crossroads: If he can't regain bat speed, stick a fork in him.

Kevin Frandsen (Second Base)

PA	R	H	2B	3B	HR	RBI	SO	BB	SB	CS	BA	OBP	SLG	OPS	3 Yr	Fld	F$
425	49	107	23	3	3	37	45	20	6	4	.280	.332	.379	.711	.012	C	$1

Swings a decent contact-hitter stick, wields a competent middle-infielder glove. Has a future as a journeyman, perhaps a regular, but no star potential.

Ryan Klesko (First Base)

PA	R	H	2B	3B	HR	RBI	SO	BB	SB	CS	BA	OBP	SLG	OPS	Fld	F$
438	51	99	24	2	6	41	75	49	5	2	.260	.343	.380	.723	C	$1

Gave the Giants a good half-season as a platoon first baseman in 2007, then went south in the second half. If he has a future, it'll be as a backup/pinch-hitting specialist.

Fred Lewis (Center Fielder)

PA	R	H	2B	3B	HR	RBI	SO	BB	SB	CS	BA	OBP	SLG	OPS	3 Yr	Fld	F$
434	54	99	18	6	8	41	87	44	9	4	.260	.338	.401	.739	-.012	B	$1

Moderate all-around skill set: A decent hitter with a little power, a little speed, and a useful outfield glove. Can make a contribution as a utility player, but no upside beyond that.

Scott McClain (First Base)

PA	R	H	2B	3B	HR	RBI	SO	BB	SB	CS	BA	OBP	SLG	OPS	Fld	F$
516	64	118	27	1	23	77	101	45	1	1	.255	.320	.467	.787	B	$1

Big, strong, veteran career minor leaguer with legitimate power. Was good enough to have been a major league journeyman, but the breaks never came. Could be useful in a backup role.

Bengie Molina (Catcher)

PA	R	H	2B	3B	HR	RBI	SO	BB	SB	CS	BA	OBP	SLG	OPS	3 Yr	Fld	F$
481	57	128	22	1	16	65	51	26	0	1	.288	.325	.449	.774	-.040	C	$3

Swings a dependable line-drive bat with nice power, yet without any semblance of strike zone discipline. Comically slow on the basepaths. Was once a standout defensive catcher, but those days are gone.

Lance Niekro (First Base)

PA	R	H	2B	3B	HR	RBI	SO	BB	SB	CS	BA	OBP	SLG	OPS	3 Yr	Fld	F$
287	35	72	15	2	11	41	52	17	0	1	.271	.314	.467	.781	-.026	A	$1

Has proven to be less than a major league-quality hitter.

Dave Roberts (Center Field)

PA	R	H	2B	3B	HR	RBI	SO	BB	SB	CS	BA	OBP	SLG	OPS	Fld	F$
468	63	113	19	8	1	32	60	45	30	6	.274	.344	.366	.710	B	$1

Still runs remarkably well, but may have reached the end of the line as a platoon-regular. Could still be helpful as a bench player.

Guillermo Rodriguez (Catcher)

PA	R	H	2B	3B	HR	RBI	SO	BB	SB	CS	BA	OBP	SLG	OPS	3 Yr	Fld	F$
289	33	65	15	2	7	32	46	20	2	1	.252	.315	.407	.722	-.048	C	$1

A 29-year-old rookie in 2007. Throws pretty well; otherwise a generic backup catcher.

Aaron Rowand (Center Field)

PA	R	H	2B	3B	HR	RBI	SO	BB	SB	CS	BA	OBP	SLG	OPS	3 Yr	Fld	F$
573	73	145	32	3	14	69	97	34	7	3	.281	.340	.436	.776	-.033	C	$9

Everything points toward 2007 as being Rowand's career year—he played half his games in the hitter-friendly Citizens Bank Park, where his OPS was nearly 100 points higher than on the road. Rowand will be a good fit for the Giants; credit some of Rowand's clubhouse intangibles as having a small part in the Phils gutting out a division title.

Nate Schierholtz (Right Field)

PA	R	H	2B	3B	HR	RBI	SO	BB	SB	CS	BA	OBP	SLG	OPS	3 Yr	Fld	F$
564	71	153	32	8	13	67	89	20	7	4	.288	.318	.452	.770	.044	B	$1

As with so many Giants "prospects," a pretty good hitter but utterly lacking in plate discipline. Big and strong, yet his power is only so-so. Formerly a third baseman, now a corner outfielder, and not good defensively.

Omar Vizquel (Shortstop)

PA	R	H	2B	3B	HR	RBI	SO	BB	SB	CS	BA	OBP	SLG	OPS	Fld	F$
561	61	133	22	5	0	37	50	47	15	6	.270	.334	.335	.669	B	$1

Still as elegant as ever with the glove, but at 40 his slap-hitting bat had a hard time finding holes. While an offensive rebound isn't out of the question, it isn't probable. Most likely Vizquel has reached the point at which he could still add value as a utility infielder, but as a regular he'll be problematic.

Randy Winn (Right Field)

PA	R	H	2B	3B	HR	RBI	SO	BB	SB	CS	BA	OBP	SLG	OPS	3 Yr	Fld	F$
594	72	151	35	3	10	64	76	45	9	3	.283	.341	.416	.757	-.035	A	$1

Solid, unexciting pro. Would be an asset as a fourth outfielder, but doesn't cut the mustard as a regular. Lacks the range of a good center fielder, and lacks the power of a good corner outfielder.

Pitchers

Scott Atchison (Relief Pitcher)

W	L	ERA	TBF	IP	Hit	HR	SO	BB	HBP	3 Yr	F$
5	3	3.71	306	73	69	6	55	23	2	0.35	$1

Veteran Quad-A who could be of service in the back end of a bullpen.

Matt Cain (Starting Pitcher)

W	L	ERA	TBF	IP	Hit	HR	SO	BB	HBP	3 Yr	F$
13	7	3.37	762	183	148	15	151	76	5	-0.16	$17

Improved his control in 2007 and emerged as one of the league's better starters at 22. Exhibits a full repertoire of explosive stuff, bull-like strength, and poise beyond his years. All that's required is one further incremental improvement in command, and major stardom is his.

Vinnie Chulk (Relief Pitcher)

W	L	ERA	TBF	IP	Hit	HR	SO	BB	HBP	3 Yr	F$
4	3	3.77	267	63	57	6	51	24	2	0.46	$1

Garden-variety middle reliever, unremarkable in every regard.

Kevin Correia (Starting Pitcher)

W	L	ERA	TBF	IP	Hit	HR	SO	BB	HBP	3 Yr	F$
5	5	4.08	392	91	87	9	70	38	3	0.13	$1

Has spent several years on the verge major league success, as the Giants haven't seemed to figure out quite what to do with him. Performed splendidly in the starting rotation in late 2007, and perhaps has finally found his niche. A strong all-around pitcher.

Dan Giese (Relief Pitcher)

W	L	ERA	TBF	IP	Hit	HR	SO	BB	HBP	3 Yr	F$
4	4	3.99	290	69	69	7	53	19	2	0.25	$1

Veteran career minor leaguer with excellent control but unimpressive stuff. Back-of-bullpen filler.

Brad Hennessey (Relief Pitcher)

W	L	ERA	TBF	IP	Hit	HR	SO	BB	HBP	3 Yr	F$
4	5	4.13	328	76	76	7	42	29	3	0.09	$1

A soft-tosser who found moderate success in the closer role for much of 2007. Nothing special, but a solidly useful talent.

Tim Lincecum (Starting Pitcher)

W	L	ERA	TBF	IP	Hit	HR	SO	BB	HBP	3 Yr	F$
10	7	3.63	635	150	130	14	152	64	4	-0.07	$10

With just 209 professional innings under his belt, Lincecum is a work in progress. But what a work it is. Exceptional two-seam fastball/hard-curve combination. Obviously there are plenty of ways in which things could go haywire, but this is the sort of talent that penetrates immovable obstacles.

Noah Lowry (Starting Pitcher)

W	L	ERA	TBF	IP	Hit	HR	SO	BB	HBP	3 Yr	F$
9	9	4.20	689	158	156	15	92	69	5	0.10	$1

A change-up artist with genuine talent. But arm trouble has bothered him for two straight seasons, and his rapidly deteriorating strikeout-to-walk ratio (K/BB) is festooned with scarlet flags.

Randy Messenger (Relief Pitcher)

W	L	ERA	TBF	IP	Hit	HR	SO	BB	HBP	3 Yr	F$
4	4	4.20	296	68	70	6	41	26	2	0.06	$1

Huge, but doesn't throw hard at all. Spent most of 2007 holding his own, but suffered a broken left hand when struck by a line drive, and upon his return from the DL was pummeled for 19 hits and 13 runs in six innings to close out the season.

Patrick Misch (Relief Pitcher)

W	L	ERA	TBF	IP	Hit	HR	SO	BB	HBP	3 Yr	F$
5	6	4.63	440	100	110	13	72	35	5	0.05	$1

Left hander has displayed dazzling K/BB ratios in extensive experience in Double-A and Triple-A. Worked mostly as a reliever in 2007, strictly as a starter until then. Upside isn't likely as a major league star, but seems a solid big league talent.

Russ Ortiz (Starting Pitcher)

W	L	ERA	TBF	IP	Hit	HR	SO	BB	HBP	3 Yr	F$
4	6	4.99	407	91	99	12	50	40	4	0.39	$1

Reclamation project had a few solid games for the Giants in 2007, but mostly displayed a silver fork stuck into his well-done backside.

Jonathan Sanchez (Relief Pitcher)

W	L	ERA	TBF	IP	Hit	HR	SO	BB	HBP	3 Yr	F$
5	4	4.30	361	82	78	8	84	40	4	-0.04	$1

Tall, slim southpaw with intriguing talent. Has worked mostly as a starter in the minors (with 333 strikeouts in 252 innings), mostly as a reliever in the majors. Still a bit raw, but his ceiling is very high.

Jack Taschner (Relief Pitcher)

W	L	ERA	TBF	IP	Hit	HR	SO	BB	HBP	3 Yr	F$
4	3	4.11	264	61	55	6	59	30	2	0.53	$1

Few things are quite as maddening as a LOOGY with an intense reverse platoon split. Another would be a pitcher with stuff that's dominating one outing, and completely hittable the next.

Tyler Walker (Relief Pitcher)

W	L	ERA	TBF	IP	Hit	HR	SO	BB	HBP	3 Yr	F$
3	3	3.69	212	50	45	5	40	20	2	0.34	$1

Returned from Tommy John surgery late in 2007 displaying impressive velocity. Could be a surprise.

Brian Wilson (Relief Pitcher)

W	L	ERA	TBF	IP	Hit	HR	SO	BB	HBP	3 Yr	F$
4	3	3.64	267	62	54	4	50	31	3	-0.06	$1

Has been entirely inconsistent, as his control is intermittently ragged. But his stuff is top-drawer. Emergence as a dependable set-up man or closer isn't unrealistic.

Barry Zito (Starting Pitcher)

W	L	ERA	TBF	IP	Hit	HR	SO	BB	HBP	3 Yr	F$
11	9	3.97	784	183	169	21	134	76	6	0.47	$6

In his inaugural San Francisco campaign, Zito's signature 12-to-6 Uncle Charlie was as wicked as ever. But for most of the season Zito had a devil of a time keeping that chattering relative in the strike zone. Down the stretch the old consistency was more in evidence, giving reason to believe that perhaps his 2008 won't be quite so dismal.

Seattle Mariners

by Jeff Sullivan of Lookout Landing (lookoutlanding.com)

2008 Projections

Record: 77-85
Division Rank: 3rd, 12 games back
Runs Scored: 725
Runs Allowed: 779

2007 in a Nutshell

Powered by an effective offense, a shutdown bullpen, and a pocket full of dreams, the Mariners stood at 20 games over .500 as late as Aug. 24. With Seattle just one game back of the division-leading Angels and three ahead of New York for the wild card, the good people at CoolStandings.com gave the M's a 56.4 percent chance of making the playoffs, and for the first time in years, the mood around the team and its fans was entirely positive, if cautiously so.

That's when the Mariners embarked on a dismal two-week voyage that I lovingly refer to as the Hope Destroyer, a period during which the bullpen fell apart, the offense stopped hitting, and the rotation remembered that it wasn't any good.

After dropping two against Texas, Seattle returned home for a highly anticipated three-game set against LA and promptly got swept. Then they lost a makeup game to Cleveland. Then they got swept by Toronto. When it was all said and done, the M's had lost 13 of 14, dropping their playoff odds all the way down to 1 percent. The race was over. With unprecedented speed, the Mariners had fallen from contenders to also-rans, and frustrated, cynical fans were wondering why they ever believed in the team in the first place. It was just the latest crushing disappointment in a series of crushing disappointments.

General Comments

Team Strengths

The biggest—and perhaps only—real team strength is the bullpen. J.J. Putz is one of the most dominating closers in the game, and armed with a supporting cast of George Sherrill, Sean Green, Ryan Rowland-Smith and others, there's at least one pitcher out there capable of providing whatever the Mariners need, be it a strike-out, a ground ball, or a good at-bat against a tough lefty. And for good measure, the whole group will cost less money this year than Randy Winn.

Manager John McLaren would have you believe that the team's experience and chemistry are two more of its strengths, but McLaren also would have you believe that left is right and cardboard is delicious, so whatever.

Team Weaknesses

Until Carlos Silva was signed, the rotation looked like a glaring weakness. Now it just looks mediocre, with the potential to be a glaring weakness.

The team's biggest problem is that it's set to get substandard production from the should-be gimme trifecta of left field/first base/designated hitter. Raul Ibanez's defense is so bad in the outfield, and he gives away so many of the runs he creates at the plate, that overall he's not a good player. Richie Sexson is arguably the worst defensive first baseman in baseball, and he just put up a .694 OPS. And Jose Vidro's a DH who hits like a middle infielder.

It'd be one thing if Ibanez or Sexson could mash like a legitimate cleanup bat, but they can't, so the Mariners will be going forward with three holes in what are supposed to be the three easiest positions in the lineup to fill with strong hitters. That puts them at a distinct disadvantage.

The General Manager is Known for...

Say the name "Bill Bavasi" to anyone who follows baseball reasonably closely and they'll probably come back with "that's the guy that traded the good reliever for Horacio Ramirez, right?"

Bavasi's a stand-up guy who loves to interact with fans of the team, and his heart's in the right place. But God bless 'im, he just isn't that good a GM. Too often he gets wrapped up in labels of things the team needs—No. 1 starter" or "veteran reliever" or "proven innings-eater"—and goes after players who fit those labels instead of simply trying to improve the team's run differential by whatever means necessary.

We've seen it again this offseason. Instead of doing simple things to make the team better, like dumping Sexson, moving Ibanez to first base, and bringing in an actual outfielder, Bavasi focused on addressing what he considered to be the team's biggest flaw—starting pitching—and threw a ton of money at Carlos Silva while partaking in a heated pursuit of Erik Bedard. (As of this writing, that one is unresolved.) In short, he gets too wrapped up in specific ideas or players he thinks the team needs, and once he does that, he's seemingly unwilling to think about anyone or anything else.

It's also worth noting that Bavasi badly overvalues the middle class. In 2008, the Mariners will be paying roughly $57 million to Ibanez, Vidro, Sexson, Silva, Jarrod Washburn and Miguel Batista. That's an overpoweringly mediocre group of players who, combined, will be taking up half the team payroll.

It's a virtual given that any contract Bavasi hands out will be for too much money and too many years, especially when you consider that there are always decent approximations on the market who cost basically a few pennies. Were it not for Bavasi's bullpen-building acumen and strong relationship with scouting director Bob Fontaine, I'm not sure he'd still be alive.

The Manager is Known for...

Said McLaren on Horacio Ramirez one day in August, when Ramirez's ERA stood at 7.12 after 13 starts:

"You know what? Take away a couple of pitches, and his outings have been pretty good."

McLaren really isn't so different from predecessor Mike Hargrove in terms of in-game strategy, but he's just a little bit worse at everything, to the extent that people calling for Hargrove's head earlier in the summer came to regret their wishes. McLaren believes way too much in chemistry and veteran entitlement, and he has an uncanny knack for using the worst reliever in the bullpen at the worst possible moment.

It might be that he was just getting his feet wet and is still a managerial work in progress, but considering the amount of time he's spent in the dugout next to guys like Hargrove and Lou Piniella, it's not like we're talking about a rookie here. Bottom line, if 90 percent of all the managers in baseball don't make a difference, and 10 percent actively cost their teams wins, McLaren is right on the border.

Ballpark Characteristics

Safeco's a pitcher-friendly environment, but it's not Petco. While left field is huge and boasts a power alley only in name, right field is actually quite generous to left-handed pull hitters, which is what's kept Ibanez from being a total disaster. Guys who stand to benefit the most from playing in Seattle are those with bats like Ibanez and southpaw flyball pitchers like Washburn. Guys who stand to benefit the least are right-handed groundball pitchers and Mike Cameron.

The Minor League System is...

It's underrated. Adam Jones is the obvious jewel, an A-grade prospect who'd play a strong center field for any team that doesn't already have Ichiro. Behind him, high-level guys or recent graduates like Brandon Morrow, Jeff Clement, Wladimir Balentien and Rowland-Smith are pretty close to being able to contribute consistently in the big leagues.

It gets more interesting the further down you go, though. The next wave of pitching prospects is about a year away from getting serious attention, and Carlos Triunfel is one of the best 18-year-olds on the planet. I know every team thinks it has a load of raw talent in the lower levels, but for the Mariners I think it's legitimately true. If the Mariners are going to keep throwing too much money at established veterans, they'll need to fill a lot of roster spots with cheap youth, and for the first time in a while, they're nearing a point where they might realistically be able to pull that off on a yearly basis.

Favorite Team Blogs

USS Mariner (www.ussmariner.com/)
Prospect Insider (www.prospectinsider.com/)

Keys for 2008

Players Lost from Last Year's Team

Most of the team is staying together. The big names going out the door are Jose Guillen and Jeff Weaver. Guillen was a solid hitter all year long, but leg problems hampered his defense, and Jones' overall blend of ability should make him the better player by a considerable margin. Weaver allowed 105 runs in 146.2 innings. His legacy will be to serve as a reminder that, while we may not be fond of a certain new starting pitcher, "at least he's not Jeff Weaver." This role was previously occupied by Joel Pineiro.

Ramirez could be taking his 7.16 ERA elsewhere as well, but since he was tendered a contract and remains in the running for the No. 5 rotation spot, I can't make any promises. Needless to say, not even Horacio Ramirez could be as bad as Horacio Ramirez was in 2007.

Players Acquired

While the Mariners are still hunting for another starting pitcher and a role player or two, so far the only guys they've brought in are R.A. Dickey and Carlos Silva.

Dickey, a Rule 5 pick, is interesting because he throws a knuckleball, but in the unlikely event that he sticks on the roster, he won't get much more than mop-up work. Silva's obviously the bigger name, being the nominal top free agent arm on the market, but for a guy who cost $48 million, he's remarkably boring. The low walk rate is nice, but he doesn't strike anyone out, and, like Washburn, he's a No. 4 starter getting paid like a No. 2. He's not Jeff Weaver, though, so he'll make the team better, even if it's only the baseball equivalent of putting a couple towels on the floor after your water heater explodes.

Reasons to be Optimistic

The team shouldn't be taking backward strides this year in any facet. The pitching will improve—removing Weaver drops the team ERA by 17 points and removing Ramirez drops it another 21. The defense will improve, since Jones is light years ahead of Guillen, and Yuniesky Betancourt doesn't figure to go through another early-season error spell. And the offense, even if it doesn't improve, shouldn't be getting any worse. There's enough upside here that, if Felix Hernandez gets his act together and Jones has a huge first full season, the Mariners could be in the thick of things down the stretch again.

Reasons to be Pessimistic

The Mariners had a negative run differential last year. Their Pythagorean record was 79-83—11 games worse than the Angels, who have gotten better over the offseason. Jones and Silva are neat upgrades, but they're not even close to representing 11-plus wins by themselves. Considering that winning the division is really this team's only shot, with the wild card coming down to whoever loses the East and Central, things don't look real good.

An awful lot has to go right in 2008 for the Mariners to make the playoffs, and if Felix doesn't pitch like an ace from the beginning, or if Putz struggles for a month or two, then the race'll be over before it even begins. As is, it's a long shot.

Due for a Better Season

Sexson is the obvious candidate here. It's one thing to decline; it's quite another to fall apart completely. Sexson's 84 OPS+ was second-worst on the team, ahead of only Jose Lopez, and 17 points behind his previous career low. At 33 years old, and without any crippling injuries, there's little reason to believe that Sexson's as finished as his raw batting line says he is. While his line drive rate was among the lowest in the league, his .217 batting average on balls in play was far and away the worst in baseball, and figures to improve even if the contact remains as poor.

Sexson's clearly beyond his peak as a fearsome slugger, but he should be able to get back to an OPS somewhere around the mid- to high-.700s, which will help offset some of the other expected regressions in the lineup.

I'd call Lopez due, too, but honestly, I'm not entirely sure. Lopez has a lot of talent in his bat, and players usually don't get worse when they turn 23, but his approach sucks, and by the end of the year his swing was all wrists. I'll peg him for a slight improvement, with the potential for much more than that.

Likely to Have a Worse Season

Vidro was the opposite of Sexson—his BABIP (.342) was too high for his line drive rate (19.5 percent). Ordinarily, BABIP is about 120 points higher than LD percentage, with some give either way depending on the player's foot speed. Vidro couldn't outrun a shelf. Based on his history, his BABIP should be 90-100 points higher than his line drive percentage instead of 147, and based on this projected regression, Vidro will likely go from being an average DH to a problem one.

Using J.C. Bradbury's PrOPS metric (predicted OPS based on batted ball profile), Vidro should've put up a batting line around .290/.360/.390 last year. That looks much closer to the truth than his actual numbers.

Other candidates of note: Ibanez should decline, because I've been saying this for four years, and it's bound to come true eventually. Ichiro probably won't hit .351 again. Putz's ERA should climb a little, as he's unlikely to keep stranding 94 percent of his baserunners. And Batista's ERA could go up, too, even if his overall skill set stays the same.

Still Left to Do

If the season started now, the Mariners could field a complete team. That said, the front office is still working to add a few more pieces. There's talk that Sexson might be dumped on someone else, but even if that doesn't happen, Bavasi's likely to bring in a veteran bench bat to fill Ben Broussard's vacant role. And you can't put it past him to sign an experienced reliever to do whatever it was Chris Reitsma was supposed to do in 2007.

More significantly, the M's continue to think about bringing in another starter instead of trying to pick one out of the current Morrow/Ramirez/Cha Seung Baek/Rowland-Smith/Ryan Feierabend/whoever pile du jour. They've been talking with Baltimore about Bedard, and those discussions aren't dead. They've also kicked the tires on a handful of other guys, so by no means is the No. 5 slot guaranteed to be up for grabs come spring training.

Most Likely Team Outcome

Second place, no playoffs, 84-88 wins. It's a good roster, and the A's and Rangers are still at least a year away from making some noise, but the gap between Seattle and the AL elite is just too large for Silva to close. As a Mariners fan, I plan to have another fun July and another dull September. Ah, routine.

Player Projections

Batters

Adrian Beltre (Third Base)

PA	R	H	2B	3B	HR	RBI	SO	BB	SB	CS	BA	OBP	SLG	OPS	3 Yr	Fld	F$
593	77	146	34	2	22	84	98	43	11	2	.272	.329	.466	.795	-.035	B	$14

At some point, it became fashionable to call Beltre's contract a bust. But Beltre's a good hitter—better than Safeco allows him to look—and his defense at third base is as good as anyone's in the American League. He's underrated, and his last day as a Mariner will be a sad one indeed.

Yuniesky Betancourt (Shortstop)

PA	R	H	2B	3B	HR	RBI	SO	BB	SB	CS	BA	OBP	SLG	OPS	3 Yr	Fld	F$
540	61	142	29	5	8	56	52	20	8	6	.280	.308	.404	.712	.018	C	$2

The Yunibomber's been the subject of a lot of interesting discussion over the past two years, as the advanced defensive metrics fail to support the visual observation that he's flipping awesome in the field. Everyone can agree on one thing, though: The man isn't much of a hitter. He'll make contact and slap a bunch of singles, but if his glovework isn't really what we thought it was when he first showed up, then we have to reconsider just how valuable a player he actually is.

Willie Bloomquist (Utility Guy)

PA	R	H	2B	3B	HR	RBI	SO	BB	SB	CS	BA	OBP	SLG	OPS	3 Yr	Fld	F$
285	32	67	12	1	2	23	45	19	11	3	.262	.318	.341	.659	-.027	C	$1

Since 2004, the Mariners have a .464 winning percentage in games that Willie Bloomquist starts, and a .492 winning percentage in games that he doesn't.

Jamie Burke (Catcher)

PA	R	H	2B	3B	HR	RBI	SO	BB	SB	CS	BA	OBP	SLG	OPS	Fld	F$
289	30	66	15	0	4	28	42	18	0	1	.259	.316	.365	.681	D	$1

He's easily the coolest Mariners backup catcher since Tom Lampkin, and anyone who didn't beam like an idiot when he hit his first career home run on the last day of the season is a cold-hearted grinch. His big numbers all but guaranteed the end of Rene Rivera, and for this I am forever grateful.

Jeff Clement (Catcher)

PA	R	H	2B	3B	HR	RBI	SO	BB	SB	CS	BA	OBP	SLG	OPS	3 Yr	Fld	F$
444	54	100	23	2	13	53	82	38	1	1	.255	.331	.423	.754	.029	D	$1

While a lot of Clement's future value depends on whether he's able to remain behind the plate, a cursory glance at the Tacoma first basemen and designated hitters over the years is enough to explain why his bat is so intriguing, regardless of where he plays. A lefty with good power and the kind of discipline that's a rare find in this system, he's not far off from being able to hit in the big leagues, and his swing is built for Safeco Field.

Raul Ibanez (Left Field)

PA	R	H	2B	3B	HR	RBI	SO	BB	SB	CS	BA	OBP	SLG	OPS	Fld	F$
599	77	148	30	3	21	81	94	62	2	2	.281	.356	.469	.825	C	$13

No matter which stat you prefer, they'll all tell you the same thing—Raul Ibanez is an absolutely godawful defensive left fielder who's going to cost the Mariners 20-30 runs with his unsightly lack of range. And this defensive penalty takes away a lot of what he contributes at the plate, to the point where you're talking about a below-average player. A lot of the Mariners' problems could be solved by dumping Sexson and moving Ibanez to first base, but as of right now, no dice.

Seattle Mariners

Kenji Johjima (Catcher)

PA	R	H	2B	3B	HR	RBI	SO	BB	SB	CS	BA	OBP	SLG	OPS	3 Yr	Fld	F$
500	59	132	26	1	14	64	50	20	1	2	.284	.324	.435	.759	-.044	A	$1

The fact that Johjima plays half his games in Safeco Field is the only reason more people don't mention him when discussing the best catchers. A right-handed pull hitter, he hits a lot of fly balls that die in the cavernous left-center power alley. On the road, Johjima's been an .800+ OPS bat since coming over from Japan, and having improved his defensive technique, he's easily the top backstop in the division.

Adam Jones (Right Field)

PA	R	H	2B	3B	HR	RBI	SO	BB	SB	CS	BA	OBP	SLG	OPS	3 Yr	Fld	F$
542	73	138	30	5	21	78	126	32	7	4	.279	.331	.488	.819	.068	C	$11

Jacoby Ellsbury gets all the press, but Jones is the better prospect with the higher ceiling. Already a success in Triple-A a year ago, this time around he thoroughly abused the Pacific Coast League despite just having turned 22 in August. He's rapidly developing into a complete player capable of hitting for both average and power while playing Gold Glove-caliber defense in the outfield.

Jones is going to be a good player, and quickly. There aren't too many prospects out there for whom a comparison to Torii Hunter wouldn't necessarily be a compliment.

Jose Lopez (Second Base)

PA	R	H	2B	3B	HR	RBI	SO	BB	SB	CS	BA	OBP	SLG	OPS	3 Yr	Fld	F$
529	60	135	28	3	10	58	64	23	3	3	.279	.316	.411	.727	.021	C	$1

Once again, Lopez started hot and finished cold, and by the end his swing looked nothing like the one that got him into the 2006 All-Star Game. Still just 24, he still has a lot of untapped talent and potential, but he's beginning to smell an awful lot like Cristian Guzman. On a short leash.

Richie Sexson (First Base)

PA	R	H	2B	3B	HR	RBI	SO	BB	SB	CS	BA	OBP	SLG	OPS	3 Yr	Fld	F$
521	67	112	27	0	25	79	118	61	1	1	.249	.342	.476	.818	-.036	C	$4

John McLaren kept putting Sexson in the lineup nearly every day, citing the fact that he's historically been a second-half player, but the second-half push never arrived. At the end of the year, Sexson had put up one of the most disappointing batting lines in recent Mariners history.

That said, there is reason for optimism—Sexson's 2007 BABIP was unbelievably low, and forecasts to rise, taking the rest of his numbers with it. I don't know that he'll reach the .818 OPS projected here, but he's unlikely to repeat as such a hopeless black hole.

Ichiro Suzuki (Center Field)

PA	R	H	2B	3B	HR	RBI	SO	BB	SB	CS	BA	OBP	SLG	OPS	3 Yr	Fld	F$
663	90	185	21	7	6	59	68	58	31	6	.312	.374	.402	.776	-.048	A	$24

During Ichiro's first years in Seattle, McLaren was Lou Piniella's bench coach, and he and Ichiro instantly bonded. When Mike Hargrove walked away and McLaren became the new manager of the Mariners this past July, it made Ichiro a lot more willing to sign the five-year extension that Bill Bavasi had put on the table. This is the only good thing that I will ever say about McLaren.

Jose Vidro (Designated Hitter)

PA	R	H	2B	3B	HR	RBI	SO	BB	SB	CS	BA	OBP	SLG	OPS	3 Yr	F$
534	59	135	26	1	6	51	56	53	1	1	.288	.360	.386	.746	-.049	$1

If you've ever wondered what Ichiro would look like if you told him to gain a few hundred pounds and devour his glove, wonder no more. Vidro basically has the same offensive profile, but because he's a slow oaf, he has to rely a lot less on beating out infield singles and a lot more on luck. If, at the end, 2007 isn't Vidro's high point as a Mariner, I'll be shocked.

176

Brad Wilkerson (Left Field)

PA	R	H	2B	3B	HR	RBI	SO	BB	SB	CS	BA	OBP	SLG	OPS	3 Yr	Fld	F$
424	52	88	21	2	15	53	110	49	4	3	.242	.333	.434	.767	-0.031	B	$1

The Guy Traded For Alfonso Soriano infuriated Rangers fans with his preposterous strikeout rate (30 percent) and mediocre production. Wilkerson still has some pop (35 homers over two injury-plagued seasons) and is patient to a fault. If he can drag his average above .260, he's useful. If not, he's yet another mediocre corner outfielder.

Pitchers

Cha Baek (Starting Pitcher)

W	L	ERA	TBF	IP	Hit	HR	SO	BB	HBP	3 Yr	F$
6	8	4.97	551	126	140	18	71	42	6	0.11	$1

Baek throws a bunch of pitches, but none of them are particularly good, and he puts the ball in the air pretty often. Still, he throws strikes and misses a handful of bats from time to time, so the Mariners could do a lot worse.

Miguel Batista (Starting Pitcher)

W	L	ERA	TBF	IP	Hit	HR	SO	BB	HBP	F$
9	10	4.64	759	172	184	18	103	73	7	$1

In Batista's return to the AL, his strikeout rate increased by more than 25 percent while his fly balls jumped by nearly 40 percent. Pitchers who are 36 years old aren't supposed to change their pitching identities this much at the drop of a hat. Blessed with stuff good enough that he can get away with a few mistakes, Batista doesn't appear to be on the verge of being anything less than a durable No. 4, and odds are he'll be finding new ways to survive long after Washburn has outlived his usefulness.

Sean Green (Relief Pitcher)

W	L	ERA	TBF	IP	Hit	HR	SO	BB	HBP	3 Yr	F$
4	4	4.32	331	74	76	4	48	41	4	0.32	$1

Before the year began, Green was a one-trick pony, a righty with a heavy fastball that he used to get ground ball after ground ball. Somewhere along the line, though, he dropped his arm angle, putting more tilt on what used to be a show-me slider and allowing Green to use it as a weapon. The result? A ton more strikeouts. All of a sudden, he went from generic Quad-A arm to effective high-leverage reliever.

Felix Hernandez (Starting Pitcher)

W	L	ERA	TBF	IP	Hit	HR	SO	BB	HBP	3 Yr	F$
12	8	3.46	747	180	171	15	152	56	6	-0.17	$15

It's hard to believe he's still only 21 years old. Frustrating at times, Felix nevertheless posts some of the strongest peripherals in either league, and as he matures it's only a matter of time before his ERA starts to reflect that.

The way he started his 2007 season wasn't a fluke. That early DL stint did funny things to his confidence and made him wary of throwing his slider, but over time he got better, and once again, barring further injury, Felix will be as good going forward as he wants to be. Were I building a team from scratch, there would be a very short list of players I'd take over the King.

Brandon Morrow (Starting/Relief Pitcher)

W	L	ERA	TBF	IP	Hit	HR	SO	BB	HBP	3 Yr	F$
4	4	4.28	302	68	61	6	61	41	3	-0.12	$1

When the Mariners scouted this guy before the 2006 draft, his report must've read "minor league development optional," because they thrust him right into the big league bullpen out of spring training last year. Results were mixed; Morrow was borderline unhittable when he was spotting his high-90s fastball, but he frequently had no idea where it was going, leading to a ghastly walk rate. Now the team wants him to start. How well he does will depend on the improvement of his command and secondary pitches. It doesn't seem like a winning equation, but the M's are determined to find out. Odds are against Morrow being much of a contributor in 2008.

Eric O'Flaherty (Relief Pitcher)

W	L	ERA	TBF	IP	Hit	HR	SO	BB	HBP	3 Yr	F$
4	3	4.10	270	61	61	5	42	27	4	-0.28	$1

Another effective middle reliever who costs close to the league minimum. The Mariners have these guys coming out of their ears. O'Flaherty is only 23, so there's reason to believe he's still on the way up. His slider just feeds lefties their lunch.

J.J. Putz (Relief Pitcher)

W	L	ERA	TBF	IP	Hit	HR	SO	BB	HBP	3 Yr	F$
6	2	2.59	280	71	54	5	77	18	2	0.19	$20

Eddie Guardado didn't have the best final season in Seattle, but it's because of him that Putz has become one of the most unhittable relievers in the league. It was early in 2006 when Guardado taught JJ how to throw a split, and ever since that point, JJ's been unbelievable. It's hard enough to hit a 97 mph fastball when you don't have to protect against an 88 mph splitter that drops off the table.

Horacio Ramirez (Starting Pitcher)

W	L	ERA	TBF	IP	Hit	HR	SO	BB	HBP	3 Yr	F$
6	8	5.05	552	124	144	15	50	50	5	0.45	$1

Seattle hasn't had a rotation arm this bad since Matt Wagner. Horacio can't miss bats, struggles to throw strikes and doesn't have a repertoire with any upside. All he can do is get a few ground balls, and he doesn't even do that as often as advertised.

Ryan Rowland-Smith (Relief Pitcher)

W	L	ERA	TBF	IP	Hit	HR	SO	BB	HBP	3 Yr	F$
4	4	4.61	325	73	70	8	63	39	4	-0.12	$1

Hyphen had an eye-opening rookie season, striking out more than a batter an inning and throwing pretty consistent strikes. Why he isn't getting more attention as a long-term starting option is beyond me. As a flyball lefty with three pitches and a good idea of the strike zone, he's exactly the right fit for the ballpark.

George Sherrill (Relief Pitcher)

W	L	ERA	TBF	IP	Hit	HR	SO	BB	HBP	3 Yr	F$
4	2	3.19	228	55	40	5	59	25	2	0.22	$2

Already a shutdown LOOGY thanks to his massive sweeping slurve, Sherrill improved his fastball command in 2007, and the result was that he had success against both lefties and righties. Suddenly, the man who was little but an afterthought when he came over from the Indy League a few years ago blossomed into a legitimate eighth-inning set-up guy without any crippling weaknesses. There aren't too many left-handed relievers around the league who look like better bets for the next few years than The Governor.

Carlos Silva (Starting Pitcher)

W	L	ERA	TBF	IP	Hit	HR	SO	BB	HBP	3 Yr	F$
10	10	4.42	768	181	206	25	80	35	6	0.37	$1

Sometimes, being average can be very valuable. For example, if a team is trotting out Horacio Ramirez once every five days, then a league average pitcher just might be worth $48 million in his place. Silva's performance is very variable because so much of what he does is out of his control. If a team is too aggressive at the plate, he can look great. On the other hand, if his command is off, he can look atrocious.

Jarrod Washburn (Starting Pitcher)

W	L	ERA	TBF	IP	Hit	HR	SO	BB	HBP	3 Yr	F$
10	10	4.31	763	178	181	21	99	59	8	0.37	$2

Not good + left-handed + flyball-prone + Safeco = good. If Washburn knows what's good for him, he'll never leave Seattle. Not on purpose.

Sean White (Relief Pitcher)

W	L	ERA	TBF	IP	Hit	HR	SO	BB	HBP	3 Yr	F$
2	5	5.95	276	59	72	7	24	32	4	0.10	$1

A Rule 5 addition a year ago, White predictably didn't do much in Seattle, but not all hope is lost. He throws a good, sinking fastball, and with a track record of getting grounders, he's a few small improvements in command and off-speed stuff away from being able to help out in the majors.

FEARLESS PREDICTIONS, 2008: ICHIRO-CAM (YEAH, RIGHT...)

St. Louis Cardinals

by Larry Borowsky of Viva El Birdos (vivaelbirdos.com)

2008 Projections

Record: 78-84
Division Rank: 4th, 10 games back
Runs Scored: 790
Runs Allowed: 830

2007 in a Nutshell

Chris Carpenter got hurt, Josh Hancock died, Scott Rolen and Jim Edmonds showed their age, and the defending champions barely contended in baseball's weakest division. We also now know just how unhappy the clubhouse was—Rolen and (to a lesser extent) Edmonds were at odds with the manager, and everyone was frustrated that Kip Wells was the big addition to a pitching staff that had lost Jeff Suppan, Jason Marquis and Jeff Weaver.

General Comments

Team Strengths

Albert Pujols, the bullpen … and that's about it. If they played in a halfway decent division, this team wouldn't be remotely considered a contender.

Team Weaknesses

Starting pitching is the glaring one. Two-fifths of the Cards' projected rotation (Mark Mulder and Matt Clement) are pitching with rebuilt shoulders and can't be relied upon to deliver innings in bulk. A third member (Joel Pineiro) was dumped last July.

The other major flaw is the Cardinals' lack of a presentable leadoff hitter—Cesar Izturis, Adam Kennedy, Skip Schumaker and Aaron Miles probably will get most of the at-bats there. The defense was uncharacteristically bad in 2007 (St. Louis allowed nearly 100 unearned runs), and the loss of Rolen's glove surely won't help; neither will the presence of another inexperienced outfielder (Rick Ankiel) alongside Chris Duncan.

The General Manager is Known for...

Inheriting the mess Walt Jocketty left behind, John Mozeliak didn't make a splashy acquisition in his first few months on the job, but he did implement two overdue changes. First and foremost, he integrated the Cardinals' sabermetric unit (which Jocketty shunned) into the big-league decision-making process.

Second—and as a consequence of the first change—he began shedding expensive past-prime veterans (including the beloved Edmonds, Rolen, and David Eckstein) to create openings for younger players with greater upside. And he put the Rolen vs. La Russa feud to rest with aplomb, shedding a bad contract while adding a 30-homer bat (Troy Glaus).

The Manager is Known for...

He's feisty. The Cardinals rehired La Russa before identifying Jocketty's replacement, a questionable decision. Tony promptly escalated his long-running spat with Rolen, just at the point the Cards were trying to stir up a market for the player; he also lobbied the front office (successfully) to re-sign Miles and pushed other terrible ideas such as Juan Gonzalez and Josh Fogg. Never known for his patience, La Russa may not be the leader best suited to the Cardinals' youth movement.

Ballpark Characteristics

After two seasons, Busch III appears to be a mild pitchers' park that stifles home runs. It has been a godsend for the Cardinals' ragtag staffs the last couple of years: They posted a 4.05 home ERA in 2006-07 versus a 5.20 mark on the road. Biggest home/road splits last year (pay attention, fantasy owners): Braden Looper (3.34 home, 6.81 road) and Pineiro (3.38 home, 4.46 road in a small sample).

The Minor League System is...

It's improving. The Cardinals' Double-A team finished first in both halves of the Texas League schedule and featured three top-flight, near-ready prospects: centerfielder Colby Rasmus, catcher Bryan Anderson and closer Chris Perez.

Favorite Team Blogs

Future Redbirds (http://futureredbirds.com/)
Whiteyball (http://whiteyball.wordpress.com/)
Get Up Baby (www.getupbaby.net/)
Bird Land (http://www.stltoday.com/blogzone/bird-land/)

Keys for 2008

Players Lost from Last Year's Team

Pitchers Kip Wells, Mike Maroth and Troy Percival, catcher Gary Bennett, third baseman Scott Rolen, shortstop David Eckstein, outfielders Edmonds and So Taguchi.

Players Acquired

Third baseman Troy Glaus, shortstop Cesar Izturis, catcher Jason LaRue, infielder D'Angelo Jimenez.

Reasons to be Optimistic

Sabermetric thinking has moved front and center in the Cardinals front office. The Cards are younger and ought to be healthier, and they might be getting Carpenter back in time for the stretch run. But the biggest reason for hope is the competition: 86 wins can go a long way in the NL Central.

Reasons to be Pessimistic

The Cardinals were outscored by more than 100 runs last year, their worst run differential since the 1910s. They need to improve by leaps and bounds in 2008 just to get back to .500. Pujols has been playing with a damaged right elbow since 2003; at some point it's going to require surgery; if that happens in 2008, the Cards might finish last. The rotation is full of long-shot gambles for the second straight year—and for the second straight year, Plan B consists of whoever floats past on the waiver wire. And the competition isn't quite as flimsy as it used to be—Milwaukee and Chicago look better than St. Louis on paper, and Cincinnati has enough upside to pass the Cardinals.

Due for a Better Season

Anthony Reyes, Adam Kennedy.

Likely to Have a Worse Season

Ryan Franklin, Russ Springer, Skip Schumaker.

Still Left to Do

Find out if Ankiel can be a league-average (or better) regular; get Rasmus' career off the ground; have a good draft in June.

Most Likely Team Outcome

75 wins, fourth place

Player Projections

Batters

Rick Ankiel (Right Field)

PA	R	H	2B	3B	HR	RBI	SO	BB	SB	CS	BA	OBP	SLG	OPS	3 Yr	Fld	F$
446	59	105	18	2	25	74	92	31	3	2	.259	.312	.498	.810	-.014	C	$1

Baseball's answer to Britney Spears and Anna Nicole Smith—you never know what the next headline will be, but you're damn sure it'll be a doozy. Ankiel has legitimate power (THT projects 25 homers), but still must silence doubts about his defense and on-base ability. La Russa loves Ankiel like a son, so he'll get every benefit of the doubt.

Chris Duncan (Left Field)

PA	R	H	2B	3B	HR	RBI	SO	BB	SB	CS	BA	OBP	SLG	OPS	3 Yr	Fld	F$
458	60	105	20	2	21	67	113	53	1	2	.263	.350	.482	.832	.004	D	$4

He can't play the outfield and can't hit left-handers, but hits right-handers well enough to earn his spot on the roster. Duncan played through a sports hernia for several weeks before shutting it down for good in mid-September. When healthy and properly platooned, he's a bona fide .500 slugger.

Troy Glaus (Third Base)

PA	R	H	2B	3B	HR	RBI	SO	BB	SB	CS	BA	OBP	SLG	OPS	3 Yr	Fld	F$
499	68	112	23	0	26	80	102	67	0	2	.265	.367	.505	.872	-.031	C	$9

Questions will linger regarding his hitting being real or chemical. Further, Glaus' injuries of the last two seasons are of the steroid variety (brittle tendons), so it would be a reach to expect him to play 130 games. If he can duplicate last season's percentages (.262/.366/.473), the Cardinals should be happy. His days of slugging .550-ish are long gone.

Cesar Izturis (Shortstop)

PA	R	H	2B	3B	HR	RBI	SO	BB	SB	CS	BA	OBP	SLG	OPS	3 Yr	Fld	F$
371	37	90	16	2	1	28	28	22	3	3	.265	.310	.332	.642	-.008	C	$1

He's honestly one of the worst hitters in the game. He's got no power, no plate patience, nothing. What the Cardinals see in him is a mystery, especially with much better options available via free agency or trade.

Ryan Ludwick (Left Field)

PA	R	H	2B	3B	HR	RBI	SO	BB	SB	CS	BA	OBP	SLG	OPS	3 Yr	Fld	F$
455	57	103	25	1	19	66	107	35	3	2	.254	.321	.462	.783	-.027	B	$1

His line after 100 at-bats last year—a .222 average with two walks and 26 strikeouts—was no different from the lines in all his previous (failed) big-league trials. But after July 1 he stopped swinging at everything. The result: 24 walks in 236 plate appearances, and a .289/.380/.520 line. He's always had decent minor-league walk rates, which suggests that Ludwick's performance last year wasn't entirely a fluke. On the contrary, it may be that he finally got a large enough sample of at-bats to show his true level of ability.

Adam Kennedy (Second Base)

PA	R	H	2B	3B	HR	RBI	SO	BB	SB	CS	BA	OBP	SLG	OPS	3 Yr	Fld	F$
395	46	95	19	2	3	34	51	32	11	4	.269	.333	.360	.693	-.026	B	$1

He played all season on a bum knee, which required season-ending surgery in mid-August. The Cardinals hope that explains why Kennedy sucked so bad in 2007. He still has decent range; he simply needs to muster a .340 OBP to earn his keep.

Jason LaRue (Catcher)

PA	R	H	2B	3B	HR	RBI	SO	BB	SB	CS	BA	OBP	SLG	OPS	3 Yr	Fld	F$
293	33	58	13	0	8	32	69	30	1	1	.234	.331	.383	.714	-.040	C	$1

LaRue was paid $5.2 million to hit .148 in 66 games for the Royals last season. He belongs to St. Louis now, and fans in Kansas City are pretty darned happy about that.

Aaron Miles (Second Base)

PA	R	H	2B	3B	HR	RBI	SO	BB	SB	CS	BA	OBP	SLG	OPS	3 Yr	Fld	F$
445	44	113	18	3	0	32	44	24	2	1	.275	.317	.334	.651	-.030	D	$1

Hits quite a number of singles but doesn't walk, hit for power, or play defense. The Cards nontendered Miles, then reconsidered and re-signed him for $1.4 million. Scrappiness still pays.

Yadier Molina (Catcher)

PA	R	H	2B	3B	HR	RBI	SO	BB	SB	CS	BA	OBP	SLG	OPS	3 Yr	Fld	F$
426	45	101	21	1	6	41	44	31	1	2	.264	.322	.372	.694	.008	C	$1

He raised his batting average 59 points. More encouraging, he raised his walk rate to nine percent. The improved strike-zone mastery suggests that these are sustainable offensive gains. And since Molina will be 25 this year, continued improvement is not out of the question. He's too slow to bat much above .280, but he may capable of slugging 12 to 15 homers.

Josh Phelps (First Base)

PA	R	H	2B	3B	HR	RBI	SO	BB	SB	CS	BA	OBP	SLG	OPS	3 Yr	Fld	F$
335	44	82	16	2	14	48	77	27	0	1	.275	.344	.483	.827	-.029	B	$1

In very limited duty with the Bucs last year, Phelps mauled the ball. The Pirates chose to designate him for assignment after the season. Phelps probably would be a decent backup DH/platoon first baseman for an AL team.

Albert Pujols (First Base)

PA	R	H	2B	3B	HR	RBI	SO	BB	SB	CS	BA	OBP	SLG	OPS	3 Yr	Fld	F$
618	97	165	32	1	34	109	93	59	4	3	.322	.426	.587	1.013	-.002	A+	$35

With his worst season as a big leaguer, he finished second in the NL in Win Shares (32) and WSAB (19). Caution to fantasy owners/bidders: If the Cardinals fall out of the race early, Pujols may shut himself down to get long-overdue elbow surgery.

Colby Rasmus (Center Field)

PA	R	H	2B	3B	HR	RBI	SO	BB	SB	CS	BA	OBP	SLG	OPS	3 Yr	Fld	F$
522	71	122	28	5	19	70	96	49	7	1	.266	.342	.474	.816	.080	D	$1

He's the main reason Edmonds asked for a trade: The Cards told Edmonds he would move to right field (or to the bench) as soon as Rasmus was ready to play in the bigs. That may happen as soon as Opening Day. At age 20, Rasmus led all Double-A hitters with 29 homers last year, then starred last autumn for Team USA. He tends to start slowly and reportedly still hasn't learned to hit to the opposite field, so it might take him a while to adjust to big-league pitching.

Brendan Ryan (Shortstop)

PA	R	H	2B	3B	HR	RBI	SO	BB	SB	CS	BA	OBP	SLG	OPS	3 Yr	Fld	F$
519	61	127	23	3	4	44	69	34	18	3	.270	.321	.357	.678	.009	D	$1

He'll compete with Cesar Izturis for playing time at shortstop and spell Kennedy at second base against left-handed pitchers. Ryan is a clear upgrade over Eckstein defensively, but he's very unlikely to reproduce the .753 OPS he compiled in a small sample last year. Fantasy factoid: Ryan was 7-for-7 as a base stealer in limited duty.

Skip Schumaker (Center Field)

PA	R	H	2B	3B	HR	RBI	SO	BB	SB	CS	BA	OBP	SLG	OPS	3 Yr	Fld	F$
456	50	118	22	3	5	43	60	27	4	2	.282	.325	.384	.709	-.006	D	$1

He was batting .193 as of July 1, then batted .400 in 120 second-half at-bats to raise his final average to .333. Fluke.

Scott Spiezio (Third Base)

PA	R	H	2B	3B	HR	RBI	SO	BB	SB	CS	BA	OBP	SLG	OPS	Fld	F$
308	37	72	16	1	8	36	53	32	0	1	.269	.351	.425	.776	D	$1

Cool beard, smokin' wife, decent batting eye.

Pitchers

Chris Carpenter (Starting Pitcher)

W	L	ERA	TBF	IP	Hit	HR	SO	BB	HBP	3 Yr	F$
7	4	2.98	95	383	85	8	77	20	4	0.28	$9

He had Tommy John surgery last August and won't be ready to pitch until August 2008 at the earliest. There's a good chance he won't pitch at all for the Cardinals this season.

Randy Flores (Relief Pitcher)

W	L	ERA	TBF	IP	Hit	HR	SO	BB	HBP	3 Yr	F$
4	3	3.78	263	62	60	5	50	22	2	0.33	$1

Getting left-handers out is supposed to be his specialty. Left-handers batted .326 against him last year.

Ryan Franklin (Relief Pitcher)

W	L	ERA	TBF	IP	Hit	HR	SO	BB	HBP	3 Yr	F$
5	4	4.09	335	79	82	9	43	23	3	0.37	$1

Franklin stripped down his repertoire at pitching coach Dave Duncan's behest and had an Eckersley-like resurrection—until September, when he went 0-2 with a 9.49 ERA. His low strikeout rate and flukishly low batting average on balls in play (.249) strongly suggest that Franklin will regress to the mean in 2008. It's not inconceivable that, like Adam Wainwright, he could return to the rotation after a successful one-year run in the setup role.

Jaime Garcia (Starting Pitcher)

W	L	ERA	TBF	IP	Hit	HR	SO	BB	HBP	3 Yr	F$
7	7	4.49	554	127	134	15	85	52	6	-0.52	$1

The Cards' top pitching prospect missed the last month of 2007 with a tender elbow. Between that and his age (he's only 21), Garcia probably will start 2008 at Double-A, but in a system this short on pitching, he could rise rapidly.

Jason Isringhausen (Relief Pitcher)

W	L	ERA	TBF	IP	Hit	HR	SO	BB	HBP	F$
4	3	3.71	278	65	56	6	54	32	2	$7

He bounced back nicely from hip surgery to have one of his best seasons. He's in the last year of his contract and the organization is well stocked with closer candidates in the minors, so if the Cardinals are out of the race at midseason—and if Izzy agrees to waive his no-trade rights—he might be moved.

Tyler Johnson (Relief Pitcher)

W	L	ERA	TBF	IP	Hit	HR	SO	BB	HBP	3 Yr	F$
3	3	4.35	222	51	50	6	38	23	3	0.08	$1

He embraced the Cardinals' pitch-to-contact philosophy, missing way fewer bats but improving his control. There was some talk (probably idle) of trying him out as a starting pitcher in 2008.

Braden Looper (Starting Pitcher)

W	L	ERA	TBF	IP	Hit	HR	SO	BB	HBP	3 Yr	F$
8	9	4.28	649	152	160	17	76	48	5	0.37	$1

One of the few success stories of the Cards' 2007 season, Looper effectively replaced Jeff Suppan for a fraction of the cost. He was worth four WSAB, about what Suppan averaged (five) in his three years with St. Louis, and he threw 175 innings and turned in 18 quality starts, almost identical to Suppan's three-year averages. THT projects him to a 4.28 ERA in 152 innings. If he hits that projection, he'll more than earn his $5.5 million salary.

Mark Mulder (Starting Pitcher)

W	L	ERA	TBF	IP	Hit	HR	SO	BB	HBP	3 Yr	F$
4	5	4.63	366	84	92	10	41	30	3	0.29	$1

He had shoulder surgery for the second September in a row. He vows to be ready by Opening Day, but May 1 is a more realistic target. But that's just the date when Mulder is likely to start facing big-league hitters again, not necessarily the date he'll start getting them out.

Chris Perez (Relief Pitcher)

W	L	ERA	TBF	IP	Hit	HR	SO	BB	HBP	3 Yr	F$
4	2	3.71	250	58	44	5	59	34	4	-0.07	$1

The presumed heir to Jason Isringhausen, Perez still hasn't learned to throw strikes—he walked a man an inning in his six-week stint at Triple-A last year—but if he can solve that problem he looks like a monster. At Double-A/Triple-A last year (his first full season of pro ball), Perez struck out 13 men per nine innings and held opposing hitters to a .125 average. He lost his job as closer with Team USA last fall, but the Cards are writing that off to fatigue. He's almost certain to see time in St. Louis in 2008.

Joel Pineiro (Starting Pitcher)

W	L	ERA	TBF	IP	Hit	HR	SO	BB	HBP	3 Yr	F$
6	7	4.41	510	118	128	14	71	38	4	0.61	$1

Dumped by the Red Sox, Pineiro went 6-4 in 11 starts for the Cardinals after Aug. 1. His strong strikeout-to-walk ratio numbers in those two months suggest that Pineiro may find a home in the National League, but he had an awful homer ratio (1.55 per nine innings) and benefited from an unsustainably high strand rate (80 percent). He seems capable of posting a league-average ERA, but probably not much better.

Anthony Reyes (Starting Pitcher)

W	L	ERA	TBF	IP	Hit	HR	SO	BB	HBP	3 Yr	F$
8	9	4.39	631	148	143	22	113	50	8	0.07	$3

La Russa and Duncan had him change his mechanics to keep the ball down, but Reyes simply isn't that type of pitcher. The altered delivery took a few miles per hour off Reyes' signature four-seam fastball, leaving him pretty much defenseless. He also suffered from awful run support and one of the worst strand rates in the league (60 percent). Better luck in the latter two regards would make him close to a .500 pitcher. If he gets a fresh start in a new organization, he might yet salvage his career.

Russ Springer (Relief Pitcher)

W	L	ERA	TBF	IP	Hit	HR	SO	BB	HBP	F$
4	3	3.53	272	66	56	8	58	21	3	$3

Springer cut his home run rate by two thirds, owing either to luck or the St. Louis ballpark. He set career highs in games, wins and ERA.

Brad Thompson (Relief Pitcher)

W	L	ERA	TBF	IP	Hit	HR	SO	BB	HBP	3 Yr	F$
6	7	4.23	497	116	122	13	56	37	7	-0.12	$1

The Cardinals went 12-5 in his starts, but only because their hitters gave him nearly six runs of support per start. Thompson has just one big-league pitch (a sinker), and hitters are sitting on it. They slugged .505 against Thompson last year; left-handers slugged .570. Hard-throwing young relievers are starting to pile up at the top of the St. Louis farm system, and Thompson is closing in on arbitration eligibility. Quad-A purgatory lies dead ahead.

Adam Wainwright (Starting Pitcher)

W	L	ERA	TBF	IP	Hit	HR	SO	BB	HBP	3 Yr	F$
10	9	4.22	741	172	182	17	119	59	7	0.12	$1

Wainwright struggled early last year due to a sore elbow, and/or jitters over moving to the rotation. But from June 1 forward, he was as good as anybody in the National League—only Brandon Webb had a better ERA over that span. Wainwright reminds Cardinals fans of Matt Morris during his 2001-03 peak: He has a killer curveball, makes good adjustments, and doesn't back down. If he stays healthy, he should enjoy a pretty good run of successful seasons.

Todd Wellemeyer (Starting/Relief Pitcher)

W	L	ERA	TBF	IP	Hit	HR	SO	BB	HBP	3 Yr	F$
5	5	4.50	393	89	85	10	68	47	4	0.53	$1

He started to throw strikes once Duncan got hold of him. Although he made 11 starts for the Cardinals, Wellemeyer was much better as a reliever (1.26 ERA, 2.5/1 strikeout-to-walk ratio) and should be kept in that role. He's only 29 years old and could still have an Al Reyes-type career.

Tampa Bay Rays

by Cork Gaines of Rays Index (raysindex.com)

Team Projections

Record: 75-87
Division Rank: 4th, 22 games back
Runs Scored: 773
Runs Allowed: 843

2007 in a Nutshell

We could pick apart the numbers and delve deeper into New Age statistics. However, for fear of overanalyzing, we will now summarize the 2007 Tampa Bay Devil Rays with two numbers ... Ready? Here goes ... 66 and 96. As in 66 wins and 96 losses. As in at least 90 losses for the 10th straight season. As in a last-place finish in the AL East for the ninth time in 10 seasons.

The biggest culprit was the pile of poop on the mound most nights that management tried to pass off as a pitching staff. Three of the (statistically) 10 worst pitchers in baseball were members of the Rays rotation. The Axis of Evil (Casey Fossum, Jae Seo and Edwin Jackson) combined for a first-half stat line of 9-20 with a 7.57 ERA, and yet Fossum and Seo kept their jobs until June and Jackson remained in the rotation the entire season. The bullpen overall ranked as the worst in the history of baseball in several statistical categories. And the defense often played as if endorsing cement shoes.

It is a miracle the Devil Rays won 66 games. The Devil Rays were bad—96 losses bad. Done. Let's move on.

General Comments

Team Strengths

Top-of-the-rotation pitching: We all knew how good Scott Kazmir could be, but before the season began many wondered if there was another major league starting pitcher in the rotation. James Shields surprised many with his dominating performance, regularly working into the seventh inning. A strikeout-to-walk ratio (K/BB) of greater than five-to-one suggests that 2007 was not a fluke.

And, there was young offensive talent. Carl Crawford again was one of the best all-around offensive threats in baseball. The difference in 2007 was that he received help from some surprising sources in the lineup, including B.J. Upton, Carlos Pena and Dioner Navarro.

Upton finally took the step forward that many were looking for. After beginning the season as the everyday second baseman, Upton was moved to center. While he looked uncomfortable at times defensively, he took well to the switch and flourished at the plate, hitting .300-24-82 with 22 steals despite missing more than 30 games.

Pena finally realized he does not need to pull every pitch to hit home runs, and he tallied 46 and became the offensive force many envisioned when he was one of the top prospects in baseball. The biggest surprise may have been the emergence of Navarro, whose first half numbers had people wondering if he would ever be a legitimate major league catcher. Navi entered the All-Star break with a .492 OPS. However, in the second half, when most catchers begin to tire, his OPS jumped to .815.

Team Weaknesses

At the front, back-of-the-rotation starting pitching: As good as Kazmir and Shields were, the rest of the rotation was bad. Seo and Fossum finally pitched their ways out of the rotation with first-half ERAs north of 7.00, and were replaced by Jason Hammel and Andy Sonnanstine. Hammel was inconsistent and probably will be in the bullpen in 2008 while Sonnanstine experienced growing pains but showed signs of potential.

Edwin Jackson managed to keep his job all season despite only five wins (31 starts) and a 5.76 ERA. The farm system is deep in pitching talent, but unfortunately for the Rays, it is not available yet.

The bullpen, as a group, sported an ERA of 6.16, nearly two runs higher than the AL average of 4.30. The relievers also allowed opponents an OPS of .875 and blew 21 of 49 save opportunities.

The Devil Rays had the worst defensive efficiency in baseball in 2007, converting only 66.2 percent of batted balls into outs. Five of the seven positions behind the pitcher had range factors below the league average. The Rays were particularly bad up the middle, where defense is most important. Shortstop and second base were manned most often by Brendan Harris, Josh Harris and Ben Zobrist, all below average defensively. In center field, Upton showed flashes of brilliance, but was tentative; he often played near the warning track, unsure of his ability to go back on balls.

The General Manager is Known for...

Under the tutelage of Gerry Hunsicker, Andrew Friedman has grown into his role very quickly. The team laid out a plan from the beginning and has not been afraid to stick to it. Through development and trades and more development, Friedman has built a franchise that now boasts at least 10 players with All-Star potential on the major league roster, backed by the best farm system in baseball, with at least five top-level prospects.

In just two years under Friedman and Co., the Rays have gone from perennial laughingstock to a team on the verge of competing in the toughest division in baseball.

The Manager is Known for...

Joe Maddon has rose tinted glasses and an amazing ability to see only the good in anything. If he had been the captain of the Titanic, he would tell you the ship put up a great fight against the iceberg. He is extremely patient with his players, often to a fault, as long as they put forth maximum effort. He is a shrewd tactician and like the new generation of general managers (and unlike most managers) he is a big believer in letting numbers dictate strategy.

Despite consecutive seasons with the worst record in baseball, the Rays picked up Maddon's two-year option. But the Rays need to show marked improvement in 2008 or the keys to the Trop will be handed over to somebody else in 2009. Team management made it clear that wins and losses were a secondary concern in 2006 and 2007; the primary goal was player development and auditioning. With the core of the team now firmly entrenched, the front office has shifted its attention away from acquiring prospects and toward the acquisition of major league talent to fill the remaining holes, with the goal of winning now.

Ballpark Characteristics

Tropicana Field (The Trop) is a fair park to both hitters and pitchers. A switch to the next generation of FieldTurf before the 2007 season slowed ground balls down and helped the Trop play more like a grass surface. Unfortunately, though, batters and fielders often must deal with the catwalks that regularly come into play on fly balls and give the players a sense they are playing putt-putt and having to navigate past a windmill.

On the bright side, it appears that the Trop's days are numbered. The Rays have proposed a new open-air stadium to be built along the waterfront in downtown St. Petersburg. The new stadium would feature a state-of-the-art retractable fabric roof that will maintain an open-air feel while keeping most seats dry when it is raining and the field considerably cooler than the outside temperatures when it is hot.

The Minor League System is...

In an organization once known for its offensive talent, most of the top hitters already have made their way to the big leagues. The cream of the crop, Evan Longoria, will make his debut in 2008. On the other hand, the Rays now have an enormous depth of starting pitching at every level of the minors that grades out as major league prospects. Foremost is David Price, the top pick in the 2007 draft, who has yet to make his professional debut, but could be in the Rays rotation as early as the second half of 2008.

Favorite Team Blogs

DRays Bay (http://www.draysbay.com/)

Keys for 2008

Players Lost from Last Year's Team

The purge of the wicked and the damned began during the season, including Fossum, Seo, Camp, Jorge Cantu and Ty Wigginton. Since the end of the season, the only player of significance lost is Delmon Young.

Players Acquired

The Rays have young players with All-Star potential throughout the roster, and a farm system stocked major league prospects.

With the core in place, the front office has begun to acquire major league talent to fill the holes that remain on the major league roster. The first move was trading Young and two pieces with no future in the organization (Harris and Jason Pridie) to the Twins for Matt Garza, Jason Bartlett and a minor leaguer. Garza gives the Rays three legitimate major league pitchers in the rotation and strengthens the back end of the rotation; Jackson and Sonnanstine slot much better in the No. 4 and No. 5 holes. Bartlett gives the Rays a stud defensive shortstop. With Akinori Iwamura moving from third base to second, the Rays have improved their team defense and at the same time strengthened the team pitching.

For the first time in recent memory, the Rays signed a real major league relief pitcher, Troy Percival. This moves the rest of the bullpen down a slot, giving Al Reyes the eighth inning and Dan Wheeler the seventh, positions where they should be more effective. In addition, the acquisition of Garza moves Jason Hammel to the bullpen to be the team's long reliever, an instant upgrade over the frauds who manned the spot last season.

The last major piece acquired was Cliff Floyd. He will share time with Rocco Baldelli and Jonny Gomes in right field and at DH. He gives the team another left-handed bat in the lineup and a veteran presence in the clubhouse. With Maddon able to play match-ups, those three should easily replace the production lost from Young's departure.

Reasons to be Optimistic

Winning is about three things: pitching, pitching and pitching. For the first time in franchise history, the Rays will feature three starting pitchers (Kazmir, Shields and Garza) who have the ability to win anytime they take the mound. And for the first time in team history, the back end of the rotation will be filled through competition and not by default.

The season likely will open with Jackson and Sonnanstine in the final two spots of the rotation. While Jackson has enormous ability, he has never come close to approaching that potential. Sonnanstine is a pitcher who must be perfect to be successful. If either or both prove unable to win consistently, a number of top prospects are close to being ready to push them aside, including Jeff Niemann, Jake McGee, Wade Davis and Price.

In the bullpen, the additions of Percival and Hammel give the Rays a legitimate closer and a long reliever and solidify a unit that was anything but solid in 2007.

Offensively the team will score early and often. While the Rays were third in the AL in home runs, too many were of the solo variety. With the subtraction of Young and the additions of Floyd and Longoria, two players who will take a walk when needed, the Rays' team OBP should improve. The everyday lineup will be deep with Baldelli and Longoria likely hitting in the No. 6 and No. 7 slots.

Defensively, the Rays were atrocious last season. With the addition of Bartlett and Iwamura's move to second base, the Rays will be considerably stronger up the middle, further strengthening a pitching unit that often was let down by those behind them in 2007.

Reasons to be Pessimistic

While it is certainly improved, there are still holes in the pitching staff. A 100 percent improvement of very little is still not very much. While Kazmir, Shields and Garza represent a formidable 1-2-3, the Rays still will be underdogs on most nights that Jackson and Sonnanstine take the mound. Jackson has a world of talent, but outside of one start in which he threw a four-hit shutout, he was allergic to the strike zone and rarely worked past the sixth inning. Sonnanstine, a young Orlando Hernandez, can pound the strike zone with pinpoint control from a variety of arm angles, but unless he is perfect The Duke is imminently hittable.

The bullpen is stronger, but the eighth and ninth innings are in the hands of a pitcher whose history includes two Tommy John surgeries (Reyes) and a pitcher who was retired at the beginning of the 2007 season (Percival). Their experience and talent will go a long way toward shoring up a weak spot, but it is hard to imagine that both will be healthy all season.

Due for a Better Season

It may be difficult to believe, but Crawford is due for a breakout season. Suffering from sore wrists each of the past two seasons, CC has yet to add power to his already stocked arsenal. With more consistent offensive talent around him in 2008, there will be less pressure on Crawford, and it would not surprise us if at the end of the season his stat line looks like .325-25-110 with 60 stolen bases.

On the surface it appears Iwamura struggled to adjust in 2007, but actually, only his home run totals were off his career averages in Japan. With a season under his belt, look for Aki to develop into a legitimate leadoff hitter and post a .400 OBP while increasing his home run total closer to 20.

Navarro was strong in the second half of 2007, when most catchers are beginning to break down. He will never hit 30 home runs, but look for .300-plus in 2008.

Sonnanstine was let down by the team's poor defense more than any other in 2007. With experience and an improved defense in 2008, he could develop into a solid back-of-the-rotation pitcher. The question will be whether it will be good enough to save his job when the next wave of pitching prospects is ready.

Likely to Have a Worse Season

Nobody denies that Pena is a talented baseball player, but it is difficult to believe that he will match his 2007 totals. With more talented hitters behind him in the lineup in 2008 (Floyd, Baldelli, Longoria), the drop-off will not be significant. Expect most of his numbers to hold steady but his home run totals will likely fall to the low 30s.

Still Left to Do

The thing left to do is for the Rays' young talent to start playing with more consistency and more confidence.

Most Likely Team Outcome

Think 84-78. Despite an opening day payroll only around $40 million (up 40 percent from 2007), the Rays have the talent to overtake Baltimore and Toronto in the AL East. With one good hot streak and a few lucky bounces, it is not out of the realm of possibility that the Tampa Bay Rays could be in the wild card hunt in September. Seriously.

Player Projections

Batters

Jason Bartlett (Shortstop)

PA	R	H	2B	3B	HR	RBI	SO	BB	SB	CS	BA	OBP	SLG	OPS	3 Yr	Fld	F$
540	66	130	24	5	5	46	72	42	16	3	.269	.334	.371	.705	-.022	B	$1

He consistently rates well on defensive metrics despite having a propensity to botch some easy plays. He has very good range to his right and should really help solidify Tampa Bay's defense.

Carl Crawford (Left Field)

PA	R	H	2B	3B	HR	RBI	SO	BB	SB	CS	BA	OBP	SLG	OPS	3 Yr	Fld	F$
585	87	160	28	9	14	68	91	37	44	0	.300	.347	.464	.811	.005	A	$25

To most, Crawford is one of the most talented players in baseball. To Rays fans, he is a bit of an enigma. In 2007, CC posted a career-best .315 average and .355 OBP, improving both numbers for the fifth consecutive season. He also stole 50 bases for the fourth time. Still, Crawford, who will not turn 26 until July, has yet to have a breakout season. At 6-foot-3, 220 pounds, he has the size to hit 30 home runs and become one of the top five hitters in baseball.

Cliff Floyd (Right Field)

PA	R	H	2B	3B	HR	RBI	SO	BB	SB	CS	BA	OBP	SLG	OPS	Fld	F$
395	48	88	16	1	12	47	64	42	2	1	.257	.347	.415	.762	D	$1

Floyd brings a tremendous attitude toward the game to the table, but little else. He's no longer an effective every-day outfielder due to his failure to win the battle with injuries. Floyd figures to be a spare outfielder for the Tampa Bay Rays, who signed him in the offseason, and he should provide some power off the bench. He isn't a pinch hitter due to his long stroke, but a move to the American League opens up the opportunity for him to DH.

Jonny Gomes (Right Field)

PA	R	H	2B	3B	HR	RBI	SO	BB	SB	CS	BA	OBP	SLG	OPS	3 Yr	Fld	F$
438	63	94	20	3	21	64	116	50	9	3	.251	.347	.489	.836	-.001	D	$5

In 2008, Jonny Gomes will see time at DH and in right field, sharing time at both positions. Considering the health history of both Rocco Baldelli and Cliff Floyd, Gomes will see plenty of playing time. He is an old-school, all-or-nothing hitter who is prone to long slumps. If given regular at bats, Gomes is a .260 hitter who will hit 25 home runs, but it would not surprise us if one of these seasons, he gets on a roll and belts 40-plus.

Akinori Iwamura (Second Base)

PA	R	H	2B	3B	HR	RBI	SO	BB	SB	CS	BA	OBP	SLG	OPS	3 Yr	Fld	F$
522	64	125	22	7	7	47	93	51	12	6	.272	.345	.396	.741	-.026	D	$2

Iwamura proved in 2007 that he can hit major league pitching, hitting .285 with a .359 OBP, but he also proved that his power numbers in Japan (career high 44 home runs) do not translate to the majors; he hit just seven home runs. If his move to second base in 2008 can be accompanied by an adjustment that leads to 20-home run power, Aki could become one of the top hitting second basemen in baseball.

Evan Longoria (Third Base)

PA	R	H	2B	3B	HR	RBI	SO	BB	SB	CS	BA	OBP	SLG	OPS	3 Yr	Fld	F$
523	67	123	24	2	20	71	102	47	3	1	.267	.341	.457	.798	.070	B	$1

The Dirtbag was born to hit a baseball. The third overall pick in the 2006 draft, Longoria posted a .934 OPS in his first 198 professional games, working his way all the way up to Triple-A in just his second season. The only knock is that he strikes out too much, but that should be of little concern; he does know how to work a walk. In 2007, he posted a decent 110/73 K/BB across two levels.

The Rays have moved Akinori Iwamura to second base, opening the door for Longoria to begin the season at the big league level. If he does, he will be there for good; he is too good a hitter to fail. He should be a lock to hit 25 home runs with a .270 average and .350 OBP.

Dioner Navarro (Catcher)

PA	R	H	2B	3B	HR	RBI	SO	BB	SB	CS	BA	OBP	SLG	OPS	3 Yr	Fld	F$
517	58	117	24	2	11	54	74	49	3	2	.259	.332	.394	.726	.044	C	$1

In the first half of 2007, Navarro looked like a catcher who belonged back in the minors, hitting .177/.238/.254. Still, his line drive percentage suggested he was suffering from a bit of bad luck and in the second half, Navarro started to show why he was once the Yankees' top prospect, hitting .285/.340/.475. He will never be a power hitter—the ball does not jump off his bat—but in the next year or two, Navi, 24, will break out and hit .320.

Carlos Pena (First Base)

PA	R	H	2B	3B	HR	RBI	SO	BB	SB	CS	BA	OBP	SLG	OPS	3 Yr	Fld	F$
536	80	120	23	2	32	91	116	81	2	2	.273	.391	.552	.943	-.031	B	$17

Pena is most likely not a 46-home run hitter. Few expect Pena to repeat the success that resurrected his career in 2007, when as a non-roster invitee to spring training he posted a 172 OPS+, second only to Alex Rodriguez in all of baseball. While the numbers scream "fluke," what we saw from Pena in 2007 was a more mature hitter who for the first time in his career was not trying to pull every pitch down the right field line. This year, Cliff Floyd, a healthy Rocco Baldelli and Evan Longoria will likely hit behind Pena in the lineup, so opposing teams will not pitch around him.

Justin Ruggiano (Right Field)

PA	R	H	2B	3B	HR	RBI	SO	BB	SB	CS	BA	OBP	SLG	OPS	3 Yr	F$
500	65	113	24	4	13	56	130	45	14	6	.257	.333	.418	.751	.027	$1

Ruggiano may be the biggest mystery in the Rays system. While none of his five tools are great, he is above average in all. Since being acquired from the Dodgers midway through 2006, he has hit .313 with 24 home runs and 30 steals in 158 games between Double-A and Triple-A. He also led Team USA in home runs during the World Cup. Still, he will be 26 in 2008 and it is hard to imagine he will be more than a replacement-level player in the big leagues. With the Rays' outfield depth, it will take more than one injury for him to see any regular playing time in 2008.

B.J. Upton (Center Field)

PA	R	H	2B	3B	HR	RBI	SO	BB	SB	CS	BA	OBP	SLG	OPS	3 Yr	Fld	F$
579	82	138	26	4	17	70	144	64	26	7	.274	.358	.443	.801	.040	C	$2

In 2007, Upton finally showed why he once was considered one of the top prospects in baseball, posting a 136 OPS+ while hitting 24 home runs and stealing 22 bases despite missing a month due to injury. Many point to his 154 strikeouts as a warning of future struggles, but he does hit the ball as hard as anybody when he makes contact.

Of bigger concern is his stamina. Upton slowed considerably in August (.826 OPS) and September (.741) after posting a .975 OPS in the first four months. At 23, Upton has yet to fill out his frame. When he does, his power numbers will jump and he will become a more consistent hitter.

Ben Zobrist (Shortstop)

PA	R	H	2B	3B	HR	RBI	SO	BB	SB	CS	BA	OBP	SLG	OPS	3 Yr	Fld	F$
454	49	93	18	4	3	32	73	48	6	2	.238	.326	.328	.654	.007	D	$1

A career minor league OPS of .881, as well as a 176/234 K/BB suggest that Zobrist should develop into a decent hitting major league shortstop. However, he is an average defensive shortstop at best, and so far has posted only a .509 OPS in parts of two major league seasons. He could be the Rays utility infielder in 2008, but will not see regular at-bats.

Pitchers

Wade Davis (Starting Pitcher)

W	L	ERA	TBF	IP	Hit	HR	SO	BB	HBP	3 Yr	F$
8	8	4.79	649	147	148	17	114	69	9	-0.26	$1

While many think that his teammate Jake McGee is the better prospect, Davis is the more polished of the two and now looks like the better lock to be a strong major league starting pitcher. A hard-throwing righty, his curveball is his best pitch. Despite efforts by the Rays to treat Davis and McGee with kid gloves, both have forced the Rays' hand. Only 22, Davis will begin the season in Double-A but will be in Triple-A shortly and will compete for a job in the Rays rotation in 2009.

Scott Dohmann (Relief Pitcher)

W	L	ERA	TBF	IP	Hit	HR	SO	BB	HBP	3 Yr	F$
3	5	5.04	308	68	69	9	58	39	3	0.54	$1

He pitched very well for the Rays once called-up from Triple-A. Dohmann is another key element in the Rays' much-improved bullpen. With the additions of Percival and Hammel, the fact that Dohmann will have to compete with Salas and Gary Glover just to earn a spot in the bullpen is a strong indication that the bullpen is more talented and much deeper in 2008.

Matt Garza (Starting Pitcher)

W	L	ERA	TBF	IP	Hit	HR	SO	BB	HBP	3 Yr	F$
8	10	4.80	698	159	165	19	121	65	9	-0.20	$1

Hampered by poor run support, Garza was very effective with the Twins after being recalled from the minors in July. He still is harnessing his feel for pitching and gets a little too obsessed with his fastball, but he will slot in nicely behind Scott Kazmir and James Shields in Tampa Bay's rotation. If healthy, there is no way he does not have an ERA better than his projection.

Jason Hammel (Relief Pitcher)

W	L	ERA	TBF	IP	Hit	HR	SO	BB	HBP	3 Yr	F$
7	9	5.13	654	147	159	18	103	67	8	-0.08	$1

Like most of the Rays pitchers, Hammel was a victim of the poor defense behind him (.333 BABIP), but that is only part of the problem. With the acquisition of Garza, Hammel will move to the bullpen to strengthen a team weakness. It is doubtful that Hammel will ever be given another shot as a major league starting pitcher, outside the occasional spot start. He is a favorite of Joe Maddon and could flourish as the Rays' long reliever.

Edwin Jackson (Starting Pitcher)

W	L	ERA	TBF	IP	Hit	HR	SO	BB	HBP	3 Yr	F$
7	10	5.29	688	152	165	18	105	82	6	-0.26	$1

Jackson is the perfect example of a pitcher with top-level talent and zero results. His 98 mph fastball was only good enough for 7.16 strikeouts per nine innings. A much-improved second half in 2007 will give him one more chance at the beginning of 2008. However, if he is unable to find another pitch to complement his fastball, and if he cannot improve on his 1.45 strikeout-to-walk ratio, his time in the rotation will be short-lived. With top prospects ready as early as the second half of 2008, Jackson is a strong candidate to be traded at some point.

Scott Kazmir (Starting Pitcher)

W	L	ERA	TBF	IP	Hit	HR	SO	BB	HBP	3 Yr	F$
12	8	3.66	771	183	159	17	196	77	7	0.02	$16

It is hard to believe that at age 24 Kazmir already has made 97 career starts. Still, Kid K has work to do before he becomes one of the best pitchers in baseball, as many are predicting. His biggest downfall in 2007 was his pitch count. Despite averaging only six innings per start, Kazmir was fourth in baseball with 3,609 pitches (106 per game started). Too often Kazmir is pushing the 100-pitch mark in the fifth inning, a risky proposition with the bullpen that the Rays sported in 2007.

If he can keep his pitch counts in check, Kazmir should be a lock for 18 wins every year. In 2008, he will have a much-improved bullpen backing him up and a much-improved defense behind him. Last year, the defense led to a very unlucky .339 BABIP, which suggests he was even better than the 3.48 ERA he posted in 2007.

Jeff Niemann (Starting Pitcher)

W	L	ERA	TBF	IP	Hit	HR	SO	BB	HBP	3 Yr	F$
6	8	5.25	568	127	133	17	83	60	9	-0.30	$1

Niemann will be 25 in 2008, and with Jake McGee, Wade Davis and David Price climbing fast, it may be now or never for the former No. 4 overall selection. Last season was his first healthy one since being drafted, yet he averaged only 5.1 innings per start despite being built like an innings-eater (6-foot-9, 260 pounds). He was consistently "good" but never "great," and rarely overpowering, averaging only 8.5 strikeouts per nine innings. If Niemann fails to win a starting job with the Rays in spring training, we will start to hear rumblings of a move to the bullpen to become a closer.

Chad Orvella (Relief Pitcher)

W	L	ERA	TBF	IP	Hit	HR	SO	BB	HBP	3 Yr	F$
3	4	4.76	286	65	63	8	51	33	3	0.15	$1

A converted infielder, Orvella has posted some nasty numbers in the minors that have yet to translate at the major league level despite opportunities in three different seasons. In the minors Orvella has a career mark of 12 strikeouts per nine innings and an even more impressive six strikeouts per walk. In the majors, those numbers have dropped to 7.2 and 1.2, respectively. A change in his mechanics may have led to his 2007 struggles. He likely will get one more opportunity, since 2008 marks only his fifth season as a full-time pitcher.

Troy Percival (Relief Pitcher)

W	L	ERA	TBF	IP	Hit	HR	SO	BB	HBP	F$
4	3	3.51	65	269	54	7	55	23	2	$11

Percival can still touch the mid-90s, but he misses fewer bats than he did in his heyday. You wouldn't know it from his stat line, though: Opposing hitters batted just .171/.227 /.279 against him. Percival benefited from Tony La Russa's careful handling; he pitched on consecutive days only three times last year.

Al Reyes (Relief Pitcher)

W	L	ERA	TBF	IP	Hit	HR	SO	BB	HBP	F$
4	3	3.75	60	250	48	8	59	23	2	$5

Reyes missed all of 2006 due to Tommy John surgery, and his comeback in '07 left something to be desired. The strikeouts were there and the walk rate was fine, but Reyes' groundball rate, never very good, fell to an incredibly low 20%. As a result, Reyes allowed 13 home runs in just 60.7 innings and posted a 4.95 ERA. If he can keep the ball down in 2008, Reyes should lower that number by a run-and-a-half.

Juan Salas (Relief Pitcher)

W	L	ERA	TBF	IP	Hit	HR	SO	BB	HBP	3 Yr	F$
3	3	4.82	231	52	49	7	42	28	3	0.52	$1

This season will mark Salas' fourth as a pitcher. The former third baseman is considered to have the stuff to be a major league closer, with a cut fastball that has been compared to that of Mariano Rivera. Still, Salas will be 29 in 2008 and will have to compete just to earn a job in the bullpen out of spring training. Whether he begins the season in Tampa Bay or Durham, Salas will see considerable playing time at the major league level in 2008 and will have an opportunity to close for the Rays as early as 2009.

James Shields (Starting Pitcher)

W	L	ERA	TBF	IP	Hit	HR	SO	BB	HBP	3 Yr	F$
11	9	4.14	764	182	184	23	153	47	9	0.10	$10

While he is not left-handed, does not throw as hard and does not have the upside of Kazmir, right now James the Greater is the better pitcher. With his dominating change-up, Shields was second in baseball with 5.11 strikeouts per walk. He also proved consistent, averaging seven innings per start en route to 12 wins and a 3.85 ERA. His only drawback in 2007 was his propensity to allow the long ball, to the tune of 28 homers in 31 starts. With a stronger bullpen and better defense, Shields should be an 18-game winner in 2008.

Andrew Sonnanstine (Starting Pitcher)

W	L	ERA	TBF	IP	Hit	HR	SO	BB	HBP	3 Yr	F$
9	10	5.00	753	173	192	25	115	53	8	-0.30	$1

Nicknamed The Duke because of his similarities to El Duque Hernandez, Sonnanstine overcomes a fastball that tops out in the upper 80s with pinpoint control, change of pace and pitches that can be thrown for strikes from multiple arm angles. A strikeout-to-walk ratio of 6.2/1 in the minors has yet to translate at the major league level (3.7:1), and as a contact pitcher, he was a victim of the Rays' poor defense in 2007 (.333 BABIP).

While he does not have the stuff to win many games by himself, he will keep his team in most games and will be a serviceable starting pitcher for years to come. The only question is whether he can hold a spot in the Rays rotation for all of 2008 with the likes of Wade Davis, Jake McGee, David Price and Jeff Niemann knocking on the door.

Dan Wheeler (Relief Pitcher)

W	L	ERA	TBF	IP	Hit	HR	SO	BB	HBP	3 Yr	F$
4	4	4.01	309	73	66	8	64	28	3	0.28	$1

Wheeler struggled with the Rays after being acquired from the Astros. However, with the addition of Troy Percival to the back end of the bullpen, less will be asked of Wheeler. Al Reyes will be moved to the eighth inning and Wheeler will now assume seventh-inning duties. All that can change; both Percival and Reyes are 38 and have histories of injury. In addition, Reyes is in the final year of his contract and likely to be traded during the season. With all those factors, there is a good chance Wheeler will be given opportunities to close for the Rays in 2008.

FEARLESS PREDICTIONS, 2008: TIM McCLELLAND MISSES ANOTHER BIG ONE...

Texas Rangers

by Scott Lucas of The Ranger Rundown (rangers.scottlucas.com)

2008 Projections

Record: 79-83
Division Rank: 2nd, 10 games back
Runs Scored: 832
Runs Allowed: 855

2007 in a Nutshell

Texas staggered to its seventh losing season in the last eight. A dark-horse division-champ pick, Texas began the season with three straight losses to Los Angeles and soon commenced a torpid 19-37 stretch that forced the focus on 2008 by mid-May. In July, Texas traded first baseman Mark Teixeira, outfielder Kenny Lofton and closer Eric Gagne for nine prospects, then played .500 ball thereafter.

General Comments

Team Strengths

The bullpen should still be effective despite the losses of Eric Gagne and Aki Otsuka, and the outfield defense should be much improved. The up-the-middle group of Saltalamacchia, Kinsler, Young and Hamilton could rank among the game's best by season's end.

The real strength is in the future. The Rangers have a deep farm system, low payroll and no albatross contracts. They'll be perfectly positioned to sign or trade for premier talent when the time comes.

Team Weaknesses

This isn't the homer-happy team of the past decade. If Josh Hamilton misses significant time or Hank Blalock reverts to his subpar form of 2005-2006, power generation could be a serious problem.

Even if fully healthy, the rotation doesn't inspire confidence. Kevin Millwood would qualify as the ace for, at most, two other teams.

The General Manager Is Known For...

Fearlessness. For three consecutive seasons, Jon Daniels has consummated shocking trades in the days before Christmas. The 2005 trade of Chris Young and Adrian Gonzalez was a disaster almost upon inception. The jury is still out on the 2006 acquisition of Brandon McCarthy and the recent addition of Josh Hamilton. While the major league team still struggles, Daniels has rebuilt a weak farm system with several trades and a re-emphasis on Latin players. His admin-

istration is neither traditional nor stat-dominated, but rather a synthesis of sabermetric ideas and plenty of old-fashioned scouting.

The Manager is Known for...

He's a work in progress. Ron Washington's upbeat, energetic personality was a badly needed change from the sometimes taciturn Buck Showalter, but his supposedly superior communication skills need some polishing. He publicly gave himself an "A" grade despite the team's cataleptic start, and made several other indiscreet comments. That said, he fought through a very tough season and seemed to gain the players' favor toward the end.

Though he favors an aggressive approach with more stolen bases and sacrifice bunts than Showalter would have countenanced, he also preaches patience at the plate. His situational use of relievers was occasionally baffling.

Ballpark Characteristics

Typically, Rangers Ballpark in Arlington (still just "The Ballpark" to fans, especially during the embarrassing Ameriquest years) ranks among the most hitter-friendly parks in baseball. Though its dimensions aren't small, the stadium layout often creates a steady jet stream to center field, turning medium fly balls into doubles and deep flies to homers. However, a mild summer led to an amazingly pitcher-friendly 2007. The Rangers and their opponents actually scored more runs on the road last year.

The Minor League System is...

It's among the best in baseball after a couple of years in the bottom half. Three July trades and five of the first 54 picks in last year's draft have replenished the system. Starting pitching, catching and third base are organizational strengths, while outfield remains a concern.

Right-handed pitcher Eric Hurley struggled at times after his promotion to Triple-A, but remains the top prospect and could join the rotation by summer. Lefty Matt Harrison (acquired in the Teixeira trade), catcher Taylor Teagarden, second baseman German Duran and third baseman Chris Davis also have a chance to contribute as early as this year.

Highly regarded but further away are left-hander Kasey Kiker, right-hander Omar Poveda, and shortstop Elvis Andrus (another return for Teixeira).

Favorite Team Blogs

The Newberg Report (http://www.newbergreport.com/)

Lone Star Ball (http://www.lonestarball.com/)

Keys for 2008

Players Lost From Last Year's Team

Texas traded Teixeira, Lofton, and Gagne last July for several prospects. In the offseason, Edinson Volquez, Otsuka, Brad Wilkerson and Sosa were the significant departures.

Players Acquired

Talented, mercurial, and oft-injured outfielder Milton Bradley was the top free-agent acquisition. Reliever Kaz Fukumori, starter Jason Jennings and first baseman Ben Broussard also joined the team.

Reasons To Be Optimistic

The team went 28-28 after the trading deadline, indicating that the youngsters can compete. There's no reason Kevin Millwood and Vicente Padilla can't be league-average starters. Hamilton could become the best center fielder in the history of the franchise. Texas is slowly building the optimum combination of youth and experience and has plenty of cash to spend on free agents.

Reasons To Be Pessimistic

Manager Washington expects a 10-win improvement, but the team is unlikely to win half of its games. Several players are more potential than results at this point, and expecting both Bradley and Hamilton to be healthy and effective is a dicey proposition. Tom Hicks isn't the most patient owner on the planet, so another 90-loss season could result in organizational restructuring regardless of what the future holds.

Due For A Better Season

Millwood and Padilla had the worst seasons of their careers and should offer improvement, if not excellence.

Likely To Have A Worse Season

Thanks to a .451 batting average on balls in play, Marlon Byrd batted .356/.406/.510 in last season's first half. His second-half line of .269/.310/.417 provides a more realistic indicator of his hitting prowess. Likewise, newcomer David Murphy had a .410 BABIP and batted .343/.384/.552 in 46 games. Both are useful bench players, but overextended as regulars.

Most Likely Team Outcome

Texas has a chance at a .500 record, but catching Los Angeles is beyond hope. The Rangers will probably amble to 75-77 wins as they break in the youngsters and look toward 2009.

Player Projections

Batters

Hank Blalock (Third Base)

PA	R	H	2B	3B	HR	RBI	SO	BB	SB	CS	BA	OBP	SLG	OPS	3 Yr	Fld	F$
402	51	99	20	2	14	54	67	35	3	1	.275	.339	.458	.797	-.003	D	$1

Labeled "the next George Brett" while still a prospect, Blalock has taken a circuitous route to fulfilling that promise. From 2003 until the middle of 2004, he hit 52 homers and looked more like the next Mike Schmidt. Then, through 2006, he was one of the worst-hitting third basemen in the majors. A shoulder injury limited him to 58 games in 2007, during which he displayed the better Hank of old. Typically egregious against lefties (career .226/.280/.349) and on the road (.243/.301/.398), Blalock maintained his dignity in those categories last year, giving hope he finally can become a complete hitter.

Milton Bradley (Left Field)

PA	R	H	2B	3B	HR	RBI	SO	BB	SB	CS	BA	OBP	SLG	OPS	3 Yr	Fld	F$
337	47	84	15	2	14	49	55	37	7	2	.286	.368	.494	.862	-.049	B	$3

If it weren't for Bradley, the Padres wouldn't have remained in the playoff picture as long as they did. Before umpire Mike Winters goaded him into a season-ending implosion, Bradley carried the team on his back in a way no one had since probably Greg Vaughn in 1998. If healthy—always a question with Bradley, who tore his ACL in that bizarre sequence—he'll provide the Rangers with tremendous value.

Ben Broussard (First Base)

PA	R	H	2B	3B	HR	RBI	SO	BB	SB	CS	BA	OBP	SLG	OPS	3 Yr	Fld	F$
371	47	93	19	2	15	54	72	27	2	1	.276	.332	.479	.811	-.035	B	$1

In 2006, when the Mariners needed a DH, Broussard was brought over from Cleveland to plug the hole. The Mariners figured that his pull-happy left-handed swing would be perfect for Safeco's forgiving right field porch. They figured wrong. For whatever reason, Broussard never got comfortable, and a guy who could've been a huge asset was never able to establish himself. Off to Texas, I'm pretty confident that he'll be able to lift enough fly balls into those swirling winds to help.

Marlon Byrd (Center Field)

PA	R	H	2B	3B	HR	RBI	SO	BB	SB	CS	BA	OBP	SLG	OPS	3 Yr	Fld	F$
526	67	134	28	4	13	62	96	37	5	3	.282	.341	.440	.781	-.025	B	$1

Called up in May, Byrd captivated fans with a .398/.438/.582 June, fueled by a .462 average on balls in play. Reality beckoned, however, resulting in the type of second half (.259/.304/.410) that cost him his starting job in Philadelphia. Byrd is a dandy fourth outfielder and backup center fielder, but unless he summons the Ghost of Gary Matthews Jr. Past, he's no everyday player.

Frank Catalanotto (Left Field)

PA	R	H	2B	3B	HR	RBI	SO	BB	SB	CS	BA	OBP	SLG	OPS	3 Yr	Fld	F$
425	54	106	24	3	8	46	43	40	2	1	.288	.365	.435	.800	-.040	D	$1

In the first season of a four-year deal, Catalanotto contributed heavily to Texas' premature burial with a line of .197/.286/.395 through June. During the second half, he did what he always does: bat .290 with enough walks and power to be useful but not exceptional. Once a true super-utility player, Little Cat now is frequently the DH and isn't a defensive asset at his remaining positions of first base and left field.

Nelson Cruz (Right Field)

PA	R	H	2B	3B	HR	RBI	SO	BB	SB	CS	BA	OBP	SLG	OPS	3 Yr	Fld	F$
507	66	121	25	2	23	76	121	43	4	3	.268	.336	.485	.821	-.009	A	$8

Cruz displays as sweet a batting-practice swing as you'll ever see. Sad to say, it hasn't translated to a remotely acceptable real-life performance. An extended tryout has revealed him as devastating on mistake pitches, devastated by most everything else, and unable or unwilling to make necessary adjustments. He needs a league populated by Matt Kinneys and Ryan O'Malleys to succeed; unfortunately, that league is the PCL.

Cruz is out of options and may not fit onto the Opening Day roster. His decent range and plus arm make him a solid defensive right fielder.

German Duran (Second Base)

PA	R	H	2B	3B	HR	RBI	SO	BB	SB	CS	BA	OBP	SLG	OPS	3 Yr	Fld	F$
556	63	133	28	4	15	66	92	22	5	2	.256	.288	.412	.700	.050	C	$1

Drafted in the eighth round in 2004, Duran has quietly risen from just another guy to a top-10 team prospect. Duran batted .300/.352/.525 with 11 steals for Double-A Frisco and exhibited solid defense at second base. The only missing weapon is patience; Duran's walk rate has hovered around six percent his entire career. The Rangers believe he could merit a trip to Arlington as early as April. Envisioning him (at least temporarily) as the player Catalanotto used to be, the Rangers moved him all over the diamond in the Arizona Fall League and will even test him in the outfield.

Josh Hamilton (Center Field)

PA	R	H	2B	3B	HR	RBI	SO	BB	SB	CS	BA	OBP	SLG	OPS	3 Yr	Fld	F$
398	56	100	20	3	19	62	77	39	4	3	.285	.360	.522	.882	.008	F	$6

Was there any greater story in sports last year than this guy? With just 50 at-bats since 2002 (in A-ball no less), he plays his way into the lineup by the second week of the season, and finishes with a .922 OPS. He's a true five-tool player. Right field is his natural position, but he was competent in center. Granted, his record consists of just 337 plate appearances, but his peripherals look in line with his performance numbers. Moving to Arlington could result in MVP-caliber numbers this season … assuming he can stay healthy. He had three stints on the disabled list last season, and his injury history dates back well into his minor league career.

Ian Kinsler (Second Base)

PA	R	H	2B	3B	HR	RBI	SO	BB	SB	CS	BA	OBP	SLG	OPS	3 Yr	Fld	F$
519	72	127	26	2	19	71	75	49	16	3	.281	.355	.474	.829	.020	C	$13

Kinsler began the season as one of the few Rangers not in a horrific batting slump. Despite missing 30 games, his 20 homers led all AL second basemen, and his 62 walks trailed only Brian Roberts. He'll bat first or second for Texas and will move into the tier of near-elite second basemen (the elite tier consisting solely of Chase Utley) with some improvement in his road performance (.215/.313/.362). Kinsler played shortstop in the minors and defends well at second, though he was prone to mental errors last year. Texas would love to sign him long-term.

Gerald Laird (Catcher)

PA	R	H	2B	3B	HR	RBI	SO	BB	SB	CS	BA	OBP	SLG	OPS	3 Yr	Fld	F$
406	49	94	21	2	12	50	85	30	5	1	.258	.316	.426	.742	-.019	A+	$1

Handed the starting catcher role after three years as Rod Barajas' caddy, Laird batted his way into no more than a time-sharing arrangement (.224/.278/.349) for 2008. Laird has shown contact ability, patience and power at the plate, but never at the same time. He's also a terrific defender, so he might yet have value in a trade as a first-string catcher or prompt a position switch for Jarrod Saltalamacchia.

David Murphy (Center Field)

PA	R	H	2B	3B	HR	RBI	SO	BB	SB	CS	BA	OBP	SLG	OPS	3 Yr	Fld	F$
522	57	117	26	5	9	50	92	39	5	3	.246	.301	.378	.679	-.003	D	$1

The classic tweener, Murphy doesn't quite merit regular duty in center and doesn't hit well enough for a corner. His .340/.382/.534 in 43 games as a Ranger was built on an unsustainable .410 average on balls in play. His reliably bland .274/.341/.432 in three seasons in the high minors provides a better indication of his future.

Jarrod Saltalamacchia (Catcher)

PA	R	H	2B	3B	HR	RBI	SO	BB	SB	CS	BA	OBP	SLG	OPS	3 Yr	Fld	F$
504	60	115	25	2	17	65	106	43	2	1	.255	.322	.432	.754	.059	C	$1

The grand prize of the Mark Teixeira trade is younger than several of Texas' top prospects and would easily top the list if he still qualified. Aside from a troubled 2006, Saltalamacchia has torn through the minors, showing ridiculous patience and steadily increasing power. He made his MLB debut on his 22nd birthday and understandably struggled at times, but the upside remains firmly in place: a .280 hitter with oodles of walks and 20 homers.

His defense behind the plate is still a work in progress, and he'll never be a plus defender, but for now, Texas intends to leave him there, where he provides the most value.

Michael Young (Shortstop)

PA	R	H	2B	3B	HR	RBI	SO	BB	SB	CS	BA	OBP	SLG	OPS	3 Yr	Fld	F$
636	80	178	37	3	13	76	92	46	8	2	.307	.357	.448	.805	-.037	D	$17

A fifth consecutive season of 200 hits whitewashed Young's lowest slugging percentage (.418) since 2002 and just one homer on the road. That said, he's still a valuable hitter, just not from his typical No. 3 spot. Young moved to shortstop back in 2004 to accommodate Soriano. He's acceptable for now, but Texas ought to be thinking about where he might play in the not-too-distant future.

Young has an impeccable work ethic and horse-like stamina, so he's likely to age well. He'd better, because his five-year, $80 million extension doesn't begin until 2009.

Pitchers

Joaquin Benoit (Relief Pitcher)

W	L	ERA	TBF	IP	Hit	HR	SO	BB	HBP	3 Yr	F$
5	4	3.68	325	77	66	7	74	32	2	0.26	$3

The unsung hero of the bullpen, Benoit finally lived up to his potential after several years in which his very status on the 40-man roster was in question. In the past, he relied too heavily on a hot but erratic fastball, allowing walks and homers by the shipload. In 2007, with better control and an effective slider and change-up in tow, he shared closing duties with C.J. Wilson by season's end. Texas bought out his final year of arbitration and first year of free agency for a relatively modest $5.5 million.

Frank Francisco (Relief Pitcher)

W	L	ERA	TBF	IP	Hit	HR	SO	BB	HBP	3 Yr	F$
4	3	4.39	260	59	54	6	47	32	2	0.38	$1

Francisco returned to action after missing most of 2005-2006 with a slow recovery from Tommy John surgery. He pulverized Triple-A competition in a brief tune-up (23 batters faced, 14 strikeouts), but had middling results back in the majors. He tends to overthrow a fastball that can hit 95 mph regularly, leading to too many hitters' counts, an alarmingly high walk rate, and plenty of wild pitches. That said, Francisco tends to pitch better in money situations, as he allowed only three of 44 inherited runners to score.

Kason Gabbard (Starting Pitcher)

W	L	ERA	TBF	IP	Hit	HR	SO	BB	HBP	3 Yr	F$
7	9	5.24	653	145	157	19	90	76	9	-0.10	$1

Among the softest tossers in the majors, lefty Gabbard relies heavily on a curve and change to augment his 87 mph fastball. His peripherals deteriorated badly in the jump from Triple-A, and he tended to nibble the plate with men on base. He doesn't seem likely to enjoy a long career—a nice ground ball/fly ball ratio carries you only so far—but with better control he could imitate Kenny Rogers for a while.

Eddie Guardado (Relief Pitcher)

W	L	ERA	TBF	IP	Hit	HR	SO	BB	HBP	F$
2	2	4.50	173	40	40	6	29	14	2	$1

Everyday Eddie worked hard to come back from Tommy John surgery, but 2007 didn't go very well for him. With the Reds, he was only a pale imitation of his former self, with dramatically lower strikeout rates and yet the same proclivity for fly balls. He did seem better over his final five or six appearances, so perhaps he still has something left in the tank.

Eric Hurley (Starting Pitcher)

W	L	ERA	TBF	IP	Hit	HR	SO	BB	HBP	3 Yr	F$
6	10	6.47	651	142	163	30	81	71	8	-0.59	$1

The 30th player selected in the 2004 draft, Hurley has a slight chance to make his major league debut in April and certainly will appear at some point during 2008. He shows good control of four pitches (two-seam and four-seam fastball, slider, change-up) and poise beyond his 22 years. Hurley tends to induce fly balls and allows more than his fair share of homers, so preventing extra baserunners is especially important to his success. He should become a strong No. 3 starter, which in 2007 would have made him Texas's ace.

Jason Jennings (Starting Pitcher)

W	L	ERA	TBF	IP	Hit	HR	SO	BB	HBP	3 Yr	F$
6	8	5.24	569	128	140	17	72	58	3	0.60	$1

Jennings was one of the five worst starting pitchers in the NL last year. Of course, he had a bad elbow all season, and may have been injured when he was obtained from the Rockies. It's unknown how well he will pitch after his surgery this past winter.

Wes Littleton (Relief Pitcher)

W	L	ERA	TBF	IP	Hit	HR	SO	BB	HBP	3 Yr	F$
4	4	4.79	320	73	81	9	40	28	4	-0.11	$1

With his weird, rapid-fire, sidearm delivery and heavy sinker, Littleton simply refuses to let hitters get air under the ball. Development of a plus change-up gave him an effectiveness against lefties sorely lacking in 2006. Littleton has the stamina to work multiple innings and should be quietly effective for years to come.

Kameron Loe (Starting Pitcher)

W	L	ERA	TBF	IP	Hit	HR	SO	BB	HBP	3 Yr	F$
7	8	5.03	591	134	154	15	72	53	4	0.10	$1

The 6-foot-8 Loe doesn't throw terribly hard, relying on a sinker to induce grounders. Batters tend to catch up with him after the first run through the order, and lefties chewed him up in 2007, so a switch to relief holds the most promise.

Brandon McCarthy (Starting Pitcher)

W	L	ERA	TBF	IP	Hit	HR	SO	BB	HBP	3 Yr	F$
7	7	5.02	538	123	129	17	82	51	4	-0.28	$1

Detractors of the controversial John Danks-for-McCarthy trade smelled blood when McCarthy limped out of the gate to an 11.40 ERA after four starts. He dropped his second-half ERA to 3.67 from a first-half 5.70, belying a quite modest improvement in his peripherals. McCarthy had trouble throwing first-pitch strikes and was unsurprisingly clobbered after 1-0 counts (.290/.407/.455). He cut his homer rate in half from 2006 but also displayed a new-found inability to get third strikes and suffered several minor injuries. All that said, he's still just 24 and has the potential to become a capable starter.

Kevin Millwood (Starting Pitcher)

W	L	ERA	TBF	IP	Hit	HR	SO	BB	HBP	3 Yr	F$
10	9	4.45	749	175	185	20	119	56	6	0.40	$2

At the midway point of a season in which the Rangers considered themselves contenders, their alleged ace had a 6.16 ERA and an opposing line of .323/.393/.521. Culprits included a sore hamstring and reported lack of physical fitness (inexcusable if true) that dropped his fastball into the high 80s. He pitched to expectations in the second half (4.29 ERA) and could add three wins to the 2008 ledger simply by being adequate. Signed for two more years at $19.5 million plus a $12 million vesting option, not excessive in today's market, he could also find himself in a different uniform by the end of the summer.

A.J. Murray (Starting Pitcher)

W	L	ERA	TBF	IP	Hit	HR	SO	BB	HBP	3 Yr	F$
3	5	5.33	314	70	77	9	48	35	3	-0.08	$1

Arlington John Murray (yes, really) doesn't have much mileage on his arm for a 26-year-old, having missed all of 2004 and 2006 with shoulder problems. He spent almost all of 2007 as a reliever in Triple-A, where he greatly impressed despite a few too many walks. Texas then gave him a couple of late-season starts and plans to acclimate him to a rotation role in Triple-A. Murray augments an ordinary fastball and curve with a plus change-up.

Akinori Otsuka (Relief Pitcher)

W	L	ERA	TBF	IP	Hit	HR	SO	BB	HBP	F$
3	3	3.72	213	51	49	4	37	18	2	$1

The only worthwhile return on the trade of Chris Young and Adrian Gonzalez gave Texas 92 innings of excellent relief over two seasons. Otsuka missed the second half of 2007 with a sore elbow and hadn't recovered by December, so Texas reluctantly declined to offer arbitration. As he's aged, he's compensated for a declining strikeout rate with pinpoint command. He still features one of the best sliders in the game.

Vicente Padilla (Starting Pitcher)

W	L	ERA	TBF	IP	Hit	HR	SO	BB	HBP	3 Yr	F$
8	8	5.05	656	148	162	18	93	62	8	0.33	$1

Padilla washed out in the first year of his three-year, $33 million deal. A nagging triceps problem limited him to 120 innings, and he finished the season on the suspended list after a first-inning ejection for drilling Nick Swisher. The injury didn't take anything off his 95 mph heater, however, and doesn't fully explain his atrocious 5.76 ERA or declining peripherals. When on, his fastball-slider combo makes him a legitimate No. 2 starter. Lefties tend to chew him up (.329/.410/.468 in 2007).

John Rheinecker (Relief Pitcher)

W	L	ERA	TBF	IP	Hit	HR	SO	BB	HBP	3 Yr	F$
6	7	5.01	505	114	133	13	57	46	4	0.39	$1

Two stints in the rotation proved that Rheinecker has no business facing right-handed batters. Banished to relief, his slider bedeviled lefties enough to give him a chance at drawing major league pay for a few years. Rheinecker never will be more than a back-end type and always will be a few bad outings from demotion.

Robinson Tejeda (Starting Pitcher)

W	L	ERA	TBF	IP	Hit	HR	SO	BB	HBP	3 Yr	F$
7	8	5.32	598	132	136	17	90	76	5	-0.09	$1

Texas handed Tejeda a rotation spot after the promising end to his 2006 season. He completely collapsed after a solid first month, surpassing five innings in only three of his last 13 starts, with a 17 percent walk rate. Banishment to Triple-A in July didn't produce any improvement in his control, nor did winter in the Dominican Republic. Tejeda can dial his fastball up to 95, but in which direction is often anybody's guess. Now out of options, he must excel in spring or face designation.

C.J. Wilson (Relief Pitcher)

W	L	ERA	TBF	IP	Hit	HR	SO	BB	HBP	3 Yr	F$
4	3	4.20	291	67	64	7	57	30	4	0.12	$6

Honest and opinionated like Curt Schilling but lacking the pomposity, Wilson openly campaigned for the closer role rather than employ the "I'll pitch wherever they need me" cliche. Given the opportunity upon Eric Gagne's departure, he earned 12 saves in 14 attempts and should be first in line for the ninth inning this season. Wilson uses his hard sinker, curve and gyroball to destroy lefties, but righties often had his number (.381 OBP). He also struggled when pitching without a day's rest.

Toronto Blue Jays

by John Brattain of The Hardball Times

Team Projections

Record: 84-78
Division Rank: 3rd, 13 games back
Runs Scored: 774
Runs Allowed: 742

2007 in a Nutshell

It was "opposite day" for 162 games for the Toronto Blue Jays. With the addition of Frank Thomas, the club felt its offense would be potent and starting pitching an ongoing concern. General manager J.P. Ricciardi had signed three league average-ish starters in John Thomson, Tomokazu Ohka and Victor Zambrano hoping to solidify the rotation.

A wave of injuries/illnesses deprived the Jays of Roy Halladay (appendicitis), A.J. Burnett, Gustavo Chacin, Brandon League, Davis Romero, Zambrano, B.J. Ryan, Gregg Zaun, Lyle Overbay, Troy Glaus and Reed Johnson for large parts of the season while Vernon Wells struggled all year with a bad shoulder.

The injuries forced manager John Gibbons to use too many barely replacement-level hitters to fill in with predictable results. Meanwhile, the injuries to the pitching staff obligated the skipper to rely on the kiddie corps of Dustin McGowan, Shaun Marcum and Jesse Litsch and pressed Jeremy Accardo into the closer's role with Casey Janssen as his primary setup man. Those pitchers acquitted themselves far above everybody's expectations. By season's end, the Blue Jays had one of the best pitching staffs in the American League and one of the most impotent offenses.

General Comments

Team Strengths

The Jays rotation that finished 2007 (Halladay, Burnett, McGowan, Marcum and Litsch) enabled Toronto to finish with the second-best ERA (4.24) in the AL East (fourth in the AL) among the division's starting staffs. The quintet chipped in an aggregate earned run mark of 3.89 while the rest of the arms pressed into rotation service posted an ERA of 6.00 in 168 innings.

The bullpen, anchored by Accardo, was the second best in the AL (to the World Champion Red Sox) with a sparkling earned run mark of 3.46.

Team Weaknesses

The offense struggled save for the very beginning and end of 2007. In the 139 games from April 12-Sept. 15, the Jays scored four or fewer runs 91 times (65 percent of the games in that period), three or fewer 65 times, two or fewer 47 times. They played 18 contests scoring one or no runs, including four shutouts.

The prime culprits were Wells' shoulder injury (85 OPS+), Johnson's back injury (66 OPS+), Overbay's broken hand (85 OPS+), Thomas' slow start (.226/.370/.392 going into game 70 of the schedule, .310/.381/.539 thereafter). And they gave more than 1,300 at-bats to players with nothing in their past to indicate they could contribute (save Adam Lind, who does have a future). The Jays' "backup crew" batted an aggregate .231/.279/.323 and whiffed (271) almost as often as they hit (301). Of the 16 homers they struck, 11 were off the bat of prospect Lind. Absent him, the the bottom 10 was an even worse .229/.280/.295.

The General Manager is Known for...

Ricciardi is known for not admitting and addressing mistakes. He occasionally struggles with reality, as seen by his remark last season: "A left fielder, a catcher, a setup guy, a closer, a (bleep) third baseman–who's got those replacements? ... The Red Sox got those (bleep) replacements?" He said that John McDonald (OPS+ of 73 at the time), Jason Smith (45 OPS+), Lind (79 OPS+), Jason Phillips (67 OPS+), Sal Fasano (45 OPS+) and Royce Clayton (74 OPS+) constituted adequate replacements.

A club can pick up that kind of production anywhere and Ricciardi thought players 25-50 percent below league average were solid? Perhaps he was confusing "replacements" with "replacement-level."

The Manager is Known for...

Gibbons gets his charges to play hard, but all too often doesn't have a fallback plan when Plan A proves faulty. He occasionally leaves starters in, running up their pitch counts, after the game's outcome has been decided or has no impact on the season.

Ballpark Characteristics

The Rogers Center is a good power park for doubles and home runs. The ball seems to carry best when the roof is closed. The FieldTurf is faster than grass but gives a more consistent bounce for infielders.

The Minor League System is...

At the beginning of 2007, the Blue Jays system was middle of the road. Travis Snider is a slugging corner outfielder being watched very closely; his bat is highly touted, but his defense has DH written all over it. Ricciardi usually prefers college players to high-ceiling/high-risk high school players, but in 2007 Toronto left that philosophy behind and looked closely at the high school crop.

Because second base is set with Aaron Hill, the Jays drafted two middle infielders, Kevin Ahrens and Justin Jackson, hoping one will excel at short. They also added to their depth of catching prospects (Robinzon Diaz or Curtis Thigpen could make their presence felt in '08), tabbing backstop J.P. Arencibia. The Jays hope Arencibia and left-handed pitcher Brett Cecil will have a short minor league apprenticeship, because catcher Gregg Zaun will be 37 this season and Chacin is the only real hope of having an in-house southpaw starter.

The Jays rolled the dice and won, getting Eric Eiland to give up Texas A&M to sign with Toronto. He projects as a center fielder and while incumbent Wells is untradeable due to the massive contract extension he signed, the Jays will cross that bridge when they come to it.

At the moment, the Jays have no immediate organizational depth at shortstop or third base and will likely require a trade should they wish to upgrade those spots.

Favorite Team Blogs

The Jays Nest (http://mvn.com/mlb-bluejays/)
Batters Box (www.battersbox.ca/)
Blue Bird Banter (www.bluebirdbanter.com/)
The Mockingbird (http://bjays.wordpress.com/)
Drunk Jays Fans (http://drunkjaysfans.blogspot.com/)

Keys for 2008

Players Lost from Last Year's Team

Since opening day 2007, the Jays have said goodbye to the following who were on the 25-man roster at some point last season: pitchers Josh Towers, Ty Taubenheim, Victor Zambrano, Joe Kennedy and Tomokazu Ohka, infielders Troy Glaus, Royce Clayton, Jason Smith and Howie Clark, catcher Jason Phillips and outfielder John-Ford Griffin.

Players Acquired

Infielders Scott Rolen, Marcos Scutaro and David Eckstein, right-hander Randy Wells (Rule 5 draft) and utilityman Buck Coats.

Reasons to be Optimistic

The Jays have four solid starters in Halladay, Burnett, McGowan and Marcum plus several options for the No. 5 starters job in Litsch, Janssen and Chacin. They will have a beyond-excellent bullpen if Davis Romero, B.J. Ryan and Brandon League are healthy and effective. They should have adequate pitching depth to withstand another wave of injuries.

Offensively, the Jays should have better bench strength than they did in '07. Also, there's no reason this club won't again be a top-tier defensive unit. The Jays will not be giving opposing teams many extra at-bats.

Reasons to be Pessimistic

While the offense cannot possibly be worse than it was in 2007, it will struggle to be league average. Thomas, Matt Stairs and Zaun will be a year older. Those who have suffered back trauma know all too well that it never goes away. It cost Don Mattingly a Hall of Fame career, so we can expect Johnson to have ongoing issues stemming from this. Another concern is Wells; while his shoulder injury affected his production, he has been about league average offensively in all but two of his full major league seasons.

Due for a Better Season

Vernon Wells, Alex Rios, Roy Halladay, Dustin McGowan, Lyle Overbay, Adam Lind and Aaron Hill.

Likely to Have a Worse Season

Greg Zaun, Matt Stairs, Pat Litsch.

Still Left to Do

Find a big lefty bat, decide who will start in left field and settle on Zaun's caddy.

Most Likely Team Outcome

88-74. Optimistic prediction 92-70; pessimistic prediction 82-80.

Player Projections

Batters

David Eckstein (Shortstop)

PA	R	H	2B	3B	HR	RBI	SO	BB	SB	CS	BA	OBP	SLG	OPS	3 Yr	Fld	F$
502	56	129	21	3	2	40	40	28	6	2	.285	.338	.358	.696	-.034	D	$1

Despite the laments of many, this wasn't a terrible signing. When you consider that the various Jays who manned shortstop in '07 hovered around replacement level, a career line of .286/.351/.362 with an OBP of .360 since 2005 is a marked improvement. As long as he doesn't spend outs like last season's motley crew of out machines—and is subbed for defensively in close games where the Jays are ahead—he'll be an asset. Fielding is a concern. He was so bad afield (20 errors and an obvious loss of range) that St. Louis made only a token effort to re-sign him.

Aaron Hill (Second Base)

PA	R	H	2B	3B	HR	RBI	SO	BB	SB	CS	BA	OBP	SLG	OPS	3 Yr	Fld	F$
581	70	152	35	3	13	70	79	40	3	2	.290	.343	.442	.785	.021	B	$9

Hill sacrificed contact for power last year, setting a team record for second basemen with 47 doubles. He finished with 17 homers, but had two pulled back by Joey Gathright in consecutive games in Kansas City in August. However, his OBP fell from .349 to .333 from 2006 to 2007 and he cracked the century mark in strikeouts. His superb defense with a maturing bat will make him one to watch this season.

Reed Johnson (Left Field)

PA	R	H	2B	3B	HR	RBI	SO	BB	SB	CS	BA	OBP	SLG	OPS	3 Yr	Fld	F$
394	48	96	20	3	7	41	66	23	3	2	.275	.339	.409	.748	-.033	C	$1

After a solid .319/.390/.479 (124 OPS+) in 2006, a back injury slowed Johnson considerably in 2007. While '06 was probably a career year, Johnson should be capable of getting on base 35 percent of the time with a bit of pop and solid defense in left. The Jays signed him to a one-year pact to see if 2006 was a complete aberration or a demonstration that he can be better than league average. Back injuries never go away completely, so this season should be a good indicator of how much his will affect him.

Adam Lind (Left Field)

PA	R	H	2B	3B	HR	RBI	SO	BB	SB	CS	BA	OBP	SLG	OPS	3 Yr	Fld	F$
505	59	121	25	2	16	64	109	34	1	2	.262	.314	.429	.743	.025	C	$1

Lind probably will start the year in Triple-A until the Jays see how Johnson's back responds to treatment and conditioning. A former first baseman, Lind still is learning the nuances of outfield play. He can hit and hit with power, although his OBP is still batting average-dependent. Word has gotten around the league that he cannot hit (or lay off) the high fastball. Until he learns to lay off it, he'll be a good mistake hitter, but never reach base on a consistent basis.

John McDonald (Shortstop)

PA	R	H	2B	3B	HR	RBI	SO	BB	SB	CS	BA	OBP	SLG	OPS	3 Yr	Fld	F$
355	37	81	16	2	2	27	50	20	6	2	.254	.301	.336	.637	-.033	A	$1

The Prime Minister of Defense put on a clinic of spectacular play at short in 2007. Pairing him with Hill, the Blue Jays enjoyed superlative defense up the middle of the infield. McDonald worked on his legs and stamina during the 2006-07 offseason and it enabled him to provide Gold Glove-quality defense. He said he would work on forearm strength and hitting during this offseason, so expect improvement on his anemic .251/.279/.333 line of last season.

With Eckstein being tabbed as the starter, expect the PMoD to make Gibbons' shortstop decision in the spring a lot more difficult—especially if Eckstein struggles in his return to the AL.

Lyle Overbay (First Base)

PA	R	H	2B	3B	HR	RBI	SO	BB	SB	CS	BA	OBP	SLG	OPS	3 Yr	Fld	F$
510	63	124	31	1	14	64	82	53	1	1	.276	.351	.442	.793	-.025	B	$2

A hand injury sapped much of his power last season. Expect him to put up an OPS+ in the 120 range with 40+ doubles and about 20 home runs and solid-to-Gold Glove level defense.

Alex Rios (Right Field)

PA	R	H	2B	3B	HR	RBI	SO	BB	SB	CS	BA	OBP	SLG	OPS	3 Yr	Fld	F$
585	82	152	34	6	20	80	97	45	14	5	.288	.345	.489	.834	.004	B	$18

For the second consecutive year, Rios saw his homer totals dip in the second half. In 2006, it was the lingering effects of a staph infection. There was no discernible cause for it in '07. (Home Run Derby hangover?) He actually made better contact in the second half last year (.294/.350/.520, 17 home runs vs .300/.360/.471, 7 HR). Whether this will be a trend will bear watching. Rios' OBP is largely batting average-driven, so he'll need to keep working on his selectivity at the plate to get to the next level.

Scott Rolen (Third Base)

PA	R	H	2B	3B	HR	RBI	SO	BB	SB	CS	BA	OBP	SLG	OPS	3 Yr	Fld	F$
452	55	105	29	1	12	55	68	41	3	2	.263	.336	.431	.767	-.028	A+	$1

Surgery took care of one of his main complaints last year, scar tissue in his chronically sore right shoulder. The trade took care of his other big problem, Tony La Russa. A healthier, happier Rolen should be better than the player who contributed just two WSAB last season, but the fact remains that he's 33 years old and has had three shoulder surgeries in the last three years. He hasn't good a good second half since 2003; if he starts strong (and he very well might), fantasy owners should look to trade him at the All-Star break.

Marco Scutaro (Infield)

PA	R	H	2B	3B	HR	RBI	SO	BB	SB	CS	BA	OBP	SLG	OPS	3 Yr	Fld	F$
410	49	95	20	3	9	44	56	42	2	1	.264	.340	.412	.752	-.039	D	$1

In 2007, Scutaro would have been perfect for the Blue Jays. The versatile infielder and fan favorite batted .348/.464/.565 with runners in scoring position and two out. Obviously, that is unlikely to be duplicated, but he enjoys a reputation as a guy who can hit or somehow get on base in key situations. He can play any infield position, but his so-so range and modest arm make him best suited to second base. While a .333 OBP since 2007 is league average, it's still about a 50-point upgrade on the Jays bench last season.

Matt Stairs (First Base)

PA	R	H	2B	3B	HR	RBI	SO	BB	SB	CS	BA	OBP	SLG	OPS	Fld	F$
416	56	99	23	1	17	61	69	51	2	2	.278	.370	.491	.861	F	$1

Stairs is coming off his best season since '03. Like Thomas, he'll be 40 this year and it would be unrealistic to see a repeat of his .289/.368/.549 effort of '07. But he should come reasonably close to his career norms (.267/.359/.488) while filling in at the infield and outfield corners and DH. His booming left-handed bat will ensure that he'll see more than 300 at-bats.

Frank Thomas (Designated Hitter)

PA	R	H	2B	3B	HR	RBI	SO	BB	SB	CS	BA	OBP	SLG	OPS	F$
523	74	120	24	0	29	87	87	73	0	1	.275	.381	.529	.910	$13

It was a tale of two seasons for The Big Hurt. It was his second consecutive season with a slow start. If Thomas can hit at a steady .280/.380/.500 clip from April through October, it will help the Blue Jays. Are his 30-home run seasons a thing of the past? I guess we'll just have to see. He topped .500 in slugging from 2003-2006 (albeit with two injury-shortened seasons), so it wouldn't be a shock to see him reach those levels once more.

Vernon Wells (Center Field)

PA	R	H	2B	3B	HR	RBI	SO	BB	SB	CS	BA	OBP	SLG	OPS	3 Yr	Fld	F$
596	78	146	33	3	22	83	84	49	11	3	.272	.332	.468	.800	-.039	F	$16

While 2007 was marred by a lingering shoulder injury, Wells' OPS+ numbers since '02 are 96, 132, 105, 104, 129 and 85. One cannot help but wonder if Wells is a real deal. Is he the superstar of 2003 and 2006, or is he a slightly above league average-hitting superb fly-chaser? Maybe we'll get a better idea this season—Ricciardi is praying that his pricey Blue Jay doesn't become an expensive albatross.

Gregg Zaun (Catcher)

PA	R	H	2B	3B	HR	RBI	SO	BB	SB	CS	BA	OBP	SLG	OPS	Fld	F$
412	50	91	20	1	11	47	56	56	1	1	.262	.365	.420	.785	F	$1

Missing all of May allowed Zaun to finish strong in 2007. While he scuffled getting his swing going when he returned from the DL, the switch-hitting catcher batted .300/.446/.538 over his final 100 plate appearances. He's given Toronto yeoman's service, posting a .358 OBP during his tenure with the Jays. He has developed a bit of pop in Canada, hitting 33 of his 72 career homers since 2005.

He's too good to be a backup, but cannot handle the rigors of everyday catching duties. His defense is generally good save for throwing out base thieves. He's Pat Borders with better plate discipline.

Pitchers

Jeremy Accardo (Relief Pitcher)

W	L	ERA	TBF	IP	Hit	HR	SO	BB	HBP	3 Yr	F$
4	3	3.89	286	67	65	6	52	25	3	0.07	$8

Accardo performed well in his first stint as closer and will likely open 2008 in that role as B.J. Ryan continues to return from Tommy John surgery. He lost command of his split-fingered fastball as the season went on (walking 13 of his 24 in June and July), but still managed to save 30 games with a tidy ERA of 2.14.

A.J. Burnett (Starting Pitcher)

W	L	ERA	TBF	IP	Hit	HR	SO	BB	HBP	3 Yr	F$
10	8	3.88	678	160	149	16	147	59	8	0.27	$10

Both the Blue Jays and Burnett would like to get at least 30 starts this season, but Burnett's track record undeniably demonstrates that consistently high pitch counts translate into time on the disabled list. He has had 30-plus starts exactly once in his career. He threw 696 pitches over six starts (including 130 in the last of those) before he landed on the DL in June. He wrapped up '07 with 707 over six starts before being yanked after 105 pitches. The Jays have to be smarter in handling him.

Gustavo Chacin (Starting Pitcher)

W	L	ERA	TBF	IP	Hit	HR	SO	BB	HBP	3 Yr	F$
5	5	5.08	395	90	100	14	48	32	4	0.13	$1

Rarely has one player tumbled so deep on a team's depth chart in such a short period of time. At one point, he was thought to be the No. 3 starter in the Jays' rotation. Now he'll be battling for a job. Chacin never has been a strikeout pitcher or a control artist. He gives up more hits than innings pitched and has been commended by PETA for his generous feeding of gophers. He has been quite injury-prone of late as well. Good thing he's young (27) and left handed—he'll get plenty of chances because of that. Will he be getting those chances in Toronto?

Scott Downs (Relief Pitcher)

W	L	ERA	TBF	IP	Hit	HR	SO	BB	HBP	3 Yr	F$
4	3	4.22	286	66	66	7	55	27	3	0.41	$1

Despite a solid season in which he whiffed close to a batter per inning with a 2.17 ERA, Downs struggled finishing off innings. Opposing players hit .407/.467/.444 with runners in scoring position and two out. Of course, relief pitcher results are wildly unpredictable. We do know Downs has nasty stuff and was unusually stingy with the long ball, but he struggles with control. Regardless, he'll be a useful cog in the Blue Jays bullpen in 2008.

Jason Frasor (Relief Pitcher)

W	L	ERA	TBF	IP	Hit	HR	SO	BB	HBP	3 Yr	F$
4	3	4.01	275	64	60	6	61	26	3	0.27	$1

He has a tremendous arm, but muscles up when under pressure, causing his pitches to flatten out. He has closer's stuff, but cannot be effective in that role. He needs to think less when on the mound and trust his stuff. Ideally, Gibbons needs to use him in low-leverage situations to showcase him for a trade. There's always a team that thinks it can correct his flaw and Ricciardi needs to find that team.

Roy Halladay (Starting Pitcher)

W	L	ERA	TBF	IP	Hit	HR	SO	BB	HBP	3 Yr	F$
13	9	3.54	802	195	199	16	119	40	6	0.27	$16

Despite what you may think, Halladay is not injury prone. He is snake-bitten however. In 2005 it was a Kevin Mench line drive off his shin, in 2006 he was shut down early as a precaution (it never hurts to take good care of the crown jewels) and last year it was appendicitis.

He was much better than his ERA would indicate. He had three starts that could be linked to his appendix—two before, one after his operation—in which he posted a 13.21 ERA in 13.2 innings. He had another rough skid in late June-early July, posting a 6.85 ERA over four turns. Halladay finished the season strong, going 6-3, 2.75 ERA over his last 14 starts. Absent any mishaps, expect a run at the Cy Young Award.

Casey Janssen (Starting/Relief Pitcher)

W	L	ERA	TBF	IP	Hit	HR	SO	BB	HBP	3 Yr	F$
4	5	4.58	336	78	86	9	43	23	4	0.06	$1

After he gave Toronto a tremendous year as Accardo's right-handed setup man, the Jays will be looking at Janssen as a potential No. 5 starter. He had 45 starts in the minors, going 17-10, 2.93 ERA and averaging a mere 1.4 walks per nine innings (BB/9) and a minuscule .37 home runs per nine innings (HR/9). Although he didn't strike out players as frequently as he did in the bushes, where he posted 7.9 strikeouts per nine innings (K/9), he'll likely better his 4.8 K/9 of '07.

Brandon League (Relief Pitcher)

W	L	ERA	TBF	IP	Hit	HR	SO	BB	HBP	3 Yr	F$
3	3	4.52	228	52	58	4	30	20	3	-0.28	$1

He was to open 2007 as Ryan's main setup man, but a winter of poorly structured weight training robbed him of his blazing fastball. He demonstrated in 2006 that he has command; the questions are whether he can get his fastball back and whether he cost himself development time. If he's back to his '06 form, he'll make Jason Frasor expendable.

Jesse Litsch (Starting Pitcher)

W	L	ERA	TBF	IP	Hit	HR	SO	BB	HBP	3 Yr	F$
8	10	5.06	723	165	187	22	76	54	12	-0.53	$1

You'd think 20 starts of 3.81 ERA would be enough to nail down the final spot in the rotation for '08. However a hits-per-nine inning of 9.4, and a K/9 of 4.1 usually doesn't translate into an ERA below four. To his credit, Litsch was stingy with walks (2.9 BB/9) and kept the ball in the park (HR/9 of 1.1). He certainly improved his location on the depth chart–not bad for a 22-year old kid drafted in the 24th round with just 310 minor league innings under his belt.

Shaun Marcum (Starting Pitcher)

W	L	ERA	TBF	IP	Hit	HR	SO	BB	HBP	3 Yr	F$
7	9	4.97	605	140	148	24	109	46	6	0.08	$1

Marcum finally translated his minor league performance into a major league pitching effort. As a major league starter, Marcum was 11-3, 3.45 ERA through the end of August with a BB/9 of 2.37 but walked 10 in 17.1 innings until he was shut down in September. Marcum struck out almost seven per nine innings but had a HR/9 of 1.53. He has to keep the ball in the park and work on his fitness. When he tires, his command slips noticeably.

Dustin McGowan (Starting Pitcher)

W	L	ERA	TBF	IP	Hit	HR	SO	BB	HBP	3 Yr	F$
9	9	4.41	702	162	161	19	134	70	6	-0.05	$1

When he was on, opponents lamented that it was like facing Halladay. Before the Yankees touched him for six earned runs in 4.1 innings on Sept. 23, McGowan had pitched 2.72 ERA ball over 12 starts, winning six. His stuff is top shelf, but he needs to work on his command and the mental aspect of his game. Barring injury, he should have a fine 2008 campaign.

Davis Romero (Relief Pitcher)

W	L	ERA	TBF	IP	Hit	HR	SO	BB	HBP	3 Yr	F$
4	8	6.96	527	111	136	21	57	65	7	-0.62	$1

Romero, out for all of 2007 with a torn labrum, has been used as both a starter and reliever in the minors. He has an electric left arm (9.8 K/9) and surprising command for one so young (2.4 BB/9), drawing comparisons to Cole Hamels. The Jays aren't expecting Hamels, but they hope to work him in slowly as a reliever until they see how his shoulder responds in the coming season.

B.J. Ryan (Relief Pitcher)

W	L	ERA	TBF	IP	Hit	HR	SO	BB	HBP	3 Yr	F$
3	1	3.10	38	155	30	3	45	13	1	0.29	$1

It'll make things interesting in Toronto when he gets back up to speed. It takes time to fully recover from Tommy John surgery, so Ryan likely will be eased into the closer's role (or he or Accardo will be dealt) as the season goes on. All bets are off as regards Ryan's 2008.

Brian Tallet (Relief Pitcher)

W	L	ERA	TBF	IP	Hit	HR	SO	BB	HBP	3 Yr	F$
3	4	5.17	296	66	68	9	47	34	4	0.33	$1

Tallet blows hot and cold. He was brilliant in May to early July, when he struck out 33 in 36 innings with a 2.25 ERA in 24 outings. But Tallet can lose the strike zone completely for prolonged stretches. As with Downs, he'll be an asset in the bullpen or a valuable trading chip in '08.

Washington Nationals

by Chris Needham of Capitol Punishment (dcbb.blogspot.com)

2008 Projections

Record: 70-92
Division Rank: 4th, 22 games back
Runs Scored: 740
Runs Allowed: 849

2007 in a Nutshell

On May 9, the Nationals slunk out of Milwaukee, a victim of a three-game sweep that dropped the team's record to an abysmal 9-25. Buster Olney's sneering scouts, who had predicted that the Nats would be a historically bad team, undoubtedly twirled their mustaches in their fingers and cackled. Nothing had gone right. The Nats became the first team since 1901 to go down 4-0 in each of their first six games and they are the proud holders of the National League record for their 22-game season-opening streak of not scoring in the first inning. They were behind early in almost every game and, more importantly, behind at the end, getting outscored by 55 runs in the first month alone.

To make matters worse, four of the five original starting pitchers went down for the count in May, pressing Jason Simontacchi, Mike Bacsik, Levale Speigner and Micah Bowie into a rotation that was "led" by rookie Matt Chico. But a funny thing happened on the way to 120 losses: They started winning! The offense, which couldn't knock any runs in because nobody was on base in the first place, started humming along, led by deserving All-Star and reform-school graduate Dmitri Young. When he returned from a nagging foot injury in mid-May, he went on a spree, batting .419 through the end of June and carrying the team on his massive, lumpy shoulders.

As the months went on, the team would tread water right around the .500 mark each month. Thanks to a 15-12 September, the Nationals exceeded 2006's win total. The Nats' September stretch featured an end-of-season domination of the Mets, taking five out of six in the last two weeks, but most importantly (to Nats fans, at least), pushing the team above and beyond the Florida Marlins into a surprising fourth-place finish.

The scout who told Buster that the team would lose 120 games was 28 off. Eight MLB teams finished with worse records. The Nats certainly proved that it's entirely possible to wildly exceed expectations without being any good at all.

General Comments

Team Strengths

The Nationals featured relief pitching and the occasional defensive gem. When the Nats held a lead in the middle innings, or when it was close late, manager Manny Acta turned to his three big arms over and over again. Jon Rauch led the NL with 88 appearances and the wildly unknown Saul Rivera finished second with 85 despite spending the first two weeks of the season traipsing around Columbus. Closer Chad Cordero chipped in another 76 appearances. The Nats starters weren't very good, but the relievers were effective enough to give the Nats' meager bats enough time to get the big hit or two they needed to steal the close game.

On defense, they were led by two legitimate Gold Glove candidates, Ryan Zimmerman and Austin Kearns. Kearns played a terrific right field, showing tremendous range and hustle. He always seemed to be in position to make the tough running catch or to cut the ball off from splitting the gap. At the hot corner, naysayers will point to Zimmerman's high error total, but they're missing the immobile, inflexible target he was throwing to at first. A better fielding first baseman would've cut off five or so of those errors and voters would've focused on what he did well: everything else.

Perhaps Zimmerman's greatest strength isn't his catlike reflexes or the jump that gives him an extra step-and-a-half, but his aggressiveness. If there's even a glimmer of a chance of him getting the lead runner on a play, he's making the tough throw, and the Nats were able to turn a number of jaw-dropping double plays when most third basemen would've been content with the ol' 5-3. When you throw in Nook Logan who, for whatever his faults with the bat, was a fly catcher in a pasture of a center field, the Nats weren't doing so badly. (As long as you ignore Young, Felipe Lopez and Cristian Guzman.)

Team Weaknesses

It's easy to say offense since they finished last, 90 runs below the average NL team, but that doesn't account for the incredibly depressive effect of RFK Stadium. On the road, the Nats were a slightly less terrible 13th in runs scored. Instead, as most expected, it was the starting pitching that was the Achilles heel of this team.

Because of injuries, only one starting pitcher—Chico and his 4.63 ERA—qualified for the ERA race and only three cracked the 100-inning mark. However, given the 5.11 ERA starting pitchers had in that very same pitcher's haven of a ballpark, that might not have been a bad thing.

Shawn Hill, their best starter, battled shoulder injuries and arm pain. Jason Bergmann had a dominant stretch early in the season as a new grip on his pitches turned him into a monster, but the strain of throwing a crisp, tight slider crippled his arm, sending him to the DL. The surprise ace of 2005, John Patterson, had his annual bout with arm pain, this one sending him to Canada for experimental treatment. Simontacchi blew out his elbow. Bowie blew out his hip. Joel Hanrahan just blew. It wasn't pretty, but Acta and pitching coach Randy St. Claire managed it beautifully, lessening the damage they could and playing to the team's strengths.

The General Manager is Known for...

His reputation is for general buffoonery and his toolsy outfielder fetish, especially for former Reds. But he really should be known for being a pretty savvy GM. Statheads don't care if their players don't model jeans, but they obsess if their GMs wear leather pants. Especially since Stan Kasten took over as team president and seemingly held him back from making those cringe-inducing pronouncements, GM Jim Bowden has had a new direction, shaping the roster for the long term and overseeing a scouting and player development process that appears to be one of the best in the league. He's shown a willingness and ability to pull off a creative trade or three and has undoubtedly made the franchise significantly stronger than it was when he took over from Omar Minaya.

The Manager is Known for...

Acta is relentlessly optimistic. After the team started 9-25, his ceaseless positive attitude kept the clubhouse afloat, preventing the team from just giving up. The team constantly played hard for him—with midgame yanking for players who didn't—and he got maximum effort from every man on the roster, even if those efforts weren't especially good.

Acta doesn't like to bunt and rarely steals, referencing the stat-based reasons for most of those moves. On the pitching side, with a gimpy, mediocre staff, he had a quick hook, getting those starters out and turning over the game to his excellent workhorse bullpen at the earliest opportunity.

Ballpark Characteristics

RFK was a canyon with 390-foot power alleys and a rounded symmetrical shape that killed any well-struck ball not pulled down the lines. It, as much as anything, shaded the offensive value of most Nats batters and brightly colored the Nationals' pitching performance. As they stroll into a new park south of the Capitol, nobody is quite sure how it will play, but the dimensions are much smaller and even if it's neutral, it's still going to be a shock to the batters and pitchers.

The Minor League System is...

It's in a different universe than before. After Bud Selig and Omar Minaya's stewardship plundered and pillaged every prospect and stripped the system bare, making it difficult for them to even find new prospects, there was nowhere to go but up. When the Lerners took over as owners, one of the first pronouncements they made was about the need to invest in the farm system, and they've hired experienced personnel, such as Mike Rizzo from Arizona, to lead the operation.

The difference in quality of the top prospect list between now and two years ago is amazing. Although the Nationals don't have any developed high-level prospects, the potential of players such as Chris Marrero, Michael Burgess and Ross Detwiler is enough to make Nats fans look forward to 2010.

Favorite Team Blogs

Nationals Farm Authority (http://www.farmauthority.dcsportsnet.com/)

Oleanders and Morning Glories (http://mvn.com/mlb-nationals/)

District of Baseball (http://www.districtofbaseball.com/)

Nats 320 (http://nats320.blogspot.com/)

Keys for 2008

Players Lost from Last Year's Team

Does losing Logan really count as a loss? The Nats will miss Brian Schneider's glove and Ryan Church's defense and gap power.

Players Acquired

Elijah Dukes scares the team's fans, but he has potential that, if tapped, will significantly help the Nats offense. Paul Lo Duca brings his heart-and-soul act to D.C. and should will the team to ten more wins with the power of his personality. Lastings Milledge rounds out what should be a much-improved outfield.

Reasons to be Optimistic

The team is like a coiled spring, with tons of potential energy. If the spring uncoils and those players live up to their potential, it's going to be a surprisingly good offense. Patterson and Hill have No. 1-No. 2-type stuff and could show it if they stay healthy.

Reasons to be Pessimistic

That "if they stay healthy" part never seems to come true, does it? This team was last in the league in runs scored, and has a pitching staff that seems even more fragile than a year ago, when many were predicting more than 100 losses.

Due for a Better Season

Kearns was one of the big disappointments of last season. Early on, he hit into bad luck, then messed up his swing. Once he got it back, he had a great second half, and is one of the batters most likely to be helped by the move out of RFK.

Likely to Have a Worse Season

Young's story—from washed-up vet to deserving All-Star—certainly got its share of ink. But can a poorly conditioned, 34-year-old first baseman with no defensive value really be expected to produce another .320/.378/.491 season?

Still Left to Do

As Bowden is wont to say, "pitching, pitching, pitching." The staff has lots of question marks and lots of candidates that the Nats are going to need to sift through, to find those who are ready to contribute immediately and who need more development. The Nats are always looking for rebound cases, and there's a strong possibility that they'll kick the tires of one of the injured pitchers licking their wounds on the free agent pile.

Most Likely Team Outcome

Nobody's going to predict "historically bad" again this year, and with the upgrades they've made in the outfield (dumping the deadweight at-bats of Logan and Ryan Langerhans), the offense is going to be much better. If the pitching holds out as well as last year, and given how long the Nationals played .500 ball last season, 81 wins looks fairly reasonable. And if Patterson or Hill (or both) stay healthy … Let's not get ahead of ourselves!

Player Projections

Batters

Ronnie Belliard (Second Base)

PA	R	H	2B	3B	HR	RBI	SO	BB	SB	CS	BA	OBP	SLG	OPS	3 Yr	Fld	F$
533	60	133	29	1	10	59	69	36	2	1	.275	.326	.402	.728	-.028	C	$1

He was signed as a backup before spring training, but Cristian Guzman's injury thrust him into a starting role. He always had a bit of a doubles stroke, so RFK was a decent match for him, and it'll be interesting to see how the new park affects him. Defensively, he played extremely deep, often beyond the grass in short right field, perhaps to compensate for some diminished range. Regardless, he made the plays he should have, and was good at turning the double play. He is penciled in as the starter at second (although that seems more like a motivational ploy with Felipe Lopez), and he is sure to see time at all four infield positions—a perfect NL bench player.

Aaron Boone (First/Third Base)

PA	R	H	2B	3B	HR	RBI	SO	BB	SB	CS	BA	OBP	SLG	OPS	3 Yr	Fld	F$
348	40	76	16	1	7	35	57	29	3	1	.249	.327	.377	.704	-.039	B	$1

Boone was excellent for the Marlins in a utility infield role, batting .286/.329/.429. Unfortunately his season was cut short when he injured his knee at the start of July and required season-ending knee surgery.

Humberto Cota (Catcher)

PA	R	H	2B	3B	HR	RBI	SO	BB	SB	CS	BA	OBP	SLG	OPS	3 Yr	Fld	F$
222	22	50	11	1	2	19	39	15	2	1	.248	.304	.343	.647	-.023	F	$1

The Pirates actually dumped him around May last year, then retired the number that he wore when he was with the club (No. 11, Paul Waner's number). It was probably a coincidence, but it seemed funny nonetheless.

Elijah Dukes (Center Field)

PA	R	H	2B	3B	HR	RBI	SO	BB	SB	CS	BA	OBP	SLG	OPS	3 Yr	Fld	F$
470	59	103	18	4	15	55	82	51	6	4	.252	.339	.425	.764	.034	D	$1

Milton Bradley? Carl Everett? Before being deactivated, Dukes was leading all rookies with 10 home runs. Among those who saw both Dukes and Delmon Young in the minors, some considered Dukes the better prospect.

The only question is whether he can stay out of trouble and on the diamond. If he cannot, the more apt comparison may be Lawrence Phillips.

Jesus Flores (Catcher)

PA	R	H	2B	3B	HR	RBI	SO	BB	SB	CS	BA	OBP	SLG	OPS	3 Yr	Fld	F$
470	49	103	23	2	12	52	112	16	1	2	.235	.273	.379	.652	.050	C	$1

Perhaps the one good move Omar Minaya made for this franchise, Flores emerged as a pleasant surprise for the Nats. He had an amazing knack for huge hits, with four of the team's five biggest plays as measured by Win Probability Added. He was the perfect complement to Brian Schneider, hitting lefties very effectively, though his struggles against righties have to be a concern. With Paul Lo Duca there to suck up some of the playing time, Flores has the chance to continue to learn and develop on the fly.

Cristian Guzman (Shortstop)

PA	R	H	2B	3B	HR	RBI	SO	BB	SB	CS	BA	OBP	SLG	OPS	3 Yr	Fld	F$
368	42	91	15	5	3	30	48	26	4	2	.270	.324	.371	.695	-.043	C	$1

It's easy to point to his career high .360 BABIP as the reason for his success. And you'd be right. But there's also reason to believe that he's a somewhat different hitter than in previous seasons. Before his lost '06 season, he had laser eye surgery. Then he had surgery on his shoulder, something which had been affecting him (and presumably his swing) for a few seasons. And he followed that up with a completely new swing, which had him driving the ball, using his legs as a base, instead of slapping the ball while playing pepper with the infielders. In the last season of his disastrous four-year contract —Bowden's last folly—there's reason to believe that he'll please Nats fans, even if he doesn't reach last year's limited heights.

Austin Kearns (Right Field)

PA	R	H	2B	3B	HR	RBI	SO	BB	SB	CS	BA	OBP	SLG	OPS	3 Yr	Fld	F$
595	74	135	33	2	18	74	111	64	1	2	.262	.350	.438	.788	.002	B	$1

I'd bet the over on this projection. He was probably the hitter most affected by RFK's massive dimensions, and he hit a pretty solid .301/.378/.454 on the road. He struggled most of the first half, where bad luck (lots of liners into gloves) and a change in hitting coach led to some bad tweaks to his swing. After working on it, he rebounded in the second half, putting up a .285/.390/.461 line that is more like what we had expected. Free of RFK, that is probably the starting point for what he can do. Given his tremendous defense in right field, he has a chance to quietly be one of the three or four best right fielders in the league this season.

Paul Lo Duca (Catcher)

PA	R	H	2B	3B	HR	RBI	SO	BB	SB	CS	BA	OBP	SLG	OPS	Fld	F$
492	53	127	26	2	4	45	42	27	2	1	.282	.328	.376	.704	D	$1

Don't be fooled by Lo Duca's batting average. He has very little offensive value, and his defense behind the plate is subpar. Once hailed as the Dodgers' clubhouse leader, Lo Duca was the center of a lot of steroids action in the Mitchell report. I guess that's one definition of "clubhouse leader."

Nook Logan (Center Field)

PA	R	H	2B	3B	HR	RBI	SO	BB	SB	CS	BA	OBP	SLG	OPS	3 Yr	Fld	F$
365	40	80	15	3	1	25	79	25	17	3	.242	.297	.315	.612	-.024	A	$1

Halfway through the season, Logan finally gave up his switch-hitting experiment, something he held on to for too long, despite no evidence that he could do it, because it took away some of the threat of the bunt single. Although he continued to struggle against right-handed pitching, he hit well enough (.305/.352/.427) against lefties—in line with his career numbers—to be somewhat interesting, especially when you consider his tremendous defense in center, and his base stealing. He was not tenderd a contract by the Nationals.

Felipe Lopez (Shortstop/Second Base)

PA	R	H	2B	3B	HR	RBI	SO	BB	SB	CS	BA	OBP	SLG	OPS	3 Yr	Fld	F$
612	79	143	26	4	9	57	103	53	36	11	.263	.328	.375	.703	-.008	F	$14

A season lost, it has been partially explained by ongoing, unspecified off-the-field distractions. There were certainly times that he played as if his mind were elsewhere. His isolated numbers aren't so different from past seasons, but he set a career low in batting average on balls in play at .288, a drop of roughly 70 points from the previous season. A move toward his career average—in the .320ish range—and he'll be the player the Nats thought they acquired, even with his scattershot throwing arm.

Lastings Milledge (Right Field)

PA	R	H	2B	3B	HR	RBI	SO	BB	SB	CS	BA	OBP	SLG	OPS	3 Yr	Fld	F$
466	56	109	23	3	9	48	90	32	6	5	.263	.332	.398	.730	.065	C	$1

Reportedly, some Mets veterans chastised Milledge in 2006 for slapping high fives with fans after hitting a home run. What the heck is wrong with a little baseball celebration? Isn't it time to let some enthusiasm into the game? Milledge is a five-tool talent, ready to prove himself at the major league level.

Wily Mo Pena (Left Field)

PA	R	H	2B	3B	HR	RBI	SO	BB	SB	CS	BA	OBP	SLG	OPS	3 Yr	Fld	F$
355	46	85	17	1	16	53	95	28	1	1	.267	.333	.477	.810	.030	F	$1

GM Jim Bowden finally scratched his itch. Pena displayed impressive power early, and the Nats believe he can improve his pitch recognition. There's some evidence that he was willing to cut down on his swing, going with pitches, especially when behind in the count, but a full season is going to show whether that was just a short-term lesson or a permanent change.

Dmitri Young (First Base)

PA	R	H	2B	3B	HR	RBI	SO	BB	SB	CS	BA	OBP	SLG	OPS	3 Yr	Fld	F$
440	53	109	24	1	12	55	73	39	0	1	.278	.346	.436	.782	-.046	D	$1

He sprayed line drives all over the field in the first half. After missing time with one of his many nagging leg and foot injuries, he hit a stunning .404/.434/.601 from May 18 to July 18. While his rebound was impressive, his lack of conditioning, nagging injuries and near-career-high stats make him a good candidate to take a step back this season. But even if he hits his projection, the Nats will be happy, given the influence they think he'll have on Lastings Milledge and Elijah Dukes.

Ryan Zimmerman (Third Base)

PA	R	H	2B	3B	HR	RBI	SO	BB	SB	CS	BA	OBP	SLG	OPS	3 Yr	Fld	F$
608	77	152	36	3	18	79	104	49	5	4	.277	.337	.452	.789	.064	A	$10

Even given a sophomore slump, his package of offense and defense pushed him into the second tier of third basemen. Zimmerman appeared to try to do too much at times last year, especially with some of the other bats struggling around him. He will have to be more selective at the plate—as he was in 2006—to improve. There is some concern that offseason surgery to remove a hamate bone will affect his power stroke, but the move out of RFK is likely to shade that.

Pitchers

Mike Bacsik (Starting Pitcher)

W	L	ERA	TBF	IP	Hit	HR	SO	BB	HBP	3 Yr	F$
6	9	5.06	592	136	156	21	68	39	7	0.34	$1

If Bacsik ever pitched to Rob Deer, the universe might explode. Bacsik took the pitch-to-contact strategy to its illogical extreme, walking nobody and striking out even fewer. With an array of mediocre pitches, he lobbed the ball in there and hoped the defense caught the liners. When it did, opposing batters gritted their teeth on the way back to the dugout. When they didn't get caught, it was ugly. He gave up an ungodly number of homers: His 26 homers in 118 innings were the eighth most of any pitcher with 120 or fewer innings, and among pitchers who started 20 or more games in a season, his two homers per nine innings was the 12th highest of all time. If he gets 20 starts again this season, the Nats are in big trouble.

Jason Bergmann (Starting Pitcher)

W	L	ERA	TBF	IP	Hit	HR	SO	BB	HBP	3 Yr	F$
7	8	4.59	599	140	133	19	110	54	6	0.13	$1

Always a hard thrower, his lack of command has held him back. After a six-walk first start, Bowden read him the riot act, and Randy St. Claire taught him a new grip for his slider. The combo worked. His high-riding, mid-90s fastball contrasted nicely with a crisp breaking slider that dived down and a slower curve, which zipped even further below. But his arm couldn't take the strain of the new breakers and he missed a long stretch of time with arm problems. He never was able to get the breaking pitches back, and he struggled to close the season, raising his ERA to 4.33 up from the 2.76 it was before the injuries started.

Matt Chico (Starting Pitcher)

W	L	ERA	TBF	IP	Hit	HR	SO	BB	HBP	3 Yr	F$
8	10	4.87	702	161	165	22	90	66	8	-0.43	$1

He battled. Fresh out of Double-A, he held his own, emerging as the "ace" of a mediocre staff—or at least its most consistent starter. None of Chico's pitches really jump out as being plus pitches and that led to too few strikeouts and *way* too many homers. When the ball stayed in the park, he was helped by being a flyballer in a huge park with a good defensive outfield, but those walls in the new park are going to seem miles closer for him this season.

Jesus Colome (Relief Pitcher)

W	L	ERA	TBF	IP	Hit	HR	SO	BB	HBP	3 Yr	F$
4	3	4.20	276	64	62	6	42	26	2	0.30	$1

When he was healthy, he was quite the mid-inning workhorse. But he missed a good chunk of time in the middle of the season with (no, I'm not making this up), a hole in his butt. Colome struggled at times with his control, which is nothing new for him.

Chad Cordero (Relief Pitcher)

W	L	ERA	TBF	IP	Hit	HR	SO	BB	HBP	3 Yr	F$
5	3	3.75	310	75	65	8	62	26	3	-0.08	$10

Some Nats fans are upset that he's not better than he is, since he blows the occasional save, but they don't realize that most closers blow the occasional save. He's not especially overpowering, and he has a tendency to get into jams, but overall, he's quite effective. Cordero gets away with a decent low-90s fastball that he pairs with a slider that's not all that much slower. When he's controlling both, he succeeds, but if he's slipping on one, he's getting hit hard, leaving that bad impression in Nats' fans minds.

Joel Hanrahan (Starting Pitcher)

W	L	ERA	TBF	IP	Hit	HR	SO	BB	HBP	3 Yr	F$
6	9	5.43	609	134	136	20	98	78	8	0.08	$1

The knock on the former top Dodgers pitching prospect has been his lack of control. And how! A hard thrower, he struck out a decent 6.8 batters per nine, but he also walked six. He seemingly has little idea where his big pitches are going to go, and when he takes something off to lay it in there, he gets hit hard (nine homers in 51 innings). There is talk of moving him to the pen, with hopes of that a more consistent delivery will ease some of those control problems.

Shawn Hill (Starting Pitcher)

W	L	ERA	TBF	IP	Hit	HR	SO	BB	HBP	3 Yr	F$
7	6	4.03	505	120	124	11	73	33	7	0.09	$1

The really poor man's Brandon Webb just couldn't stay healthy, with one of his big injuries coming to his non-throwing shoulder when he dived into a base wrong, jamming it. His big sinking fastball got a slew of grounders, but it's his change-up and breaking pitches that give him his success. Unfortunately, some of the elbow injuries he has had have tempered the effectiveness of those breaking pitches. If his elbow is sound and those pitches are moving, he's a legit No. 2 starter—which seems funny to say of someone with 143 career innings and a 4.53 career ERA.

John Lannan (Starting Pitcher)

W	L	ERA	TBF	IP	Hit	HR	SO	BB	HBP	3 Yr	F$
6	10	5.17	639	142	158	15	56	70	7	-0.63	$1

His debut game, in which he was ejected after hitting Chase Utley—breaking his hand—and Ryan Howard with pitches in back-to-back plate appearances, was certainly memorable. He blazed through the Nats' barren minor leagues last season, pitching effectively without being dominant at every level. He's succeeded by keeping the ball in the park and with pretty decent control, and he's a candidate for a call-up at midseason once one of the other starters breaks down.

John Patterson (Starting Pitcher)

W	L	ERA	TBF	IP	Hit	HR	SO	BB	HBP	3 Yr	F$
5	5	4.53	385	90	87	12	71	35	4	0.67	$1

In 2005, he showed what he's capable of if he can stay healthy. His fastball/curveball combo was dominant enough to make him one of the league's better starting pitchers. After a 2006 lost to nerve problems in his right elbow, there was a glimmer of hope in spring training. Unfortunately his velocity was down, and the curveball had lost some of its bite. After a few disastrous starts early in the season, Patterson shut it down, trying to find a cure for his barking elbow, which took him to Canada for some experimental treatment. The Nats haves brought him back for one more try to see if he'll be able to hold off the injuries and tap that potential.

Jon Rauch (Relief Pitcher)

W	L	ERA	TBF	IP	Hit	HR	SO	BB	HBP	3 Yr	F$
5	4	3.82	329	79	70	9	67	28	3	0.44	$2

The iron man of the Nats pen, he led the NL in games with 88 and locked down most eighth innings (and the occasional ninth when Cordero wasn't available). If the Nats ever do trade Cordero (which they've been tempted to do each of the last two seasons), he'd be the logical choice to step in. Like Cordero, he's not dominant, but he's successful, and like Cordero, his one weakness is the occasional gopher ball.

Tim Redding (Starting Pitcher)

W	L	ERA	TBF	IP	Hit	HR	SO	BB	HBP	3 Yr	F$
7	11	5.01	699	159	171	21	96	66	7	0.66	$1

He had a Fielding Independent Pitching mark nearly two runs higher than his actual ERA, and the projected 5.01 ERA here seems more in line with his career numbers. The Nats better hope that the further he gets from his surgeries, the stronger his arm gets. Otherwise, they might be in for a rude awakening if they are expecting another 3-something ERA.

Saul Rivera (Relief Pitcher)

W	L	ERA	TBF	IP	Hit	HR	SO	BB	HBP	3 Yr	F$
4	5	4.21	356	81	81	5	55	38	4	0.32	$1

By the end of the season, I was expecting his arm to fly off toward the plate with the ball. He finished second to Rauch in the NL in games pitched and second in all of MLB (by two outs) in relief innings pitched. Rivera succeeds because he keeps the ball in the park, which might be slightly harder in the new stadium.

Star Maps

by John Burnson

The following two pages offer graphical depictions of the values and contributions of the top fantasy hitters. Each graph is a field with three "poles:" HR (top), BA (bottom left), and SB (bottom right). Each pole attracts hitters who contribute to that category.

Players are represented as stars. The magnitude of a star indicates the player's overall worth. The location of the star shows his relative contributions to the three categories. The closer a player is to a pole, the greater is his relative personal contribution to that category. A player can be caught between two or three poles if he makes positive contributions to all the respective categories.

Stars that are situated in the middle of the graph contribute in some measure to all three categories. Stars situated between two poles, or at one pole, contribute disproportionately to those categories. (It is possible for a player to be situated beyond a pole or pair of poles; in

that case, the player contributes below replacement level to the opposing categories and is effectively "repulsed" by those distant poles.)

These graphs help you to find needed talent during the draft in a jiffy. If you're looking for a player who contributes to all three categories, check the middle of the graph for a star that suits your budget and positional needs. Later in the draft, if you care only about one or two of the categories, focus your attention on players near or between those poles. Remember, smaller stars are less pricey hitters.

For a wealth of other baseball-related graphs, including Star Maps for pitchers as well as graphical profiles of over 750 players, check out the 2008 Graphical Player, featuring the work of THT contributors Jeff Sackmann and Craig Brown. You can order the book at www.BaseballHQ.com/gp.shtml and view sample pages at www.HeaterMagazine.com/TheRundown.

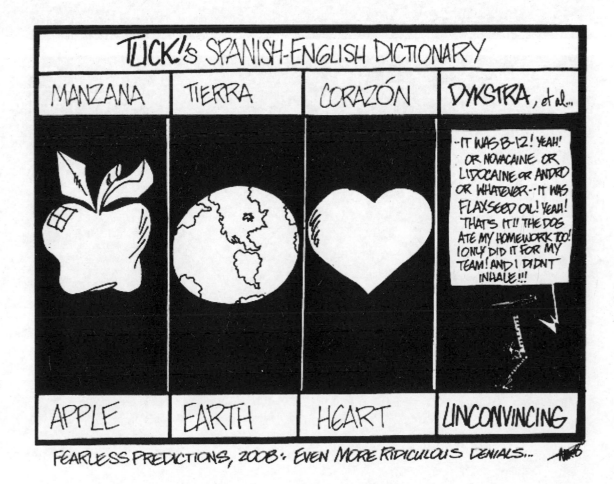

Star Maps

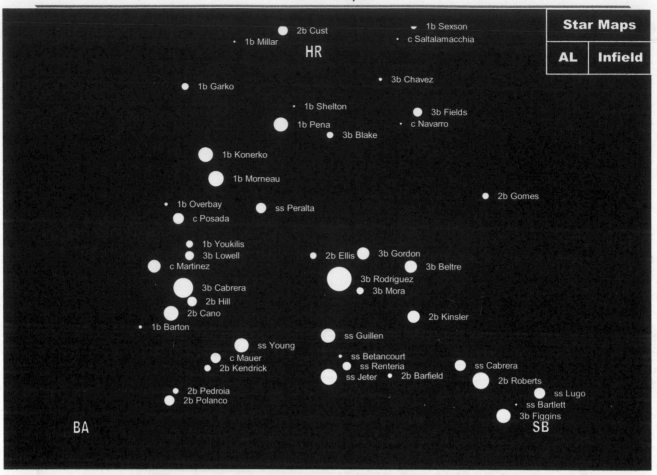

HR

• 2b Cust
• 1b Millar
• 1b Sexson
• c Saltalamacchia

• 3b Chavez
• 1b Garko
• 1b Shelton
• 3b Fields
• 1b Pena
• c Navarro
• 3b Blake

• 1b Konerko
• 1b Morneau

• 1b Overbay
• 2b Gomes
• c Posada
• ss Peralta

• 1b Youkilis
• 3b Lowell
• 2b Ellis
• 3b Gordon
• c Martinez
• 3b Beltre
• 3b Rodriguez
• 3b Cabrera
• 3b Mora
• 2b Hill
• 2b Cano
• 1b Barton
• 2b Kinsler

• ss Guillen
• ss Young
• ss Betancourt
• c Mauer
• ss Renteria
• ss Cabrera
• 2b Kendrick
• ss Jeter
• 2b Barfield
• 2b Roberts
• ss Lugo
• 2b Pedroia
• ss Bartlett
• 2b Polanco
• 3b Figgins

BA
SB

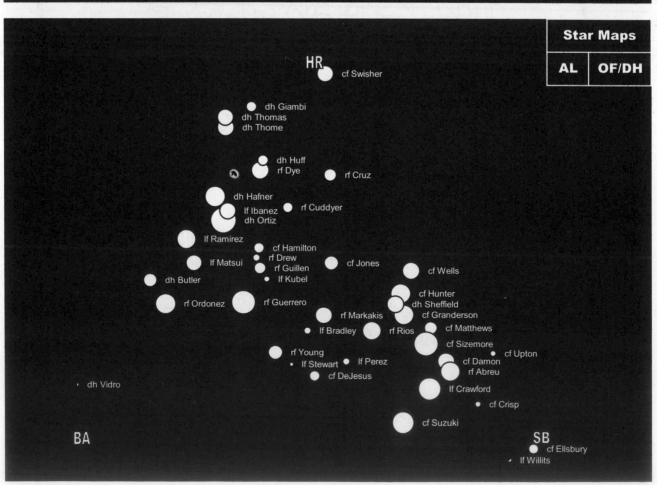

HR
• cf Swisher

• dh Giambi
• dh Thomas
• dh Thome

• dh Huff
• rf Dye
• rf Cruz

• dh Hafner
• lf Ibanez
• rf Cuddyer
• dh Ortiz
• lf Ramirez

• cf Hamilton
• rf Drew
• lf Matsui
• rf Guillen
• cf Jones
• lf Kubel
• cf Wells
• dh Butler
• cf Hunter
• rf Ordonez
• rf Guerrero
• dh Sheffield
• cf Granderson
• rf Markakis
• cf Matthews
• lf Bradley
• rf Rios
• cf Sizemore
• rf Young
• cf Upton
• lf Stewart
• lf Perez
• cf Damon
• rf Abreu
• dh Vidro
• cf DeJesus
• lf Crawford
• cf Crisp

• cf Suzuki

BA
SB
• cf Ellsbury
• lf Willits

The Hardball Times Season Preview 2008

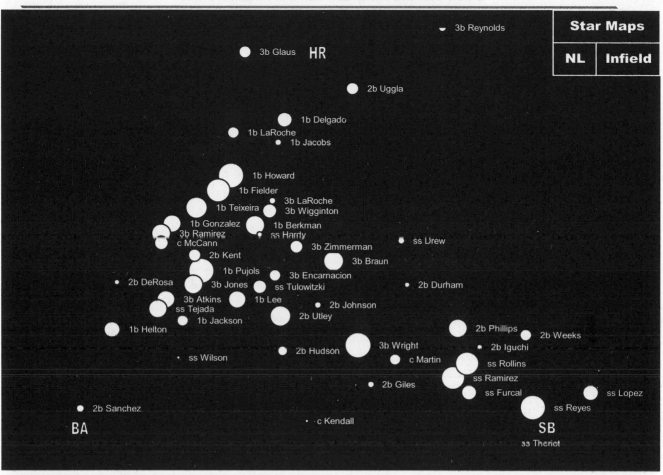

Star Maps

NL | **Infield**

HR

3b Reynolds

3b Glaus

2b Uggla

1b Delgado

1b LaRoche

1b Jacobs

1b Howard

1b Fielder

3b LaRoche

1b Teixeira

3b Wigginton

1b Gonzalez

1b Berkman

3b Ramirez

ss Hardy

c McCann

ss Drew

3b Zimmerman

2b Kent

3b Braun

1b Pujols

3b Encarnacion

2b DeRosa

3b Jones

ss Tulowitzki

2b Durham

3b Atkins

1b Lee

2b Johnson

ss Tejada

1b Jackson

2b Utley

1b Helton

2b Phillips

2b Weeks

2b Hudson

3b Wright

2b Iguchi

ss Wilson

c Martin

ss Rollins

ss Ramirez

2b Giles

ss Furcal

ss Lopez

ss Reyes

2b Sanchez

BA

c Kendall

SB

ss Theriot

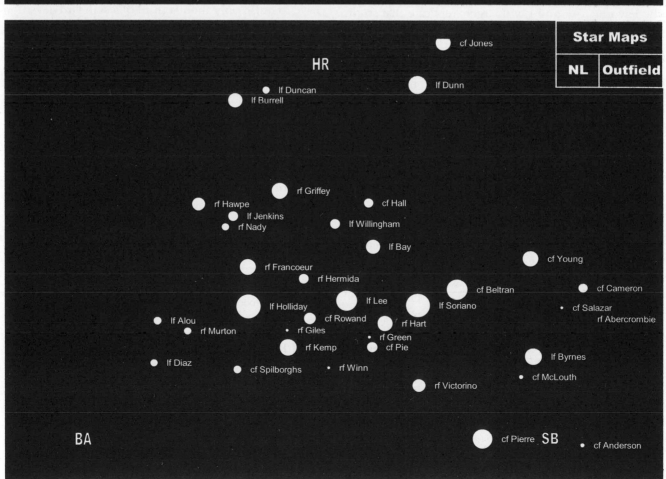

Star Maps

NL | **Outfield**

cf Jones

HR

lf Duncan

lf Dunn

lf Burrell

rf Griffey

cf Hall

rf Hawpe

lf Jenkins

lf Willingham

rf Nady

lf Bay

cf Young

rf Francoeur

rf Hermida

cf Beltran

cf Cameron

lf Lee

cf Salazar

lf Holliday

lf Soriano

rf Abercrombie

lf Alou

cf Rowand

rf Hart

rf Murton

rf Giles

rf Green

lf Kemp

cf Pie

lf Byrnes

lf Diaz

cf Spilborghs

rf Winn

cf McLouth

rf Victorino

BA

cf Pierre

SB

cf Anderson

Projecting Career Statistics

by David Gassko

On August 4, 2007, Alex Rodriguez became the youngest player ever to reach the 500 home run milestone, almost a full year younger than previous record holder Jimmie Foxx. He tacked on 18 more home runs before the year's end, and he starts 2008 more than two-thirds of the way to setting a new record, all at only 32 years old. Obviously, that is a potent combination, but just how potent is it? What are Rodriguez's odds of breaking Barry Bonds' mark? How many home runs should we expect him to hit when all is said and done? Those are good questions; let's try to answer them.

Of course, as with most questions about baseball statistics, the idea of projecting career numbers was first thought of by Bill James, who devised his own system, "The Favorite Toy," to project how a player would fare before retiring. But the Favorite Toy, while elegant in its logic and simplicity, is also flawed, making projections that are generally very optimistic (see *Beyond the Favorite Toy* at Baseball Think Factory online). As far as I am aware, there has been only one attempt to improve the Favorite Toy, and I will largely replicate that study. In that study, Jesse Frey, now a professor at Villanova, used a statistical technique known as regression analysis to predict how many home runs a player would hit over the rest of his career given his age and home run totals in the previous three years. I'm going to extend that technique to hits as well as wins for pitchers. In one paragraph, here is my method.

First, I put together a database of all major league players who debuted after World War II and retired by 2006. I then found every string of three consecutive seasons for every hitter in my database and every string of two consecutive seasons for every pitcher (as a third season proved to be unnecessary). I grouped the players by age and found how many home runs, hits, or wins they had remaining in their career at a given age. Then I ran a regression trying to predict that number based on the number of hits, home runs, or wins they had in the previous few seasons. For very young or old players, only more recent seasons proved to be significant, so that's all I used. Players younger than 20 or older than 40 in their most recent season were excluded because of the miniscule sample sizes.

Here's an example of how the system works. A 28-year-old player's remaining home runs can be projected by multiplying his home runs in the most recent season by 3.475; the year before that by 1.239; and the year before that by 0.939. So Adam Dunn, who will have a seasonal age of 28 in 2008 and has hit 40 home runs each of the past three seasons, is projected to hit $3.475*40 + 1.239*40 + 0.939*40 = 226$ home runs in the rest of his career. With 238 career home runs already to his credit, the system projects that he will hit 464 career home runs. The Favorite Toy, meanwhile, predicts 526 home runs, while Frey's system projects 437.

But just projecting career home run totals is kind of boring. If Dunn ends up with 400 some-odd home runs, he will go down as a very good home run hitter, but nothing more—Dave Kingman with more walks. What we really want to know are Dunn's chances of hitting some historic number, say 500 home runs or even 763. Luckily, statistics provide us with a simple way of estimating that: the standard error, which is what news organizations use to give you the margin of error associated with their polls. In Dunn's case, the standard error is around 111 home runs, meaning that he would have to finish only about a third of a standard deviation away from his projection to hit 500 career home runs, but 2.7 standard deviations away to hit 763. In plain English, that translates to a 38 percent chance of hitting 500 home runs, but less than a 4% chance of breaking Barry Bonds' all-time record.

How does this all impact Rodriguez? Well, we project that he will finish his career with 685 home runs, but that there is about a one-in-four chance that he hits 763. Does that seem low? Perhaps, but don't forget that a lot of things can change suddenly as a hitter ages. Here, for example, are all the players who hit at least 400 home runs by the seasonal age of 31 and how their careers ended:

Player	HR at 31	Career HR
Alex Rodriguez	518	?
Jimmie Foxx	464	534
Ken Griffey Jr.	460	593
Eddie Mathews	422	512
Mickey Mantle	419	536
Frank Robinson	403	586

Obviously, Jr. is still playing; we project he will finish his career with 639 home runs.

On average, these guys, Griffey excluded, padded their career totals by 27 percent before retiring, which would give A-Rod 658 home runs. Astute readers might notice that if I expanded this list by one spot, it would include Hank Aaron, who had 398 home runs at age 31 and of course ended his career with 755, but then I could just as easily lower the threshold by just one more homer and put Juan Gonzalez, who finished his career with 434 home runs, on the list as well. With those two added, we would project 695 home runs for Rodriguez, not much different from what our system says.

The funny thing is that A-Rod is *not* the hitter most likely to break Bonds' record, according to the system. That honor goes to Prince Fielder, who we project to finish with 530 career home runs and with an astounding 37 percent chance at hitting 763. How does that happen? Well, first of all, Fielder accomplished something this year that no one has ever done, becoming the youngest player to 50 home runs in a season. Young players' accomplishments are multiplied out many, many times and so we end up predicting that Fielder will knock out 450 more bombs in his career. Moreover, since the error bars rise with our predictions, the system sees a lot of different but fairly likely outcomes to Fielder's career—one of them involving him setting the all-time record. It works both ways: Manny Ramirez is projected to finish with a similar career total to Fielder (537 home runs), but his chances of hitting 500 are about three-in-four, whereas Fielder's are barely over 50 percent since Manny needs to hit 410 fewer home runs than Fielder to get there.

Only Fielder and Rodriguez register better than a five percent chance at besting Bonds' career mark, but just out of interest, here's the whole top 10:

Name	763 Chance
Prince Fielder	37.0%
Alex Rodriguez	23.3%
Miguel Cabrera	4.9%
Ken Griffey	4.6%
Albert Pujols	4.1%
Adam Dunn	3.7%
Ryan Howard	3.1%
Jim Thome	3.1%
Andruw Jones	3.0%
David Wright	2.5%

Overall, our system tells us that the probability of Bonds' current record being broken are better than 80 percent, a number that should satisfy those who feel that mark has been tainted by steroid suspicions.

Let's move away from home runs and look at hits. Now that Craig Biggio has retired and Barry Bonds' career seems to have ended, it may be a while before we see a player get his 3,000th hit. Here are the players with the best chances of doing that (remember that players younger than 20 or older than 40 in 2007 are excluded from this analysis):

Name	3000 Chance
Derek Jeter	42.1%
Alex Rodriguez	36.1%
Delmon Young	32.4%
Miguel Cabrera	30.1%
Ryan Zimmerman	27.4%
Ivan Rodriguez	27.4%
Jose Reyes	26.2%
Ken Griffey	23.5%
David Wright	23.3%
Hanley Ramirez	21.3%

A-Rod again shows up second, but he is bested by The Captain himself, Derek Jeter. I'll admit that the odds for some of the younger players, Young and Zimmerman in particular, look really high. Young has one full major league season under his belt, Zimmerman has two. Neither has even broken the 190-hit mark yet. So how come our system says that the probability of one of the two gathering 3,000 hits are better than the probability that neither does? Once more, it all comes down to two effects: the high multipliers for extremely young players and the high error bars associated with those kinds of projections. Young was just 21 years old in 2007; Zimmerman was 22. We end up projecting that both will end up with around 2300 hits and the huge standard errors mean that their chances of ending up at 3000 are pretty good.

The Favorite Toy sees things very differently. It tells us that Zimmerman has around an 11 percent chance at 3,000 hits and places Young's chances at zero. On the other hand, it gives Jeter an 86 percent chance at hitting 3,000 and Rodriguez a 79 percent shot. Overall, both systems see about 10 active players who were between the ages of 20 and 40 in '07 ending up with 3,000 hits, an encouraging sign since research has shown that the

Favorite Toy does a pretty good job at projecting how many players will end up with 3,000 hits (though I will admit that number sounds high to me).

Care to switch gears from hitters to pitchers? Let's do it. A lot was written after Tom Glavine won his 300th game this season that he would be the last 300-game winner. Reminds me of the US patent office chief who said at the turn of the 20th century that the office could be closed down because everything had already been invented. Our numbers tell us that about five active players will eventually win 300 games (the odds that none of them do? About 1 in 220.), though in defense of the writers, only Mike Mussina is particularly close. Here are the 10 guys with the best shot at reaching 300:

Name	300 Chance
Mike Mussina	28.9%
Andy Pettitte	12.1%
Felix Hernandez	9.7%
C.C. Sabathia	9.3%
Carlos Zambrano	8.0%
John Smoltz	8.0%
Josh Beckett	7.4%
Justin Verlander	6.9%
Jake Peavy	6.8%
Johan Santana	5.9%

The list is dominated by younger pitchers, indicating that the real story here is not how few players are close to winning 300 games, but how many great young hurlers may get there eventually. At the seasonal age of 26, Sabathia has 100 wins, 21 more than Glavine had at the same age. Beckett's postseason record rivals Sandy Koufax's. And Felix Hernandez established himself as one of the best pitchers in the major leagues before he could even legally drink. They're far off from winning 300 games, but that just makes the journey all the more exciting. And the numbers tell us that one pitcher from the above list will probably join that exclusive club.

For more information about the accuracy of the Favorite Toy, read "Toying with 'The Favorite' Toy" by Shane Holmes (http://www.philbirnbaum.com/btn2003-05.pdf) and "Beyond the Favorite Toy" by Jesse Frey (http://www.baseballthinkfactory.org/files/primate_studies/discussion/jfrey_2003-09-18_0/).

For those who care about the statistical details: I could not use a general standard error because the estimates exhibited heteroskedasticity, which is an increase in error bars as the predictions get bigger. I tried a few well-known statistical methods for dealing with the issue, but it persisted, so I settled on a kind of ad-hoc solution, using regression analysis to project the standard errors at various prediction levels. So as the total number of home runs, hits, or wins remaining goes up, so do the error bars.

Batter Career Probabilities

Here is a table of projected career hits and home runs for all major league batters projected to have at least 1,500 hits or 150 home runs. We've also included each batter's probability of reaching 3,000 hits, 500 home runs and 763 home runs. You can download a spreadsheet that contains all major league players from the URL mentioned in the book's introduction.

Name	Hits	HR	3000 %	500 %	763 %
Bobby Abreu	2,209	262	6%	1%	0%
Moises Alou	2,229	343	1%	0%	0%
Garret Anderson	2,477	290	7%	1%	0%
Garrett Atkins	1,537	203	4%	2%	0%
Rich Aurilia	1,621	189	0%	0%	0%
Brad Ausmus	1,613	79	0%	0%	0%
Tony Batista	1,207	227	0%	0%	0%
Jason Bay	1,336	249	2%	3%	0%
Ron Belliard	1,626	125	2%	0%	0%
Carlos Beltran	1,987	350	4%	9%	1%
Adrian Beltre	2,215	340	10%	8%	1%
Lance Berkman	1,789	378	3%	12%	1%
Casey Blake	1,102	155	1%	0%	0%
Hank Blalock	1,302	202	1%	1%	0%
Russell Branyan	535	160	0%	0%	0%
Ryan Braun	1,057	299	2%	12%	2%
John Buck	817	155	1%	1%	0%
Pat Burrell	1,490	335	1%	7%	1%
Eric Byrnes	1,268	165	1%	1%	0%
Melky Cabrera	1,838	116	13%	1%	0%
Miguel Cabrera	2,485	413	30%	30%	5%
Orlando Cabrera	2,022	120	5%	0%	0%
Mike Cameron	1,702	266	1%	1%	0%
Robinson Cano	2,052	206	16%	3%	0%
Sean Casey	1,861	144	2%	0%	0%
Luis Castillo	2,148	28	6%	0%	0%
Eric Chavez	1,659	313	2%	4%	0%
Jeff Cirillo	1,669	114	0%	0%	0%
Tony Clark	1,235	275	0%	0%	0%
Royce Clayton	1,975	111	0%	0%	0%
Carl Crawford	2,322	170	20%	1%	0%
Joe Crede	948	181	0%	1%	0%
Jose Cruz	1,295	218	0%	0%	0%
Michael Cuddyer	1,259	157	2%	1%	0%
Johnny Damon	2,499	207	12%	0%	0%
Carlos Delgado	2,144	486	3%	41%	1%
J.D. Drew	1,436	217	1%	1%	0%
Chris Duncan	707	168	1%	2%	0%
Adam Dunn	1,561	464	3%	38%	4%
Ray Durham	2,173	213	2%	0%	0%
Jermaine Dye	1,851	351	2%	7%	1%

Name	Hits	HR	3000 %	500 %	763 %
Damion Easley	1,382	172	0%	0%	0%
Jim Edmonds	1,947	382	1%	1%	0%
Edwin Encarnacion	1,354	183	3%	2%	0%
Juan Encarnacion	1,591	195	1%	0%	0%
Morgan Ensberg	801	165	0%	1%	0%
Darin Erstad	1,721	124	0%	0%	0%
Pedro Feliz	1,138	168	1%	1%	0%
Prince Fielder	1,732	530	9%	52%	37%
Josh Fields	643	153	1%	1%	0%
Cliff Floyd	1,595	243	0%	0%	0%
Jeff Francoeur	2,090	279	19%	7%	1%
Rafael Furcal	1,987	122	6%	0%	0%
Nomar Garciaparra	1,991	246	2%	0%	0%
Jason Giambi	1,824	395	0%	3%	0%
Jay Gibbons	999	167	0%	0%	0%
Brian Giles	1,948	296	1%	0%	0%
Troy Glaus	1,530	381	1%	12%	1%
Jonny Gomes	792	178	1%	2%	0%
Adrian Gonzalez	1,572	258	5%	5%	1%
Alex Gonzalez	1,378	151	1%	0%	0%
Luis Gonzalez	2,661	363	9%	0%	0%
Curtis Granderson	1,430	183	4%	2%	0%
Shawn Green	2,321	353	5%	1%	0%
Khalil Greene	1,247	200	2%	2%	0%
Ken Griffey	2,797	639	24%	100%	5%
Mark Grudzielanek	2,134	96	2%	0%	0%
Vladimir Guerrero	2,588	462	21%	33%	2%
Carlos Guillen	1,590	157	2%	1%	0%
Jose Guillen	1,682	233	2%	1%	0%
Travis Hafner	1,201	253	1%	3%	0%
Bill Hall	1,212	189	1%	2%	0%
J.J. Hardy	1,451	199	4%	2%	0%
Corey Hart	1,065	171	2%	2%	0%
Brad Hawpe	1,047	183	1%	2%	0%
Todd Helton	2,337	346	8%	2%	0%
Jeremy Hermida	1,203	182	2%	2%	0%
Ramon Hernandez	1,261	163	1%	0%	0%
Aaron Hill	1,618	124	6%	1%	0%
Matt Holliday	1,782	288	7%	6%	1%
Ryan Howard	1,212	385	2%	22%	3%
Aubrey Huff	1,622	223	2%	1%	0%

Name	Hits	HR	3000 %	500 %	763 %
Torii Hunter	1,748	283	3%	3%	0%
Raul Ibanez	1,549	207	1%	1%	0%
Mike Jacobs	932	160	1%	1%	0%
Geoff Jenkins	1,539	272	1%	2%	0%
Derek Jeter	2,911	228	42%	0%	0%
Andruw Jones	2,174	502	6%	51%	3%
Chipper Jones	2,476	446	10%	22%	1%
Jacque Jones	1,642	196	1%	0%	0%
Austin Kearns	1,421	197	2%	2%	0%
Jason Kendall	2,181	76	4%	0%	0%
Jeff Kent	2,523	388	5%	1%	0%
Ian Kinsler	1,047	156	1%	1%	0%
Ryan Klesko	1,708	286	0%	0%	0%
Paul Konerko	1,927	387	3%	13%	1%
Mark Kotsay	1,645	114	1%	0%	0%
Adam LaRoche	1,285	217	2%	2%	0%
Carlos Lee	2,112	364	7%	10%	1%
Derrek Lee	1,835	310	3%	3%	0%
Mike Lieberthal	1,189	152	0%	0%	0%
Kenny Lofton	2,573	136	5%	0%	0%
Felipe Lopez	1,537	132	3%	1%	0%
Jose Lopez	1,674	141	7%	1%	0%
Mark Loretta	1,896	80	2%	0%	0%
Mike Lowell	1,805	239	3%	1%	0%
Julio Lugo	1,503	104	1%	0%	0%
Nick Markakis	1,837	257	12%	5%	1%
Russell Martin	1,313	169	3%	2%	0%
Victor Martinez	1,544	197	3%	2%	0%
Hideki Matsui	1,070	156	0%	0%	0%
Joe Mauer	1,611	124	5%	1%	0%
Brian McCann	1,587	245	6%	4%	1%
Kevin Millar	1,357	177	0%	0%	0%
Bengie Molina	1,343	157	1%	0%	0%
Craig Monroe	1,007	166	0%	1%	0%
Melvin Mora	1,408	162	1%	0%	0%
Justin Morneau	1,573	312	4%	8%	1%
Xavier Nady	1,001	152	1%	1%	0%
Magglio Ordonez	2,194	318	7%	4%	0%
David Ortiz	1,794	402	3%	18%	1%
Corey Patterson	1,453	154	2%	1%	0%
Carlos Pena	908	237	0%	2%	0%
Wily Mo Pena	907	186	1%	2%	0%
Jhonny Peralta	1,606	222	5%	3%	1%
Brandon Phillips	1,441	206	4%	2%	0%
Mike Piazza	2,255	445	1%	5%	0%
Juan Pierre	2,258	16	12%	0%	0%

Name	Hits	HR	3000 %	500 %	763 %
Placido Polanco	1,910	97	4%	0%	0%
Jorge Posada	1,687	261	1%	1%	0%
Albert Pujols	2,339	492	16%	47%	4%
Aramis Ramirez	1,902	359	5%	11%	1%
Hanley Ramirez	2,121	312	21%	13%	2%
Manny Ramirez	2,514	537	10%	74%	1%
Edgar Renteria	2,479	156	14%	0%	0%
Jose Reyes	2,360	181	26%	2%	0%
Mark Reynolds	748	153	1%	1%	0%
Alexis Rios	1,662	188	5%	2%	0%
Brian Roberts	1,640	105	3%	0%	0%
Alex Rodriguez	2,835	685	36%	100%	23%
Ivan Rodriguez	2,804	311	27%	0%	0%
Scott Rolen	1,872	291	2%	0%	0%
Jimmy Rollins	2,299	243	15%	3%	0%
Aaron Rowand	1,430	174	2%	1%	0%
Reggie Sanders	1,688	307	0%	0%	0%
Richie Sexson	1,494	368	1%	8%	1%
Gary Sheffield	2,723	507	15%	58%	0%
Grady Sizemore	2,117	309	18%	10%	1%
Alfonso Soriano	1,833	363	3%	10%	1%
Sammy Sosa	2,566	629	5%	100%	1%
Matt Stairs	1,353	265	0%	0%	0%
Shannon Stewart	1,948	137	2%	0%	0%
Ichiro Suzuki	2,217	84	9%	0%	0%
Mike Sweeney	1,553	215	0%	0%	0%
Nick Swisher	1,261	245	2%	4%	1%
Mark Teixeira	1,682	356	4%	12%	1%
Miguel Tejada	2,293	325	9%	4%	0%
Frank Thomas	2,591	542	7%	100%	0%
Jim Thome	2,162	573	2%	100%	3%
Troy Tulowitzki	1,645	201	8%	3%	0%
Dan Uggla	1,098	199	1%	2%	0%
B.J. Upton	1,477	205	5%	3%	1%
Juan Uribe	1,415	215	2%	2%	0%
Chase Utley	1,501	224	3%	3%	0%
Jose Valentin	1,405	257	0%	0%	0%
Jason Varitek	1,286	181	0%	0%	0%
Jose Vidro	1,963	138	4%	0%	0%
Omar Vizquel	2,724	80	10%	0%	0%
Rickie Weeks	1,106	155	2%	1%	0%
Vernon Wells	1,829	266	5%	3%	0%
Rondell White	1,564	206	0%	0%	0%
Ty Wigginton	1,130	172	1%	1%	0%
Brad Wilkerson	1,036	182	0%	1%	0%
Jack Wilson	1,602	96	2%	0%	0%

Name	Hits	HR	3000 %	500 %	763 %
Preston Wilson	1,100	207	0%	0%	0%
Randy Winn	1,831	128	2%	0%	0%
David Wright	2,266	351	23%	17%	2%
Chris Young	1,035	288	2%	10%	2%

Name	Hits	HR	3000 %	500 %	763 %
Delmon Young	2,306	187	32%	2%	0%
Dmitri Young	1,639	196	1%	0%	0%
Michael Young	2,074	155	8%	0%	0%
Ryan Zimmerman	2,250	305	27%	12%	2%

Pitcher Career Probabilities

Following is a table of projected career wins for all major league pitchers projected to win at least 50 games in their career. We've also included each pitcher's probability of reaching 300 wins.

Name	Wins	300 %
Tony Armas	72	1%
Bronson Arroyo	91	1%
Homer Bailey	58	2%
Scott Baker	63	1%
Brian Bannister	58	1%
Miguel Batista	121	2%
Josh Beckett	162	7%
Erik Bedard	97	2%
Chad Billingsley	111	5%
Joe Blanton	114	4%
Jeremy Bonderman	129	4%
Boof Bonser	59	1%
Doug Brocail	54	0%
Mark Buehrle	152	3%
A.J. Burnett	106	2%
David Bush	87	2%
Paul Byrd	131	2%
Daniel Cabrera	84	2%
Matt Cain	93	3%
Matt Capps	57	1%
Chris Capuano	72	1%
Fausto Carmona	118	6%
Chris Carpenter	107	0%
Shawn Chacon	64	1%
Bartolo Colon	154	1%
Jose Contreras	83	1%
Aaron Cook	71	1%
Rheal Cormier	71	0%
John Danks	56	1%
Kyle Davies	65	2%
Doug Davis	116	2%
Ryan Dempster	66	0%
Elmer Dessens	50	0%
Zach Duke	59	1%
Adam Eaton	99	1%

Name	Wins	300 %
Scott Elarton	65	0%
Kelvim Escobar	151	4%
Josh Fogg	97	1%
Casey Fossum	57	1%
Jeff Francis	125	5%
Ryan Franklin	54	0%
Yovani Gallardo	83	3%
Freddy Garcia	127	1%
Jon Garland	145	4%
Chad Gaudin	74	2%
Edgar Gonzalez	56	1%
Tom Gordon	136	0%
Tom Gorzelanny	78	2%
Zack Greinke	67	1%
Roy Halladay	169	5%
Cole Hamels	115	5%
Aaron Harang	124	3%
Danny Haren	121	4%
LaTroy Hawkins	58	0%
Mark Hendrickson	53	0%
Felix Hernandez	152	10%
Livan Hernandez	167	3%
Rich Hill	60	1%
Trevor Hoffman	59	0%
Tim Hudson	184	6%
Philip Hughes	63	2%
Jason Isringhausen	51	0%
Chuck James	81	2%
Jason Jennings	79	1%
Todd Jones	54	0%
Jair Jurrjens	53	1%
Scott Kazmir	119	5%
Kyle Kendrick	83	3%
Joe Kennedy	60	0%
Byung-Hyun Kim	93	1%

Name	Wins	300 %
John Lackey	149	5%
Brian Lawrence	52	0%
Cliff Lee	89	1%
Jon Lester	52	1%
Jon Lieber	137	1%
Ted Lilly	124	3%
Tim Lincecum	51	1%
Jesse Litsch	63	2%
Esteban Loaiza	128	0%
Kameron Loe	51	1%
Kyle Lohse	94	1%
Braden Looper	80	1%
Rodrigo Lopez	87	1%
Derek Lowe	145	2%
Noah Lowry	98	3%
Ryan Madson	52	1%
Paul Maholm	74	2%
John Maine	83	2%
Shaun Marcum	72	2%
Mike Maroth	69	1%
Jason Marquis	121	3%
Sean Marshall	58	1%
Pedro Martinez	215	2%
Daisuke Matsuzaka	66	2%
Brandon McCarthy	53	1%
Dustin McGowan	70	2%
Gil Meche	105	2%
Wade Miller	62	0%
Kevin Millwood	165	3%
Eric Milton	98	0%
Brian Moehler	64	0%
Franklin Morales	53	1%
Matt Morris	150	2%
Mark Mulder	109	0%
Mike Mussina	280	29%

Name	Wins	300 %
Brett Myers	94	1%
Joe Nathan	56	0%
Eric O'Flaherty	63	2%
Tomokazu Ohka	59	0%
Darren Oliver	98	0%
Scott Olsen	97	3%
Ramon Ortiz	100	1%
Russ Ortiz	112	0%
Roy Oswalt	166	5%
Vicente Padilla	104	1%
Chan Ho Park	115	0%
Carl Pavano	64	0%
Jake Peavy	157	7%
Brad Penny	149	4%
Odalis Perez	94	1%
Oliver Perez	115	4%
Andy Pettitte	240	12%
Joel Pineiro	96	1%
Sidney Ponson	90	0%
Horacio Ramirez	70	1%
Mark Redman	75	0%
Mariano Rivera	67	0%
Nate Robertson	80	1%
Wandy Rodriguez	65	1%
C.C. Sabathia	183	9%

Name	Wins	300 %
Ervin Santana	98	3%
Johan Santana	162	6%
Joe Saunders	53	1%
Curt Schilling	234	6%
Jason Schmidt	136	1%
Aaron Sele	155	1%
Ben Sheets	114	2%
James Shields	77	2%
Scot Shields	56	0%
Carlos Silva	106	2%
John Smoltz	234	8%
Ian Snell	77	2%
Jorge Sosa	66	1%
Mike Stanton	70	0%
Huston Street	55	1%
Jeff Suppan	153	3%
Julian Tavarez	98	1%
Brad Thompson	52	1%
John Thomson	64	0%
Brett Tomko	104	1%
Josh Towers	62	0%
Steve Trachsel	161	2%
Claudio Vargas	86	2%
Javier Vazquez	168	5%
Justin Verlander	137	7%

Name	Wins	300 %
Carlos Villanueva	61	2%
Ron Villone	55	0%
Luis Vizcaino	55	1%
Adam Wainwright	81	2%
Tim Wakefield	201	5%
Chien-Ming Wang	131	5%
Jarrod Washburn	121	1%
Dave Weathers	67	0%
Jeff Weaver	119	1%
Jered Weaver	98	3%
Brandon Webb	137	5%
Kip Wells	87	1%
Jake Westbrook	94	1%
Bob Wickman	65	0%
Woody Williams	148	1%
Dontrelle Willis	124	3%
Randy Wolf	108	1%
Kerry Wood	76	0%
Jamey Wright	84	0%
Jaret Wright	83	1%
Chris Young	76	1%
Carlos Zambrano	168	8%
Barry Zito	160	4%

Rookies to Watch in 2008

by Chris Constancio

Welcome to our annual top rookies list. Whether you are a fantasy baseball player looking to draft an undervalued rookie or a fan of major league baseball who wants to know more about the new names you will be hearing in 2008, this list is for you. The following players have an opportunity to make an impact on the 2008 season. Last year's rookie preview highlighted eventual Rookie of the Year award winners Ryan Braun and Dustin Pedroia, and this year's list is not short on potential stars.

This is not a list of baseball's top prospects. There are plenty of great young players, such as the Dodgers' Clayton Kershaw and the Rays' Reid Brignac, who were excluded from this list simply because I don't think they will play at least half a season in the major leagues this year. There is a lot of uncertainty in projecting roles for these young players. It is difficult to assess players' value before they have established roles on their 2008 clubs, so I won't even rank the rookies. Instead, think of this list as a collection of names you should definitely know heading into the 2008 season.

I will identify strengths and weaknesses for each player in my comments, but you can also find projections and comments for most of the players in the team sections that follow.

Matt Antonelli

2B | San Diego Padres | 23

The 17th overall pick from the 2006 draft experienced a breakout season in the California League and Texas League last year. Like most Padres prospects, Antonelli has plenty of patience at the plate and should post a good on-base percentage even if he is aggressively promoted to the big leagues this year. He has speed and power potential and is projected to hit 15 home runs while playing half his games at pitcher-friendly Petco Park in 2008.

Homer Bailey

RHP | Cincinnati Reds | 22

If you picked up last year's preview, you knew one of the most heralded young pitchers of 2007 was at risk of disappointing due to control issues. A nagging groin injury certainly had something to do with his lackluster debut with Cincinnati, but he also wasn't finding the strike zone regularly enough when he was healthy. His stuff is so good that he will get big-league batters to swing and miss often enough to ensure average results even if his control doesn't improve much this year.

Wladimir Balentien

OF | Seattle Mariners | 23

Balentien has always demonstrated excellent raw power and is clearly capable of hitting 30 home runs in a major league season. Over the past two years, he improved his contact rate and walk rate to the point where he is now much more than a one-dimensional hitter. There is no obvious job opening for Balentien in Seattle, so he may need to wait for a trade before getting the chance to face major league pitchers on a regular basis.

Nick Blackburn

RHP | Minnesota Twins | 26

One of the lesser-known prospects on this list, Blackburn has struggled to stay healthy and put together any eye-catching performances at a young age. He can throw hard, but he tends to pitch to contact and won't collect many strikeouts over the course of a season. Blackburn's exceptional command and ability to induce weak contact could lead to the kind of results the Twins got from Carlos Silva over the past three seasons.

Daric Barton

1B | Oakland Athletics | 22

Barton never produced the kind of power typically expected from first basemen and designated hitters during his minor league career, but he did launch four home runs for Oakland in September. Even if he only matches our projection of nine home runs in 2008, he will still collect plenty of base hits and doubles this year. His superb on-base skills warrant a starting role in Oakland.

Lance Broadway

RHP | Chicago White Sox | 24

A first-round pick from the 2005 draft, Broadway has made steady progress in the White Sox system and will compete for a job in the starting rotation this spring. Broadway has a strong set of secondary pitches, but he doesn't throw very hard and he allows a lot of batted balls in play. His control was terrible at times during the 2007 season, and he won't last long in the Chicago rotation if he doesn't show improvement in that this year.

Jay Bruce

OF | Cincinnati Reds | 21

Bruce is probably the best prospect in all of baseball right now. The first-round pick from the 2005 draft is athletic enough to handle center field and has hit at every stop of his minor league career. Bruce hits the ball hard; 22 percent of his batted balls were line drives at Triple-A Sarasota. But he also strikes out often enough to prevent a high batting average this year. His outstanding power potential in Cincinnati's hitter-friendly context makes him an early favorite for the National League Rookie of the Year Award.

Clay Buchholz

RHP | Boston Red Sox | 23

Buchholz struck out over one-third of opposing batters at each minor league level last year. Then he pitched a no-hitter for Boston. Buchholz has a deep repertoire of above-average pitches and could easily outpace his projected 4.71 ERA under the guidance of Jason Varitek. He is among the early favorites for the American League Rookie of the Year award in 2008.

Joba Chamberlain

RHP | New York Yankees | 22

Another Rookie of the Year contender, Chamberlain will get a chance to show off more than his fastball as a starting pitcher for the Yankees. His projected 4.19 ERA may sound underwhelming after he posted a 0.38 ERA over 24 innings pitched last year, but keep in mind a 4.19 ERA is above-average among starting pitchers in the American League and would probably be enough to earn 15 or more wins if he stays healthy all season long.

Jeff Clement

C | Seattle Mariners | 24

Clement showed off his complete skill set during his 2007 season with Triple-A Tacoma. He hit 20 home runs while demonstrating above-average on-base skills, but he isn't more than an average receiver behind the plate. We project a .331 OBP and 13 home runs from Clement while he shares catching duties with Kenji Johjima this year.

Johnny Cueto

RHP | Cincinnati Reds | 22

He doesn't get the attention that Homer Bailey does, but Cueto might outperform Bailey in the near future as he is a power pitcher with exceptional control that should lead to a smooth transition to the major leagues. Cueto relies on a mid-90s four-seam fastball, so my only major concern with him is his tendency to allow fly balls. Among pitchers with at least 60 innings pitched in the Southern League, Cueto had the second-highest proportion of batted balls hit in the air. That could lead to home run troubles in the context of Great American Ballpark in Cincinnati.

Eulogio de la Cruz

RHP | Florida Marlins | 24

A usable curveball and a fastball that has touched 100 mph in the past should be enough to bring de la Cruz into the Marlins bullpen in 2008. Although his fastball has lacked the movement needed to strike out a lot of batters during his minor league career, the humid air of southern Florida should help add some life to his pitches.

Jacoby Ellsbury

OF | Boston Red Sox | 24

The speedy Ellsbury is unlikely to repeat the .353 batting average and .394 OBP he compiled during his stint with the Red Sox in 2007. In fact, he is projected to be a below-average major league hitter in 2008 as he doesn't hit for any power, isn't particularly patient at the plate, and hits most of his batted balls on the ground. That said, he is an exciting player to watch and could certainly add a lot of value on the bases and in the field.

Kosuke Fukudome

OF | Chicago Cubs | 30

Fukudome doesn't project to hit for much power relative to other corner outfielders in the U.S. He has posted an OBP over .400 in four of his last five seasons in Japan's Central League, and he has a chance to score over 100 runs if the Cubs have the sense to bat him ahead of their sluggers in the lineup.

Carlos Gonzalez

OF | Oakland Athletics | 22

Gonzalez was the centerpiece of the package the Diamondbacks sent to Oakland in exchange for Dan Haren. He's a five-tool player with good power potential and the ability to play any outfield position. The Athletics have parted with most of their outfielders from the 2007 season and Gonzalez could start there this season, but he could also use some more time in the minor leagues as his plate discipline was mediocre at Double-A Mobile last year.

Gio Gonzalez

LHP | Oakland Athletics | 22

Gonzalez used a low-90s fastball and excellent curveball to post a 3.18 ERA and strike out nearly 30 percent of opposing batters while repeating Double-A last year. He does have a history of below-average control, and this is reflected in our underwhelming projection for the 2008 season. Oakland will give him plenty of chances to succeed; he has a good chance of becoming at least an average starting pitcher within the next couple years.

Carlos Gomez

OF | Minnesota Twins | 22

Gomez is a five-tool athlete with excellent range in the outfield and a plate approach that remains a work in progress. While he improved his contact rate and walked more often than ever in 2007, he also saw a significant drop in power production. His projected power might not arrive this year; Gomez had minor wrist surgery last summer and this has been known to temporarily sap power from hitters.

Chase Headley

3B | San Diego Padres | 23

The switch-hitter posted a .437 OBP while launching over 60 extra-base hits at Double-A San Antonio in 2007. He's the Padres' top prospect, but they already have young players at their corner infield positions. They will try out Headley in left field this spring, and he should be starting every day at some position by midseason.

Jair Jurrjens

RHP | Atlanta Braves | 22

Jurrjens arrived in Atlanta as part of the Edgar Renteria deal with Detroit. His control is excellent. While he won't be anything more than an average strikeout pitcher, he is able to get weak contact on his two-seam fastball. Jurrjens' durability is of some concern, but if he can stay healthy he should be able to log plenty of innings in the back of the Braves rotation.

Ian Kennedy

RHP | New York Yankees | 23

Kennedy rapidly ascended through the Yankees system and may have had the most impressive performance of any minor league pitcher in 2007. Our system projects a more modest 5.19 ERA over 149 innings pitched, largely due to his fly ball tendencies and potential home run troubles.

Andy LaRoche

OF | Los Angeles Dodgers | 24

LaRoche doesn't project to be an above-average power hitter, but he is a strong contact hitter with a disciplined approach at the plate. He is a safe bet to hit for a high batting average and post an above-average on-base percentage in 2008 and beyond.

Evan Longoria

3B | Tampa Bay Rays | 22

Longoria is a complete hitter. His disciplined plate approach should result in solid on-base skills. He also has plenty of power potential and projects to hit 20 home runs this year. His 23 percent line drive rate and .528 slugging percentage led all hitters with at least 400 plate appearances in the pitcher-dominated Southern League last year. Longoria is a converted shortstop, and at third base he ranks above-average using our play-by-play fielding metric for minor leaguers.

Jed Lowrie

SS | Boston Red Sox | 23

Lowrie bounced back from an injury-riddled 2006 season to hit for impressive power in the upper minor leagues. He also has the ability to hit for a respectable average and was among the league leaders in walk rate for Double-A Portland in 2007. He might be a better overall offensive player than the more highly touted Ellsbury in Boston, but Lowrie lacks a clear opportunity to start in the major leagues. He will likely begin the season in Triple-A Pawtucket until a trade sends him to a team that needs a middle infielder or opens up a spot for him in Boston.

Cameron Maybin

OF | Florida Marlins | 21

He's a gifted athlete who will get every chance to succeed in his new organization. I just don't think he's ready in 2008. Watch for high strikeout totals and a low batting average if he doesn't find success on infield hits like he did against less experienced fielders in the lower minor leagues.

Andrew McCutchen

OF | Pittsburgh Pirates | 21

The 11th overall pick from the 2005 draft could probably use more time in the minor leagues, but who else will the Pirates start in center field? McCutchen is a similar type of offensive player as Jacoby Ellsbury (see above), except that McCutchen projects to hit for a lower batting average and a bit more power. He has outstanding speed, but he doesn't attempt to steal bases particularly often.

Adam Miller

RHP | Cleveland Indians | 23

Miller is a complete pitcher; he has good control, stuff that gets hitters to swing and miss, and a two-seam fastballs that can get ground balls when he needs them. Arm trouble has slowed his rise to the major leagues, but he could earn a role in the Cleveland bullpen with a healthy spring.

Franklin Morales

LHP | Colorado Rockies | 22

The hard-throwing southpaw played an important role in the Rockies rotation during their improbable late-season run to the postseason. Morales has a history of inconsistent control and problems with walking batters, but he demonstrated some improvement in that respect during the second half of the 2007 season. If he can maintain those gains, he could easily beat our modest expectations that are dragged down by a projection of 86 walks in only 138 innings pitched.

Eduardo Morlan

RHP | Tampa Bay Rays | 22

Morlan is a power reliever with the potential to be the Rays' closer some day. His mid-90s fastball and slider combination induce a lot of strikeouts and fly balls. He doesn't have much experience beyond the Class A level, but he is close to reaching his full potential, and the Rays don't have many better options for the bullpen in 2008.

Jeff Niemann

RHP | Tampa Bay Rays | 25

Niemann improved his walk rate while continuing to strike out over 20 percent of opposing batters after a promotion to Triple-A Durham in 2007. Most importantly, Niemann stayed healthy throughout most of the season. The big right-handed pitcher will finally have the opportunity to use his power repertoire in Tampa this year.

Troy Patton

LHP | Baltimore Orioles | 22

Patton was the top prospect traded in the Miguel Tejada deal, and he is expected to compete for a role in the Baltimore rotation this year. Patton throws strikes and has a solid four-pitch repertoire, but his strikeout rate has declined over the past two years and when he does allow contact it tends to be hit in the air. His high contact rate and fly ball tendencies could lead to home run struggles in his rookie season.

Manny Parra

LHP | Milwaukee Brewers | 25

Parra has finally recovered from a shoulder injury and reclaimed his status as a top pitching prospect in the Brewers system. Parra demonstrated above-average control throughout his minor league career, and last year he located his low-90s fastball well enough to strike out nearly a quarter of all batters faced at the Double-A and Triple-A levels. He should find a role in the back of the rotation this year, where we project Parra will contribute a 4.80 ERA for the Brewers.

Steven Pearce

1B/OF | Pittsburgh Pirates | 25

Pearce earned attention by hitting 11 home runs in the first month of minor league baseball last year. He continued to hit for a high average while slugging extra-base hits at each level of competition in 2007. The Pirates are going to try Pearce in right field so he can get playing time while Adam LaRoche handles first base duties for the team. Our projection system forecasts 22 home runs from Pearce this year.

Chris Perez

RHP | St. Louis Cardinals | 22

A power fastball/slider pitcher, Perez is widely viewed as the closer of the future for the Cardinals. His control is in need of improvement, as he walked 28 batters in only 40 innings for Double-A Springfield last year. So far, he has missed bats and induced weak contact often enough to succeed despite his inconsistent control. The Cardinals will close out games with Jason Isringhausen this year, but Chris Perez could be ready to take over later this year or in 2009.

Colby Rasmus

OF | St. Louis Cardinals | 21

The Cardinals' trade of Jim Edmonds clears the way for Rasmus, their best prospect, to take over center field at some point in 2008. Rasmus might not hit for a high average at first, but the athletic center fielder hit the ball in the air more than any other Texas League hitter and led the league in isolated power (slugging percentage minus batting average) last year. We project 19 home runs and a solid OBP of .342 in his rookie season.

Ryan Sweeney

OF | Oakland Athletics | 23

Sweeney has an opportunity to fulfill his potential as a member of Oakland's new youth movement, and he might need a breakout season to earn a spot in the organization's long-term plans. He probably can't stick in center field, but he also has not yet hit for the kind of power most teams expect from a corner outfielder. Sweeney played his home games at one of the International League's most hitter-friendly parks and only hit a total of 23 home runs from 2006 through 2007.

Geovany Soto

C | Chicago Cubs | 25

Soto would be a strong enough defensive catcher to warrant a role on a major league team even if he couldn't hit much. And he couldn't hit much until he got stronger and suddenly started to pace the International League in home runs last year. Soto has always had reasonably good on-base skills, and if he can maintain his power production he could be an above-average catcher in the National League as soon as this year.

Ian Stewart

3B | Colorado Rockies | 23

Stewart didn't hit for the power everyone expected even though he played in some hitter-friendly home parks during his ascent through the upper minor leagues. Still, he has a quick bat and the discipline to reach or exceed our projected OBP of .336. He deserves a place in the Rockies lineup, but they will have to get creative to find a spot for him on the field.

J.R. Towles

C | Houston Astros | 24

Injuries slowed down Towles in 2005 and 2006, but he stayed healthy and moved from Class A Advanced all the way to the major leagues in 2007. He is a strong contact hitter who has hit above .300 and posted an OBP above .375 at every major stop of his minor league career. Towles struggled to throw out base runners last year, but he is widely considered a good defensive catcher overall.

Neil Walker

3B | Pittsburgh Pirates | 22

Walker converted from catcher to third base in 2007, and he made impressive progress on the field while posting solid offensive numbers at Double-A Altoona. Walker has not hit for much power in his career, but he is a strong contact hitter who improved his plate patience last year. Because he is still new to third base, he may need more time refining his glove work in the minor leagues before earning a promotion to Pittsburgh later this year.

Brandon Wood

3B | Los Angeles Angels | 23

Wood gained notoriety when he slugged over 100 extra-base hits in 2005. Since then, he has maintained his power production in the upper minor leagues while continuing to strike out at high rates. We do project 24 home runs from Wood in 2008, but we also project a .254 batting average and a modest .308 OBP. Wood played shortstop during most of his career, but the Angels have better fielders available at those positions and Wood will likely earn a regular role as a third baseman.

Joey Votto

1B | Cincinnati Reds | 24

Votto will get a chance win the first base job in spring training this year. He probably won't post outstanding home run totals, but he makes contact fairly often and posted the highest line drive rate of all International League players under the age of 25 last year. He is capable of the kind of offensive numbers that Cincinnati fans saw from Sean Casey four or five years ago.

Player Index

Following is an index of all the players with projections and comments in the *Season Preview*, and the team section each one is listed within.

Player	Team
Abreu, Bobby	Yankees
Abreu, Tony	Angels
Accardo, Jeremy	Blue Jays
Affeldt, Jeremy	Reds
Albers, Matt	Orioles
Alfonzo, Eliezer	Giants
Alou, Moises	Mets
Amezaga, Alfredo	Marlins
Anderson, Brian	White Sox
Anderson, Garret	Dodgers
Anderson, Josh	Braves
Anderson, Marlon	Mets
Ankiel, Rick	Cardinals
Antonelli, Matt	Padres
Arroyo, Bronson	Reds
Atchison, Scott	Giants
Atkins, Garrett	Rockies
Aurilia, Rich	Giants
Ausmus, Brad	Astros
Aybar, Erick	Dodgers
Backe, Brandon	Astros
Bacsik, Mike	Nationals
Baek, Cha Seung	Mariners
Baez, Danys	Orioles
Bailey, Homer	Reds
Baker, Jeff	Rockies
Baker, Scott	Twins
Bako, Paul	Orioles
Bale, John	Royals
Bannister, Brian	Royals
Bard, Josh	Padres
Barfield, Josh	Indians
Barmes, Clint	Rockies
Barrett, Michael	Padres
Bartlett, Jason	Rays
Barton, Daric	A's
Batista, Miguel	Mariners
Bautista, Denny	Tigers
Bautista, Jose	Pirates
Bay, Jason	Pirates
Bayliss, Jonah	Pirates
Bazardo, Yorman	Tigers
Beckett, Josh	Red Sox

Player	Team
Bedard, Erik	Orioles
Beimel, Joe	Angels
Belisle, Matt	Reds
Bell, Heath	Padres
Bell, Rob	Orioles
Belliard, Ronnie	Nationals
Beltran, Carlos	Mets
Beltre, Adrian	Mariners
Benoit, Joaquin	Rangers
Bergmann, Jason	Nationals
Berkman, Lance	Astros
Betancourt, Rafael	Indians
Betancourt, Yuniesky	Mariners
Betemit, Wilson	Yankees
Billingsley, Chad	Angels
Blake, Casey	Indians
Blalock, Hank	Rangers
Blanco, Henry	Cubs
Blanton, Joe	A's
Bloomquist, Willie	Mariners
Bonderman, Jeremy	Tigers
Bonds, Barry	Giants
Bonifacio, Emilio	Dbacks
Bonser, Boof	Twins
Boone, Aaron	Nationals
Bootcheck, Chris	Dodgers
Borkowski, Dave	Astros
Borowski, Joe	Indians
Bourn, Michael	Astros
Bowen, Rob	A's
Boyer, Blaine	Braves
Braden, Dallas	A's
Bradford, Chad	Orioles
Bradley, Milton	Rangers
Braun, Ryan	Brewers
Bray, Bill	Reds
Britton, Chris	Yankees
Brocail, Doug	Astros
Broussard, Ben	Rangers
Brown, Andrew	A's
Brown, Emil	A's
Broxton, Jonathan	Angels
Bruce, Jay	Reds

Player	Team
Bruney, Brian	Yankees
Buchholz, Clay	Red Sox
Buchholz, Taylor	Rockies
Buck, John	Royals
Buck, Travis	A's
Buehrle, Mark	White Sox
Burke, Chris	Dbacks
Burke, Jamie	Mariners
Burnett, A.J.	Blue Jays
Burrell, Pat	Phillies
Burres, Brian	Orioles
Burton, Jared	Reds
Bush, Dave	Brewers
Butler, Billy	Royals
Bynum, Freddie	Orioles
Byrd, Marlon	Rangers
Byrd, Paul	Indians
Byrdak, Tim	Tigers
Byrnes, Eric	Dbacks
Cabrera, Asdrubal	Indians
Cabrera, Daniel	Orioles
Cabrera, Melky	Yankees
Cabrera, Miguel	Tigers
Cabrera, Orlando	White Sox
Cain, Matt	Giants
Calero, Kiko	A's
Callaspo, Alberto	Royals
Cameron, Kevin	Padres
Cameron, Mike	Brewers
Cano, Robinson	Yankees
Capps, Matt	Pirates
Capuano, Chris	Brewers
Carlyle, Buddy	Braves
Carmona, Fausto	Indians
Carpenter, Chris	Cardinals
Casilla, Alexi	Twins
Casilla, Santiago	A's
Castillo, Jose	Marlins
Castillo, Luis	Mets
Castro, Ramon	Mets
Catalanotto, Frank	Rangers
Cedeno, Ronny	Cubs
Chacin, Gustavo	Blue Jays
Chacon, Shawn	Pirates
Chamberlain, Joba	Yankees
Chavez, Endy	Mets
Chavez, Eric	A's

Player	Team
Chico, Matt	Nationals
Chulk, Vinnie	Giants
Church, Ryan	Mets
Clark, Tony	Dbacks
Clemens, Roger	Yankees
Clement, Jeff	Mariners
Coffey, Todd	Reds
Colome, Jesus	Nationals
Colon, Bartolo	Dodgers
Contreras, Jose	White Sox
Cook, Aaron	Rockies
Cora, Alex	Red Sox
Cordero, Chad	Nationals
Cordero, Francisco	Reds
Corpas, Manny	Rockies
Correia, Kevin	Giants
Coste, Chris	Phillies
Cota, Humberto	Nationals
Counsell, Craig	Brewers
Coutlangus, Jon	Reds
Crain, Jesse	Twins
Crawford, Carl	Rays
Crede, Joe	White Sox
Crisp, Coco	Red Sox
Crosby, Bobby	A's
Cruz, Juan	Dbacks
Cruz, Nelson	Rangers
Cuddyer, Michael	Twins
Cueto, Johnny	Reds
Cust, Jack	A's
Damon, Johnny	Yankees
Danks, John	White Sox
Davidson, Dave	Pirates
Davies, Kyle	Royals
Davis, Doug	Dbacks
Davis, Rajai	Giants
Day, Dewon	White Sox
De Aza, Alejandro	Marlins
De La Cruz, Eulogio	Marlins
De La Rosa, Jorge	Royals
DeJesus, David	Royals
Delcarmen, Manny	Red Sox
Delgado, Carlos	Mets
Dellucci, David	Indians
Dempster, Ryan	Cubs
DeRosa, Mark	Cubs
Devine, Joey	A's

Player	Team
Diaz, Matt	Braves
DiNardo, Lenny	A's
Dobbs, Greg	Phillies
Dohmann, Scott	Rays
Donnelly, Brendan	Red Sox
Doumit, Ryan	Pirates
Downs, Scott	Blue Jays
Drew, J.D.	Red Sox
Drew, Stephen	Dbacks
Duchscherer, Justin	A's
Duckworth, Brandon	Royals
Duensing, Brian	Twins
Duffy, Chris	Pirates
Duke, Zach	Pirates
Dukes, Elijah	Nationals
Duncan, Chris	Cardinals
Duncan, Shelley	Yankees
Dunn, Adam	Reds
Duran, German	Rangers
Durbin, Chad	Phillies
Durham, Ray	Giants
Dye, Jermaine	White Sox
Easley, Damion	Mets
Eaton, Adam	Phillies
Eckstein, David	Blue Jays
Edmonds, Jim	Padres
Ellis, Mark	A's
Ellsbury, Jacoby	Red Sox
Embree, Alan	A's
Encarnacion, Edwin	Reds
Erstad, Darin	Astros
Escobar, Kelvim	Dodgers
Escobar, Yunel	Braves
Estrada, Paul	Astros
Ethier, Andre	Angels
Everett, Adam	Twins
Eyre, Scott	Cubs
Fahey, Brandon	Orioles
Farnsworth, Kyle	Yankees
Feliciano, Pedro	Mets
Feliz, Pedro	Phillies
Fielder, Prince	Brewers
Fields, Josh	White Sox
Figgins, Chone	Dodgers
Flores, Jesus	Nationals
Flores, Randy	Cardinals
Floyd, Cliff	Rays
Floyd, Gavin	White Sox

Player	Team
Fogg, Josh	Rockies
Fontenot, Mike	Cubs
Francis, Jeff	Rockies
Francisco, Ben	Indians
Francisco, Frank	Rangers
Francoeur, Jeff	Braves
Frandsen, Kevin	Giants
Franklin, Ryan	Cardinals
Frasor, Jason	Blue Jays
Freel, Ryan	Reds
Fuentes, Brian	Rockies
Fukudome, Kosuke	Cubs
Fultz, Aaron	Indians
Furcal, Rafael	Angels
Gabbard, Kason	Rangers
Gagne, Eric	Brewers
Gallardo, Yovani	Brewers
Garcia, Jaime	Cardinals
Garciaparra, Nomar	Angels
Gardner, Lee	Marlins
Garko, Ryan	Indians
Garland, Jon	Dodgers
Garza, Matt	Rays
Gathright, Joey	Royals
Gaudin, Chad	A's
Geary, Geoff	Astros
German, Esteban	Royals
Germano, Justin	Padres
Giambi, Jason	Yankees
Gibbons, Jay	Orioles
Giese, Dan	Giants
Giles, Brian	Padres
Giles, Marcus	Rockies
Glaus, Troy	Cardinals
Glavine, Tom	Braves
Gload, Ross	Royals
Gobble, Jimmy	Royals
Gomes, Jonny	Rays
Gomez, Carlos	Twins
Gonzalez, Adrian	Padres
Gonzalez, Alex	Reds
Gonzalez, Edgar	Dbacks
Gonzalez, Mike	Braves
Gordon, Alex	Royals
Gordon, Tom	Phillies
Gorzelanny, Tom	Pirates
Gotay, Ruben	Mets
Grabow, John	Pirates

Player	Team
Granderson, Curtis	Tigers
Green, Sean	Mariners
Greene, Khalil	Padres
Gregg, Kevin	Marlins
Greinke, Zack	Royals
Griffey, Ken	Reds
Grilli, Jason	Tigers
Gross, Gabe	Brewers
Grudzielanek, Mark	Royals
Guardado, Eddie	Rangers
Guerrero, Vladimir	Dodgers
Guerrier, Matt	Twins
Guillen, Carlos	Tigers
Guillen, Jose	Royals
Guthrie, Jeremy	Orioles
Gutierrez, Franklin	Indians
Guzman, Cristian	Nationals
Gwynn, Tony	Brewers
Haeger, Charlie	White Sox
Hafner, Travis	Indians
Hairston, Scott	Padres
Hall, Bill	Brewers
Hall, Toby	White Sox
Halladay, Roy	Blue Jays
Hamels, Cole	Phillies
Hamilton, Josh	Rangers
Hammel, Jason	Rays
Hampson, Justin	Padres
Hampton, Mike	Braves
Hannahan, Jack	A's
Hanrahan, Joel	Nationals
Harang, Aaron	Reds
Harden, Rich	A's
Hardy, J.J.	Brewers
Haren, Dan	Dbacks
Harris, Brendan	Twins
Hart, Corey	Brewers
Hatteberg, Scott	Reds
Hawkins, LaTroy	Yankees
Hawpe, Brad	Rockies
Headley, Chase	Padres
Heilman, Aaron	Mets
Helms, Wes	Phillies
Helton, Todd	Rockies
Hennessey, Brad	Giants
Hensley, Clay	Padres
Herges, Matt	Rockies

Player	Team
Hermida, Jeremy	Marlins
Hernandez, Felix	Mariners
Hernandez, Livan	Dbacks
Hernandez, Orlando	Mets
Hernandez, Ramon	Orioles
Hill, Aaron	Blue Jays
Hill, Rich	Cubs
Hill, Shawn	Nationals
Hinske, Eric	Red Sox
Hirsh, Jason	Rockies
Hochevar, Luke	Royals
Hoffman, Trevor	Padres
Holliday, Matt	Rockies
Hopper, Norris	Reds
Howard, Ryan	Phillies
Howry, Bob	Cubs
Hudson, Orlando	Dbacks
Hudson, Tim	Braves
Huff, Aubrey	Orioles
Hughes, Philip	Yankees
Hull, Eric	Angels
Humber, Philip	Twins
Hunter, Torii	Dodgers
Hurley, Eric	Rangers
Iannetta, Chris	Rockies
Ibanez, Raul	Mariners
Iguchi, Tadahito	Padres
Infante, Omar	Braves
Inge, Brandon	Tigers
Isringhausen, Jason	Cardinals
Iwamura, Akinori	Rays
Izturis, Cesar	Cardinals
Izturis, Maicer	Dodgers
Jackson, Conor	Dbacks
Jackson, Edwin	Rays
Jacobs, Mike	Marlins
James, Chuck	Braves
Janssen, Casey	Blue Jays
Jenkins, Geoff	Phillies
Jenks, Bobby	White Sox
Jennings, Jason	Rangers
Jeter, Derek	Yankees
Jimenez, Ubaldo	Rockies
Johjima, Kenji	Mariners
Johnson, Dan	A's
Johnson, Josh	Marlins
Johnson, Kelly	Braves

Player	Team
Johnson, Randy	Dbacks
Johnson, Reed	Blue Jays
Johnson, Tyler	Cardinals
Jones, Adam	Mariners
Jones, Andruw	Angels
Jones, Chipper	Braves
Jones, Jacque	Tigers
Jones, Todd	Tigers
Jurrjens, Jair	Braves
Kazmir, Scott	Rays
Kearns, Austin	Nationals
Kemp, Matt	Angels
Kendall, Jason	Brewers
Kendrick, Howie	Dodgers
Kendrick, Kyle	Phillies
Kennedy, Adam	Cardinals
Kennedy, Ian	Yankees
Kensing, Logan	Marlins
Kent, Jeff	Angels
Keppinger, Jeff	Reds
Kim, Byung-Hyun	Marlins
Kinsler, Ian	Rangers
Klesko, Ryan	Giants
Kobayashi, Masahide	Indians
Konerko, Paul	White Sox
Koshansky, Joseph	Rockies
Kotchman, Casey	Dodgers
Kotsay, Mark	Braves
Kouzmanoff, Kevin	Padres
Kubel, Jason	Twins
Kuo, Hong-Chih	Angels
Kuroda, Hiroki	Angels
Lackey, John	Dodgers
Laffey, Aaron	Indians
Laird, Gerald	Rangers
Lamb, Mike	Twins
Lannan, John	Nationals
LaRoche, Adam	Pirates
LaRoche, Andy	Angels
LaRue, Jason	Cardinals
League, Brandon	Blue Jays
Ledezma, Wilfredo	Padres
Lee, Carlos	Astros
Lee, Cliff	Indians
Lee, Derrek	Cubs
Lester, Jon	Red Sox
Lewis, Colby	A's
Lewis, Fred	Giants

Player	Team
Lewis, Jensen	Indians
Lidge, Brad	Phillies
Lieber, Jon	Cubs
Lilly, Ted	Cubs
Lincecum, Tim	Giants
Lind, Adam	Blue Jays
Linebrink, Scott	White Sox
Liriano, Francisco	Twins
Litsch, Jesse	Blue Jays
Littleton, Wes	Rangers
Livingston, Bobby	Reds
Liz, Radhames	Orioles
Lo Duca, Paul	Nationals
Loaiza, Esteban	Angels
Loe, Kameron	Rangers
Loewen, Adam	Orioles
Lofton, Kenny	Indians
Logan, Boone	White Sox
Logan, Nook	Nationals
Lohse, Kyle	Phillies
Loney, James	Angels
Longoria, Evan	Rays
Looper, Braden	Cardinals
Lopez, Felipe	Nationals
Lopez, Javier	Red Sox
Lopez, Jose	Mariners
Loretta, Mark	Astros
Lowe, Derek	Angels
Lowell, Mike	Red Sox
Lowry, Noah	Giants
Ludwick, Ryan	Cardinals
Lugo, Julio	Red Sox
Lyon, Brandon	Dbacks
MacDougal, Mike	White Sox
Maddux, Greg	Padres
Madson, Ryan	Phillies
Maholm, Paul	Pirates
Maine, John	Mets
Majewski, Gary	Reds
Marcum, Shaun	Blue Jays
Markakis, Nick	Orioles
Marmol, Carlos	Cubs
Marquis, Jason	Cubs
Marshall, Jay	A's
Marshall, Sean	Cubs
Marte, Andy	Indians
Marte, Damaso	Pirates
Martin, Russell	Angels

Player	Team
Martinez, Pedro	Mets
Martinez, Victor	Indians
Mastny, Tom	Indians
Mathis, Jeff	Dodgers
Matsui, Hideki	Yankees
Matsui, Kazuo	Astros
Matsuzaka, Daisuke	Red Sox
Matthews, Gary	Dodgers
Mauer, Joe	Twins
Maybin, Cameron	Marlins
McAnulty, Paul	Padres
McBride, Macay	Tigers
McCann, Brian	Braves
McCarthy, Brandon	Rangers
McClain, Scott	Giants
McClung, Seth	Brewers
McDonald, John	Blue Jays
McGowan, Dustin	Blue Jays
McLemore, Mark	Astros
McLouth, Nate	Pirates
Meche, Gil	Royals
Medders, Brandon	Dbacks
Meloan, Jonathan	Angels
Meredith, Cla	Padres
Messenger, Randy	Giants
Michaels, Jason	Indians
Mientkiewicz, Doug	Yankees
Miles, Aaron	Cardinals
Millar, Kevin	Orioles
Milledge, Lastings	Nationals
Miller, Andrew	Marlins
Miller, Justin	Marlins
Miller, Trever	Astros
Millwood, Kevin	Rangers
Miner, Zach	Tigers
Mirabelli, Doug	Red Sox
Misch, Patrick	Giants
Mitre, Sergio	Marlins
Moehler, Brian	Astros
Molina, Bengie	Giants
Molina, Jose	Yankees
Molina, Yadier	Cardinals
Montero, Miguel	Dbacks
Mora, Melvin	Orioles
Morales, Franklin	Rockies
Morales, Kendry	Dodgers
Morneau, Justin	Twins

Player	Team
Morris, Matt	Pirates
Morrow, Brandon	Mariners
Moseley, Dustin	Dodgers
Moss, Brandon	Red Sox
Mota, Guillermo	Brewers
Moyer, Jamie	Phillies
Moylan, Peter	Braves
Mulder, Mark	Cardinals
Murphy, David	Rangers
Murray, A.J.	Rangers
Murton, Matt	Cubs
Mussina, Mike	Yankees
Myers, Brett	Phillies
Nady, Xavier	Pirates
Napoli, Mike	Dodgers
Nathan, Joe	Twins
Navarro, Dioner	Rays
Neshek, Pat	Twins
Niekro, Lance	Giants
Niemann, Jeff	Rays
Nieve, Fernando	Astros
Nippert, Dustin	Dbacks
Nix, Jayson	Rockies
Nolasco, Ricky	Marlins
Nunez, Leo	Royals
O'Flaherty, Eric	Mariners
Ohlendorf, Ross	Yankees
Ojeda, Augie	Dbacks
Okajima, Hideki	Red Sox
Oliver, Darren	Dodgers
Olivo, Miguel	Royals
Olsen, Scott	Marlins
Olson, Garrett	Orioles
Ordonez, Magglio	Tigers
Ortiz, David	Red Sox
Ortiz, Russ	Giants
Orvella, Chad	Rays
Osoria, Franquelis	Pirates
Oswalt, Roy	Astros
Otsuka, Akinori	Rangers
Overbay, Lyle	Blue Jays
Owens, Henry	Marlins
Owens, Jerry	White Sox
Owings, Micah	Dbacks
Ozuna, Pablo	White Sox
Padilla, Vicente	Rangers
Palmeiro, Orlando	Astros

Player	Team
Papelbon, Jonathan	Red Sox
Paronto, Chad	Braves
Parra, Manny	Brewers
Patterson, Corey	Orioles
Patterson, John	Nationals
Paulino, Felipe	Astros
Paulino, Ronny	Pirates
Payton, Jay	Orioles
Pearce, Steven	Pirates
Peavy, Jake	Padres
Pedroia, Dustin	Red Sox
Peguero, Jailen	Dbacks
Pelfrey, Mike	Mets
Pena, Carlos	Rays
Pena, Tony	Dbacks
Pena, Tony	Royals
Pena, Wily Mo	Nationals
Pence, Hunter	Astros
Penny, Brad	Angels
Peralta, Jhonny	Indians
Peralta, Joel	Royals
Percival, Troy	Rays
Perez, Christopher	Cardinals
Perez, Odalis	Royals
Perez, Oliver	Mets
Perez, Rafael	Indians
Perkins, Glen	Twins
Petit, Yusmeiro	Dbacks
Pettitte, Andy	Yankees
Phelps, Josh	Cardinals
Phillips, Andy	Reds
Phillips, Brandon	Reds
Pie, Felix	Cubs
Pierre, Juan	Angels
Pierzynski, A.J.	White Sox
Pineiro, Joel	Cardinals
Pino, Yohan	Twins
Plouffe, Trevor	Twins
Polanco, Placido	Tigers
Posada, Jorge	Yankees
Prior, Mark	Padres
Proctor, Scott	Angels
Pujols, Albert	Cardinals
Punto, Nick	Twins
Putz, J.J.	Mariners
Qualls, Chad	Dbacks
Quentin, Carlos	White Sox
Quinlan, Robb	Dodgers

Player	Team
Quintero, Humberto	Astros
Raburn, Ryan	Tigers
Ramirez, Aramis	Cubs
Ramirez, Edwar	Yankees
Ramirez, Hanley	Marlins
Ramirez, Horacio	Mariners
Ramirez, Manny	Red Sox
Ramirez, Ramon	Rockies
Randolph, Stephen	Astros
Ransom, Cody	Astros
Rasmus, Colby	Cardinals
Rauch, Jon	Nationals
Ray, Chris	Orioles
Redding, Tim	Nationals
Redman, Mark	Rockies
Redman, Tike	Orioles
Redmond, Mike	Twins
Renteria, Edgar	Tigers
Reyes, Al	Rays
Reyes, Anthony	Cardinals
Reyes, Dennys	Twins
Reyes, Jo-Jo	Braves
Reyes, Jose	Mets
Reynolds, Gregory	Rockies
Reynolds, Mark	Dbacks
Rheinecker, John	Rangers
Richar, Danny	White Sox
Rincon, Juan	Twins
Rios, Alex	Blue Jays
Riske, David	Brewers
Rivera, Juan	Dodgers
Rivera, Mariano	Yankees
Rivera, Saul	Nationals
Roberts, Brian	Orioles
Roberts, Dave	Giants
Robertson, Nate	Tigers
Rodney, Fernando	Tigers
Rodriguez, Alex	Yankees
Rodriguez, Francisco	Dodgers
Rodriguez, Guillermo	Giants
Rodriguez, Ivan	Tigers
Rodriguez, Wandy	Astros
Rogers, Kenny	Tigers
Rolen, Scott	Blue Jays
Rollins, Jimmy	Phillies
Romero, J.C.	Phillies
Romero, Ricky	Blue Jays
Ross, Cody	Marlins

Player	Team
Ross, David	Reds
Rowand, Aaron	Giants
Rowland-Smith, Ryan	Mariners
Ruggiano, Justin	Rays
Ruiz, Carlos	Phillies
Ryan, B.J.	Blue Jays
Ryan, Brendan	Cardinals
Sabathia, C.C.	Indians
Saito, Takashi	Angels
Salas, Juan	Rays
Salazar, Jeff	Dbacks
Saltalamacchia, Jarrod	Rangers
Sampson, Chris	Astros
Sanchez, Anibal	Marlins
Sanchez, Duaner	Mets
Sanchez, Freddy	Pirates
Sanchez, Jonathan	Giants
Sanchez, Romulo	Pirates
Santana, Ervin	Dodgers
Santana, Johan	Mets
Saunders, Joe	Dodgers
Schierholtz, Nate	Giants
Schilling, Curt	Red Sox
Schmidt, Jason	Angels
Schneider, Brian	Mets
Schoeneweis, Scott	Mets
Schumaker, Skip	Cardinals
Scott, Luke	Orioles
Scutaro, Marco	Blue Jays
Sexson, Richie	Mariners
Shealy, Ryan	Royals
Sheets, Ben	Brewers
Sheffield, Gary	Tigers
Sherrill, George	Mariners
Shields, James	Rays
Shields, Scot	Dodgers
Shoppach, Kelly	Indians
Shouse, Brian	Brewers
Silva, Carlos	Mariners
Sisco, Andrew	White Sox
Sizemore, Grady	Indians
Slaten, Doug	Dbacks
Slowey, Kevin	Twins
Smith, Jason	Royals
Smith, Joseph	Mets
Smith, Seth	Rockies
Smoltz, John	Braves

Player	Team
Snell, Ian	Pirates
Snyder, Chris	Dbacks
Snyder, Kyle	Red Sox
Sonnanstine, Andrew	Rays
Soria, Joakim	Royals
Soriano, Alfonso	Cubs
Soriano, Rafael	Braves
Sosa, Jorge	Mets
Soto, Geovany	Cubs
Sowers, Jeremy	Indians
Speier, Justin	Dodgers
Spiezio, Scott	Cardinals
Spilborghs, Ryan	Rockies
Springer, Russ	Cardinals
Stairs, Matt	Blue Jays
Stanton, Mike	Reds
Stauffer, Tim	Padres
Stewart, Shannon	A's
Street, Huston	A's
Suppan, Jeff	Brewers
Suzuki, Ichiro	Mariners
Suzuki, Kurt	A's
Swisher, Nick	White Sox
Taguchi, So	Phillies
Tallet, Brian	Blue Jays
Tankersley, Taylor	Marlins
Taschner, Jack	Giants
Tavarez, Julian	Red Sox
Taveras, Willy	Rockies
Teahen, Mark	Royals
Teixeira, Mark	Braves
Tejada, Miguel	Astros
Tejeda, Robinson	Rangers
Thames, Marcus	Tigers
Thatcher, Joe	Padres
Theriot, Ryan	Cubs
Thomas, Frank	Blue Jays
Thome, Jim	White Sox
Thompson, Brad	Cardinals
Thorman, Scott	Braves
Thornton, Matt	White Sox
Timlin, Mike	Red Sox
Torrealba, Yorvit	Rockies
Towers, Josh	Rockies
Towles, Justin	Astros
Tracy, Chad	Dbacks
Treanor, Matt	Marlins

Player	Team
Tulowitzki, Troy	Rockies
Turnbow, Derrick	Brewers
Uggla, Dan	Marlins
Upton, B.J.	Rays
Upton, Justin	Dbacks
Uribe, Juan	White Sox
Utley, Chase	Phillies
Valentin, Javier	Reds
Valverde, Jose	Astros
Van Benschoten, John	Pirates
VandenHurk, Rick	Marlins
Vargas, Claudio	Brewers
Varitek, Jason	Red Sox
Vazquez, Javier	White Sox
Verlander, Justin	Tigers
Victorino, Shane	Phillies
Vidro, Jose	Mariners
Villanueva, Carlos	Brewers
Villarreal, Oscar	Astros
Vizcaino, Luis	Rockies
Vizquel, Omar	Giants
Volquez, Edinson	Reds
Votto, Joey	Reds
Wagner, Billy	Mets
Wainwright, Adam	Cardinals
Wakefield, Tim	Red Sox
Walker, Jamie	Orioles
Walker, Tyler	Giants
Wang, Chien-Ming	Yankees
Ward, Daryle	Cubs
Washburn, Jarrod	Mariners
Weathers, Casey	Rockies
Weathers, David	Reds
Weaver, Jered	Dodgers
Webb, Brandon	Dbacks
Weeks, Rickie	Brewers
Wellemeyer, Todd	Cardinals

Player	Team
Wells, Kip	Rockies
Wells, Vernon	Blue Jays
Werth, Jayson	Phillies
Westbrook, Jake	Indians
Wheeler, Dan	Rays
White, Sean	Mariners
Wigginton, Ty	Astros
Wilkerson, Brad	Mariners
Williams, Woody	Astros
Willingham, Josh	Marlins
Willis, Dontrelle	Tigers
Willits, Reggie	Dodgers
Wilson, Brian	Giants
Wilson, C.J.	Rangers
Wilson, Jack	Pirates
Winn, Randy	Giants
Wise, Matt	Mets
Wolf, Randy	Padres
Wood, Brandon	Dodgers
Wood, Kerry	Cubs
Wright, David	Mets
Wuertz, Michael	Cubs
Yates, Tyler	Braves
Youkilis, Kevin	Red Sox
Young, Chris	Padres
Young, Chris	Dbacks
Young, Delmon	Twins
Young, Dmitri	Nationals
Young, Michael	Rangers
Zagurski, Michael	Phillies
Zambrano, Carlos	Cubs
Zaun, Gregg	Blue Jays
Zimmerman, Ryan	Nationals
Zito, Barry	Giants
Zobrist, Ben	Rays
Zumaya, Joel	Tigers